Painting Masterclass

Quantum
Books

A QUANTUM BOOK

This book is produced by
Quantum Publishing Ltd
6 Blundell Street
London N7 9BH

ISBN 0-681-04856-5

QUMTPM2

Manufactured in Singapore by
Pica Digital Pte Ltd
Printed in Singapore by
Star Standard Industries (Pte) Ltd

ARTISTS' CREDITS

Ian Sidway pp 28 34, 35, 36, 39, 42, 46 (left), 50 (top),
62-65, 80-83, 94-103, 124-127; Elaine Mills pp 45, 106,
109-111; Stan Smith pp 44, 50 (bottom), 52, 76-79;
Kate Gwynn p 57 (top right); Ann Verney pp 29-61;
Mark Winer pp 70, 71, 88, 108, 122, 123; Sally Michel
pp 87, 89-93; Jane Wisner pp 112-115;
John Devane pp 116, 117.

CONTENTS

PAINTING IN OILS

PAINTING THE NUDE

Painting
in
Watercolor

Introduction

"I don't do watercolor; it's far too difficult" is a
remark often heard from amateur painters, even those
who regard themselves as reasonably proficient in
other media, such as oils. It cannot be denied that
some people find watercolors a little harder to use than
oils. This very attractive medium is sometimes
unpredictable, but this very unpredictability should be
regarded as a virtue, not a drawback. What people
really mean when they make this kind of remark is that
watercolors cannot be altered over and over again as
oils can; a color or wash, once laid down on the paper,
must stay there. To some extent this is true, and it is
understandable that people should feel a certain
nervousness when approaching a watercolor. But, in
fact, many alterations can be made, and often are, as a
painting progresses: a wash in a color that has not
come out quite right can be changed dramatically by
applying another wash on top of it; areas can be
sponged out or worked over; and if the worst comes to
the worst the whole painting can be put under running
water and washed away.

OPPOSITE The main body of Samuel
Palmer's work was in oil. It was highly
accomplished, but uninspired. His early
watercolors, drawings, and etchings,
however, were works of true poetic
imagination and owed much to the
influence of William Blake, whom he met
in 1824. Paintings such as the one shown
here, The Magic Apple Tree, have their
starting points in nature, but go far
beyond it to create dream-like fantasy
worlds, personal visions expressed in
strange, emotive colors and almost
Expressionist brush work. Unlike the 18th-
century watercolorists, Palmer used semi-
opaque paint. But this handling of it was
so sure that the colors never became
muddy or muted, as they often do with
gouache paints in less skilful hands.

Watercolor has many virtues, its main attraction for artists being its freshness and translucence, making it ideal for a variety of subjects, especially landscapes and flower paintings. As its name implies, pure watercolor is mixed with water and is transparent, so that it must be applied from light to dark, unlike oil paint or acrylics which are opaque and can be built up from dark to light. Highlights consist of areas of the paper left white or very pale washes surrounded by darker ones. A certain amount of preplanning is necessary at an early stage to work out where the highlights are to be, but some planning is always needed for any painting or drawing, whatever medium is being used.

No one ever quite knows how watercolor will behave, and many watercolor artists find this very unpredictability one of its greatest assets. The medium itself will often begin to "take over" a painting, suggesting ways of creating interesting effects and lending a sparkle and spontaneity to the work. Experience is needed to make the most of the chance effects that occur in watercolor painting. A real feeling for the medium may not be achieved until several attempts have been abandoned, but there are many ways of using watercolor and with perseverance you will evolve your own style and method. The purely practical advantages of watercolor painting are that you need little expensive equipment, the painting can be done more or less anywhere provided there is enough light, and paints can be cleared up quickly, leaving no mess. Since the paper is relatively cheap,

experiments and mistakes are not very expensive.

THE MEDIUM

Watercolor, like all paint, is made by mixing pigment with a binding agent, in this case gum arabic, which is soluble in water. There are two types of watercolor, "pure" or "classical" watercolor, which is transparent, and gouache, or "body color," which is the same pigment made opaque by adding white pigment to the binder. The technique of gouache painting is similar to that of oil or acrylic, since light color can be laid over dark, and is outside the scope of this book; but gouache is quite frequently used in conjunction with pure watercolor. Its use is a source of constant controversy among watercolorists: some claim that it destroys the character of the medium—its luminosity—and should never be used; others combine the two with considerable success. Nowadays there is a general trend toward mixing different media, and watercolor is often used with pastel, pen and ink, pencils, or crayons (see Chapter 2). It can be a useful exercise, when a watercolor has "gone wrong", to draw into it

with inks or pastels to see the effects that can be achieved.

THE HISTORY OF WATERCOLOR PAINTING

It is commonly believed that watercolor was invented by the English landscape painters of the

18th century, but this is far from so. Watercolor has been in use in various forms for many centuries. Indeed the ancient Egyptians used a form of it for painting on plaster to decorate their tombs; the great frescoes of Renaissance Italy were painted in a kind of watercolor; it

was used by medieval manuscript illuminators, both in its "pure" form and mixed with body color; the great German artist, Albrecht Dürer (1471–1528), made use of it extensively, and so did many botanical illustrators of the 16th century and the Dutch flower

ABOVE John Sell Cotman was the leading watercolorist of the 18th century British School. In paintings like this one, *St Benet's Abbey, Norfolk*, he used paint in a bold, free, and imaginative way to create marvelous effects of space, light, and texture. Notice particularly the broad, overlapping brush strokes in the foreground and the swirling, directional ones in the sky.

ABOVE John Sell Cotman worked on a fairly small scale, but his landscapes and seascapes give an impressive feeling of space, strength, and power, and are extraordinarily modern in approach. Many have an almost abstract quality, as in this painting, The Dismastered Brig, where the rain-swept sky has been treated in bold,

broad masses, and the swirling movement of the waves has been used to make his geometric pattern of different-sized triangles.

RIGHT Albrecht Dürer, who painted this painting, which has come to be known as The Great Piece of Turf, found watercolor a

particularly sympathetic medium for detailed studies of nature. We cannotbe sure of his precise method, but he probably began by using transparent washes to establish broad areas, such as the large leaves, and then built up intricate details with tiny strokes of opaque paint (or body color).

painters of the 17th century.

It was, even so, in 18th-century England that watercolor painting was elevated to the status of a national art. A new interest in landscape painting for its own sake culminated in the work of John Constable (1776–1837), the forerunner of the Impressionists. Landscape had hitherto been purely topographical—a truthful and detailed record of a particular place—but in the hands of artists such as Paul Sandby (1725–1809), John Cozens (1752–97), Thomas Girtin (1775–1802), Francis Towne (1740–1816), John Sell Cotman (1782–1842), and Peter de Wint (1784–1849) it became much more than that. Watercolor was at last

fully exploited and given the recognition that was its due.

Most of these artists worked in watercolor alone, regarding it as the perfect medium for creating the light, airy, atmospheric effects they sought; Constable used watercolor mainly for quick sketches of skies. The greatest watercolorist of all, J M W Turner (1775–1851) achieved his fame as an oil painter, but he produced watercolors; of an amazing depth and richness. Quite uninhibited by any "rules," he exploited accidental effects like thumbprints and haphazard blobs of paint, turning them into some of the most magical depictions of light and color that have ever been seen in paint.

Throughout the 19th century the techniques of watercolor continued to be developed and the subject matter became more varied. The poet and artist, William Blake (1757–1827), evolved his own method of conveying his poetic vision in watercolor, as did his follower, Samuel Palmer (1805–81), who used swirls and blocks of opaque color in his visionary and symbolic landscapes. With the end of the Napoleonic Wars in 1815, travel once again became easier, and the topographical tradition reached new heights in the work of artists like Samuel Prout (1783–1852), a superlative draftsman who painted the buildings and scenery of western Europe in faithful detail.

CHAPTER ONE

Materials and Equipment

Perhaps the greatest single adventure of watercolor painting is that only a small amount of equipment is needed, equipment that is easy to store. Paints and brushes, although not cheap, last for a long time; indeed, brushes should last virtually for ever if looked after properly. Hand-made paper is, of course, expensive, but beginners will find that many perfectly satisfactory machine-made papers are available from artist's suppliers.

OPPOSITE This paintbox might be regarded by some as messy, but this artist finds that he achieves a greater unity of color by allowing traces of old color to remain on the palette. He cleans the mixing trays only when the colors become muddied or when a different range of colors is required.

Payne's gray and cadmium yellow.	Prussian blue and cadmium yellow.	Cobalt and cadmium yellow.	Prussian blue and lemon yellow.	Viridian and lemon.	Black and cadmium yellow.

Cobalt blue and alizarin crimson.	Payne's gray and alizarin crimson.	Prussian blue and alizarin crimson.	Cobalt blue and Payne's gray.	Black and Prussian blue.	Black and alizarin crimson.

Cadmium yellow and cadmium red.	Alizarin crimson and cadmium yellow.	Lemon yellow and cadmium red.	Burnt umber and black.	Payne's gray and cadmium red.	Burnt umber and cobalt blue.

PAINTS AND COLORS

Ready-made watercolor paint is sold in various forms, the commonest being tubes, pans, and half-pans. These all contain glycerine and are known as semi-moist colors, unlike the traditional dry cakes, which are still available in some artist's suppliers, but are not much used today. Dry cakes require considerable rubbing with water before the color is released. It is a slow process, but the paints are therefore economical.

Gouache paints, or designer's colors as they are sometimes called, are normally sold in tubes. These paints, and the cheaper versions of them, poster colors and powder paints, have chalk added to the pigment to thicken it, and are thus opaque, unlike true watercolor. Watercolors themselves can be mixed with Chinese white to make them opaque or semi-opaque, so that they become a softer and more subtle form of gouache.

Success in watercolor painting depends so much on applying layers of transparent, but rich, color that it is a mistake to buy any but the best-quality paints, known as "artist's quality." There are cheaper paints, sold for " sketching," but since these contain a filler to extend the pigment, the color is weaker and the paint tends to be chalky and unpredictable in use.

Whether to use pans, half-pans, or tubes is a personal choice. Each type has its advantages and disadvantages. Tubes are excellent for those who work mainly indoors on a fairly large scale, as any quantity of paint can be squeezed out of them on to the palette. Any paint left on the palette after a painting is completed can be used again later, simply by moistening it with a wet brush. Pans and half-pans, which can be bought in sets in their own palette and are easy to carry, are the most popular choice for working out of doors on a small scale. Watercolors can also be bought in concentrated form in bottles, with droppers to transfer the paint to the palette. These are eminently suitable for broad washes which require a large

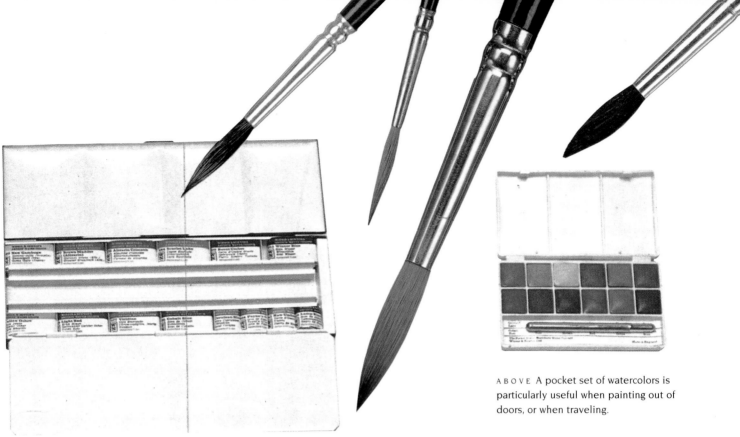

ABOVE A pocket set of watercolors is particularly useful when painting out of doors, or when traveling.

LEFT These swatches show some of the effects that can be achieved by mixing in a limited color range.

ABOVE semi-moist pans must be carried in tins and boxes, which can then be used as palettes.

BELOW MIDDLE Half-pans are available individually as well as in sets. The artist can replace the most frequently used colors, and also build up a palette to suit his own style.

ABOVE Bottled watercolors are concentrated, and quicker to use than dry cakes or semi-moist pans when a large area of wash is required.

RIGHT Watercolor in tube form is popular and convenient. Do not squeeze too many colors onto your palette at a time, or they will run together.

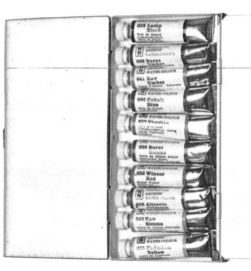

LEFT Gouache is available in tube or pot form in an enormous range of colors. From left to right: lamp black, zinc white, burnt sienna, raw umber, yellow ocher, cadmium red (pale), Winsor emerald, cobalt blue.

quantity of paint, but they are less easy to mix than the other types.

The choice of colors is also personal, though there are some colors that everyone must have. Nowadays there is such a vast range of colors to choose from that a beginner is justified in feeling somewhat bewildered, but, in fact, only a few are really necessary. One point to bear in mind is that some colors are considerably less permanent than others, which may not be an important consideration for quick sketches and "note-taking," but clearly is for any painting that is intended to be hung or exhibited. A wise course, therefore, is to rule out any colors classified as "fugitive." All the major paint manufacturers have systems of grading permanence. These are not always marked on the tubes or pans, but they appear on the manufacturers' color charts; if in doubt, ask the shopkeeper or manager for advice. The tubes or pans will also bear a code indicating the relative price of each color, some being more expensive than others according to the cost of the pigment used.

The golden rule when choosing a range of colors, or "palette" as professionals call it, is to keep it as simple as possible. Few watercolorists use more than a dozen colors. For landscape painting, useful additions to the basic palette are sap green, Hooker's green, raw umber, and cerulean blue, while monastral blue (called Winsor blue in the Winsor and Newton range) is sometimes recommended instead of Prussian blue. For flower painting the basic range might be enlarged by the addition of cobalt violet and lemon yellow.

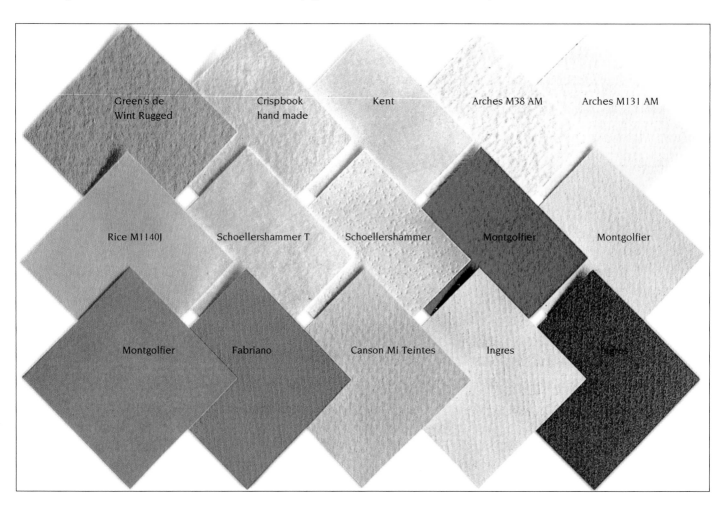

Green's de Wint Rugged

Crispbook hand made

Kent

Arches M38 AM

Arches M131 AM

Rice M1140J

Schoellershammer T

Schoellershammer

Montgolfier

Montgolfier

Montgolfier

Fabriano

Canson Mi Teintes

Ingres

Ingres

ABOVE The range of papers available is vast and can be bewildering even for the experianced artist. In order to find the paper which suits your particular style and immediate needs, buy only a few sheets at a time. The heavier papers are more expensive but can absorb large amounts of water; they do not, therefore, need stretching, which makes them useful for outdoor work.

Toned papers provide a convenient middle ground for some subjects, from which to work darks and lights.

PAPER

The traditional support—the term used for the surface on which any painting is done—is white or pale-colored paper, which reflects back through the transparent paint to give the translucent quality so characteristic of watercolors. There are many types of watercolor paper. Each individual will probably need to try several before establishing which one suits his method of working, though sometimes a particular paper may be chosen to create a special effect.

The three main types of machine-made paper are hotpressed (HP), cold-pressed (CP), which is also rather quaintly known as "not" for "not hot-pressed" and rough. Hot-pressed paper is very smooth and, although suitable for drawing or pen-and-wash, is not a good choice for building up layers of washes in the standard watercolor technique as it becomes clogged very quickly. Coldpressed paper, which is slightly textured, is the most popular and is suitable for both broad washes and fine detail. Rough paper, as its name implies, is much more heavily textured, and the paint will settle in the "troughs" while sliding off the "peaks," giving a speckled effect which can be effective for some subjects but is difficult to exploit successfully. Among the best-known makes of good watercolor papers are Saunders, Fabriano, Arches, Bockingford, Strathmore in the US, Ingres in the UK, and R.W.S. (Royal Watercolor Society), some of which also include handmade papers.

Hand-made papers are made from pure linen rag and specially treated with size to provide the best possible surface for watercolor work. Such papers are sized on one side only and thus have a right and a wrong side, which can be checked by holding the paper up to the light so that the watermark becomes visible. Many of the better machine-made papers also have a watermark and hence a right and wrong side.

STRETCHING THE PAPER

Watercolor papers vary widely in weight, or thickness, and the lighter ones need to be stretched or they will buckle as soon as wet paint is applied to them. The weight is usually expressed in pounds and refers to the weight of a ream (480 sheets), not to each individual sheet. The thinner papers, ranging from 70 to 140 pounds, must be stretched; any paper weighing 200 pounds or more can be used without this treatment. Watercolor boards can be bought. These have watercolor paper mounted on heavy board, so that the stretching has already been done. They are

STRETCHING PAPER

1 Cut the paper to size and place it right-side up in a bath or tray of water. Leave it to soak for a few minutes.

2 Lift out the paper and drain off the excess water.

3 Lay the paper on a drawing board at least 1 in. (2.5 cm) larger than the paper, making sure that it is right way up.

4 Smooth the paper quite flat and stick gumstrip around the edges, starting with opposite sides.

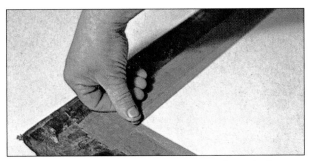

5 Finish by putting a drawing pin in each corner. Do not dry the paper in front of a fire, which will buckle it.

particularly useful for outdoor work, since no drawing board is needed.

Stretching paper is not difficult, but since the paper must be soaked, it takes some time to dry thoroughly and needs to be done at least two hours before you intend to start work. Cut the paper to the

BELOW The difference between a quality sable brush (left), or synthetic sable (middle), and the kind of cheap brush sometimes provided in watercolor boxes (right), are self evident.

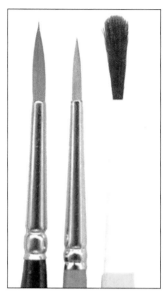

size required (if you do not want to use the whole sheet) and wet it well on both sides by laying it in a bath or tray of water. When it is well soaked, hold it up by the corners to drain off the excess water, then lay it right-side-up on a drawing board and stick down each edge with the gummed brown paper known as gumstrip (do not use masking tape or sellotape). Finally, place a drawing pin in each corner. The paper will dry taut and flat and should not buckle when paint is applied. Occasionally, however, stretching does go wrong and the paper buckles at one corner or tears away from the gumstrip; if that happens there is no other course but to repeat the process. Drying can be hastened with a hairdrier, but it is not a good practice to leave the board in front

of a fire. Ideally the paper should dry naturally.

BRUSHES

Soft brushes are normally used for watercolor. The best ones are sable, made from the tips of the tail hairs of the small rodent found chiefly in Siberia. Sable brushes are extremely expensive, but if looked after properly they should last a lifetime. Watercolor brushes are also made from squirrel-hair (known as "camel hair" for some reason) and ox-hair. These are good substitutes for sable, but have less spring. There is now a wide range of synthetic brushes, usually made of nylon or a mixture of nylon and sable, and although they do not hold the paint as well as sable and are thus less suitable for broad washes, they are

BELOW Japenese and Chinese brushes are versatile, and are very well suited to fine calligraphic work, but they require some practice and are not recommended for beginners.

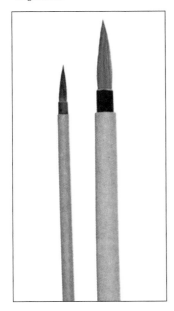

LEFT The complete range of sizes available of one make of brush.

BELOW A range of brush types used for particular techniques. From left to right: fine synthetic round, broad synthetic round, mixed fibers round, ox hair round, squirrel hair round, sable fan, sable bright, sable round, fine sable round.

excellent for finer details and are very much cheaper.

Brushes come in a variety of shapes and only by experiment will an individual discover which shapes and sizes suit him. It is not necessary to have a great many brushes for watercolor work; for most purposes three or four will be adequate, and many artists use only two. A practical range would be one large chisel-end for laying washes and two or three rounds in different sizes. Some watercolorists use ordinary household brushes for washes, but care must be taken to prevent hairs from falling out as you work.

If you want your brushes to last, it is essential to look after them well. Wash them thoroughly in running water after use—if they are still stained use a little soap. Store them upright if possible.

EASELS

Watercolors, unlike oils, are best done at close quarters, with the support held nearly horizontal, so that an easel is not really necessary for indoor work. However, an easel can be helpful. It allows you to tilt the work at different angles (many artists prefer to do preliminary drawings with the board held vertical) and to move it around to the best light, which is more difficult with a table. The most important aspects to consider—apart, of course, from price—are stability and the facility for holding the work firmly in a horizontal position. For outdoor work, the combined seat and easel, which folds and is carried by a handle, is particularly useful. For indoor work, the combination easel, which can be used both. as a drawing table and a studio easel, is more convenient. Both are adjustable to any angle from vertical to horizontal. Good easels are not cheap, however, so that it is wise to do without one until you are sure of your requirements; many professional watercolorists work at an ordinary table with their board supported by a book or brick.

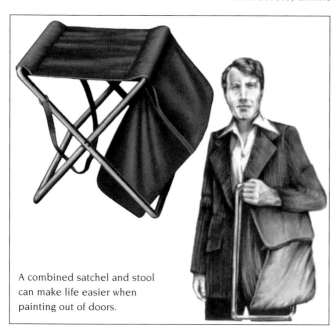

A combined satchel and stool can make life easier when painting out of doors.

FAR LEFT The combination easel functions both as a folding studio easel and a drawing table, which makes it practical for use in a small studio.

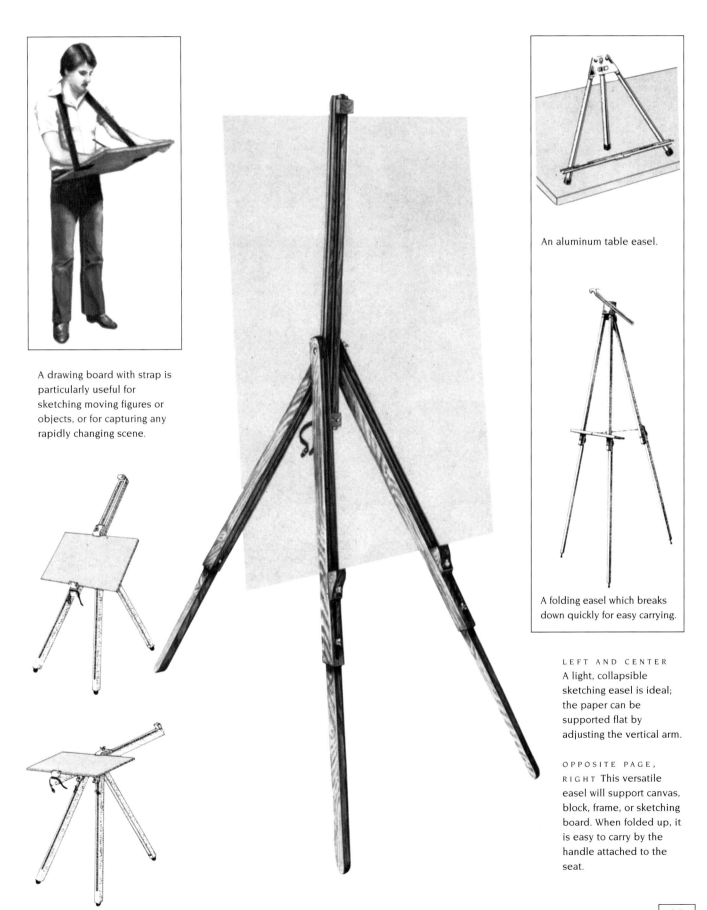

A drawing board with strap is particularly useful for sketching moving figures or objects, or for capturing any rapidly changing scene.

An aluminum table easel.

A folding easel which breaks down quickly for easy carrying.

LEFT AND CENTER A light, collapsible sketching easel is ideal; the paper can be supported flat by adjusting the vertical arm.

OPPOSITE PAGE, RIGHT This versatile easel will support canvas, block, frame, or sketching board. When folded up, it is easy to carry by the handle attached to the seat.

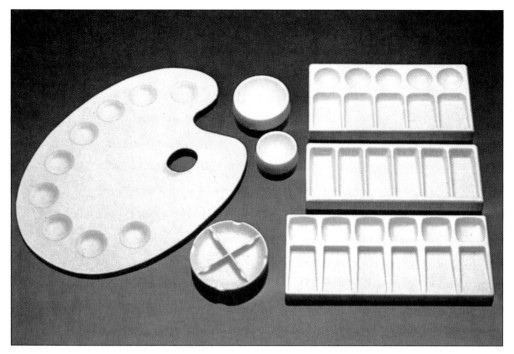

ABOVE Any plate or dish can be used for mixing watercolor, but there are several specially made palettes on the market.

The thumbhole variety is especially useful for outdoor work.

ABOVE These colors will provide a perfectly adequate range for most needs. Some artists work with fewer. From top to bottom: cobalt blue, Prussian blue, viridian, yellow ocher, cadmium yellow, lemon yellow, cadmium red, alizarin crimson, burnt umber, Payne's gray, and ivory black.

LIGHTING

For indoor work it is vital to organize a good system of lighting. Working by a window with light coming over your left shoulder (or right shoulder if you are lefthanded) can be quite satisfactory if the window faces north and gives an even and relatively unchanging light. It is less so if the window faces the sun, since the light may constantly change from brilliant to murky and may even throw distracting patches of light and shade across your work. An artificial light of the fluorescent "daylight" type will enable you to work in a poorly lit room or corner and to continue working when the light has faded—winter days can seem very short for those dependent on daylight. Such light can be used either instead of natural light or to supplement it, and there is one type with a screw base that can be fitted to the edge of a table or an adjacent shelf.

BOARDS, PALETTES, AND OTHER EQUIPMENT

You will need a drawing board, or possibly two boards of different sizes, to support the paper and stretch it where necessary. A piece of plywood or blockboard is perfectly adequate provided the surface is smooth and the wood soft enough to take drawing pins. For outdoor work a piece of hardboard can be used, with the paper clipped to it, though the paper must be heavy enough not to require stretching.

If you buy paints in paintbox

Small natural sponges are an invaluable aid to watercolor painting, both for applying paint and for correcting or modifying areas. Rags, kitchen paper, and cotton swabs should also form part of the basic equipment.

form you will already have a palette; if not, you will need one with compartments for mixing paint. Watercolor palettes are made in plastic, metal, or ceramic, in a variety of sizes, and some have a thumbhole so that they can be held in the non-painting hand when working out of doors. Water containers are another necessity for outdoor work; there is nothing worse than arriving at your chosen spot to find that you have forgotten the water. Containers can be bought, plastic soft-drink bottles can be used to carry the water and

any light (unbreakable) container such as a yogurt pot will suffice to put it in.

Various other items, though not strictly essential, can be useful and inexpensive aids for watercolor work. Small sponges can be used instead of brushes to apply washes, to sponge out areas, and to create soft, smudgy cloud effects; kitchen roll, blotting paper and cotton wool can be used in much the same way. Toothbrushes are useful for spattering paint to create textured effects, to suggest sand or pebbles on a beach, for example. A scalpel,

or a razor blade, is often used to scrape away small areas of paint in a highlight area. And both masking tape and masking fluid can serve to stop out areas while a wash is laid over the top, leaving a hard-edged area of white paper when removed. The specific uses of such aids and devices are more fully explained in the following chapter, and examples are given in the step-by-step demonstrations in the latter part of this section.

CHAPTER TWO
Technique

Pure watercolor, being transparent, must be applied
from light to dark. The paper itself is used to create the
pure white or light tones which, with opaque paints,
would be made by using white alone or mixed with
colored pigment.

OPPOSITE A detail of a French vineyard:
the artist decided that the converging
lines of the field were too heavily colored.
He loosens the color with a soft brush and
clean water, before lifting it off with tissue.

Any area required to be white is simply "reserved," or left unpainted, so that when it is surrounded with darker washes it will shine out with great brilliance. Pale tones are created in the same way, with a light-colored wash put on first and then surrounded with darker tones. Light reflected off the paper, back through these thin skins of paint known as washes, gives a watercolor painting a spontaneity and sparkle which cannot be achieved with any other medium. Hence watercolor's popularity with artists both past and present.

The two most important facts about watercolor are, first, that it is always to some extent unpredictable, even in the hands of experts, and, second, that because dark is always worked over light, some planning is needed before beginning the painting. It is not always necessary to do a detailed and complicated drawing on the paper, only enough to work out the basic shapes and design; this really should be done however, or you will begin without really knowing which areas are to be left white or pale and how they will fit into the painting as a whole.

Thus the first step in any painting is to establish where the first wash is to be applied; and the first step in watercolor technique is to learn how to put on the wash.

FLAT WASH

A flat wash in a vivid color is being laid on dampened paper with a broad, flat-ended brush. It is not strictly necessary to dampen the paper (many artists prefer the slightly "dragged" look given by working on dry paper) but dampening facilitates an even covering. Tilt the board slightly so that the brush strokes flow into one another, and work backward and forward down the paper until the whole area is covered.

LAYING A FLAT WASH

The wash is the basis of all watercolor painting, whether it is a broad, sweeping one, covering a large expanse, such as a sky or the background to a portrait, or a much smaller one laid on a particular area. Washes need not be totally flat. They can be gradated in both tone and color, or broken up and varied. But the technique of laying a flat wash must be mastered, even if you subsequently find that you seldom use it.

The support should be tilted at a slight angle so that the brush strokes flow into one another, but do not run down the paper. For a broad wash a large chisel-end brush is normally used; for a smaller one, or a wash which is to be laid against a complicated edge, a smaller round brush may be more manageable. Laying a wash must be done quickly or hard edges will form between brush strokes.

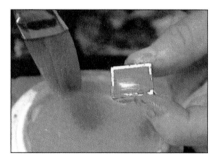

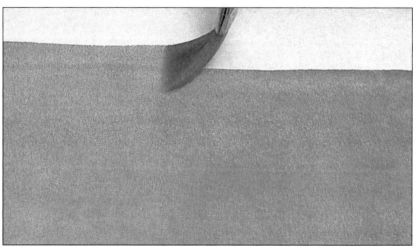

Therefore mix up more paint than you think you will need. Start by damping the paper with clear water (this is not actually essential, but helps the paint to go on evenly). Working in one direction, lay a horizontal line of color at the top of the area, then another below it, working in the opposite direction, and continue working in alternate directions until the area is covered. Never go back over the wet paint because you feel it is uneven or not dark enough, as this will result in the paint's "flooding" and leave blobs and patches. A final word of caution: if the doorbell or the telephone rings while you are in the middle of a wash, ignore it; otherwise you will return to a hard edge which is impossible, or at least very difficult to remove.

Leave the wash to dry before working on adjacent areas of the painting. Not until the wash is completely dry will you be able to

SPONGE WASH

Often a wash needs to be slightly textured or varied in strength, for which purpose a sponge is useful.
I The wash is mixed with a brush and tested on a piece of spare paper.

2 Enough paint is mixed to cover the area and the sponge is dipped into it. For a lighter covering, some of the paint can be squeezed out.

3 A variegated effect is achieved by applying the paint quite thickly with the first stroke, much more thinly with the second.

4 The final wash can be worked into with the sponge while it is still wet in order to lighten some areas and produce a soft, shimmering effect.

VARIEGATED WASH

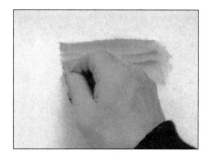

I The paper is dampened with a sponge and a thin wash of color is applied, also with a sponge.

2 A second color is then flooded on, using the tip of the sponge so that the two run together.

3 A brush is now used to touch in darker areas on the still-wet paint. Very subtle effects can be created by this wet-into-wet technique, but they are always to some extent unpredictable.

establish either how even it is or what its true color value is (watercolor dries much paler than it appears when wet). The ability to assess the precise tone of a wash comes only with experience, but it can be helpful to lay down one or two patches of flat color on a spare piece of paper and allow them to dry as a preliminary

test. Washes can be laid on top of the first one to strengthen the color or darken the tone, though too many will turn the painting muddy. Purists claim that more than three layers spoils the quality.

Another method of laying a wash is to use a sponge. This is particularly useful when a slightly

variegated or textured wash is required, as the sponge can either be filled with paint for a dense covering or used relatively dry for a paler effect. A sponge can also be used in conjunction with a brush. If you rinse it in clean water and squeeze it out you can remove some of the paint laid by a brush while it is still wet.

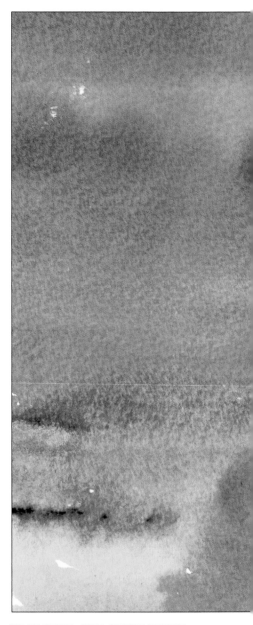

COMPLEX EDGES

Sometimes a wash must be laid against a complicated edge, for example, a group of roofs and chimneys with an intricate outline. The wash must then start from the edge rather than end at it, which may necessitate turning the board sideways or upside down. When dampening the paper before putting on the wash take care to dampen only up to this edge; otherwise the wash will flow into the areas to be reserved.

This kind of technical problem highlights the need for initial planning—the success of a painting may hinge on the precise way a certain area has been outlined by reserving. Another method for dealing with intricate shapes is to stop out the parts to be reserved with masking fluid.

GRADATED AND VARIEGATED WASHES

Colors in nature are seldom totally flat or one solid hue. It is often desirable, therefore, to lay a gradated wash, which becomes darker or lighter at the top or bottom or changes from one color to another. For a gradated wash, simply mix more water with the paint to make each successive strip lighter or more pigment to darken them.

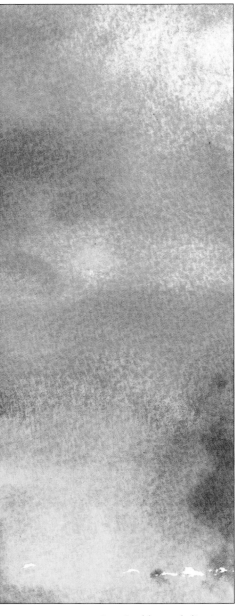

LEFT The possibilities of working wet-into-wet may be explored by producing this kind of doodle in a matter of minutes. The wet-into-wet technique is often used in the early stages of a painting, or for the background, more precise work being done at a later stage or in another area of the painting.

DRY BRUSH

Dry brush work is an excellent method of suggesting texture, such as that of grass or a cornfield, but it becomes monotonous if used too much in one painting. Here a number of similar colors have been used over a pale underlying wash to give tonal variation.

FAR LEFT Prussian blue and alizarin crimson have been allowed to run into one another, just as they would with a wash of only one color. Such effects are impossible to control accurately; the artist must be prepared for an element of "happy accident."

MIDDLE Laying one wash on top of another often gives textural variety as well as intensifying the color. Notice that the bottom band, a pale wash of Payne's gray, is quite even, while the one at the top, a third application of the same wash, shows distinct brush marks.

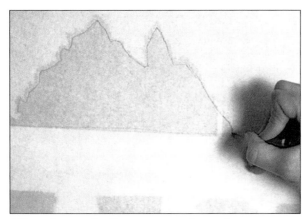

1 The artist uses detail paper to trace the area he wants to mask.

2 He then carefully cuts the mask with a scalpel.

4 More sap green, again mixed with gum water, is spattered on the area with an ordinary household brush.

5 The slightly irregular stippled effect is clear, even before the mask is peeled off.

For a variegated wash, mix up the two or more colors to be used, dampen the paper as usual, and then lay on the colors so that they blend into one another. The effect of such a wash cannot be worked out precisely in advance, even with practice—you should be prepared for a happy (or unhappy) accident. As with a flat wash, never make corrections while the paint is still wet; if you are dissatisfied when it is dry it can be sponged out and a further wash laid on top.

Some watercolorists use variegated washes in a particularly free way. Each individual arrives at his own technique by trial and error. Attractive efforts can sometimes be achieved by deliberately allowing the paint to flood in the middle of a wash, by introducing blobs of strong color to a paler wash while the paint is damp, or by laying one wash over a dry one, thus producing a slight granulation of the paper. Such effects are unpredictable. For one thing, they vary widely according to the type of paper used. But one of the great joys of watercolor is the opportunity it provides for turning accidental effects to advantage.

DRY-BRUSH AND TEXTURAL METHODS

Painting with a small amount of paint on a fine brush which is almost dry is a method most frequently used for the fine details of a painting, but dry-brush is also a technique in its own right and can be used very effectively for large areas, either over a wash which has already been laid down or straight on to white paper. For landscape work it can be used to suggest the texture of grass, trees,

USING MASKING FLUID

Masking fluid provides a way of painting in "negative," which can give very subtle and exciting effects.

1 The areas to be masked are carefully drawn and the fluid is applied with a fine brush.

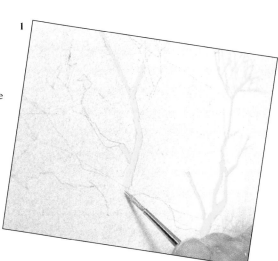

3 The mask is applied and the tree is painted in sap green, mixed with a little gum water to give it extra body and brilliance.

2 The fluid is allowed to dry and a yellow-brown wash is laid over the top.

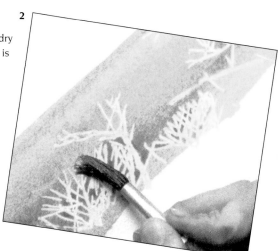

3 A blue wash for the sky is added and allowed to dry, after which the fluid is peeled off by gentle rubbing with a finger.

6 The mask is removed, leaving a sharp, clean outline. The slightly irregular texture is very effective in suggesting foliage.

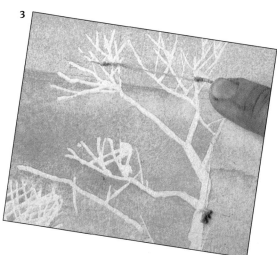

rocks, stone walls, and the like. For portraits and still-lifes it can model forms more easily than washes of wet paint can.

Like all watercolor techniques dry-brush requires practice. If the paint is too wet it will go on as a solid wash; if too dry it will not go on at all. The brush normally used for large areas of dry-brush work is a large chisel-end, with the bristles slightly splayed to produce a series of fine lines, rather like hatching and cross-hatching in drawing. One color and tone can be laid over another, and the brush strokes can be put on in different directions as the shape suggests.

The Victorian artist, William Holman Hunt (1827–1910) used this method extensively, together with stippling, in which small dots of color are applied to the paper very close together, in rather the way that the French artist, Georges Seurat (1859–91), applied oil paint. Scumbling is a method of applying fairly thick paint in a circular scrubbing motion so that the paint goes on to the paper from all directions and picks up the texture of the surface. It is effective when used for relatively small areas to provide contrast to flat washes, but if used too extensively in one painting it can become monotonous.

Another common method of suggesting texture is to spatter wet paint on to the paper with a toothbrush or bristle-brush. This technique, too, should be reserved for certain areas only, but it is an excellent way of dealing with a pebble beach, say, or a rough stone wall. The paint is usually spattered over an existing wash not directly on to white paper, and to make the result look natural care must be taken to use paint which is not much darker than the wash. Mask off surrounding areas if they are lighter in tone.

Masking tape can be used for a straight edge; for more complex shapes, a rough mask can be cut from cartridge paper.

MASKING OUT AND CREATING HIGHLIGHTS

Many watercolorists use masking fluid and masking tape for reserving areas of white paper. Masking fluid, which is specially made for the purpose, is a kind of liquid rubber sold in small bottles and applied with a brush. Purists disdain to use it, but their scorn is baseless. Very attractive and exciting effects, quite different from those produced by the classic method of laying washes around an area, can be gained by it. Stopping out with masking fluid is a method of painting in "negative," the precise and subtle shades made by the brush remain when the liquid is removed.

The paper must be quite dry before the fluid is applied, and the fluid itself must be allowed to dry before a wash is laid on top. Once the wash has dried, the fluid can be rubbed off with a finger or a soft eraser, leaving the white area, which can be modified and worked into if required. Masking fluid should never be left on the paper for longer than necessary, and care must be taken to wash the brushes immediately; otherwise fluid will harden in the hairs and ruin them. Masking fluid is not suitable for all papers, especially ones with a rough surface.

Masking tape is particularly useful for straight-edged areas, such as the light-catching side of a building or the edge of a window-sill. There is no reason why all painting should be done freehand; just as few people can draw a circle without recourse to compasses, few people can paint a really straight line without splashing paint over the edge. Masking tape enables you to use the paint freely without worrying about spoiling the area to be reserved.

ABOVE Watercolor has been used in conjunction with pastel to give liveliness and textural contrast to this painting. Both the building itself and the dark tree on the left are in pure watercolor, while the foreground grass is pure pastel. The sky is a combination of the two. Pastel combines well with watercolor, and a painting such as this often benefits from a "non-purist" approach.

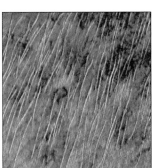

LEFT Sharp, clean lines and highlights can be made by scraping into dry paint with a scalpel or other sharp knife. Take care not to damage the paper by pressing too hard.

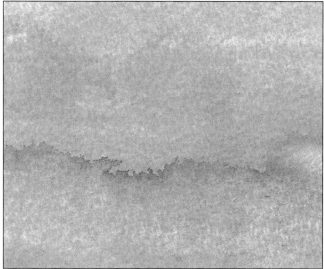

A wash which has "gone wrong" ABOVE and flooded, has been worked into to create a sky effect not originally planned TOP. One of the attractions of watercolor is that new uses of the medium are often supported by "mistakes."

Yet another way of keeping the paint away from the paper is to use wax in what is called the resist method, like that used in batik fabrics. This differs from the previous techniques in being permanent; once the wax is on the paper it cannot be removed except by laborious scraping with a razor blade. The paint, moreover, will lie on top of the wax to some extent (this varies according to the paper used), leaving a slightly textured surface. The effect can be very attractive, particularly for flowers or fabrics. An ordinary household candle can be used, or a white wax crayon for finer lines.

The best method of creating fine, delicate highlights when a painting is nearly complete is to scrape into the paint with a sharp point, of a scalpel, say, so that the white paper is revealed. Very fine lines can be drawn in this way to suggest a blade of grass or a flower stem catching the light in the foreground of a landscape. Such touches often give a painting that extra something it seems to need. They can also be achieved by applying Chinese white with a fine brush, but scraping back tends to give a cleaner line.

MIXING MEDIA

Many other media can be used in combination with watercolor; indeed, the mixing of media is now commonplace, whereas in the past it was regarded as breaking the rules. Watercolor used with pen and ink has a long history; in the days before watercolor became recognized as a medium in its own right, it was used mainly to give touches of color to drawings or to tint black and white engravings. Nowadays there are many other media—some old and some new—that can be used with watercolor to good effect.

One traditional way to change the nature of paint by thickening it is to mix it with a little gum arabic, which gives it both texture and lasting luster. Soap can be used in much the same way, and it makes the paint easier to scrape back. Soap can also be used to make imprints of objects such as leaves or flowers. Coat the object with soap, apply paint to it and then press it on to the paper.

Watercolors can be drawn into with pens, pencils, crayons, or pastels, and areas can be stressed or lightened with gouache or Chinese white. Watercolor pencils and crayons, a relatively new invention, are particularly suitable for this purpose. When dry they behave like crayons or hard pastels, but if dipped in water or used on wet paper they will dissolve, forming a wash. Using these, or ordinary pastels, on top of watercolor can turn a painting which has "gone wrong" and become dull and lifeless into something quite new and different. It is always worth experimenting with such media on a painting that you are less than happy with; you may evolve a personal technique that you can use again. Wax oil pastels can create interesting textured areas when laid underneath a wash, as can treating the paper, or parts of it, with white spirit before painting, which has a similar effect. The possibilities are almost endless, and experimentation is sure to reward you with interesting discoveries.

PROBLEM-SOLVING

Although watercolors cannot be altered so drastically or so often as paintings in any of the opaque media, changes are possible. It is a mistake to abandon a picture because a first wash has not gone on quite right.

The first thing to remember is that a wash which looks too dark or too vivid on a sheet of otherwise white paper will dry much lighter and may look quite pale when surrounded by other colors. If the first wash looks wrong, let it dry. If you are still quite sure it is not what you intended, sponge it out with a clean sponge and clear water. This may leave a slight stain on the paper, depending on the paper used and the color itself (some colors stain the paper, like a dye, while others do not) but when dry it will be too faint to spoil the new wash.

USING GUM WATER

Gum water, which is gum arabic diluted in water, adds richness to watercolors and keeps the colors bright. It can also be used, as here, as a sort of resist method to create highlights.
1 The tree and hedge are painted in with pure watercolor.
2 A further wash of green is applied, this time mixed with gum water.
3 The area of the central tree is spattered with water, flicked on with a household brush.
4 The central tree is blotted with a rag, so that wherever the water has touched, small areas of paint are lifted off, the gum being soluble in water.
5 The lighter patches of color give an extra sparkle to the tree, while the addition of the gum water imparts richness to the dark green on either side.

1

2

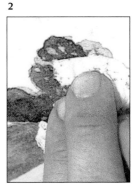

3

4

5

CHAPTER THREE

Basic Rules for Artists

Every painter, working in whatever medium, needs to understand the basic rules of his craft, even if sometimes only to break them. The underlying principles of such things as composition, perspective, drawing itself, apply to all kinds of painting. The novice watercolorist, who needs to plan his paintings especially carefully, should have a firm grasp of them from the beginning.

OPPOSITE Working out of doors. Some artists find that they work best with the subject in front of them. Others will only work from sketches or photographs, or even (more rarely), from memory.

COMPOSING AND SELECTING

Whether you are painting outdoors or indoors, whether your chosen subject is a landscape, a group of buildings, a portrait or a single flower in a vase, you need to have a clear idea of what the main elements are and of how you will place them on the paper before you begin to paint. Painting a landscape out of doors requires you to decide where the view is to begin and end, where to place the horizon, whether to emphasize or alter features in the foreground, and so on. For a portrait, still-life, or flower painting you must decide how much to show, the proportion of the figure or flower in relation to the background, the general color scheme and the balance of lights and darks. Composition and selection thus go hand in hand: an artist first selects which aspects of the subject are important and then composes the picture by placing them in a certain way.

There are well-tested mathematical rules for "good composition." The ancient Greeks, for instance, devised the system known as the Golden Section (or Golden Mean), in which the area of the painting is divided by a line in such a way that the smaller part is to the larger what the larger is to the whole. This ensures that the picture plane is divided in a balanced and symmetrical way, and countless artists have made use of the principle. The triangle is another basis for composition (many paintings are based on the framework of a single triangle) as is a series of intersecting geometric shapes such as squares, rectangles, and circles.

It is unlikely that someone sitting down to an outdoor watercolor sketch will need a full knowledge of such principles, but there are some simple and practical ones that should be

A B O V E Figure paintings are more difficult to compose than landscape because the choices are so much wider. A figure can be disposed in an almost infinite number of ways, while a landscape often needs only minor re-arranging. Here the artist has placed his subject in the center of the picture, with the diagonal of the leg balancing the angle of the head: He has allowed one leg and the legs of the chair to "bust" the frame at the bottom, thus bringing the figure forward on to the picture plane and avoiding a cramped and awkward appearance.

Painters of the Renaissance usually planned the composition of a painting on a geometric grid structure. This example, by Piero della Francesca, is based on a triangle, a common compositional device which is still much used, as are circles and rectangles. the drawing on the right shows how other triangles can be discerned within the main one formed by the figures.

 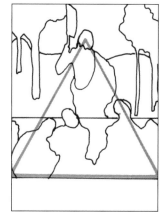 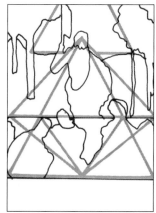

ABOVE Converging lines in landscapes are often used to lead the viewer's eye to the focal point, in this case the buildings. Unusually, the artist has divided the picture into two nearly equal parts, the land and the sky; but monotony has been avoided by allowing the buildings and trees to break into the skyline and by dividing the foreground by the broken line of white road in the middle distance.

borne in mind. Basically, a good composition is one in which there are no jarring elements; all the parts of the picture balance one another in a pleasing way, and the viewer's eye is led into the picture rather than out of it. Whatever the subject, it is almost never advisable to divide the painting into two equal halves, such as sea and land, or table-top and background in a still-life. The result is at once monotonous and disjointed. The viewer's eye should not be led to one part of the painting to the exclusion of others, but there should usually be a "focal point." For example, a group of buildings in a landscape can be used simply as a counterpoint to

other elements, such as trees and hills, or they may be what interests you most about the scene, with the trees, hills, and foreground used as a "backdrop." The buildings need not be large, nor placed directly in the center of the picture (this is not normally advisable); what matters is that the eye should be consistently led to them as the focal point. Compositional devices often used to lead the eye in this way are the curving lines of a path, stream, plowed field, or fence, along which the viewer's eye must travel. Such lines should never lead out of the picture unless for a deliberately sought effect.

The focal point of a

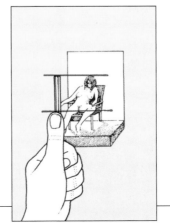

portrait is almost always the face, the eyes in particular for a front or three-quarter view, and care must be taken not to detract from it by placing too much emphasis on other elements, such as the background, or the hands. Hands and clothing are often treated in a sketchy way so that they do not assume too much importance. A figure or face should be placed in a well-considered and deliberate way against the background to create a feeling of harmony and balance. There should not be too much space at the top. Nor, usually, should the subject be placed squarely in the middle of the picture, though a central position can sometimes be effective.

Backgrounds are part of a portrait painting, as are skies in landscapes, even when they are quite plain and muted in color. If a picture is placed against a stark white background, the white areas will have their own shapes and thus make their contribution to the balance of the painting. Such flat areas are known as

When drawing a figure from life measurements and angles need constant checking. By holding up a pencil and moving your thumb up and down on it you can check proportions; angling the pencil to follow the line of the body or limb shows you the precise slope, which can be double-checked by relating it into a vertical such as a chair leg.

43

"negative space." A more decorative background, such as a boldly patterned wallpaper or still-life of a vase of flowers on a table, can be used to complement the main subject, just as the colors in the sky or the direction of clouds do in a landscape.

Many artists use viewing frames to help them work out a satisfactory composition, and some also use polaroid cameras for indoor work, taking several shots of a portrait or still-life until they find a satisfactory arrangement. A viewing frame is simply a piece of cardboard with an oblong hole cut in it (a good size of aperture is 4½ x 6 in. /11 x 15 cm), which is held up at about arm's length to work out the best placing of the subject. It is particularly useful for on-the-spot landscape work, as it is very difficult to assess large landscape subjects without some form of framing device. Making small, quick sketches, often referred to as thumbnail sketches, is another good way to work out a composition. A rough scribble, even a few lines, will often provide a clear idea of how the main shapes should be placed within the picture area.

In portraiture precise drawing is very important. It is often wise to make preliminary drawing and then transfer it to the painting surface, thus avoiding too much erasing on the surface itself. Here the artist has worked from a photograph, enlarged to the required size by means of a grid. The drawing

DRAWING

Drawing is the basis of all painting. Indeed, painting is simply drawing with a brush and color. Although much of the more detailed drawing in a watercolor is done at the final stages with a fine brush, it is nearly always necessary to make some form of pencil drawing on the paper before beginning to paint. Without this, you will have no idea where to place the first wash or which areas to reserve as paler ones. Obviously there are exceptions to this general rule. A very quick study in which color is the most important aspect or a broad and impressionistic landscape with little detail may not need a drawing. But, even so, a few lines can provide a helpful guide.

Few people draw with the ease and assurance that produce the confident and flowing lines of really fine drawings. However, a drawing which is to be used only as the guideline for a painting need not be of high quality. What matters is getting the proportions and shapes

line transferred to the support by using a form of carbon paper called iron-oxide paper, which provides a clear outline. The finished painting can be seen on page 106.

TRANSFERRING THE IMAGE

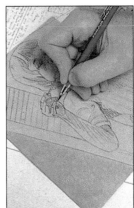

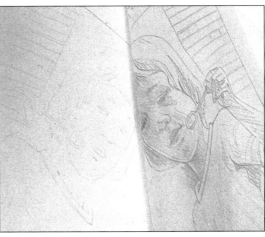

right. Everybody tends to draw what he knows, or thinks he knows, rather than what he actually sees. The first step in drawing is to take a good long look at the subject and try to get rid of any preconceptions about it. By holding a pencil up at arm's length and closing one eye it is possible to check whether a line which appears vertical or horizontal really is so; and the size of one object in relation to another can be measured in the same way. Once one part of a scene, or figure, has been described accurately all the others can be related to it. But if

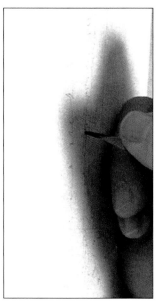

TOP RIGHT AND ABOVE Since only an outline was needed, the drawing was done directly on the support with a sharp 2B pencil. The first wash was then laid around the shapes of the building and trees.

you begin with a false "statement," misunderstanding the angle at which a roof top slopes away from you, for example, and then try to relate the other shapes and lines to it, the drawing will go progressively awry. It pays to take time over a preliminary drawing, especially if the subject is complex, otherwise you will become increasingly

frustrated when you start to paint.

Never try to draw any subject from too close a viewpoint, which distorts the view. And make sure that you do not have to move your head to see different parts of the subject. Your line of vision should be central. Try to make sure that you are reasonably

1

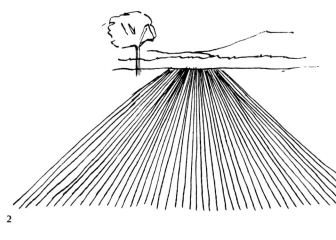

2

3

4

PERSPECTIVE

Perspective governs everything we see; even in a simple landscape of fields and hills the way in which a wall twists and narrows or the furrows of a plowed field change direction explain the lie of the land and help to create a feeling of form and recession.

1 The furrows in a plowed field run across our vision, the spaces between them becoming progressively smaller as the field recedes.

2 Now our viewpoint is altered, so that the furrows run away, converging at a vanishing point on the horizon.

3 In this mid-view, between that of the two previous examples, the lines still converge on the horizon, but the vanishing point is some way outside the picture.

4 This wide-angle view shows that we do not really perceive the lines of the furrows as straight.

5 The vanishing point must always be on the horizon—that is, at our own eye-level—if the ground is flat, but it will be within the picture area only if viewed square-on.

6 If there is a dip in the ground the furrows will follow it, thus taking their vanishing points from the angle of the indentation, which theoretically alters the horizon line. This is an important point to remember in landscape painting, as the land is seldom completely flat.

7 When viewed from a distance, the two sides of a church tower appear to be vertical

8 However, when seen more closely, the side walls seem to converge. The lower the viewpoint, the more sharply they do so.

9 When seen from above, the sides appear to converge at the bottom.

10 When the tower is seen from an angle, each side will have its own vanishing point. When drawing or painting buildings it is all too easy to forget this.

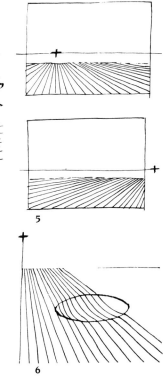

5

6

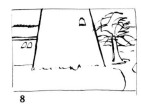

7

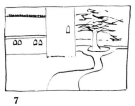

8

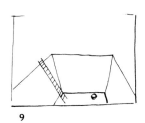

9

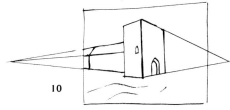

10

comfortable (not always possible when working out of doors) and hold the drawing board in such a way that it does not obscure any part of the subject. Check sizes and measurements continually by holding up your pencil and moving your thumb up and down on it, closing one eye to measure distances. Avoid making the drawing too fussy. Too many pencil marks may muddy the paint. An HB or B pencil is the best to use, as softer ones may smudge the paper. The drawing can be erased at any stage during the painting as long as the paper is quite dry. On most papers pencil marks can be erased without affecting the paint on top, though the surface of a few, rather smooth, papers may be spoiled by too much erasing.

PERSPECTIVE

Perspective is sometimes believed to be the concern only of those who paint buildings. In fact, the laws of perspective govern everything, simply because drawing and painting transfer three-dimensional shapes on to a two-dimensional surface.

In theory, a perfectly adequate drawing with a fairly accurate rendering of perspective could be produced by simply drawing what is seen. Some knowledge of the basic principles of perspective is nevertheless helpful, if only because it will enable you to know when something has gone wrong. The "golden rule," which most people learn at school, is that receding parallel lines meet at a vanishing point. That vanishing point, which is on the horizon, may be inside the picture area or outside it. The horizon itself is your own eye-level, so that if you are lying down or crouching it will be low, with a large expanse of sky, whereas if you are looking down on a scene, from a top-floor window, say, it will be very high, perhaps with no sky visible at all, and a receding parallel line of rooftops below you will slope upward. The real difficulty in drawing complex perspective subjects, such as urban scenes, is that buildings have several different planes, each with its own vanishing point, and sometimes one building or group of buildings is set at angles to another, giving yet another set of points, many of which will be outside the picture plane. These must be guessed at to some extent, but the pencil-and-thumb measuring system described earlier is helpful, or a small plastic ruler

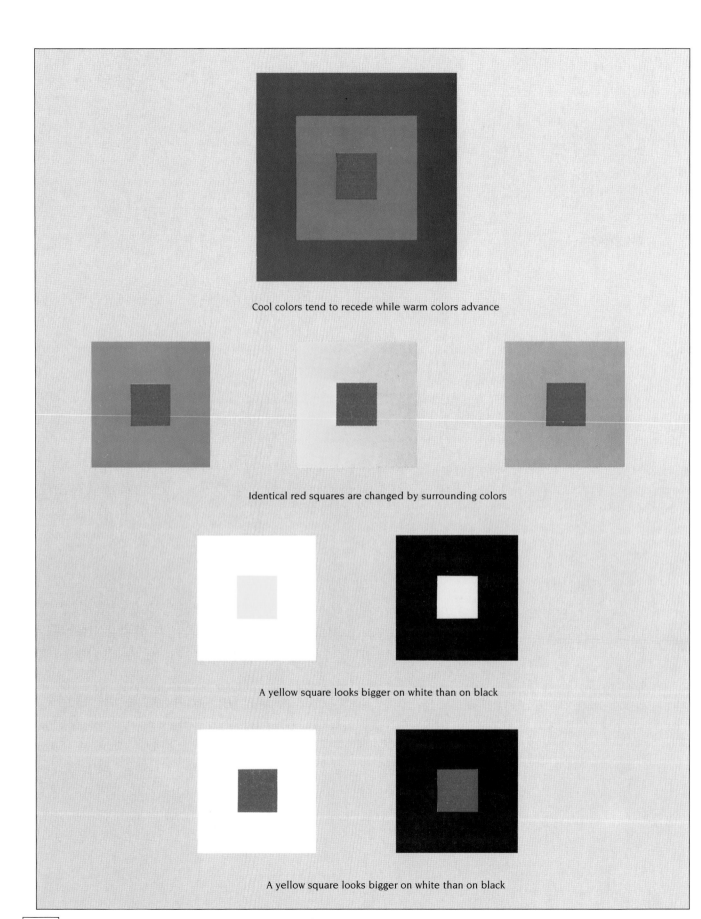

Cool colors tend to recede while warm colors advance

Identical red squares are changed by surrounding colors

A yellow square looks bigger on white than on black

A yellow square looks bigger on white than on black

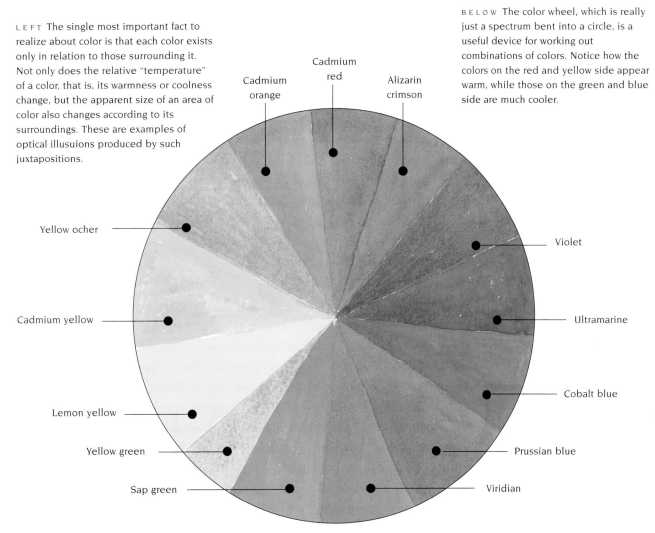

Cadmium red

Cadmium orange

Alizarin crimson

Yellow ocher

Violet

Cadmium yellow

Ultramarine

Lemon yellow

Cobalt blue

Yellow green

Prussian blue

Sap green

Viridian

TONE AND COLOR

Color theory can be enormously complicated. It is a fascinating study in itself, about which whole books have been written. But there are really only a few facts about color which the average painter needs to know. Color has two main components, tone and hue, the former being its lightness or darkness and the latter its intensity, or vividness. If you were to take both a black-and-white photograph and a color one of a landscape composed almost entirely of greens, the black-and-white one would show the tones quite clearly

can be held up to assess the angles of parallel lines.

as a series of dark grays and light grays shading to white and black. It is important to balance tones, or lights and darks, in a painting, but they can be rather hard to assess, particularly outdoors in a changing light. You may wonder whether the sky is lighter or darker than the sea or land, or whether the leaves of a tree are lighter or darker than the hills behind. Tones are much easier to judge if you half-close your eyes, thus eliminating distracting details.

In the color photograph of the landscape some of the greens will appear more vivid than others, to have a brighter hue. You may notice that the brightest colors are in the foreground, where the contrasts in tone are also the

strongest, those in the background tending to merge into one another and become barely distinguishable in places. An understanding of this phenomenon, called aerial perspective, is vitally important, especially for the landscape painter. As a landscape recedes into the middle and then the far distance, objects appear much less distinct and become paler and bluer because the light is filtered through dust and moisture in the atmosphere. It is possible to suggest distance and recession in a painting by using this kind of perspective alone, and such effects are easier to achieve in watercolor than in oil: a pale, flat wash can be put on and then the tiny differences

ABOVE In this painting all the colors are cool, just a range of blues and grays with a touch of warmer greenish brown on the left side of the building. Foregrounds are often brought forward and emphasized by using warmer colors in the front of the picture; but here the foreground has been made to "advance" by the use of much darker tones, aided by the very clear definition of the spiky foliage on the left.

RIGHT Warm colors have been used throughout this painting, those in the foreground being repeated in smaller quantities in the background. The artist's concern was with the pattern created by the various elements rather than with a strict three-dimensional representation, though the background recedes just enough to allow us to "read" the picture as an urban landscape.

in tones suggested by just a dab or two of barely tinted water.

Colors in the foreground tend to be "warmer" than those in the background as well as brighter in hue. All colors can be broadly classified as either "warm" or "cool." Reds, yellows, and oranges, for instance, are warm, and tend to push themselves forward, or "advance;" blues, and colors with blue in them, such as blue-gray and blue-green, will recede. However, colors can be perceived as colors only in relation to one another, and some blues are warmer than others while some reds are cooler. You can see this by placing ultramarine blue, which is relatively warm, next to the cold Prussian blue, or alizarin crimson, which is quite cool, next to cadmium red or orange, both of which are very warm.

Another way of using color effectively is to make use of complementary colors, those that are opposite one another on the color wheel. Red and green are complementaries, as are blue and yellow. A large expanse of green grass or blue sea can often be heightened by a small patch of bright red or yellow respectively. Landscape and seascape painters often use a figure or the sail of a boat as a means of introducing a complementary color.

Perhaps the single most important fact about color is that there is no color at all without light. The quality, strength, and direction of the light changes colors constantly, a problem when working out of doors, as a landscape which might have seemed to be composed of tones of greenish gray in the morning could by evening have become golden ocher, even red, in places. The best ways to overcome the difficulty are to work quickly, possibly making several sketches under different lights, or to decide on a color scheme and stick to it, ignoring subsequent changes.

USING REFERENCE MATERIAL

Paintings do not, of course, have to be done from life: many fine landscapes are painted in the studio, and excellent portraits are done from photographs or drawings or a combination of both. Few good paintings, however, are done from memory. Even professional artists, who are trained to observe and assess and are constantly on the lookout for visual stimulus, make use of reference material for their paintings. These may be sketches or photographs, sometimes even picture postcards. You may think that you remember a scene very well, but you will be surprised how the details escape you as soon as you sit down to paint it. It is therefore wise to amass as much reference material as possible, even if it seems to be much more than you need.

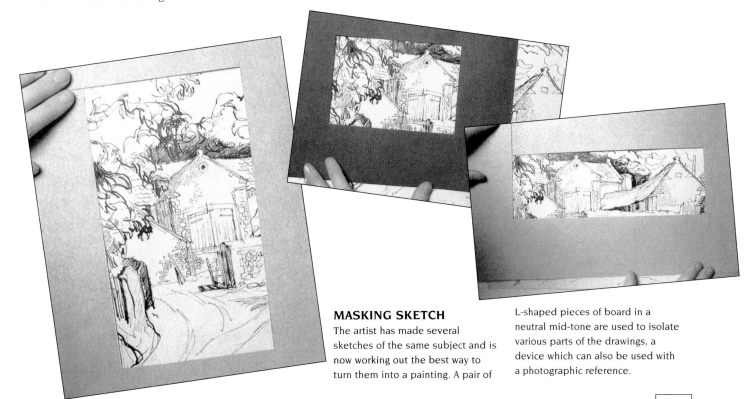

MASKING SKETCH

The artist has made several sketches of the same subject and is now working out the best way to turn them into a painting. A pair of L-shaped pieces of board in a neutral mid-tone are used to isolate various parts of the drawings, a device which can also be used with a photographic reference.

CHAPTER FOUR

Landscape and Seascape

Watercolor has always been closely associated with landscape and seascape painting, and even with today's proliferation of new media for the artist there is still none more able to render the transient and atmospheric qualities of countryside, sea, and sky.

OPPOSITE Earth colors and a vibrant green form the basic palette for this watercolor of a twisting harbor wall. The tones of the background were harmonized and blended by laying more paint into damp washes.

THE ENGLISH WATERCOLOR TRADITION

In England, the country which more than any other can claim to have founded the great tradition of landscape painting in watercolor, landscape was not really considered a suitable subject in its own right until the late 18th century. The formal, classical landscapes of the French artists, Claude Lorraine (1600–82) and Nicolas Poussill (1594–1665), were much admired by artists and discerning collectors, as were the realistic landscapes of artists of the Dutch school such as Jacob van Ruisdael (1629–82), but the general public in the main wanted portraits and historical subjects. The great English portrait painter, Thomas Gainsborough (1727–88), had a deep love of his native landscape and regarded it as his true subject, but in order to earn a living he painted many more portraits than landscapes.

The two artists who elevated landscape and seascape to the status of fine art were Constable and Turner. Their influence on painting, not only in Great Britain but all over the world, was immeasurable. By the early 19th century landscape had arrived, and at the same time watercolor, a

ABOVE Peter de Wint, an English painter of
Dutch extraction, was drawn to flat, panoramic
landscapes. His great sweeping views seem to
extend beyond the confines of the paintings
themselves. Observe the sure and confident
handling of the trees and water in *Walton-on-
Thames*, and the tiny area of unpainted paper
which give extra sparkle to the picture.

LEFT Thomas Girtin was a pioneer of watercolor
painting much admired by his contemporary,
Turner. He worked with only five colors—black,
monastral blue, yellow ocher, burnt sienna, and
light red—to create subtle evocations of
atmosphere. *The White House, Chelsea* shows
both this fine sense of composition and his
mastery of tone and color.

medium hitherto used for quick sketches and for coloring maps and prints, had become the chief medium for many landscape artists. Constable used it as his predecessors had, as a rapid means of recording impressions, but Turner used it in a new and daring way and exploited its

potential fully to express his feelings about light and color.

At much the same time John Sell Cotman, the co-founder of the school of painting known as the Norwich School after its other founder, John Crome (1768–1821), who lived in that town, was producing some of the finest

watercolor landscapes ever seen before or since. These paintings by the artists of the English watercolor school have never been surpassed; they became an inspiration to artists everywhere, and remain so today.

ABOVE A watercolor of stones at Avebury. The cool tones express the clarity of daylight and the calm grandeur of this ancient monument.

LEFT Francis Towne's work was not appreciated in the 19th century, but he has since been recognized as one of the great names of British watercolor painting. He felt a particular fascination for grand mountain landscapes, finding much of his inspiration in the wild scenery of the Alps, North Wales, and England's Lake District. This painting, *Grasmere by the Road*, is typical of his technique, in which pen outline is used to isolate areas of contrasting color.

PRACTICAL HINTS FOR OUTDOOR PAINTING

Once landscape had become an "official" subject for painters, working out of doors directly from nature became increasingly common, the more so after the French Impressionists set the example. It is not now so popular.

Photographers queueing up to record a beauty spot are a more usual sight than artists doing so. It is, however, an excellent discipline, which forces you to look hard at a subject and make rapid decisions about how to treat it and lends immediacy and spontaneity to the work itself.

Watercolor is a light and portable medium, ideally suited to outdoor work, but on-the-spot painting, whatever the medium, always presents problems. Chief among them is the weather. You may have to contend with blazing heat which dries the paint as soon as it is laid down, freezing winds which numb your hands, sudden showers which blotch your best efforts, or wash them away altogether, and changing light which confuses you and makes you doubt your initial drawing and composition. If the weather looks unpredictable, take extra clothes (a pair of old gloves with the fingers cut off the painting hand are a help in winter), a plastic bag or carrier large enough to hold your board in case of rain, and anything else you can think of for your comfort, such as a thermos of tea or coffee and a radio. If the sun is bright try to sit in a shaded place; otherwise the light will bounce back at you off the white paper, which makes it difficult or sometimes impossible to see what you are doing. If you are embarrassed by the comments of passers-by, a "walkman" serves as an efficient insulation device. Some

people also find it an aid to concentration, though others do not. Always take sufficient water and receptacles to put it in, and restrict your palette to as few colors as possible.

Although Turner's watercolors are less well known than his oils, they rank among his finest works. He was clearly extremely taken with watercolor and used it brilliantly and experimentally to express

SUMMER PAINTING

This landscape is a fine evocation of the drama of the everchanging countryside, here seen under the kind of summer squall of rain which causes the sky and hills to merge into one another. Watercolor is an ideal medium for capturing such atmospheric effects, but although the painting looks spontaneous (as the artist intended) it is actually very carefully planned.

The technique could not be more dissimilar to that used in the following example. Here an unusually large selection of colors has been used, and they have been deliberately allowed to mix on the paper to create soft, blurring effects. The natural translucence of watercolor has been exploited to the full to allow the bright colors, such as the greens of the foreground and the patch of sunlight on the hills, to shine out with brilliance and clarity.

Since the time of Turner the effects of light have been among the prime concerns of landscape painters, particularly those living in the temperate zones, where the landscape is subject to sudden changes. It is not easy, however, to capture light and atmosphere with brushes and paints, and a painting like this one relies for its success on a deliberate use of certain techniques as well as on fast working—freshness and spontaneity is quickly destroyed if the brush work becomes too labored. Here the

MATERIALS USED

SUPPORT: pre-stretched watercolor paper with a Not surface, measuring 9½ X 13 in (24 X 33 cm).
COLORS: Hookers green, oxide of chromium, Indian yellow, Naples yellow, raw sienna, raw umber, cobalt blue, ultramarine, and permanent rose, plus a little Chinese white.
BRUSHES: a selection of soft brushes and a small household brush.

brush strokes themselves form an integral part of the painting, having been used to suggest the uneven shroud of rain, with brighter and darker colors laid on in places with great accuracy and assurance. There are no totally flat washes anywhere in the painting. Even in the distant hills different tones and colors are visible, but a feeling of space and recession has been rendered by the use of very bright colors and greater tonal contrasts in the foreground.

1 The paper was stretched before use and the board was laid flat, not propped at a slight angle as it would be for laying flat washes. In this way the paint was allowed to mix on the paper without running down it uncontrollably.

his preoccupation with light and atmosphere, often making use of the semi-accidental effects that occur in watercolor painting. In *Venice from the Giudecca* he has created distance by using thin layers of paint and cool blues in the background; the darker and warmer details in the foreground are suggested lightly enough to retain the feeling of hazy, shimmering light.

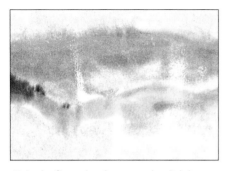

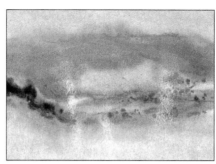

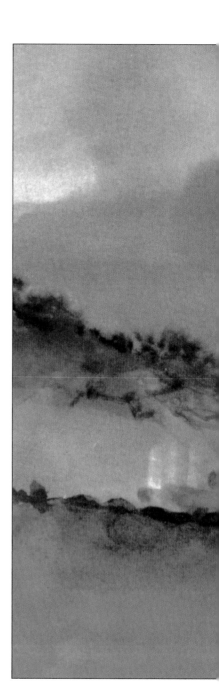

2 As the first colors began to dry slightly a warmer pink tone was introduced to the sky and touches of blue added to the middle distance. In this technique, called working wet-into-wet, the paint is never allowed to dry entirely; but if new paint is added when the first layer is too wet it will flood rather than merge softly into the other colors.

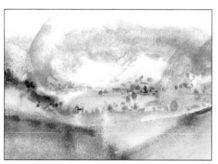

3 A broad bristle-brush was used to block in the colors for the foreground, the greens being chosen to balance the yellow-green patch of sunlight on the hills. Oil painting brushes and household brushes can often be used in watercolor painting to create particular effects.

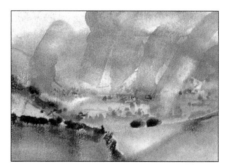

4 Next, bold brush strokes were introduced into the sky to indicate the rain clouds, and the sky was given a yellow hue and then overlaid with gray-blue. At the same time the foreground colors were strengthened and further definition was added.

5 Finished painting: to give a softer, more blurred effect to the rain, a little white has been added to the paint in the final stages. Adding white to watercolor gives an effect quite unlike the harsher one provided by gouache paints, but it should not be used until the painting is near completion; otherwise it may muddy the other colors.

Raw umber

Cobalt blue

SUMMER PAINTING

Ultramarine   Permanent rose   Hooker's green   Oxide of chromium   Indian yellow   Naples yellow   Raw sienna

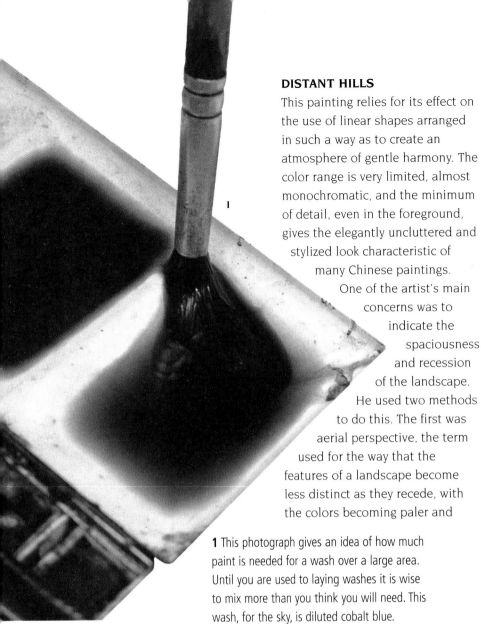

DISTANT HILLS

This painting relies for its effect on the use of linear shapes arranged in such a way as to create an atmosphere of gentle harmony. The color range is very limited, almost monochromatic, and the minimum of detail, even in the foreground, gives the elegantly uncluttered and stylized look characteristic of many Chinese paintings.

One of the artist's main concerns was to indicate the spaciousness and recession of the landscape. He used two methods to do this. The first was aerial perspective, the term used for the way that the features of a landscape become less distinct as they recede, with the colors becoming paler and cooler. Tonal contrasts are greater in the foreground, where the colors are strong and warm. The second method was to allow the tree on the right to go out of the frame at the top, thus clearly indicating that the group of trees is on the picture plane (the front of the painting).

The painting provides an excellent example of the "classical" approach to watercolor, in which the paint is laid on in a series of thin washes, allowing the brilliance of the white paper to reflect back through them. Unusually, an HP (hot-pressed) paper was used instead of the more popular Not, or cold-pressed, but this artist finds that the smoother paper suits his style, and he mixes a little gum arabic with the water to give extra body and adherence. Each wash, once laid down, has been left without any further paint being laid on top, and the painting was worked from the top downward, with the foreground trees painted over the washes for the sky and hills.

1 This photograph gives an idea of how much paint is needed for a wash over a large area. Until you are used to laying washes it is wise to mix more than you think you will need. This wash, for the sky, is diluted cobalt blue.

2 Put on with a No 10 squirrel brush, the sky was deliberately laid slightly unevenly to suggest a pale blue sky with a light cloud cover.

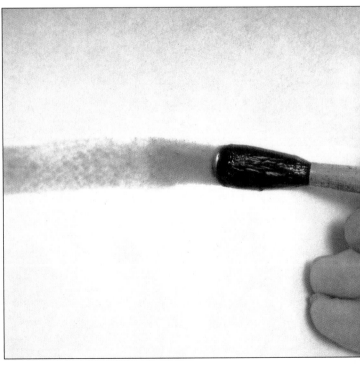

3 When dry, the same squirrel brush was used to put on a darker shade, with Payne's gray added to the cobalt blue, to the far hills.

4 The second wash had to be darker than that for the sky but not too dark, as the artist knew that he would have to increase the tonal contrasts in the middle distance to suggest its relative nearness to the picture plane.

5 & **6** As each wash has to be allowed to dry before putting on the next, in this particular technique, a hairdrier is sometimes used to hasten the process. The third and fourth washes, darker shades of the second, were laid on next, leaving the whole of the foreground and middle distance still untouched.

7 The tone of the darker area of the middle distance had to be very carefully calculated to make it appear to be in front of the far hills. This wash has been put on slightly thicker in places to suggest the shapes of the trees.

8 The trees in the foreground were worked on next, the darker paint being taken over the background and sky washes. This overlapping device is most successful when the colors are similar; overlapping two quite different colors, for instance red-brown tree trunks over bright green middle distance, would give a third color, which could provide a jarring element if not planned.

> **MATERIALS USED**
>
> SUPPORT: pre-stretched watercolor paper with an HP surface, measuring
> 14 X 21½ in. (35 X 53 cm).
> COLORS: cobalt blue, Payne's gray, raw umber, and sap green.
> BRUSHES: a No. 10 squirrel and a No. 4 sable.
> ADDITIONAL EQUIPMENT: a selection of ceramic palettes for mixing the paint; a little gum arabic for mixing with the water.

9 &**10** At this stage both the background and foreground were complete, but the area between the two was still unpainted. Because warm colors tend to advance and cool ones recede, the artist laid a warm greenish wash over this area to make it come forward toward the picture plane.

DISTANT HILLS

OLD HARRY AND HIS WIFE

A large variety of different techniques has been used to create the deceptively simple effect of this painting. The subject is bold and dramatic, and its drama has been emphasized by the juxtaposition of large, solid shapes. The tonal contrasts between the rocks and the sea are distinct enough for the rocks to stand out as light against dark, but not so great as to spoil the delicate balance. Greater contrasts might have looked overstated.

Seascapes can be tricky subjects. It is difficult to decide whether to treat the sea as a flat area or to try to show the movement of the water by "filling in" every wave and ripple. Also, when painting outside, you will see the colors constantly changing, which can give rise to uncertainty about the best approach. Here the sea has been treated fairly flat, with just enough unevenness and broken texture to suggest water; the sky hints at clouds, nothing more. The artist did not have to contend with changing colors and lights, since the painting was done in the studio. He used a photograph as his main reference for the shapes and was thus free to decide on a color scheme without external distraction. The light falling on the rock, which the photograph features very vividly, has been given a minor role in the painting, as the artist was more concerned with the texture of the rock, which is echoed in the rippling reflection below.

1 Having made a careful outline drawing of the main shapes, the artist blocked out the brightest areas of the rocks with masking fluid. This method highlights the importance of an accurate drawing, since the artist has to know where to place the masking fluid.

2 Masking fluid gives a different effect from that obtained by painting around areas to be reserved. The marks of the brush are visible when the fluid is removed. When the masking fluid was dry, a broken wash was laid over the sky area and then a darker one for the line of distant cliffs.

3 The sea was laid in with a soft brush and a dilute wash of Payne's gray. This wash was deliberately kept loose and fluid, and the paint was moved around to create different tones.

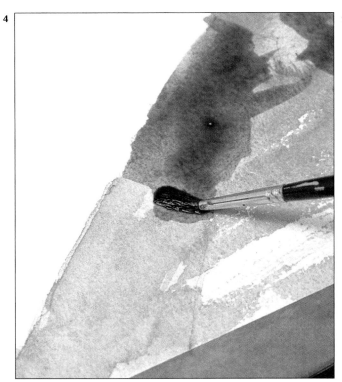

4 Here the artist is using a darker tone of Payne's gray, mixed with ultramarine, a warm blue, to darken the sea in places.

5 At this stage the entire surface has been covered and the masking fluid is still on. A pale wash of lemon yellow was laid on the reflection area and grayish washes put over the darker parts of the rocks.

6 Using diluted black paint, the artist works the darkest shadows between the rocks and at the bottom of the central rock.

7 Once the dark tones have been put on, the masking fluid is removed by rubbing gently with the finger. Masking fluid is not suitable for use on rough paper, as it sinks into the hollows and cannot be removed.

8

8 The grassy tops are now painted sap green with a fine brush. Note how the artist darkens the color at the edge to produce a crisp line of shadow.

10

9

9 Here the artist is preparing the brush for dry-brush work by spreading the bristles below the ferrule so that they will give a series of fine lines. The minimum of paint is put on the brush for this technique.

10 Another technique used for this painting was to cover an area already painted with gummed water, leave it to dry, and then gently work into it with a brush dipped in clear water to give areas of lighter tone.

11 Here the artist is using a broad bristle-brush to spatter paint on to the surface. Surrounding areas were masked off first. This is an effective texture-creating technique, but care must be taken to mix a color which is only slightly darker than that underneath; otherwise you will create a spotted, rather than an unobtrusively textured, effect.

11 As a final touch, the line of wavelets at the bottom of the rocks is added with opaque white paint, which is allowed to mix a little with the blue to give the broken effect of foamy water.

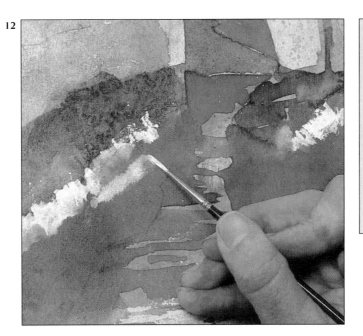

OLD HARRY AND HIS WIFE

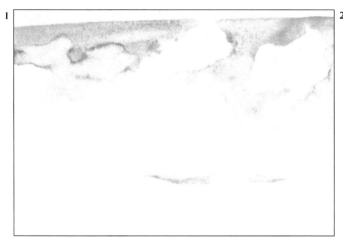

1 The artist started with some pencil lines to indicate the position of the horizon and the diagonal line of the river. He then began to lay wet washes on the sky and distant hills, using the brush as a drawing implement to describe the shapes of the clouds.

2 The artist continued to build up wet washes, keeping the middle ground fairly light at this stage, and repeating the warm pink tones on the undersides of the clouds.

3 The hills on the left have now been deepened in tone, so that they separate themselves from the more distant hills behind. At the same time further modeling has been added to the clouds by building up the mid-tones with Payne's gray, warm blue-gray, and pink.

CLOUDS

In a landscape painting, sky and land should always be seen together and in relation to one another, since the particular light cast by the sky—varying according to the amount of cloud cover and the position of the sun—has a direct influence on the colors and tones of the land below. Also, the shapes and colors of clouds can be used as an important part of a composition, perhaps to act as a counterfoil to some feature of the foreground or to echo a shape or color in the middle distance.

Watercolor lends itself very well to sky painting, since by working wet into wet effects can often be produced which resemble those seen in skies. Care must be taken, however, not to allow too many hard edges to form or the soft, rounded appearance of the clouds will be lost. Here the artist has kept the paint quite loose and fluid, using the brush to draw the cloud shapes and laying one wash over another to build up the forms. He has worked all over the painting at the same time, repeating some of the warm pinky-browns of the foreground and middle distance in the clouds themselves, so that the painting has a feeling of unity, with no artificial division between sky and land. The horizon has been placed quite low, as the sky is the main focus of interest.

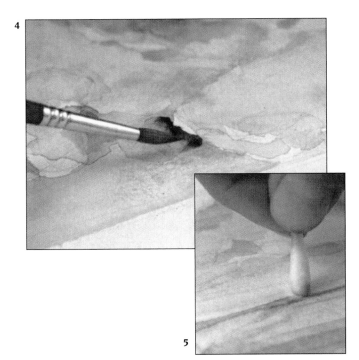

4 Here the artist is seen working wet-into-wet, adding small touches of Payne's gray to parts of the clouds. Notice how the fine lines which have formed in places where the paint has flooded have been cleverly exploited to give a crisp look to the clouds.

MATERIALS USED

SUPPORT: pre-stretched watercolor paper, measuring 10 X 14 in. (25 X 35 cm).
COLORS: ultramarine, cobalt blue, olive green, burnt sienna, cadmium yellow, alizarin crimson, and Payne's gray.
BRUSHES & OTHER EQUIPMENT: Nos. 12, 8, and 4 soft brushes, cotton swabs.

5 Sponges and cotton swabs are particularly useful for painting like this, as they can be used to soften edges, as here, or to draw paler shapes into an existing wash.

6 The final touches, which have brought the whole painting together, were to add some definition to the foreground and to increase the intensity of the blue above the clouds, so that the darker tones of land and sky are pleasingly balanced.

CLOUDS

CHAPTER FIVE
Buildings

Although paintings which take a building or a group of buildings as their subject are usually regarded as a branch of landscape painting, it is more practical to regard architectural painting and drawing as a separate subject. It presents its own problems, not the least of them being the intricacies of perspective. Obviously not all paintings of buildings need to be as accurate and precise as an architect's drawings—this is seldom desirable—but a painting of a house, church, or ruin is similar to a portrait. It is that particular building you want to paint, because you are attracted to its shape, color, or general atmosphere. It is therefore important to get the proportions and perspective right, just as you would the features of a face.

OPPOSITE Bonington's paintings, in both oil and watercolor, were much admired in his lifetime. He died of consumption at the age of 26 without having fully exploited his gift. As a colorist he was superb, and he was a pioneer in the use of watercolor, but it is said of him that he never fully understood perspective. In this painting, Castelbarco Tomb, the subject is sufficiently simple to disguise any possible weakness, and it comes across as a bold and dramatic statement of form and color.

THE TOPOGRAPHICAL TRADITION

Before the time of the great watercolor landscape painters of the later 18th and early 19th centuries, watercolor had been used mainly for quick sketches and topographical drawings, that is, precise visual records of landscapes or buildings. Many such drawings and paintings were intended as the basis for engravings or etchings, and were not really painterly in approach, color being used in flat washes to supplement a linear drawing, often in pen and ink. In the 19th century interest in buildings was stimulated by the comparative ease of travel to foreign parts. Crumbling medieval ruins, Roman remains and picturesque streets in old towns became favorite subjects for artists. By then, too, the use of watercolor had become much more daring and inventive, and artists were concerned with conveying the feeling and atmosphere of buildings, not simply recording their outward appearance and superficial details as an architect or draftsman would. Paintings such as Bonington's *Castelbarco Tomb* and Turner's *Tintern Abbey* are faithful and accurate records of the buildings, but they are also full of life and vigor, thus combining the topographical tradition with that of poetic landscape.

PRACTICAL HINTS

Some knowledge of perspective is needed to make a building look solid and convincing, but the most important factor is close and careful observation, which leads to a good foundation drawing. Try to work directly from the subject itself wherever possible: photographs, which distort the perspective, are not the ideal source of reference for architectural subjects. A photograph taken with a standard instant camera, which usually has a wide-angle lens (35–45mm focal length) will cause a tall building to look much shorter and wider; and any details in shadow, such as the top of a wall under the eaves of a roof, will probably be indistinguishable.

Watercolorists of the past sometimes paid a draftsman to make a preliminary drawing for them. They would simply put on the color! Most of us, however, have to do our own donkey-work, and with a complicated subject it can take time. Fortunately, the drawing can be done on one day (and can take as long as necessary, since changing light does not matter very much at this stage) and the actual painting on another, or even indoors. A photograph might then be used as a reference for the color only.

A small ruler is a useful addition to your usual drawing kit as it can be used to check angles, verticals, and horizontals by holding it up at arm's length and to draw guidelines on the paper. There is no reason why all drawing should be done freehand; the rather mechanical-looking lines given by ruling will be obscured once the paint is laid on. Proportions can be measured by

LEFT Turner was a master of every kind of painting he turned his hand to, and he could portray the intricate details of a building with the same skill and sensitivity that he brought to atmospheric landscapes. This detail from his *Study of Tintern Abbey* shows a combination of the topographical draftman's precision and the painter's eye for mood, tone, and color.

the pencil-and-thumb method, and all such measurements should be constantly checked and re-assessed as the work progresses.

Once the painting itself is begun, you can work in a much freer manner, altering small details to improve the composition. But architecture generally calls for a more methodical approach than landscape. Lines usually need to be crisp and clear. So allow each wash to dry before putting on the next, turning the board sideways or upside down, if need be, to fill each area.

When the first washes have been laid on, texture, such as that of brickwork or stone, can be suggested by any of the various methods described in Chapter 3 and small, precise details can be added carefully with a fine brush. Final touches are often added with a pencil or pen and ink to give a crisp definition to the painting, but they must be handled carefully. A heavy, black line can destroy the delicacy of a painting.

1 When painting on the spot, making a preliminary sketch is a good way to sort out your ideas before commiting yourself to paint. It is essential to be sure of the most important elements of a landscape. Resist the temptation to put everything in just because it is there.

2 The artist's first step was to lay a neutral wash on the foreground area. This was a mixture of raw umber, Prussian blue, and permanent yellow. He then laid a second wash over it, using the same mixture, to create slight tonal differences and texture.

VINEYARD IN ITALY

This painting is more a landscape than an architectural study. The buildings are just one of the features in a landscape, not the whole subject. They are treated quite sketchily and their appeal lies in the way that the planes of the walls catch the light and the colors of the roofs balance the greens of the foliage. However, although not drawn in any great detail, the buildings are a large part of what the painting is about, and hence its focal point, and they have been treated with sufficient attention to perspective and proportion to ensure that they look solid and convincing.

The painting was done on the spot, but the artist worked out his composition first by making a charcoal sketch, which clarified the subject for him and enabled him to see how best to treat it. He placed the group of houses slightly higher than they are in the sketch, so that almost no sky was visible, and altered the foreground so that the sweeping lines of the vineyard were made much stronger, leading the eye into the picture and up to the houses. This is a good example of the way an artist can ignore, emphasize, or alter any elements of the scene in front of him to make an interesting and lively composition. The busyness of the background, with the different shapes and colors of walls, roofs,

and foliage, is accentuated by the strong, regular and linear pattern of the foreground, so that the whole painting has a sparkling air of movement. The use of complementary colors is also exemplary: the red of the roofs and the greeen of the foliage engage in a lively interplay.

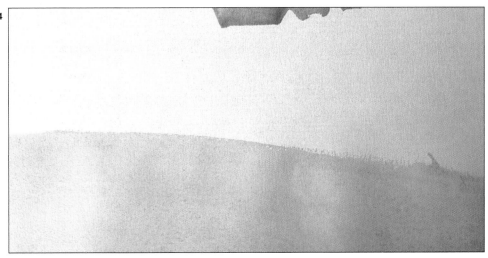

3 Having laid broad but precisely placed washes on the rooftops and shadowed sides of the buildings, the artist puts on an area of loosely applied bright green, thus juxtaposing complementary colors and establishing a key for the rest of the painting.

LAYING A WASH TO AN UNEVEN EDGE

4 & **5** Here the artist had to lay a wash against a complicated edge, the rooftops on the right-hand side of the picture. He first wet the paper only in the area to be covered, then worked paint into it, and finally dabbed it with blotting paper to absorb some of the excess paint, lighten the tone, and provide an even texture.

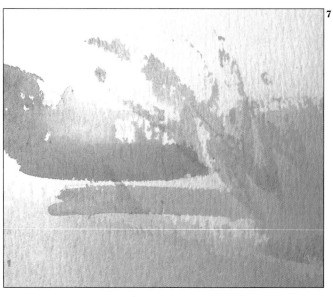

6 Here the artist is defining the shadows on the unlit sides of the buildings, allowing the paint to mix on the paper in order to produce a soft effect.

7 He uses a combination of Prussian blue and Payne's gray to achieve relatively strong tonal contrasts.

8 The paint was kept quite fluid throughout the painting, and the texture of the paper is an important element in the final effect. Here a large soft brush is used to apply dark green over the light red of the roofs and the blue of the sky, so that the colors blend into one another in a pleasing way.

9 The lines of the veins are laid on with bold brush strokes and darkened in places to hint at shadow, without describing it in detail. Strong tonal contrasts help to bring the foreground forward toward the picture plane.

10

10 The rows of vines are reinforced with a mixture of terre verte and Payne's gray. Shadows are not usually merely darker shades of the same color, but have their own colors.

MATERIALS USED

SUPPORT: pre-stretched watercolor paper, with a Not surface measuring
12 X 16 in (30 X 40 cm).
COLORS: raw umber, burnt umber, Payne's gray, terre verte, Hookers green, yellow ocher, permanent yellow, Prussian blue, and cadmium red.
BRUSHES: Nos. 4 and 11 sable.

VINEYARD IN ITALY

CHURCH IN FRANCE

Buildings present special problems to the artist, especially the watercolorist, and they demand a fairly precise and planned method of approach. In a painting such as this, where the church is the *raison d'être* of the picture rather than being just one feature in a landscape, the perspective must be convincing, the lines sharp and clear, and some suggestion made of the texture and quality of the masonry.

This artist has worked in a very deliberate way, starting with a careful outline drawing made with a sharp pencil and ruler to map out the main areas, so that he is sure where to place his first wash. He then put on a series of flat washes, the first one being laid over the sky area and the second, very pale, over the building itself. Next he began to consider the best way of suggesting the stonework, and decided on masking fluid, applied in slightly uneven brush strokes. When this was dry he washed over the top with brownish gray paint and then removed the fluid, leaving lines of paint between and around the original brush strokes. Further texture was applied at a later stage by the spattering method, and crisp lines were given to details, such as the face and hands of the clock, by drawing with a sharp pencil. The whole painting has a pleasing crispness, produced by the very sharply defined areas of light and dark; no attempt has been made to blend the paint in the shadow areas, and very distinct tonal contrasts have been used—in

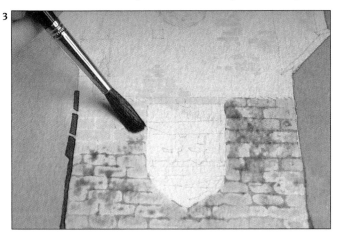

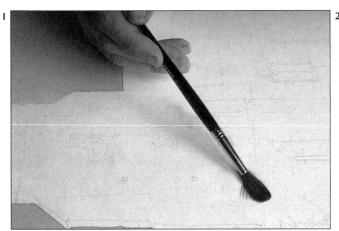

1 & 2 Here a careful outline drawing is essential. Once completed, the artist laid an almost flat wash over the sky and then a paler one over the building. These established his basic mid-tones, enabling him to gauge the tonal strength of the steeple.

3 The steeple was painted, allowed to dry, then masking fluid was put on to areas of the masonry as individual brush strokes. Fairly dark brownish paint was washed over this when dry.

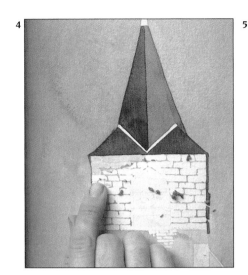

4 Here the masking fluid is being rubbed off with a finger, leaving the irregular lines of dark paint to suggest the edges of the stones. This is a more effective method than painting in the lines, and gives a much more natural look because the technique is a very slightly "random" one.

5 Here the spattering technique is being used to give further texture to the walls. It is sometimes neccessary to mask off surrounding areas so that they do not get splashed, but this artist makes use of the method quite often, and is confident of his ability to control the paint.

6 At this stage only the foreground, with the dark trees and bright grass, remain unpainted. The artist worked the painting piece by piece, as he found that having no overlapping layers of paint gave a crisper definition, but it is not a method recommended for beginners because it is difficult to judge tones and colors in isolation.

the small round tree in front of the church, for example. The artist has also avoided the temptation to put in too much detail, which might have reduced the impact and made the picture look fussy and untidy. The tiled roof consists simply of a flat wash; although there is just enough variation in the sky to avoid a mechanical look, no attempt has been made to paint actual clouds.

7 Here the hands and face of the clock are being carefully drawn in with a very sharp pencil over the original pale wash.

8 Further texture is given to the stonework by rubbing a candle over the paint. Candles or wax crayon can also be used like masking fluid, in which case they are applied before a final paint layer.

9 The mid-tones of the grass have now been laid in, providing a foil to the red-brown of the tiled roof.

10 The artist now works carefully on the shadow side of the tree, using a fine brush and very dense dark green paint.

MATERIALS USED

SUPPORT: pre-stretched 200 lb Bockingford paper
COLORS: cobalt blue, sap green, yellow ocher, raw umber, brown madder, alizarin, Payne's gray, and ivory black
BRUSHES: Nos. 2, 7, and 9 sables and a 1 in. (2.5 cm) bristle brush for spattering.
ADDITIONAL EQUIPMENT: masking fluid, a candle, and gum water.

CHURCH IN FRANCE

11 The final touches were to darken the left hand tree and paint in the straight, dark shadow in the foreground. Two small trees were also added in the shadow area at the bottom of the church.

CHAPTER SIX

Nature

From the 16th century onward watercolor became a favored medium for botanical illustration, which, with the great upsurge of interest in describing and cataloguing plants and flowers, was very much in demand. Just as it did for architecture, the medium proved ideal for the detailed and delicate work demanded by such subjects.

OPPOSITE Dürer's accurate and precise drawings and watercolors of plants and animals are possibly the best examples of natural-history painting in the entire history of art. *The Young Hare* was probably begun with broad washes of transparent paint to establish the main form. The fine details were then built up with tiny brush strokes of opaque paint; every hair and whisker has been precisely described, but the hare is still quite evidently a living, breathing creature.

NATURAL HISTORY PAINTING

In the early years of the 16th century Dürer pioneered the use of watercolor with body color for botanical subjects, and such works as *The Great Piece of Turf* and *Young Hare*, faithful renderings of nature, laid the basis for a tradition of botanical and natural history painting which has continued down to the present day.

In the 18th and 19th centuries the majority of naturalhistory painters and illustrators made their initial watercolors as bases for engravings. Some, notably the famous French flower painter, Pierre-Joseph Redout (1759–1840), mastered the art of engraving themselves, the techniques of which in turn influenced styles of painting. In America natural-history painting in watercolor reached new heights with the marvelous bird paintings of John James Audubon (1785–1851), paintings which became familiar to a wide public through the hand-colored engravings done from them. These works, although they are in the illustrative tradition of accurate observation, are now regarded as art rather than illustration and change hands at staggering prices.

Watercolor is still much used for precise botanical and natural-history illustration, but it has also come into its own as a medium for depicting nature, particularly flowers, in a more painterly way, either in its natural environment or in the studio as still-life.

The painting of water-lilies overleaf shows how superbly the medium can be used to give a feeling of life and immediacy: the water-lilies could almost be opening before your eyes.

PRACTICAL HINTS

Flowers and plants always make attractive subjects and present no particular problems other than the usual one of getting the drawing right. However, many people frequently buy a bunch of flowers and paint them at home, but do not think of going out to paint them in their natural environment. There is nothing at all wrong with the still-life approach. Countless superb paintings have been done of plants and flowers indoors. But painting or drawing on the spot is an excellent way of observing nature, and the plants or flowers do tend to look more at home in their natural setting.

RIGHT *Ring-Tailed Lemur*, by Sally Michel, has something of the quality of Dürer's work. She works in watercolor and pastel, and always from life, though she takes the occasional polaroid for reference.

Sally Michel

Animals and birds present much graver problems to the would-be wild-life painter. They simply will not sit still. For most professional wild-life artists, birds or animals are a life-long passion, and they have often made a long study of their chosen subject from books and museums before beginning to sketch and observe from nature. A family pet, however, can often be prevailed upon to stay in one place for long enough to be sketched—

especially if it has just had a good meal—and photographs can sometimes be used in combination with sketches as the basis for a painting. Anyone who decides to make animals or birds his subject should try to observe them as often and as closely as possible, both in movement and in repose. You may think you know exactly what your dog or cat looks like, but if you try to daw it from memory you will soon realize the limits of your knowledge.

ABOVE This study of waterlillies, by Marc Winer, was painted on the spot, with much use of the wet-into-wet technique. The artist allowed some colors to run into one another in a semi-random way, sometimes creating more gentle transitions, an effective way to suggest the soft wetness of the leaves and flowers floating in water.

TROPICAL FISH

It can be difficult to find natural-history subjects that remain still for long enough to be observed and studied by the artist, but fish in a tank almost beg to be looked at and admired, and although they are always on the move, at least they do not move very far. Many wild-life artists make a particular branch of the animal world their own, often because of a life-long interest. This artist has studied fish very closely, and has made a great many drawings of them over the years.

The painting was done from a series of drawings and from past observations of the structure and colors of the fish. It makes use of both the wet-into-wet technique, in which new color is applied to a wash before it is dry, and the wet-into-dry technique, in which wet washes are laid over dry ones so that they overlap in places. The hard and soft edges formed in this way create the illusion of rippling water, a very important element in the painting. The background washes had to be applied extremely carefully and accurately so that they did not spoil the crisp edges of the fishes' bodies and fins. A careful drawing was made before any paint was put on.

Although people often think of watercolors as pale and delicate, the colors can be made as vivid as you like, simply by being less diluted. In places the artist has used the paint almost pure to create bright and glowing effects.

1 This sketch is just one of many that the artist has made in the past and uses as reference for her paintings.

2 Having made a careful drawing on her stretched paper with a sharp pencil, the artist began by painting in the shapes of the fish with a mixture of cadmium orange and cadmium yellow pale. The colors and tones were varied to show the lights and darks of the bodies as well as the individual differences between the fish.

3 The background color was a mixture of black and lemon yellow, which gives a warmer color than blue and yellow. When laying the wash the artist took special care to work precisely and accurately between and around the fins and bodies in order to preserve the clean, crisp lines that are such a vital feature of the painting.

4 When the broad area of the background has been laid in with deliberately uneven washes to suggest ripples, the painting was allowed to dry. Further layers of color were then added, so that the water became darker around the fish and lighter at the top, where the proportion of yellow to black was increased.

5 Here the artist is painting the leaves with a fine brush in a very strong lemon yellow, barely diluted. This covers the original pale wash and is slightly modified by it.

6 A very fine sable brush was used to paint the delicate details of the scales, and touches of white were added in places. When doing detailed work in the center of a painting, make sure the area below is quite dry or you may ruin the painting by smudging it.

TROPICAL FISH

MATERIALS USED

SUPPORT: pre-stretched
watercolor paper with a Not
surface, measuring
14 X 20 in. (35 X 50 cm).
COLORS: cadmium red, cadmium
orange, cadmium yellow pale,
lemon yellow, yellow ocher, sap
green, Payne's gray, and black,
plus a little Chinese white.
BRUSHES: Nos. 7, 5, 3, and 00
sable.

7 Final touches deepened and enriched
the colors of the fins and tails and gave
definition to the foreground, hitherto left
as an area of water. Opaque paint
(Chinese white) was mixed with the
watercolor to produce grays and ochers,
which were then used to pick out the
pebbles. Opaque paint should be used
sparingly and only in the final stages, but
it is extremely useful for touches such as
these

PHEASANT

This painting is both a bird study and still-life, since it was painted indoors and the subject is a stuffed pheasant borrowed from an antique shop. Artists whose particular interest is wildlife can study and observe nature at second hand as well as directly from life. Natural-history books and museums both offer opportunities for gaining a thorough knowledge about structure and detail.

Because there could be no attempt to make the stuffed bird appear anything other than what it was, the painting presented a different challenge from that of representing a live bird. With a live bird the prime consideration might have been to suggest movement, while the natural background of trees or rocks might have formed part of the composition. Here the artist chose to treat the subject in a very formal way, setting it up as a rather stark still-life, but his enthusiasm for the bird itself comes across very strongly in the glowing color and the delicately painted detail.

His technique was quite free and fluid, and he worked quickly, building up the form in the early stages from loose washes and working wet into wet in places. The background shows an interesting use of watercolor: with only one

1 A very hard (F) pencil was used to make a careful outline drawing. Composition is extremely important for this subject, which relies for its impact on the way the main shape is placed. Once he had planned the composition, allowing the tail to go out of the frame so that it appears longer, the artist first laid a pale wash on the body and tail.

2 Once the first wash, a mixture of raw umber and cadmium orange, was dry, a darker one using the same colors was laid on top, after which blue and red were applied to the head and neck.

3 The same red, alizarin crimson, was put on the breast area, and the artist then began to work on the head feathers with a fine brush. He used a mixture of black, viridian, and ultramarine for this, leaving parts of the original blue showing through.

color a wide variety of tonal contrasts has been achieved. This gives the painting extra drama and excitement as well as providing a balance to the texture of the pheasant itself.

4 Some artists work all over a painting at the same time, but in this painting the bird was completed before the artist turned his attention on the background. Here the feathers are being painted, with the paint kept quite loose and fluid to prevent a cramped, overworked look.

5 This detail shows the richness and variety of both the colors and the brushwork. In the red area a darker tone has been allowed to overlap the one below, creating a series of edges which give the impression of feathers. Note how small lines of white have been left in the original wash to stand for the wing feathers.

6 The painting is now complete, and the successive washes have created exactly the rich impression that the artist wanted. When putting washes over other washes in this way it is essential to know when to stop; if the surface of the paper becomes too clogged with paint the painting will begin to look tired. Judging the strength of color needed for each wash takes some practice, since watercolor looks so much darker when it is wet.

7 Now the artist begins to work on the background, using a fairly strong mixture of Payne's gray and taking it very carefully around the bird's body. It is often necessary to turn the board sideways or upside down for this kind of work.

MATERIALS USED

SUPPORT: pre-stretched Bockingford watercolor paper, measuring
22 X 30 in. (55 X 75 cm).
COLORS: chrome orange, alizarin crimson, burnt sienna, raw umber, ulramarine, viridian, Payne's gray, and black.
BRUSHES: Nos. 12 and 2 sable and a No. 7 synthetic round.

PHEASANT

8 By varying the tones of the background wash the artist has made the bird stand out in a very three-dimensional way. The dark head is prevented from merging into the similar tone behind it by the thin line of white which has been left between the two. The white area of the table top has been carefully placed so that it is not quite central and thus provides a balance to the long, almost horizontal, line of the tail.

GERANIUM

This painting demonstrates very well how in the right hands watercolor can be an ideal medium for capturing the rich colors and strong, yet intricate, forms of flowers and foliage. The starting-point was a single bloom in a garden trough, but the artist has transformed the rather ordinary subject seen in the photograph into a highly dramatic painting with a strong element of abstract pattern. He has reduced the background to an area of dark neutral color, which allows the shapes of the leaves to stand out in bold contrast, but he has given it interest by varying the tonal contrasts while using only one color. He has done this by allowing the paint and water to mix unevenly, and even form blobs in places, and by scrubbing the paint with a stiff household brush.

Although no preliminary drawing was done, the artist had a very clear idea of the composition before he began to paint; the positioning of the flowers against the background is a vital element in the effect of the painting. The leaves have been slightly cropped by the frame on both sides, thereby bringing the flowers and leaves toward the picture plane. The almost horizontal band of lighter color in the foreground, suggesting the garden trough, adds to this effect,

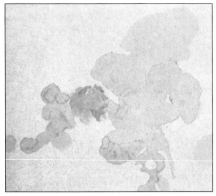

1 The colors were built up gradually from very light to very dark, and the first step was to apply dilute washes of green and red to the leaves and flower head.

2 The leaves were then darkened in places and touches of cerulean blue added to the flower head with a No. 2 sable brush.

3 Once the main shapes of the leaves and flower had been established, the artist began to paint the background, using a mixture of Payne's gray and cerulean blue and judging the tones very carefully. Assessing the strength of a dark wash takes practice, as watercolor appears much lighter when it is dry.

4 Next the artist began to darken the tones of some of the leaves, mixing the Payne's gray used for the background with cadmium green. Using only a small selection of colors helps to give unity to a painting.

5 Payne's gray was again used, this time pure, to paint the fine, delicate lines formed by the stems and veins of the leaves. A No. 2 sable brush gave the fine brush marks needed for this detailed work.

firmly "mooring" the plant in the front of the picture. It is interesting to compare the finished painting with the penultimate stage, in which the flower appears to float in space.

EXPLOITING THE WASH

The general leaf shapes were produced with a very wet green wash. The paint was then drawn out, while still wet, into thin strands to create the leaf stems.

GERANIUM

6 The red of the flower head had to be as vivid as possible, and the depth of color was achieved by laying deep washes of vermillion over paler ones in which a little blue had been added. Note how the artist has varied the intensity of the colors and left small lines of a lighter tone showing through to suggest the shapes of the petals.

MATERIALS USED

SUPPORT: pre-stretched watercolor paper with a Not surface, measuring 18 X 23 in. (45 X 57 cm).
COLORS: vermillion, yellow ocher, cadmium green, Payne's gray, cerulean blue, and black.
BRUSHES: Nos. 10, 6, and 2 sables and a small household brush for the background.

FIELD OF DAISIES

There is no better medium than watercolor for rendering the bright colors and delicate detail of flowers, but a painting like this one presents a technical problem which is not easy to overcome by traditional methods. Since watercolor must always be worked dark over light, white or pale shades are created by painting around them. Here the white shapes are smaller and more intricate than they are in most paintings, and if the artist had attempted to lay washes around them the painting would have run the risk of becoming niggly and

tired-looking. He has solved this problem by using masking fluid for the heads of the flowers, laying washes of varying intensities on top and then removing the fluid to reveal the white paper.

Some artists find masking fluid a rather mechanical device, and in the past it was more often used for illustration and other graphic work, but in fact it can be used quite freely, as it was in this painting, and can either be applied with a brush or used for spattering effects. It is difficult to draw really fine lines with it, however, as it is thick and viscous. The artist has therefore used oil pastel to draw

the stems of the flowers. This works as a resist medium in the same way as masking fluid; the oil repels the water, creating clear lines and interesting textures.

One of the most difficult decisions faced by painters attempting plant or flower studies outdoors is what to put in and leave out. Obviously, if you try to include every flower head and blade of grass, as well as large parts of background and sky, the painting will become a confused jumble.

A comparison of this painting with the reference photograph shows how the artist has simplified

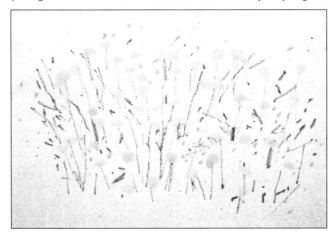

1 Without making a drawing on the support, the artist began by picking out the flower heads with masking fluid. Since this takes some time to dry, it should be done in the very early stages.

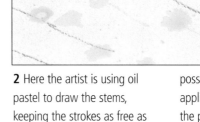

2 Here the artist is using oil pastel to draw the stems, keeping the strokes as free as possible. When the washes are applied, the paint will slide off the pastel, leaving a clear line.

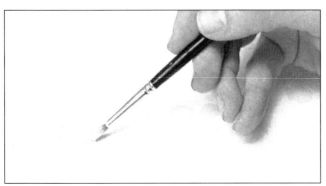

3 Before any paint was put on, the artist established the overall pattern with masking fluid and with lines and dots of oil pastel.

4 Next the whole picture area was covered with a wash of sap green and yellow, deliberately applied unevenly and loosely. The brush strokes, made with a No. 6 sable brush, were used to suggest the movement of wind-blown grass and leaves.

the subject, reducing the number of flowers to make a telling arrangement and allowing the background to become simply a dark, receding area suggestive of grass. No preliminary drawing was done, as the artist wanted to create a feeling of spontaneity, but less experienced painters would probably find an advance thumbnail sketch or two helpful in establishing the composition.

TEXTURING
The green wash is enlivened by the strong brush strokes. This is purely a textural effect: note that the color is exactly the same as the first.

5 Once the first wash was laid, the artist began to strengthen the color in places with a dark mixture of chrome green and black. A slight sheen was given to the paint by mixing it with gum water.

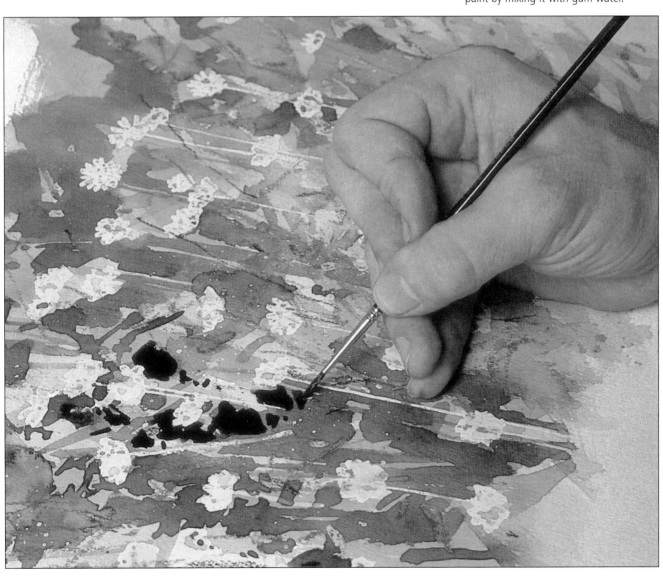

6

REMOVING MASKING FLUID

Before removing masking fluid (by gently rubbing with the finger, as the artist does here), make sure that the paint is quite dry and that no further alterations or additions are needed.

6 The deepest shadows in the foreground have now been painted and the background has been darkened. The darker green areas were carefully drawn with a fine brush, as accurate definition was needed at this stage.

MATERIALS USED

SUPPORT: Arches watercolor paper with a Not surface, measuring 12 X 18 in. (30 X 45 cm).
COLORS: watercolors in sap green, chrome green, cadmiumum yellow, and black; oil pastels in olive green and yellow.
BRUSHES & OTHER EQUIPMENT: Nos. 6 and 4 sable brushes, a small household brush for spattering, gum water, and masking fluid.

7 The final touch was to paint in the flower centers with cadmium yellow.

FIELD OF DAISIES

CHAPTER SEVEN

Portrait and Figure

As more and more artists succumb to the charms of watercolor, it is becoming an accepted medium for portraits and figure paintings, hitherto regarded as the province of oils. Its softness and translucence make it ideal for capturing the living qualities of skin and hair, but it needs particularly careful handling in this branch of painting if the surface is not to become muddy and dull. Accurate drawing is also vital, especially for portrait work. Try to draw from life wherever possible and avoid the temptation to put the paint on before the drawing is right.

OPPOSITE John Frederick Lewis's paintings were often of Middle-Eastern subjects. Like many 19th century painters he traveled widely in search of inspiration. He was attracted by the rich colors and textures of the East and in *The Harem* he rendered their bright, jewel-like quality in a painstaking technique typical of the watercolors of the period.

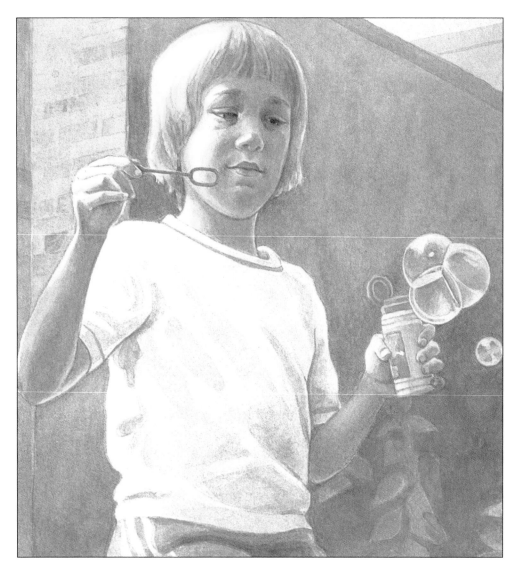

PAST AND PRESENT APPROACHES

ABOVE This portrait, *Blowing Bubbles*, by Elaine Mills, was done from a photograph. The artist wished to capture the child in movement, not in a stiff, artificial looking pose. A scaled-up drawing made from the photograph was transferred to the painting surface by means of iron-oxide paper. The painting itself was built up in a series of thin washes, the colors kept light and clean throughout. The details of the face were done last, with the point of a No. 2 sable brush.

Although artists have always used watercolor or pen-and-wash to make quick studies of faces and figures, there is really no tradition of portraiture in watercolor, and until this century paintings of the figure have also usually been in oil. The reasons for this have nothing to do with any inherent unsuitability of the medium itself. In the past portraits were the artist's bread and butter—they were seldom done for pure pleasure as they are today—and

RIGHT Edward Burra worked in watercolor because his severe arthritis made it difficult for him to handle oils. His use of the medium was truly amazing: he achieved a depth and richness of color seldom seen in watercolor, and each detail was minutely described without ever appearing over-worked. In paintings such as *Harlem* (1934) Burra's concern was with the general atmosphere and lifestyle of the people he encountered, and his juxtaposition of dark and light colors and harsh and soft textures is highly descriptive.

the sitter who paid to have his image or that of his family hung on his wall wanted a large and imposing painting as well as one that would stand up to the ravages of time. Watercolors, although we have better ways of preserving them now, as well as more permanent pigments, are prone to fade, and the paper can become mildewed and blotched. Figure paintings were also traditionally fairly large, and most artists found that they called for a slower and more deliberate approach than that normally used for watercolors. Nowadays we have a different attitude to such subjects. A rather sketchy and impressionistic treatment of a figure, either clothed or unclothed, is not only acceptable but often desirable, and can suggest light and movement more easily than a more heavily worked painting.

Figure paintings in watercolor became more usual during the 19th century, partly as a result of the far-reaching influence of William Blake's symbolic and allegorical paintings. The Pre-Raphaelites and Edward Burne-Jones (1833–98) pioneered new techniques, such as rubbing in dry color and scratching out. Burne-Jones' watercolors are barely recognizable as such; they have rather the appearance of medieval manuscripts. Another 19th-century artist, influenced by the Pre-Raphaelites though, like Burne-Jones, not actually a member of the Brotherhood, was John Frederick Lewis (1805–76), whose paintings of Middle Eastern scenes such as The Harem, (see page 104), glow with a jewel-like brilliance. A comparison of The Harem with Girl in Armchair reveals startling

differences in technique. It is difficult to believe that the same medium has been used. Painters such as Lewis used watercolor almost like oil, with the minimum use of washes and much fine-brush work, but his paintings never look tired, as an over-worked watercolor easily can. Today there is a tendency to favor the classical, broad-wash technique, but many others are also used, such as dry-brush and stippling, and some artists combine several techniques in one painting.

PRACTICAL HINTS

Photographs provide a very useful source of reference for portraiture and figure work, particularly if the subject is a figure in motion. Blowing Bubbles is an example of a painting done almost entirely from a photograph. It is advisable, even so, to work from life wherever possible, and since a watercolor study is not likely to take as long as an oil, it should not be difficult to persuade people to sit.

Good drawing is essential for human subjects, since a misplaced eye or an ill-drawn hand or foot can completely destroy the harmony of a painting. Never start painting

until you are sure that the drawing is correct; and as you draw, check proportions and measurements constantly. When you are drawing a figure, it often helps to look at the space behind the head or between limbs. If a person is standing with one hand resting on a hip, for instance, the triangle formed between the arm and the body will be a particular shape. Foreshortened limbs, an arm resting on a chair for example, are difficult to get right, but they can

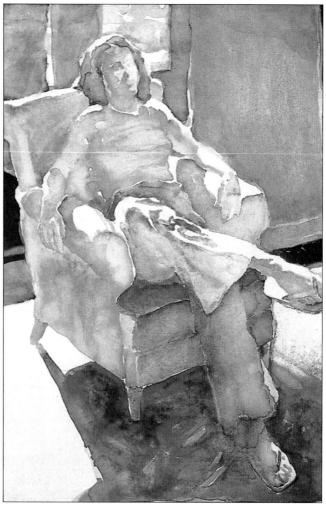

ABOVE This painting presents a striking contrast to the previous example, in both technique and the atmosphere it conveys. The artist was interested in light and color rather than in achieving a likeness, and the paint was kept fluid and free, with the minimum of detail, thus enhancing the relaxed mood of the light-flooded figure in the armchair.

usually be checked by using some part of the background as a reference point. You can see at which particular point the arm would be intersected by a vertical line formed by the wall behind, or how the hand lines up with the legs of the chair.

1 The photograph shows how different the actual colors were from those the artist has chosen. Even the strongly patterned blanket, which has been given a prominent role in the painting, is much paler and more muted.

AGAINST A STRIPED BLANKET

This is an unusually large painting for a watercolor. The head is almost life-size. The colors are gentle and muted with the minimum of tonal contrast. This type of color scheme, in which there are no dark tones or colors, is known as "high-key." Some artists always work in a high key, others always in a low one (using dark or vivid colors with strong contrasts); yet others are happy to work in both, the choice depending on their approach to the subject.

This portrait was done from life. The artist made sure that the model was really comfortable before work began, and makes the positions of her hands and feet so that she could resume exactly the same position after breaks. In a painting as subtle as this the drawing had to be very accurate and the tonal contrasts and variations extremely tightly controlled. The artist needed to observe the subject closely without being distracted by movement or complaints about discomfort.

2 The drawing was made with a mechanical lead-holder, sometimes called a clutch pencil, into which different leads can be inserted for different purposes. Any unnecessary lines were carefully removed with a soft putty eraser in order not to damage the surface of the paper.

3 The area around the eyes and brows is one of the most difficult to draw accurately, and the artist pays special attention to the structure and the way the eyes fit into the sockets. Pencil lines can either be rubbed out when the painting is partially done, but quite dry, or left as part of the image.

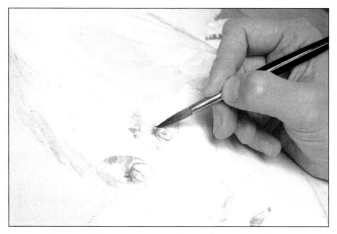

4 When the pencil drawing was complete the artist began to draw with the brush, painting below the top eyelid. The eyes are the focal point of most portraits and need very careful treatment.

5 The next step was to get rid of some of the white paper by applying a pale wash to the background. A No. 2 sable brush was used to work on separate areas right across the painting.

6 The stripes of the blanket were intensified before any further work was done on the face, being a very important part of the painting and acting as a key for the colors and tones of the face and hair.

7 Here the artist paints the darkest part of the hair, using a No. 2 sable brush and a mixture of violet, Payne's gray, and Indian red. The hair had hitherto been mainly yellow ocher with touches of Indian red.

MATERIALS USED

SUPPORT: pre-stretched Bockingford paper, measuring 18 X 16 in. (45 X 40 cm).
COLORS: Indian red, yellow ocher, violet, Payne's gray, cobalt blue, ultramarine, alizarin crimson, cadmium red, and sap green.
BRUSHES & OTHER EQUIPMENT: Nos. 6 and 4 sable brushes, a mechanical lead-holder, and a putty rubber.

8 At this stage the paper had been entirely covered, but the painting was somewhat weak and insubstantial, the flesh tones too pale and cool. The artist therefore intensified all the tones, adding warmth to the flesh and giving a more solid feel to the face. The final touches were to paint in the pattern of the blanket and add definition to the hair, forming a pleasing pattern.

AGAINST A STRIPED BLANKET

The first stage was to draw a very careful outline, establishing the composition so that each wash could be placed quickly and accurately. The pale colors, as well as the sheer size of the painting, ruled out the possibility of major alterations once the painting had begun. Drawing is particularly important in a portrait, since if the proportions of the features are wrong, or the eyes or mouth placed crookedly, the painting will not only fail as a likeness, but will also lose structural credibility. The drawing need not be elaborate— too many pencil marks can confuse rather than clarify—but it must be clear and accurate enough to provide a guide for the painting; so if you are working from life, make sure that both you and your model have enough time to spare.

PORTRAIT OF PAUL

This sensitive study is much more graphic in approach than the previous portrait. The artist is more interested in line than in color, and has used a technique which is a combination of drawing and painting, enabling her to express the character of the sitter in a way she found suited his thin, somewhat aquiline, features.

She used a quill pen made from a goose feather, a drawing tool much favored by such artists as Rembrandt, but the medium was dilute watercolor instead of the more traditional ink. A quill pen produces a less mechanical line than a metal nib, because strokes of different thicknesses can be made by turning the quill. By this means, and by varying the strength and colors of the paint itself, the artist has produced a series of contrasting lines—some thick and soft, some short and stabbing, and some fine and taut. She used a Chinese brush in combination with the quill, both to lay washes across the whole image and to soften the line in places by dipping it in a little clean water. Using watercolor gives an artist more freedom to modify or alter lines.

1 A simple pose, seen directly from the front, was chosen for the painting, because it gave the artist the opportunity to explore fully the lines and contours of the features. No preliminary pencil drawing was made, since the painting was in itself a drawing, which could be corrected as the work progressed.

2 This photograph shows how the artist varied the strength of the watercolor when drawing with the quill. She used three different mixtures: raw sienna and cobalt blue; Prussian blue and cadmium red; and yellow ocher and cadmium yellow.

3 Here the artist has found that she is not satisfied with the line of the cheekbone; so she lightens it with a brush dipped in water before redrawing it.

4 A Chinese brush was used to apply small areas of color all over the image. No attempt was made to render the colors precisely; they were applied in a spontaneous manner to create an overall effect.

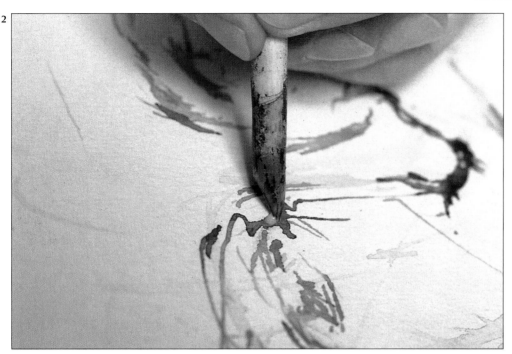

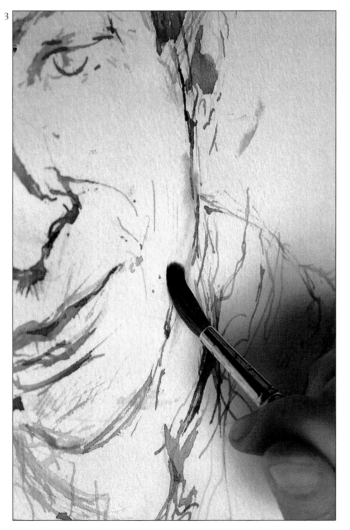

5 The artist has made little use of the traditional watercolor technique of flat washes. Instead, she has allowed the brush marks to become part of the painting. The background was applied with two different brushes, a No. 9 sable round and a Chinese brush.

6 Once the lines had been firmly established and the artist was satisfied with the drawing, she laid a loose wash over the face and neck to build up the form and add warmth to the flesh.

PORTRAIT OF PAUL

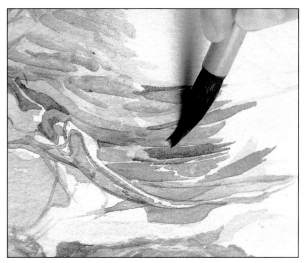

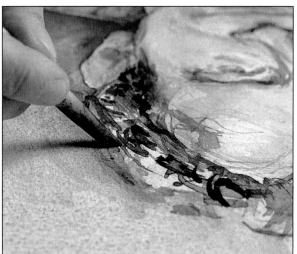

Although color is not the most important aspect of the painting, it has been used boldly and sensitively. Here the artist is using a Chinese brush to apply small patches of bright color to the clothing and darker tones to the hair.

MATERIALS USED

SUPPORT: Langton watercolor paper with a Not surface, measuring 12 X 10 in. (30 X 25 cm).
COLORS: raw sienna, cobalt blue, Prussian blue, cadmium red, cadmium yellow, and yellow ocher.
BRUSHES & OTHER EQUIPMENT: a No. 9 sable round, a Chinese brush, and a goose-feather quill pen.

1 The artist has deliberately chosen the pose to fit in with a pre-conceived composition, and he was sufficiently sure of the placing of the main shapes not to need a preliminary pencil drawing. Instead, the main lines and shapes were mapped out with much-diluted watercolor.

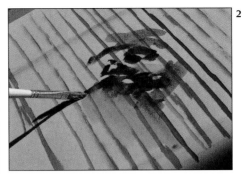

2 The tree just visible through the slats of the blind was painted in very freely over the orange-brown lines of the blind. The darker lines thus show through the green wash, giving the shimmering effect of light striking the soft, uneven form of the tree.

3 The next step was to lay a dark gray-blue wash at the top of the window area, leaving white below so that the light was chaneled through the bottom part of the window. The body was then established with a strong cadmium orange, balanced by the crimson of the skirt and the blue of the bed.

4 The artist continued to work all over the painting, modeling the outstretched leg and adding definition to the face and neck. A strong tint of raw sienna was used for the darker flesh tints in order to echo the orange-brown of the blind and window frame.

GIRL BY A WINDOW WITH A BLIND

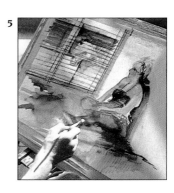

5 Although pure watercolor was used for most of the painting, some white gouche was added for the smaller highlights, such as those on the leg and face.

6 As a final touch, a deep pink flesh-tint was put on to the body, and the area of the bed was strengthened by using a wash of blue gouache with white added. Too much use of gouache with watercolor can destroy its quality, but here it has been used skilfully.

MATERIALS USED

SUPPORT: pre-stretched watercolor paper with a fine grain, measuring 18 X 28 in. (46 X 71 cm).
COLORS: lemon yellow, cadmium yellow, cadmium orange, cadmium red, alizarin crimson, raw sienna, sap green, cobalt blue, and Payne's gray, plus white gouache.
BRUSHES:
a selection of sables and a small bristle brush.

GIRL BY A WINDOW WITH BLIND

In this painting the figure is seen in the context of an interior, and the effects of light interested the artist most. Watercolor has been used very loosely in thin washes, with a large amount of paper left uncovered, and the impression of a large, spacious room lit by diffused light has been created with minimal attention to detail.

Although the paint has been used mainly pure, the artist also used gouache in the final stages for certain areas such as the blue bed and the smaller highlights on the face and body. Gouache can destroy the quality of a watercolor by giving a matt, dead surface, but here it has been used very skilfully without detriment to the painting.

The composition, with its careful arrangement of lights and darks, is well balanced. The crisp, diagonal lines of the blind contrast with the softer contours of the model, who is placed in silhouette against the white wall. It is the relationship between the figure and the window that gives the painting its interest, and the two are unified by the expanse of bright blue formed by the bed, which is in turn echoed by the cushion and shadow behind the model.

CHAPTER EIGHT
Still Life

Still life as its name implies, simply means a
composition of objects which are not moving and
which are incapable of doing so, usually arranged on a
table; the French rather depressingly call it
"dead life" (*nature morte*).

The subjects can be whatever you like, but
traditionally the objects in a still-life group are in some
way associated with each other—a vase of flowers with
fruit, a selection of vegetables with cooking vessels or
implements, and sometimes dead fish, game, or fowl
with a goblet of wine, perhaps, or a bunch of parsley.
(Culinary still lifes are less popular nowadays, possibly
because they run the risk of looking like the cover
of a cookery book.)

OPPOSITE Pierre Joseph Redouté was
primarily a flower painter, official artist to
Marie Antoinette and later to the Empress
Josephine. His detailed flower studies are
well known to us through prints; his
watercolors and drawings of other subjects
are much rarer, though equally fine. this
still life, done in 1834, towards the end of
his life, shows a wonderfully fresh and
skilful handling of watercolor.

Good paintings can be made from quite homely subjects. Vincent Van Gogh (1853–90) made a wonderful and moving still-life from nothing but a pile of books on a table. Most artists have painted still-lifes at one time or another, and several, notably Jan Vermeer (1632–75), included them in their figure paintings. In the 17th century a group of Dutch artists became obsessed with still-life to the exclusion of all other subjects, and vied with one another to produce ever more lavish portrayals of table-tops gleaming with edible produce, rare porcelain, and golden goblets. In many of these, tiny insects are visible among the foliage, blood drips from the mouths of freshly killed hares or rabbits, and bunches of grapes shine with tiny droplets of moisture, every object painted with breathtaking skill.

Because the subject of a still-life painting can be entirely controlled by the artist, as can its arrangement and lighting, still-lifes present an unusual opportunity for exploring ideas and experimenting with color and composition. The greatest master of the still-life, Paul Cézanne (1839–1906), found that the form allowed him to concentrate on such fundamental problems as form and space and the paradox of transferring the three-dimensional world to a two-dimensional surface.

The ability to control the subject of a still-life means that you can take as much time as you like to work out the composition and complete the preliminary drawing, and you can practise painting techniques at leisure, trying out new ones as you feel inspired. Oddly, watercolor was seldom used in the past for still-lifes other than flower paintings, but it is now becoming extremely popular.

SETTING UP A STILL LIFE
There are no specific problems in painting a still-life or flower piece once it has been set up. The real

LEFT Cezanne used still life to explore the relationships of forms and their interaction on various spatial planes. He usually worked in oils, but *Still Life with Chair, Bottle and Apple*, shows his understanding of watercolor.

ABOVE William Henry Hunt produced charming portraits as well as genre subjects, using his paint rather dry to depict colors and textures with great accuracy. *Plums* is an unusual approach to still life, as it has an outdoor setting but it was almost certainly done in the studio from preliminary sketches.

challenge is arranging it, and this may take some time—plonking an assortment of objects down on a table will not give you a good painting. The wisest rule to follow at first is to keep the composition simple. The more objects you have the more difficult it is to arrange them in a harmonious way. It is also best to have a theme of some kind: if the various objects are too different in kind they will look uneasy together.

Start with something you like, a bowl of fruit on a patterned tablecloth, perhaps, or a pot plant, and keep arranging and re-arranging until you are satisfied that you have achieved a good balance of shapes and colors. Drapery is often used to balance and complement the main subject, and it is useful to have a selection of fabrics or tablecloths on hand for this purpose. Many artists make small sketches or diagrams to work out whether a vertical line is needed in the background, or a table-top shown as a diagonal in the foreground. Finally, when you are fairly sure that the arrangement will do, look at it through a viewing frame to assess how well it will fill the space allotted to it. Move the frame around so that you can assess several possibilities. Often you may find that allowing one of the objects to run out of the picture actually helps the composition.

Lighting is also very important. It defines the forms, heightens the colors and casts shadows which can become a vital component in the composition.

CYCLAMEN

Flower arrangements are among the most popular of all still-life subjects. Indeed, they are often regarded as a separate branch of painting. In purely practical terms, however, they are a type of still-life, posing the same problems as well as sharing the major advantage of being a captive subject.

With any group of objects set up as a painting subject the main problem is arrangement, and hence the composition of the painting itself. Flowers in a vase, for example, do not always make a shape that fills a rectangle very well; so it is sometimes necessary to add other elements, such as a plate, some fruit, or background drapery. Here the composition is simple but very effective: the table-top, with its checked cloth, provides foreground interest to balance the pattern formed by the flowers themselves against the plain background. It also adds to the impression of solidity and its intersecting diagonal lines provide a pleasing contrast with the curved shapes. Interestingly, the tablecloth was added as an afterthought, when the artist had already painted the flower and pot; without it the character of the painting would have been quite different.

1 A drawing was made of the flowers and pot, then painted in with a mixture of cadmium red and purple lake. Attention was paid to the arrangement of the spaces created by the flowers against the background.

2 The mid-to-light tones of the leaves in the center were laid on quite freely, sharper definition being reserved for those at the sides. The colors—emerald green, sap green, Payne's gray, and a touch of raw sienna—were put on wet and allowed to mix on the paper.

3 The leaves and flowers were darkened in places and a first wash was then laid on the pot. Here, too, the colors were applied wet and moved around on the paper until the artist was satisfied with the way they had blended together.

4 A very pale wash was put on the underside of the dish, leaving the rim white to stand out against the checks. The blue used was chosen to echo the blue on the pot.

FREEDOM AND LIGHT

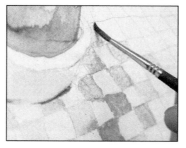

5 Here the artist is using the tip of a sable brush to paint the blue checks. Although they were painted carefully, and varied in size and color to suggest recession, the artist has not attempted to produce perfectly straight or regular lines, which would have looked mechanical and monotonous.

6 The wet-into-wet technique was used for painting the pot, giving it a lively appearance suggestive of light and texture. Widely varying colors were applied with plenty of water and blended into one another. If the paint is too wet, or blends in the wrong way, it can be dabbed off with a sponge or tissue.

CYCLAMEN

MATERIALS USED

SUPPORT: pre-stretched watercolor paper with a Not surface, measuring 12 X 16 in. (30 X 40 cm).
COLORS: cadmium red, alizarin crimson, raw sienna, purple lake, emerald green, sap green, lemon yellow, ultramarine, cobalt blue, and Payne's gray.
BRUSHES: Nos. 7 and 3 sable.

When arranging a still-life or flower piece it is helpful to make a few advance sketches, as alterations cannot always be made as easily as they were here.

STILL LIFE WITH FRUIT

The artist has used a number of different techniques to give a lively look to this bright fruit and vegetable group. His approach was unusual too, since he began by painting in the basic colors of the fruit, leaving the background and the table unpainted until a relatively late stage. This artist frequently paints piece by piece in this way, instead of adopting the more usual method of working all over the painting at the same time. It can be very successful, as it is here, but it does rely on the ability to judge tones and colors very accurately and upon having a clear idea of how the painting is to look finally.

A watercolor containing small, intricate shapes like these requires some planning, as too much overpainting and overlapping of colors can result in a muddy, tired-looking painting in which the brilliance of the colors is lost or diminished. In this case, the artist has solved the problem by using the watercolor mixed with white gouache, which gives it extra covering power without dulling the colors.

Once the colors of the fruit had been established, the warm ocher of the table top was laid on. The paint was applied around the shapes of the fruit, but quite boldly and loosely without too much concern about occasional overlapping. Texture was given to the wood by spattering opaque paint from a stiff brush and then by dragging

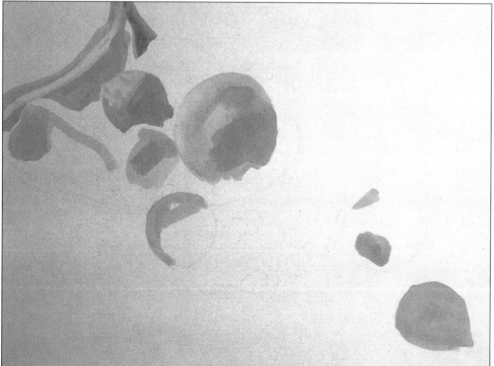

1 The artist begins by painting the lemons, using watercolor mixes with just a little white gouache.

2 By painting all the yellow areas first the artist has to a large extent established the composition. The pattern formed by the yellow shapes, interspersed with darker or more vivid forms and colors, is an important element in the painting.

the same brush, used rather dry, along the surface to suggest wood grain. The fruit was worked up and given more color and form, and then the near-black background was painted in, giving an even richer glow to the fruit and providing a diagonal which balances the composition and brings all the elements in the painting together

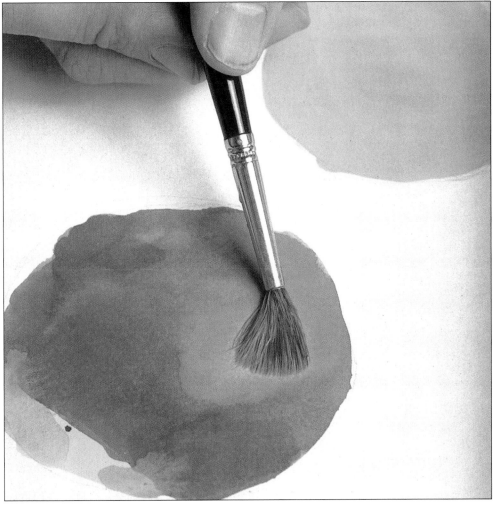

3 Here the artist is working wet-into-wet to build up the forms and colors. Because he is using semi-opaque paint, he is able to lay a lighter yellow on top of the deep orange.

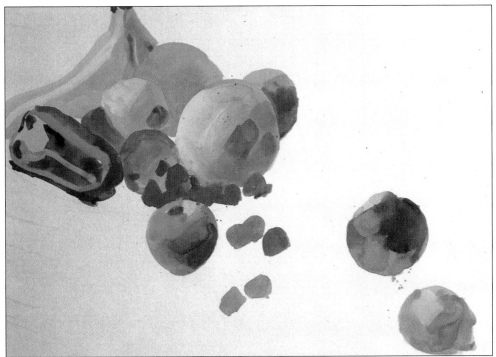

4 Now all the colors of the fruit have been laid on, although not in their final form. This enables the artist to gauge the color and tone he needs for the table top.

ADDING TEXTURE

5 Having laid on the basic color for the table top, taking it a round the edges of the fruit, the artist now uses the spatter method to give a slight textural interest.

6 The grain of the wood is suggested by dragging a stiff, broad brush over the surface, using a darker color in a slightly dry mixture.

7 This detail shows how well the solidity of the fruit has been depicted, being built up with quite broad and bold areas of the color. The dark shadows beneath them anchor them to the horizontal plane of the table.

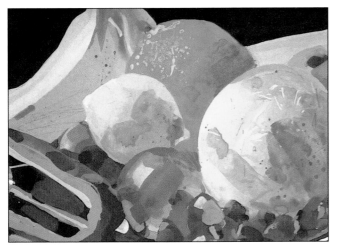

8 The addition of the black background gives a further sparkle to the clear, bright colors of the fruit. The textured highlights on the top of the orange were made by dribbling wet, opaque white paint from the brush on top of the darker color.

MATERIALS USED

SUPPORT: plain white mounting board.
COLORS: lemon yellow, cadmium yellow, cadmium red, alizarin crimson, sap green, cobalt blue, raw umber, and ivory black.
BRUSHES: Nos. 2, 7, and 9 sables and a 1 in. (2.5 cm) bristle brush.

STILL LIFE WITH FRUIT

9 The finished painting shows how important the greatly angled diagonal formed by the back edge of the table is to the composition. It balances the opposing diagonal formed by the fruit itself, a triangle with the bowl as the apex.

Painting
in
Acrylics

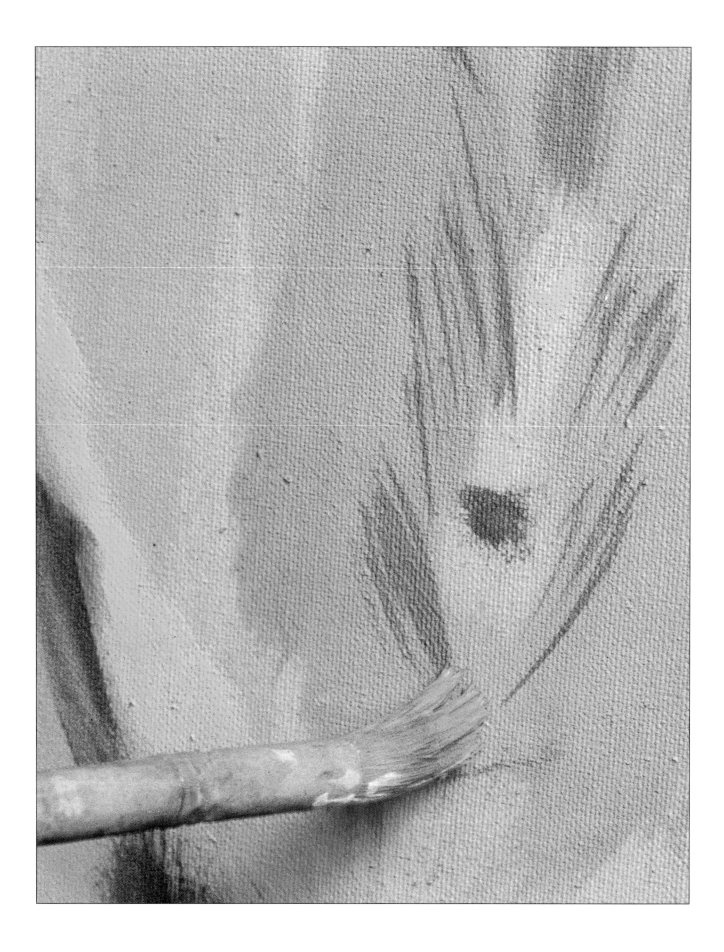

Introduction...
...Why Acrylics?

Acrylic is a relatively new paint for artists, the first for nearly 300 years. During that time, painters and designers have used mainly oil, watercolor, and tempera. In acrylic, we have a modern paint of enormous value to both artists and designers, whatever fields they are in—painting, illustration, graphic design, textiles, jewelry, mural, and interior design, even sculpture.

BELOW Detail of a mural in the Graduate School of Busuness Studies, London, by Leonard Rosoman.

THE NATURE OF PAINT

The qualities of acrylic are exceptional. It is certainly more versatile than most other paint. For one thing, it can stimulate almost exactly what they can do, in many instances better. It is clean to handle and has only a slight, pleasant aroma. No cumbersome equipment is needed, no special chemical knowledge to make it

function satisfactorily. This alone makes it ideal for those who find oil paint somewhat messy, its smell unpleasant, its use arduous and something of a performance.

Advantages of Acrylic

One of the advantages of acrylic is its speed of working. It dries rapidly, in minutes if need be, and permanently. Alternatively, drying

can be prolonged to suit individual working requirements. Acrylic dries throughout so thorougly, it can be varnished immediately with either a matt (eggshell) or glossy finish. Another advantage is that acrylic is both tough and flexible.

Why Acrylics?

They are made simple and clean to handle; flexible; water resistant;

tough. Acrylics: can simulate other paints; smell good; need little special equipment; dry fast; can be cleaned; can be repaired; adhere permanently. It does not peel, crack, or split, and it is water-resistant. The surface of dried acrylic can be gently cleaned should the need arise, and can be repaired easily if damaged.

Perhaps the most advantageous characteristics of acrylic are its adhesive qualities. It can be applied, without difficulty, to almost anything, and remain, permanently, without flaking or rubbing off. Unlike oil paint, which can damage the surface of certain materials if applied without the appropriate priming, acrylic can be used without any special preparation if the situation demands.

Among other things, it will adhere satisfactorily to all kinds of wall surfaces, cloth, paper, card (cardboard), hardboard, wood, plastic — almost any object or surface suitable for painting or decoration.

Acrylic is a multipurpose paint; it can be used as a paste as well as a liquid, enabling a variety of surface changes to be carried out and explored. From the perfectly flat, or evenly gradated kind, to the highly modeled, textured

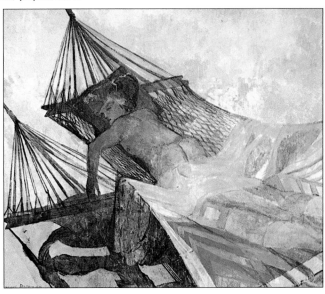

ABOVE *Girl Lying in Hammock* by Leonard Rosoman.

BENCHES I BATTERSEA PK
FOR ALL FLESH IS AS GRASS. THE GRASS WITHERETH

surface that has sand, glass, wool fiber and tissue paper added to it. For among its many accomplishments, the acrylic medium is also a powerful glue.

It will especially suit those who delight in bold, bright, clear colors. Conversely it can be reduced to subtle tones and carefully gradated tints by the usual methods of mixing.

Acrylic's simplicity of handling is a major advantage, especially for beginners. The simple equipment needed means less initial expense, a further encouragement to those who have never painted before.

Acrylic is uncomplicated to use, but it is important to learn how it behaves. Practice and experiment will teach you how to exploit the qualities of the paint. Experience

ACE PROSPECT GARD
TE 156 IN CENTRAL
DENNIS P 2082 IN TH
AN'S WALK SOUTHPO
GARDENS BOURNEM
D STEINE GARDENS
95 AND REFLECTED
ANISHEN PT 28357

III THE SAME A YEAR LATER
TOM PHILLIPS LONDON IV MCMLXX XVI IV MCMLXXI

ABOVE *Benches* by Tom Phillips. This painting is based around a series of postcards. The artist has used a number of techniques (eg stippling and hatching) and a wide range of colors.

LEFT The most convenient way to buy acrylics is in tubes.

with other mediums is not necessary; beginners are at no disadvantage to the more experienced painter in understanding acrylics, and the beginner may be less prejudiced and more adventurous than the painter skilled in other mediums. If you begin with a spirit of inquiry, you will soon grasp the potential of this exciting medium.

CHAPTER ONE

Acrylic Paint

Acrylic paint is made by mixing powdered pigment with acrylic adhesive. The adhesive looks milky when wet but becomes transparent when dry, revealing the true color of the pigment. All the ingredients are carefully weighed and tested before use. It is this painstaking precision and control during the manufacture which enables thousands of tubes of paint of almost identical color, consistency, and quality to be turned out at any time.

THE NATURE OF PAINT

Acrylic is unlike any other paint, but it has affinities with all of them, since all paints contain the same ingredient: pigment. A pigment used in watercolor is identical to that used in oil and acrylic. The quality is equally high, its brightness and durability the same, and the care used in manufacture just as thorough.

The major difference between one paint and another is not the color but something much more fundamental: the binder. The binder largely decides the character and behavior of the various paints. Binders also play a large part in permanence and drying qualities, brilliance, and speed of working. They also determine what kinds of diluents (also known as solvents) and varnishes may be used in conjunction with them. For instance, water is the diluent for watercolors and gouache, and turpentine for oil, because of the liquid binders used.

A brief look into the history and development of paint will provide valuable insight into what may be achieved when it is used with imagination.

The history of painting reveals that before the establishment of paint and equipment manufacturers and suppliers most artists made their own materials. They ground their own paint, prepared their own supports and primings, even made their own brushes.

In studios in the 15th century the apprentices who worked under the master ground the colors and made the supports. It was all part of the artist's training.

Irksome as it may appear to us today, for them it was a normal part of the process of painting to know how paints were made as well as how to use them. It gave them, in effect, an enormous respect for their materials and was instrumental in achieving a high level of craft which, in turn, richly enhanced the creativity of their work.

Today, happily, we can buy brushes and paint of a consistently high standard whenever we need them. And though we can buy every kind of support to suit all mediums, prepared for oil, tempera, or acrylic—canvas, hardboard, card (cardboard), even paper for oil paint—we can, if we prefer, make our own with ready-to-be assembled stretchers and prepare our own canvas or board with ready-made primings—not necessarily to save money, which it undoubtedly does, but for the satisfaction it will give.

Pigments

Pigments are the coloring materials of paint, and are usually made in the form of powders. From the earliest, pigments had to be bright and clear, and able to withstand prolonged exposure to light. Certain colors were apt to fade and did not produce the subtle tints and shades we would admire today, but were more likely to produce a dead or muddy effect.

Throughout history, bright color was preferred for both practical and aesthetic reasons, having close associations with joy, celebration, pleasure, and delight. To express

HOW ACRYLIC PAINT IS MADE

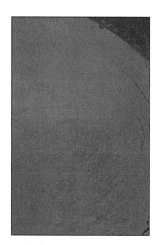

1 The first constituent is powdered pigment.

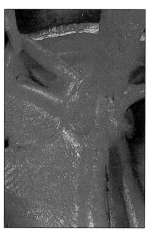

2 The pigment is then mixed with acrylic adhesive.

3 The paint is then milled between steel rollers.

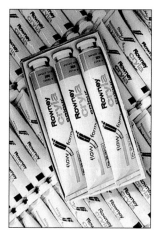

4 After it has been inspected, the paint is put into tubes.

these emotions, bright, rich hues were in constant demand, and the search for pigments that possessed these qualities has been constant over the centuries.

By the Middle Ages the range of colors was quite extensive, and put to complicated use on walls, illuminations, panels, in books, and on woodwork. An all-purpose paint like acrylic would have suited them admirably.

After the Renaissance, pigments reached a peak of brightness and variety. Thereafter a more expressive and realistic style emerged and the medium more suited to this was oil paint. Realistic paintings moved away from bright colors to rich, somber hues, which brought a new range of pigments into being. An interest in brighter color returned again in the 19th century due, in part, to Constable and Turner, the designs of William Morris, and the Impressionists.

Delight in bright color today means a wide range of pigments, and the list of those available is long. The names of pigments often echo places: burnt Sienna, Venetian red, Naples yellow, Prussian blue, Chinese vermilion; or recall the materials they are derived from: cobalt blue, rose madder, emerald green, ivory black, sap green, geranium lake and so on.

Though interesting sounding, the names give little indication of the quality or behavior of colors, and some are sold under two or three different names.

To simplify the situation, the names of absolutely necessary colors are listed further on, and you may want to look at a color chart to see the full range. The number of colors needed to produce a variety of tones and tints need not be large. Pigments today are bright, durable (unless specified), and capable of a great deal of mixing.

Briefly the requirements for a reliable pigment are that: it should be a smooth, finely divided powder; insoluble in the medium in which it is used; able to withstand the action of light without changing color under normal exposure; and it should be chemically inert and unaffected by materials with which it is mixed, or by the atmosphere. Moreover, it should possess the proper degree of opacity or transparency to suit the purpose for which it is intended, and should conform to accepted standards of color and color quality.

The raw materials used to provide the pigments are customarily classified as inorganic or organic. Inorganic materials are those of purely mineral origin such as the natural earths: ochers, raw umber, which can be calcined like burnt umber and burnt sienna, and the artificially prepared colors like cadmium yellow and zinc oxide, the basis of the famous "Chinese white" which was introduced in 1837 by

Winsor & Newton.

Organic pigments include animal and vegetable substances, as well as complex synthetic substances. Vegetable sources furnished color like gamboge, indigo (now not available), and madder. Animal sources produced cochineal which was made into carmine, and Indian yellow was an incredible color made in India from the urine of cows fed on mango leaves. It has now been replaced by synthetically made colors. Other artificially prepared organic colors include alizarin, or anilines (now largely discontinued for aritists' colors, but occasionally used as constituents of household paints and printers' inks).

Many of these organic colors are no longer produced, and have been replaced by newer and more durable colors that have been developed successfully over the years. Notable among these is the plithalocyanine range, the first of which was a very intense blue, known under the trade name of Monastral blue and a very suitable replacement for the less reliable Prussian blues, whose color effects and pigment properties it closely resembles.

The range has now increased to include yellows, reds and greens, and a splendid violet, all of them available in oil, watercolor and acrylic. These colors are classed as organic and are derived by a chemical process from an organic dyestuff. They are very intense with a high degree of durability and, like acrylic paint itself, are a modern and flexible addition to the artist's means of expression.

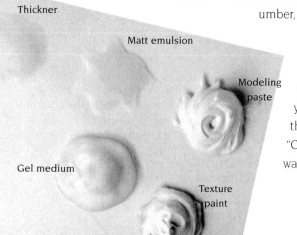

Thickner

Matt emulsion

Modeling paste

Gel medium

Texture paint

PAINTING WITH PIGMENTS

When pigments are seen as powders they are fresh and bright with a beauty all their own. When mixed with a small quantity of water a paste is formed that can be painted with. When the water dries the bloom returns, but so does the powder. In other words it reverts to its former state. What is needed is something to bind the colored grains together to make them adhere. For this purpose some kind of glue or binder must be added to the powder before it becomes paint.

The paints that have the slightest amount of binder, so that the pigment is as pure as possible, are pastels. They are, in effect, dry paint, but though beautiful to look at and work with, they are very fragile. The finished work is easily brushed off unless properly fixed, which, of course, takes away some of the original freshness, and represents the major difficulty over the centuries: to bind the paint so that the color is not impaired.

To repeat, the major difference between one paint and another is not the color or the pigment, it is the binder. Understand the nature of binders and you are half-way to understanding acrylic. This is where the mystery lies.

BINDERS

Gum

The earliest form of binder was a gum, probably gum arabic, though gum tragacanth was supposedly used by the Egyptians. Gum tragacanth is used principally to bind pastels, and gum arabic to bind water colors and gouache.

The popularity of gum arabic as a binder is probably because it dilutes well with water and does not impair the brightness of the pigments. It can also be made into small cakes of paint that are compact and easily stored, and dissolve easily when needed. The only limitation is that watercolor has little body, and is best used transparently, in washes and glazes.

As soon as white is added to the pigment it becomes more opaque. This kind of paint is known as gouache (derived from the Italian word for gum) and dries matt and bright. It is very popular with designers and often referred to as designer's gouache or poster color.

Gouache can also be bought in cake form, but is more practical in liquid form, in bottles and tubes. It is not waterproof and cannot be overpainted without picking up the color underneath. Neither will it stand up to harsh treatment or exposure. Like watercolor, the only protection is to put it immediately under glass.

Emulsions

Any sort of paint that is bound with an emulsion that contains oil, but is mixable with water, is called tempera. The tempera most frequently used throughout the Renaissance contained the yolk of an egg. Other emulsions contained casein glue, wax, and parchment size. The oil most often added to the emulsion was linseed oil.

Most of the paintings and decorations of that period, seen in museums and art galleries today, could be correctly assumed to be tempera paintings.

Egg tempera in particular, dries quickly, hardly changes color, and is fairly waterproof—sufficiently so not to pick up when over-painted. It has a good surface that wears well, provided it is treated with care. It is by far the best of the mediums, but requires technical knowledge and expertise to handle it well.

There are other drawbacks: speed of working is slow, it does not cover large areas well, and is therefore better confined to small panels. There is always the difficulty of making flat, even coats of color on a large scale because the emulsion binder cannot accommodate huge amounts of pigment—something acrylic can do with ease.

Tempera lends itself to simple Images. For more realistic forms of expression, oil paint is more suitable.

Oil

The most common oil used to bind pigment is linseed, and gave the freest possible manner of working for over 300 years. In fact until the introduction of acrylic, an artist could work on a large scale with oil paint without the limitations imposed by tempera and fresco (a pure, but temperamental binder that only functioned well in hot, dry climates) and paint as realistically—or expressively—as vision dictated.

Pigment ground with oil is slow to dry and therefore slow to use, but it brought a softer, more delicate tonality to painting, and did justice to the visual delights of light and shade. Moreover, because of its consistency, it could exploit more surface textures than tempera.

Drying could be speeded up with the addition of siccatives, like copal, dammar, and mastic, which in turn could also be used as varnishes. The addition of natural resin toughened the paint so successfully that all manner of objects and surfaces could be painted.

The practical application of oil paint outweighed its many disadvantages: that it darkens over a period of time, attracts dirt, is difficult to clean, cracks and peels, and is messy and smelly.

Oil paint has to be diluted with turpentine and brushes and palettes cleaned with white spirit and can be applied only to primed surfaces. It requires technical expertise and virtuosity and is not an easy medium to master.

ACRYLIC BINDERS, MEDIUMS, VARNISHES, RETARDERS, AND SOLVENTS

The liquid binders mainly used for oil paint, watercolor, gouache, tempera, fresco, wax encaustic, and so on, were not intended specifically to bind pigments. Linseed oil, egg, gum, wax, and lime are natural products with many other uses, and were adapted to make paint. Consequently all kinds of difficulties were apt to crop up to spoil or limit the full potential of the paint.

Acrylic binders are completely different. They are made specifically for the jobs intended for them. Chemically, acrylic binders are based on polymer resin, and classed as an emulsion into which pigments are mixed. It is, in short, a clear plastic, with great adhesive properties, and water-resistant—despite the fact that the diluent is water. For once the binder is dry, it becomes completely insoluble in water.

Acrylic binders (or more specifically, mediums) can be obtained in three consistencies. This alone makes acrylic unique. With oil paint, a number of alien products are needed to thin or thicken it. Acrylic thinners and thickeners belong to the same family. With them, not only are we able to achieve what other paints can, but a great deal more besides. These mediums, or binders, come as:

• liquid
• jelly (Gel)
• paste

They are milky-white in color when wet, but after evaporation of water, they dry to a clear, transparent film, which is fairly tough and flexible. This also ensures maximum brightness of the pigment.

When these binders are used to exploit the possibilities of acrylic paint they become in effect mediums: liquid constituents of paint, in which the pigment is suspended, or liquids with which the paint may be diluted, without decreasing its adhesive, binding, or film-forming properties.

Mediums can loosely be described as paint additions to make the paint flow or dry more variously, or to produce different results for special kinds of work (impastos, for example, where the addition of a medium will give more bulk to the paint), or, as in the case of acrylic, to transform it into a modeling material. These additions can also thin or thicken to produce a variety of visual effects such as glazes, scumbles, impastos, etc.

Although you need not try them all immediately, you may want to know something about them and

Grumbacher, Winsor and Newton, and Rowney Cryla (**2**) are just a few of the acrylic paints on sale today. Rowney Flow Formula (**1**) is used for covering large areas with flat color. The canvas should be primed with an acrylic primer (**3**) or gesso (**4**). Mediums are available in gloss (**5, 7, 11, 13**) or matt (**6, 10**) textures. Retarding medium (**16**) slows the drying time of the paint. Like mediums, varnishes can be matt (**8, 9**) or gloss. Acrylic varnishes are normally insoluble, but Rowney make a soluble gloss variety (**12**). Also useful are gel medium (**15**) and water tension breaker (**14**).

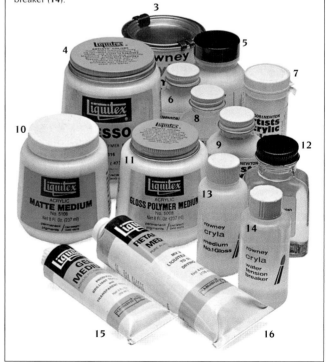

what they are capable of, to understand the possibilities of acrylic, and to experiment with them later.

Acrylic gloss medium

Acrylic gloss medium increases the translucency and gloss of acrylic colors while reducing consistency to produce thin, smooth paint layers which dry rapidly. This means that an unlimited number of glazes of exceptional brilliance, depth, and clarity can be developed and exploited.

A few drops of the medium mixed with ordinary watercolor or gouache immediately transforms them into an acrylic paint, that is, they take on many of the characteristics of acrylic paint: quick-drying, water resistant, capable of overpainting without picking up, and a gloss finish.

The acrylic gloss medium is an essential part of the acrylic artist's paintbox, as essential as water itself, for nearly all the main tasks that acrylic is capable of are much better done with a few drops of the medium added to the paint or wash. This medium has a secondary function as a gloss varnish though there is a newer and more practical and versatile product in two finishes, gloss or matt, which can between them furnish a glossy, semi-matt or eggshell, or matt finish.

Acrylic matt medium

The matt medium behaves in a similar way to the gloss, and everything said of the gloss medium also applies to the matt. It is a useful medium to have if you intend to paint matt, so that the tones of the colors can be properly mixed before painting. There is an appreciable difference in tonality between matt and glossy finishes. The pigment dispersed in either medium may be the same for both matt or gloss, but the light affects them differently. To allow for this during painting, the addition of a few drops of matt (or gloss) medium in the paint mixtures will ensure that, on drying, you get exactly the tone or tint you want.

Acrylic gel medium

Gel medium is thicker than the gloss or matt mediums. As its name implies, it is jelly-like in texture and consistency, and like the gloss medium has two distinct functions.

First, it enables thick, highly textured impastos to be produced easily while maintaining consistency of color, and second, the colors increase in translucency the greater the proportion of gel medium used. At the same time, the drying rate is retarded to some degree.

Glazes and impastos are an integral feature of acrylic painting

BELOW A painting knife is used to mix paint and gel in equal proportions.

ABOVE The consistency of the gel is thick, and so it retains the shape of the knife marks.

and, because of its fairly quick drying qualities, acrylic has an advantage over oil paint, which is by comparison a slow drier, making glazing a long drawn out operation, in which it is hard to foresee the result.

Glazes are made by laying a transparent film of color over another that has already dried. With oil it may take up to two months for a surface to dry out thoroughly for glazing to be done. With gel medium it can be done in a matter of minutes. Moreover any number of glazes can be overlaid, and not just one, as with oil paint. Glazing is a beautiful way of using color so that its brightness and purity is exploited to the full.

Both the acrylic gloss medium and gel medium can be used to make glazes. The difference is merely one of consistency. The gel medium is much thicker than the gloss, and therefore can also be used for impastos. Nevertheless it will make beautiful glazes especially with a palette knife.

Impasto is thick paint that can be textured by the movement of the brush or by the edge of the palette or painting knife.

Impasto has been a particular characteristic of oil paint, and gives tremendous vitality to the expressiveness of the image. Gel medium can achieve this effect in exactly the same way as oil paint, with just as much vitality, and is less liable to crack. It dries much quicker than oil so is less easily spoiled or damaged during painting and, once dried, it becomes very hard to dislodge.

Acrylic texture paste

The thickest, and the most powerful acrylic binder, comes in a carton. Though more dense than the other two binders, it can be watered down without any loss to its adhesive powers.

It can be used to make those very heavy impastos that Vincent Van Gogh was so fond of, for this kind of vigorous brush stroke, large brushes will be needed, or a palette or painting knife will serve

just as well.

Alternatively, instead of using this medium to make thick colored impastos, it can be formed so that other materials, for example sawdust aggregate, may be pressed or embedded into it, to create richly textured surfaces.

The Tepline paste medium has remarkable adhesive powers, and so presents numerous possibilities for design, one of which is the pleasant and simple assemblage known as collage. It presents many possibilities for design and can be used to model and, with the addition of sand, marble dust, or other aggregate to strengthen it, it can be carved or cut and even sanded when dry.

Acrylic water tension breaker

The water tension breaker is a concentrated solution of a wetting agent, which is diluted with water before use. Water tension breaker can be added to water, or matt or gloss mediums, following manufacturers' instructions in quantities depending on the effect required.

Use of this additive allows easier, more rapid thinning of colors with minimum loss of color strength. Staining effects of maximum intensity into difficult surfaces, such as unprimed canvas, are more easily attainable with color diluted in this way.

The flow and ease with which the

color may be used are increased so that flat, even washes of color can be applied to large areas of the work. This is ideal for hard-edge techniques, and for spraying acrylic colors.

It should also be very helpful for those who like to use acrylic in free-flowing washes (like watercolor for example). All that would be required is a few drops of the tension breaker in the container of water.

Acrylic gloss varnish

The main advantages of this varnish are that:

• it is not prone to bubble formation (as the acrylic gloss medium tended to do if brushed vigorously).

• it is removable by an acrylic varnish remover (the gloss medium cannot be removed, as it becomes an integral part of the painting when used as a varnish).

• it has a remarkably good flow, which means that it will spread evenly over the surface, without leaving unsightly brush marks.

This gloss varnish is water-based and dries to a flexible, transparent, extremely light-fast, glossy film. Two coats applied liberally are recommended since any parts that may be missed by the first coat will be covered by the second. On the other hand, the application of two coats necessitates waiting for at least two hours for the first coat of varnish to dry before the second can be applied.

Some manufacturers recommend slight dilution with a few drops of water to achieve good flow, but I have found that this varnish flows very evenly straight from the bottle. However, a few drops of water never does any acrylic material harm—on the contrary, it acts as a safety device for both paints and mediums to be so diluted.

The final varnish film is water-resistant and scuff-resistant and brings out the brilliance of the colors wonderfully. It both protects and enhances at the same time, which is the major reason for varnishing finished work. Varnishing consequently becomes the normal extension to painting, and should offer few problems if all these points are observed.

Acrylic gloss varnish can also be used to varnish prints and posters to protect and enhance them. The varnish should, however, be applied first to a small test area to assess suitability for use. It should also be pointed out that attempting to remove varnish film from prints is not recommended, as damage to the print may result.

Should cleaning of the varnish film be necessary, a soft cloth moistened with either water or weak soap solution can be used with complete safety to wipe the surface.

Acrylic matt varnish
For very large works—murals, wall decorations, exhibition stands and so on—it is usually the practice to varnish with a matt finish, as a glossy surface on a large scale will reflect the light unevenly, giving an unwanted shine. Irregular shine will distort the image, or impair the visual effect which can be very irritating to look at. The only answer to this is a completely matt surface.

Similarly for those who prefer blonde or high-key colors, a matt finish will be more suitable than a rich glossy one. Be careful when buying the varnish to stipulate exactly the kind of varnish you require, and to check the label on the bottle. Acrylic matt varnish has similar qualities to the gloss varnish. It is also removable. One coat will be found to be adequate, but another may be given if necessary after two hours. It can also be used on prints and posters.

Satin on eggshell finish
If you find that a glossy finish is too shiny, or a matt one too bland, there is a way of making an intermediate finish. Simply blend the gloss varnish with the matt in a saucer, or container, and brush on as directed. The resultant midway finish can be adjusted to suit individual preferences by adding either more gloss or more matt to the mixture. A prepared satin finish is also available in art supply shops.

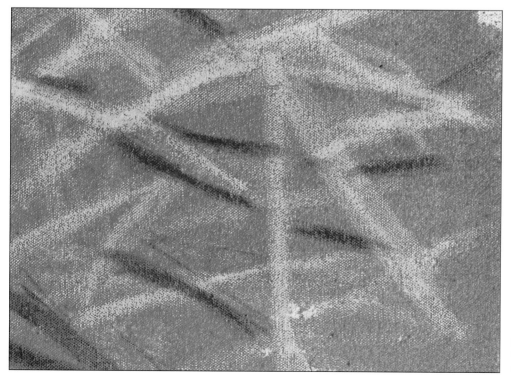

LEFT Acrylic paints can be used very effectively in combination with oil crayons.

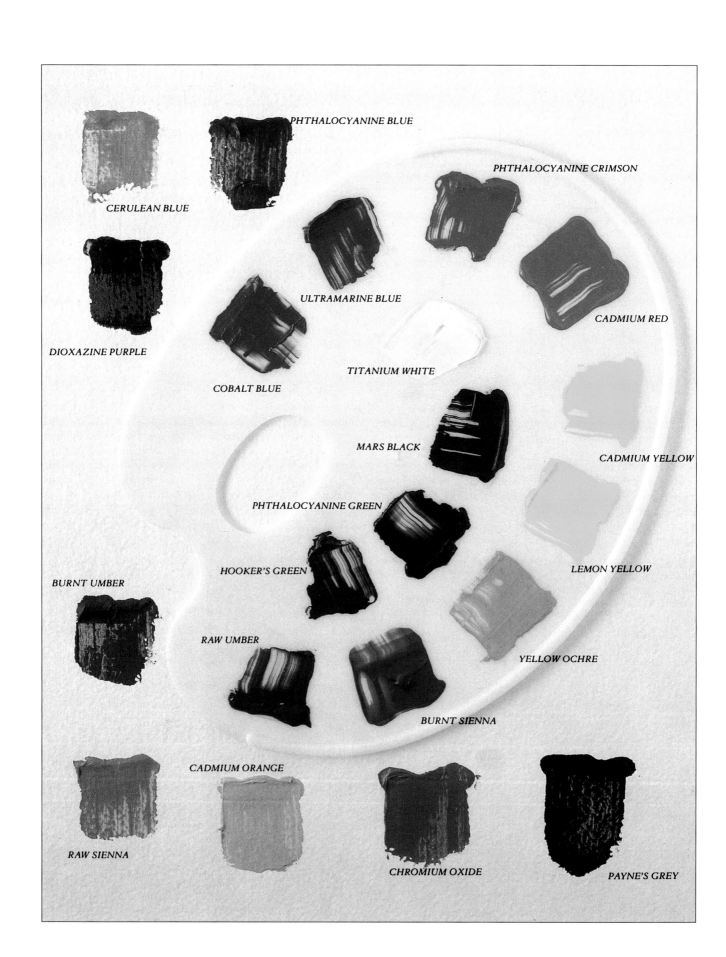

CERULEAN BLUE

PHTHALOCYANINE BLUE

PHTHALOCYANINE CRIMSON

DIOXAZINE PURPLE

ULTRAMARINE BLUE

CADMIUM RED

COBALT BLUE

TITANIUM WHITE

MARS BLACK

CADMIUM YELLOW

PHTHALOCYANINE GREEN

LEMON YELLOW

HOOKER'S GREEN

BURNT UMBER

RAW UMBER

YELLOW OCHRE

BURNT SIENNA

RAW SIENNA

CADMIUM ORANGE

CHROMIUM OXIDE

PAYNE'S GREY

CHAPTER TWO

Materials and Equipment

Painting consists of a number of specific actions, for example smearing, brushing, dabbing, swirling, tinting, staining, spraying, sponging, spattering, and spreading.

The tools needed for this job are usually brushes of varying types and sizes, knives known as painting or palette knives, sponges, airbrushes, and rollers.

The tools and equipment needed for acrylic painting are exactly the same as for oil painting, watercolor and gouache, with a few minor differences.

WATER CONTAINERS

Water is the only solvent, or diluent, needed for acrylic painting, because acrylic paints are water-based. But whether the paint is to be diluted or not, plenty of clean water is essential for keeping brushes clean, and to prevent paint drying on them. You will want glass, china, or plastic containers—jars, cups, bowls, glasses—for this job.

Brushes and palettes will dirty the water as you clean them, and will leave a deposit of sludge after a time. This will sully fresh paint and fail to clean brushes properly. So have as many containers as possible, change the water in them frequently and, if they are disposable, throw them away when they become stained.

Jam, peanut butter, instant coffee, and similar jars are also useful for keeping brushes in.

Two containers are not recommended: narrow-necked bottles which restrict movement, and any kind of tin can or container as they are liable to rust and will ruin paint and brushes if they do.

Have at least two large containers available, filled with clean water, one for diluting paint and the other for cleaning brushes. You will also need clean water to keep the paint on the palette moist. Acrylic paint dries when the water in it evaporates, and is then difficult to dislodge. To prevent this, splash a few drops of water on the paint with a brush from time to time, or use a small hand spray.

Wash out dirty water containers regularly. Dirty water will stain them if left overnight, and they will then be difficult to clean.

PALETTES

The next important piece of equipment is a palette.

The nearest object I have found to fulfil all the conditions for the ideal palette is a large china plate.

A porcelain or glazed pottery surface is easy to keep clean. If paint dries on it, it can be cleaned

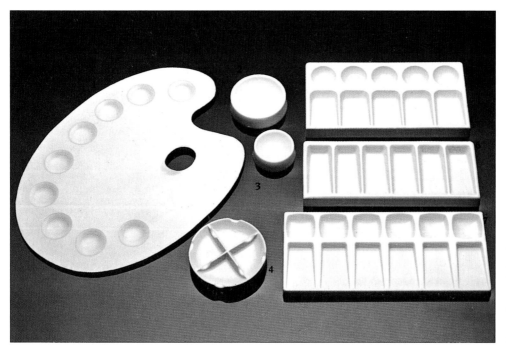

LEFT There are many forms of palette. (1) The traditional palette with thumb hole may be held in one hand while painting. (2, 3) Small pots may be used to mix colors separately. (4, 5, 6, and 7) Alternatively, you may wish to keep the colors together in a larger palette with several wells. The palette used is a matter for the artist's personal choice.

with hot water. A few minutes soaking is all that is needed. For more stubborn cases, soak for a longer time in hot water; paint should then scrape off quite easily.

A white plate is an advantage. White allows mixtures to be accurately gauged; a colored surface plays optical tricks and is best avoided.

The lip or edge on a plate is only important if the mixtures are rather liquid. For stiffer mixtures, using thicker paints, a pad of paper palettes has advantages. Mixing is done on the top layer, which can be torn off and discarded. Paper palettes are not very practical for more liquid paint, or washes, as the paper tends to wrinkle and the paint to spill over the edges.

Another possible palette is a sheet of plain white plastic. The advantage here is that it can be bought in any size. Most palettes tend to be small, useful for taking outdoors for sketching trips, but not nearly large enough for working in the studio.

A sheet of firm, white plastic, glued to an old kitchen table, will make not only a good surface for mixing paint on, but can double up as a working desk.

If there is any disadvantage in a plastic palette it might be in the way acrylic paint clings to it. Some kinds of plastic also have a tendency to stain, unless kept scrupulously clean. Plastic palettes can be obtained at most art supply shops.

Choosing a palette

The choice of palette will depend, broadly speaking, on how you paint —large or small, with thick paint or thin paint or washes.

For thick paint you will want plenty of room for mixing and holding the amount to be used. For thin paint and washes a lip or edge to the palette is mandatory, or the paint will spill. For washes, china saucers are very satisfactory and, being small, are easy to keep clean. They will stack neatly and so will not take up too much room on the painting table.

Choosing a palette will entail a certain amount of trial and error in the early stages, but from my personal experience one fact stands out sharp and clear: you cannot have too many palettes.

Palette surfaces

Many surfaces will do as palettes. A sheet of glass, though a bit slippery, with a sheet of white paper underneath, is possible. Enameled metal or marble tops will do at a pinch. But the palette to avoid is the traditional wooden kind used for oil painting. It has nearly everything wrong with it, from its color to its absorbency. It is difficult to keep clean and is generally impractical for acrylic.

Another surface to avoid is any kind of metal that is uncoated or untreated—with enamel or plastic etc. Metal is liable to corrode, and if it does, will contaminate the paint. Also avoid old or dirty surfaces, or spongy surfaces like leather or rubber.

As a last resort, a piece of ordinary hardboard, or thick cardboard, primed with white emulsion—as for supports—will serve. If it should stain, after cleaning give it another coat of emulsion, and it will be ready for use next time. Such a surface is a little more porous as a palette than plastic or china, but with successive coats of paint it will become less so.

MIXING

After palettes come the mixing implements, which can be either brushes—the most common—or palette knives—the most practical.

Like brushes, palette knives have more than one function. Both are used to mix and apply paint; the palette knife is also used to clean palettes, which makes it, on balance, a necessary piece of equipment. But this is not all. Whereas brushes may apply paint more satisfactorily, the palette knife mixes paint better. For clean, well integrated mixes, the knife remains supreme. The flat, smooth, firm metal shape is perfectly adapted for large and small mixtures. Moreover, the freshness of the colors is better preserved, because they and the mediums used will be properly amalgamated. Tones and subtle tints will then be more easily assessed as to suitability, and texture is retained.

PALETTE KNIVES

The palette knife will not only clean the palette, but is itself easily kept clean. A rub of a rag is all that is needed. Dried-on paint can be scraped off with a knife or razor blade, after softening, if necessary, with warm water or a solvent.

Scraping won't damage a palette knife, as it would a brush. A palette knife is almost indestructable, and with reasonable care should last indefinitely. (I have had a number of palette knives for well over 20 years.) A brush, by contrast, wears badly if used for all kinds of mixing —other than small amounts on the palette—and should be regarded primarily as a painting tool.

Palette knives

RIGHT (**1**) Plastic palette knife. (**2, 6**) Palette knives with rounded blades are flexible along their whole length. They produce the necessary pressure for mixing colors on the palette. They may also be used to scrape away wet paint. (**3, 4, 5**) Painting knives with small, angular blades. These are used to apply and shape small dabs or broad sweeps of paint.

1
2
3
4
5
6

For mixing (and cleaning) paint, the palette knife is a vital and necessary part of any paintbox, and you can also paint with it. For those who find brushes awkward or difficult to manage, the palette knife will provide the answer. Clean, well-mixed paint can be applied to the support with broad, vigorous strokes. For finer work, specially fashioned knives (known as painting knives) make a variety of delicate marks that are very effective. Of course, for more intricate painting and finish, brushes are the superior tools, but for certain kinds of effects, the painting knife can be extremely successful.

Knives, whether for palette or for painting, consist of a wooden handle, and a metal (or plastic) blade. They may be straight, or cranked. The straight are continuous, from the wooden handle to the blade which must be of either stainless steel or plastic. The cranked have a bend that enables them to be manipulated more easily for both mixing, painting, and cleaning.

Broad-faced knives, like putty knives and printers' mixing knives, tend to be too large and clumsy for acrylic

BELOW Brushes are made in several different materials, both natural and synthetic. These are from left to right: red sable round, Russian sable bright, red sable bright, red sable fan blender.

mixing and painting. On balance, the most suitable is a cranked knife that is not too small or too flexible, that will clean, mix, and apply paint equally well. The aim should be to use both palette knife and brush, switching from one to the other as and when the situation demands.

BRUSHES

Brushes for acrylic painting can also be used for oil painting. The range is identical.

Sable brushes

Sable brushes are delightful to work with in all mediums; they can be used for watercolor, oil, and acrylic with equal success. Having specially fashioned points, they can make the most delicate lines and strokes. In addition, they are constructed to hold the paint well, and so spread it with ease and fluency.

The advantage of a sable brush over most of the others is that it responds so sensitively to the touch, allowing the most gentle of marks to the broadest of washes to occur with the slightest pressure of the hand. Your intentions are carried out immediately with a

RIGHT Choice of brushes, as with most other equipment, is a completely personal matter. An artist may wish to use only one type of brush. In this case, he or she will need several different sizes. If the artist wishes to use all types of brushes, three sizes of each may be necessary: small, medium, and large.

sable, which in effect becomes an extension of the hand.

They are also expensive, and so must be carefully treated on all counts. If sables are used with acrylic paint, they must be scrupulously washed of all color after use. Acrylic dries hard very quickly, so always keep water handy, to make sure that there is little chance of that happening. Get into the habit of dipping your brush into the water when not in use.

The range and the variety of sable brushes may appear bewildering initially, but a good start can be made by narrowing the choice down to two: a No. 3 for fine work, and a No. 7 for broad, both round in shape. Other sizes can be added later.

To these can be added ox-hair or squirrel brushes which, though a great deal less expensive than sable, are very useful to do those jobs that would otherwise be impossible. Large areas, for example, which would need a very expensive sable to do the job,

could be done just as satisfactorily with an ox-hair or squirrel brush.

A good all-round selection of brushes must contain a few soft and hard brushes to meet all possible contingencies.

The best hard brushes are hog's-hair.

Hog's-hair brushes

Hog's -hair brushes were mainly used for oil paint, until the introduction of acrylic, for which they are admirably suited. They differ from sables in a number of ways: whereas the majority of sables are round in shape, hog's hairs come in four quite distinct shapes: round, bright (or square), flat, and filbert, which are capable of a great variety of marks.

Hog's-hair brushes are made from real bristle, and are dressed and shaped according to the natural curve of the hair. They are so skilfully put together that they always retain their shape no matter how much paint is on them and how vigorously they are used.

Though sturdier than sables, they must still be treated with care by keeping them clean, and not doing too much mixing with them.

Choosing a selection of these brushes may be done in the same way as with sables: a small and a large from each type—say a 3 or 4 small, and a 7 or 8 large, depending on individual preferences and cost.

Other brushes that may be found to be useful are household and nylon brushes.

Household brushes, the kind that are used for painting woodwork around the house, come in various sizes, and are extremely useful for the kinds of painting that are too arduous or rough for sables and hog's-hair—for example, priming supports, and painting sculpture, models, and other kinds of design, preparatory to painting with sables.

Synthetic brushes

Nylon brushes have improved a great deal since they were first introduced. They are available in a large variety of sizes and shapes, perform well, clean easily and, as sable brushes have become very expensive, are good alternatives to sable and the finer hog's-hair. Synthetic fibers are robust and wear well under vigorous use. They are cheaper than other brushes and well worth trying.

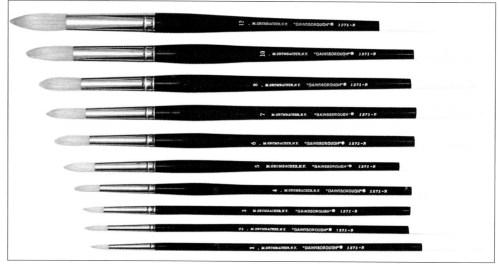

SUPPORTS AND SURFACES

Anything upon which a painting is executed is called a support. Traditionally they were wood panels, walls, and canvases; today we also use paper, card (cardboard), and hardboard.

Every painting or painted surface consists of three elements: a support—the material upon which one paints; the ground—which covers the support (also referred to as priming); the paint itself, usually put on in layers.

Supports, ideally, should be light enough to be transported without damage—unless fixed to a wall, or indeed the wall itself. Card and hardboard are light and serviceable in the smaller sizes, though hardboard is cumbersome in anything over a square yard/square meter.

A B O V E Brushes come in many sizes. Most ranges are numbered from 1 (the smallest) to 12. Extra large brushes (numbered up to 36) are also available.

For large, portable paintings, canvas remains the most convenient. Supports are always treated with a ground to preserve the support and, receive the paint satisfactorily.

Grounds are traditionally white, for the good reason that a white base will not impair the brilliance and permanence of the colors laid on it; and slightly absorbent, to ensure that the paint adheres well. The surface can be roughened or textured to do the same job.

This roughness or texture is usually referred to as the tooth. The natural grain of canvas gives a perfect tooth, and many card or hardboard supports purchased

R I G H T Types of supports (left to right): canvas board, daler board, primed paper, hardboard (smooth side), hardboard (reverse side), plywood.

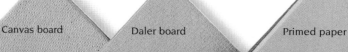

Canvas board   Daler board   Primed paper

ready-made for painting have a simulated canvas grain because it keys the paint so well.

A white base is absolutely necessary for oil painting, as oil paint goes transparent in time, and, if on a dark ground, will darken the colors subsequently. Acrylic colors do not go transparent with age, but even so, a white base is more suitable for painting on. Grounds and primings are really no more than coats of paint, and are often referred to as the undercoat or underpainting by painters and decorators.

In the past, preparing panels for tempera and canvases for oil was a skilled and exacting task, not to be undertaken lightly. Before the grounds were applied to the surface, a coat of animal glue size (usually rabbits' skin) might be needed to separate the surface from the priming. In the case of oil painting, this was mandatory as oil paint will rot unprimed canvas if placed directly upon it.

If the priming was brittle, as in the case of plaster-based primings, known as gesso, canvas could not be used at all, as it was far too flexible, and the priming was not. Gesso could only be used on a perfectly rigid support like wood, that had to be properly seasoned, otherwise warping and splitting might occur.

Making glue for primings was a long and tedious operation. A double glue boiler was needed to melt the glue, and when ready the smell could be rather strong. Furthermore it had to be applied hot.

Making gesso was equally arduous—to make as well as apply. Anything up to eight coats were normally applied, and if not done correctly would crack and flake.

With acrylic all this is avoided completely. Acrylic needs no special glues or primings. Acrylic sticks so well, it can attach itself, without harm, to almost anything. There are only two treatments for priming a support: either the acrylic medium, or white acrylic priming which can be bought ready-made.

SUPPORTS FOR ACRYLIC PAINTING

In theory, you can use almost anything as a support for acrylic painting. There should be no problem if you bear in mind these

CLEANING A BRUSH

1 Rinse the brush in a wide-necked jar of clean water.

2 Reshape the brush by drawing it backward through the palm of the hand.

3 Allow the brush to dry by storing it up-ended in a jar.

Hardboard (smooth side)   Hardboard (reverse side)   Plywood

six points:

All surfaces must be absolutely clean. Any oil or wax present, even in minute quantities, will prevent the acrylic adhering properly.

Make sure that any unprepared hardboard, or equivalent commercial board, has no oil or wax in its manufacture.

Any oil-primed wood, canvas, or board (ostensibly for oil painting) should not, under any circumstances, be overpainted with acrylic. Check the maker's instructions very carefully on this point. If in doubt do not use at all.

Very smooth surfaces, like glass, polished metal, or plastic, may appear to hold acrylic paint, but in fact may scratch easily, or even flake or peel off if in contact with dampness, unless slightly roughened before painting. Wirewool, sandpaper, or some other tool that will scratch or indent the surface can be used to give a tooth.

Avoid silk. It is rather too smooth, and not nearly robust enough for good adhesion. Also avoid unseasoned wood, as it will warp or split in time, and large sheets of hardboard, unless properly backed by battens or frame, will sustain damage at the corners unless protected.

Avoid painting on very rough surfaces. For example, murals and wall decorations should not be painted directly on to brick or concrete without some kind of treatment first. At least three or four coats may be needed.

Priming

Priming surfaces for acrylic painting requires only white acrylic primer, which is easily and quickly applied with a household brush, roller, or palette knife to wood, canvas, card (cardboard), paper, or hardboard.

Anyone who has painted a wall with emulsion paint will be able to prime a piece of hardboard or card successfully, for the job is identical.

ABOVE White arylic primer is applied to hardboard with a household brush.

HOW TO STRETCH A CANVAS

1 Wood for stretchers is available in many lengths, which can be fitted together to make rectangles of all sizes.

2 Slot the stretchers together so that the corners are at right angles—the diagonals should be of equal length.

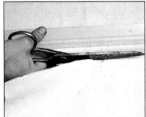

3 Cut the canvas to fit, allowing a margin of 2-3 in (5-6 cm) all round.

4 Fold the canvas over and staple it to the stretcher, starting in the middle of the longest side.

5 Staple toward the corners at 3 in (8 cm) intervals. Repeat on the opposite side and then the shorter sides.

6 Turn the corners diagonally. Staple both edges firmly into position.

7 Tap the corner wedges into place. The fabric should be tight but not taut. The fabric is now ready for priming.

The acrylic primer can be applied directly from the jar, or thinned with a little water if too thick.

Two thin coats should be sufficient to cover a piece of hardboard—the aim is to obliterate completely the color of the hardboard—whereas one coat might be sufficient for a piece of white card (cardboard). There is no need to size the hardboard, but if it is highly absorbent, it can be made less so by brushing on a thin coat of acrylic medium before priming with white. And if too shiny or smooth, it can be roughened with a piece of sandpaper to give it a tooth.

If you prefer the natural color of the support, you can brush on a thin coat of acrylic medium, matt or glossy, to seal and prime the surface. Any further painting can proceed as if it were primed with white.

Canvases

Ready-made canvases, primed for acrylic painting, can be obtained at most art supply shops. The acrylic canvases available might need an extra coat of priming to give the tooth required. Somehow (and here personal preference intrudes), I feel that canvases are best left to oil painting, and the natural and primary supports for acrylic are the more rigid and firmer supports like card (cardboard) and hardboard and, of course, paper.

The disadvantages of canvas tend to outweigh their pleasant handling qualities and lighter weight. Canvas is vulnerable. It is prone to damage, the expansion and contraction of the cloth in varying temperatures will place a great strain on the priming, and cause cracking and

flaking. The more flexible acrylic can cope with this hazard, but cannot avoid damage by denting, and the kind of wear and tear a more rigid support can sustain.

Thin coats of acrylic medium might help to stiffen the canvas a little and make it a little less fragile, as would keeping the canvas taut by knocking up the corners with the appropriate wedges whenever possible. Do not lean things against them, for any creases or dents that may occur will be very difficult to remove.

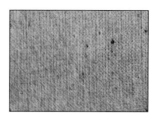

1 Unbleached calico, a cheap cotton weave.

2 A quality canvas, the next best thing to linen.

3 Hessian, always a coarse material.

4 Linen, in a close weave.

5 Linen, in a coarse weave.

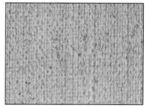

6 Linen, ready-primed with acrylic.

Bought canvases, stretched and ready for use, are convenient, but expensive. Making your own is not only cheaper, but is also more satisfying if you have the time. For make no mistake, you do need time and space to do the job properly. Either a good wide table or workbench or the floor will do, provided the canvas can lie perfectly flat, and is unimpeded, so that you can either turn the canvas satisfactorily or move around it easily.

The canvas is made up of two distinct materials, before priming: wood for the stretchers and keys (wedges), and the canvas itself,

which might be made from cotton or flax and be woven coarse, medium, or fine.

There are two kinds of stretchers: the interchangeable kind or the fixed. The interchangeable are known as wedged stretchers, and have a specially cut end that will firmly wedge together. When made up with canvas, they can be stretched tightly by the insertion of small triangular shaped pieces of wood into the specially cut slots. Gently tapping them in with a hammer will pull the canvas as tight as a drum.

Wedged stretchers come in many lengths up to several feet/meters, and up to 3 in. (8 cm) in width. They are grouped in categories according to size, and within these categories they are interchangeable. They should be easily obtainable from a good art supply shop, which should stock all sizes.

Rigid or fixed stretcher

Most painters find that the wedged stretcher is the most suitable for making their own canvases, and the most practical for working on, mainly because the canvas can be kept fully taut by the use of the wedges at the corners. If for some reason the right size cannot be obtained, making them yourself can be a problem. Wedged stretchers have a complicated cut end made to ensure accuracy. If they are badly made warping, among other things, will ensue, and it will be out of true at the corners. It is essential that, when a canvas is made up, the angles should be at 45 degrees, or else the canvas will develop folds and look unsightly.

As a substitute for a wedged stretcher you can construct a simple fixed frame, made from bought, 2 by 1 strips of wood. These can be cut to size and properly mitered and glued to ensure that it will take the strain of the taut canvas.

As these frames are rigid, they cannot be tightened at the corners with keys or wedges should the canvas become slack. This means that the only way to keep the canvas tight is to restretch it. In spite of this, many painters continue to use them especially for painting on odd-shaped canvases. Since the introduction of acrylic paint, many painters have broken away from the traditional rectangle, to exploit unusual shapes to paint on. Oil paint seemed to demand the rectangle (and the occasional oval) shape to work on. Among other things, acrylic allowed the painter to break away from conventional practices and try new approaches. The odd-shaped canvas was one of them.

Rigid frames impose a number of conditions, one of which is to make sure that the canvas is absolutely taut before priming. Many painters who use fixed canvases tell me that they try to stretch the canvas unprimed, if possible, and then give it a thin coat of acrylic medium. They maintain that this stretches the canvas taut when dry, and then a thin coat of acrylic priming can be put on without any slackening at all.

When an unusual support is required, another answer is to use hardboard, which can be constructed much more easily than a rigid stretcher. If a canvas surface is desired, it can be glued on (marouflaged) to the hardboard, and no arduous stretching will be necessary

An odd-shaped support made with hardboard can be rather heavy to transport, as it will also need strong battens at the back to prevent it from warping. Hence the popularity of canvas—even on a rigid support.

Stretching the canvas

Stretching can be done with either raw or with primed canvas. Primed canvas can be bought, but you can prime it yourself. The procedure is exactly the same as for hardboard —two thin coats straight from the jar. For a smoother finish a third coat may be added.

If done on the stretcher you can make a neater job, whereas priming un-stretched canvas can be rather messy. I usually stretch five or six unprimed canvases at a time. I can then prime them all at once, or just one or two. Acrylic priming dries comparatively quickly, which means that the tedious business of laying two or three coats can be speeded up.

To stretch either primed and unprimed canvas: cut the canvas 4 in. (8 cm) longer and wider than the stretcher, to allow for overlap. Place on a flat surface and place the stretcher on top of the canvas. Fold one edge of the canvas over the frame and tack or staple it in the center of the side. Then do the same to the opposite side, then to the two remaining sides.

When tacking is completed make certain that there are no folds or creases at the corners before priming. It is unnecessary to wedge the corners at this stage. When the priming dries out the canvas will tighten automatically, provided the priming is thinly applied.

Priming canvases can be done with brushes, knives, or rollers, as with hardboard.

EASELS

The last, important piece of equipment is the easel. The easel carries the support. For large supports, and especially canvases, the easel is best placed firmly on the floor. Ideally suited to this purpose is the radial easel.

For smaller sized supports, a table easel can be used as an alternative. Also when space is at a premium, it can be folded up neatly and put away, unlike the radial type which will take up room however

adequately for small supports, if required, and so duplicate their value.

An easel of some kind is absolutely necessary for most kinds of work. Unless you paint on a workbench or on the floor, even a block of wood will do at a pinch to prop up a support in the studio. Outdoors, because of the quick drying qualities of acrylic, the support may be rested on the lap or on the ground. However, an

easel is an essential piece of equipment.

BELOW There are many types of easel.
1 Studio easel, ideal for work on large canvases.
2 Radial easel, may be folded down and tilted backward and forward.
3 Artist's donkey, suitable for working while sitting down.
4 Table easel, best used on a low table or with a tall chair.
5 Collapsible easel, good for outdoor work.

you stack it.

The lighter, more mobile easels are designed principally for outdoor work where walking or moving about may be involved. They can, of course, be used in the studio quite

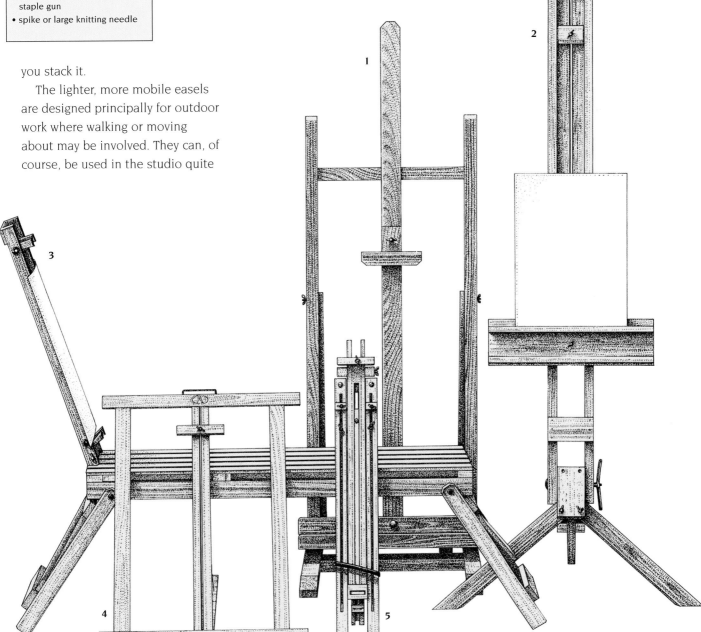

CHAPTER THREE

Painting with Acrylics

Next to watercolor, acrylics are the simplest of paints to use. The minimum amount needed is a few tubes of paint, some brushes, a palette, and water. This is not to say that watercolors or acrylics are the easiest paints to use because the equipment needed can be reduced to the bare minimum, but because of its basic simplicity, acrylic can give enjoyment from the very start.

Many painters and designers make a practice of combining acrylic with other media like colored inks, drawing, and gouache. Acrylic seems to work well with almost any conventional medium, provided it doesn't contain oil.

The reason for including information on what must seem like so much equipment is that it can be used when needed should it be required. Those who have painted with oils will know how much basic equipment is needed just to begin. Happily this is not so with acrylics.

Paints, paper, brushes, and water are all that will be needed. With experience newer items will be added and others discarded.

THE INFRASTRUCTURE OF PAINTING

Looking at a painting or design is rather like looking at an iceberg. We only see the tip. We can't see what's underneath holding it up, as it were. We know, however, that a great deal of the iceberg is beneath the water—hence its strength.

The strength of a painting, too, lies beneath the surface—and has dangers for the unwary as well as delights. If this fact isn't understood, painting will forever be a mystery.

Actually the principle is very simple and quite easy to understand. It is this: paintings are built up in layers. Even watercolors are built up with layers of washes, one transparent film over another.

This layering of one coat of paint over another varies with the function of that layer. For example the function of the primer differs from the function of a glaze: the primer, because it is a sealer and a reflector of light, is thick and opaque; the glaze is thin and transparent because its job is to let the light, or another color, come through.

For most household jobs, the paint layers would be fairly simple: sealer, undercoat, top coat.

For painting in oil or acrylic the number of coats or layers could be as many as ten. For example, starting from the bottom:

LAYERS OF A PAINTING

• support: paper, card, canvas, hardboard etc
• sealer: glue size or acrylic medium (optional for acrylic, necessary for oil)
• primer: gesso, acrylic white, lead white etc.
• wash or toned drawing
• underpainting: blocking in the main areas of color, usually thinly
• middle layer
• scumble
• impasto
• glaze
• varnish

This is precisely what painting entails: a study of the layers of paint. The success of any painting depends on how they are amalgamated. Naturally only a few of them may be used on any one painting, but to get the best out of acrylics it is essential to be acquainted with them. Fortunately acrylic dries quickly, so the process of laying one coat over another can be speeded up, and takes much of the tediousness out of painting. Oil paint, being a slower-drying paint, hasn't this advantage.

The study of paint layers goes hand in hand with a study of colors and the way they interact with each other. Before that, we have to consider another important factor—water.

WATER

A number of mediums have been suggested for use with acrylic paint to make it flow better, to give different finishes—gloss, eggshell, or satin, matt—to produce every kind of impasto from medium, to thick, to very thick, and to retard the drying rate. But the most important of these, the medium that takes precedence over them all, is the diluent itself, water.

Acrylic paint is made up from three components: pigment, binder, water. Water plays a dominant part in painting with acrylics, not only for the vital process of thinning the paint to the required consistency, but also for cleaning brushes and palette. Without water, painting with acrylics becomes irksome, if not actually impossible.

Literally one must study the behavior of water, for apart from its thinning and brush cleaning propensities, it must play its part throughout the whole of the work. Water is the life blood of acrylics, and though the other mediums extend the range of achievement, one can, at a pinch, do without them—as many of us did when acrylic paint was new and largely unknown. Consequently we were forced to examine just how much we could do with water alone.

By giving water the central role to play in acrylic painting, you learn that the amount used largely controls the rate of drying. It is essential to remember that once the water evaporates the paint hardens and cannot be redissolved with any more water (as it can with watercolor and gouache).

With experience and experiment you learn to add just the right amount of water to produce: the right consistency and the appropriate drying time to allow for working. This produces the simple rule: the more water used, the thinner the paint and the longer the drying time.

The four main forms of consistency are: thin, thick, transparent, opaque. Some of them can be amalgamated by the use of water alone: thin /transparent; thin/opaque. However, the only way to admix thick and transparent is by the use of a gel. Similarly the only way to get a really thick paint is by the addition of acrylic texture paste.

For the rest, water is sufficient.

Because acrylic is a water-based paint, it is always the practice to wet the brush before use, especially for mixing paint. As a general rule, never use a dry brush for anything pertaining to acrylic. A dry brush won't allow the paint to flow properly, will alter the drying times so that it will be harder to gauge, and won't do a sable brush much good. However if it does transpire that a dry brush has inadvertently been used, wash it out immediately afterward. (The exceptions to this rule will be seen in the section on scumbling, but here old brushes are recommended.)

This means acquiring, early on, the habit of constantly dipping the brush into water, and shaking out the excess, before beginning.

You can do the same with a palette knife—moistening it before use—though of course, the knife won't retain the water to anything like the same degree.

CHOOSING COLORS

The next, and most important, stage, is choosing colors, then mixing and applying them. The following color exercises are very basic and, to get the maximum benefit from them, thin opaque paint, rather than thick or transparent paint, is recommended. The latter kinds of paint will be gone into later, and may be adapted to the exercises

accordingly.

Choose a palette that will hold the paint well. Thin paint does have a tendency to slop about. Try the kind with wells or use a small saucer or two.

Another point to note is that once acrylic paint is mixed, it will last indefinitely so long as the water in it doesn't evaporate. Therefore any color that has been mixed, and for any reason isn't needed right away, can be kept in a small jar or container so long as it is properly stoppered. For this purpose, I use discarded film cassette canisters, which are ideal for ready-mixed paint, and are useful for taking outdoors for working. A dab of the color contained in them on the lid of the canister identifies them immediately.

Choice of colors is the very heart of painting and designing. The question is how to go about it? What are the rules, or principles, if any, that apply?

The overwhelming compunction on seeing a color chart for the first time, is to want them all—and then give up because the choice is so wide, so it is refreshing to be told that the maximum number of colors needed to make up a palette that will do practically everything is five.

FIVE ESSENTIAL COLORS

• White is absolutely mandatory in any palette, for mixing tones and tints, for repainting prior to glazing or alteration, and as a color.

• Black is essential for tones, and as

a color.

• Yellow—primary.
• Red—primary.
• Blue—primary.

The three primaries, yellow, red, and blue can be mixed to make three further colors, or secondaries: orange, green, and violet in the following way.

Yellow and red make orange.
Yellow and blue make green.
Blue and red make violet.

The secondary colors—orange, green, and violet—can be bought in tubes ready-mixed which, if preferred, will make the basic eight-color palette.

Whether you decide to have a five or eight palette, mixing primaries to make secondaries must be carried out at some time for the experience of seeing what happens.

As an aid to choosing colors it is helpful to use a color chart. Charts give the best information on the tone and range of the selection, the names of the colors, and a note or two on their use and permanence. Moreover charts are good to refer to for other reasons. By being the standard or yardstick of what pure color looks like before mixing, they will aid mixing by being a reminder of what they were. With color, the way to enhance understanding of them is to experience them often.

COLOR TEMPERATURE

Warm colors are those closer to the red end of the spectrum.

Cold colors are those closer to the blue end of the spectrum.

MIXING ACRYLIC

To get used to the way acrylic behaves, and to get the feel, as well as the visual impact of a mixture, a sound practice is to begin mixing each color—both primaries and secondaries—with white first, and then with black. Then add black to white mixes, and white to the black.

Mixing white with a color is referred to as a *tint*.

Mixing black with a color is referred to as a *tone*.

All colors, whether pure or mixed together on the palette, can be toned or tinted with the addition of black or white. To grasp the range of tones and tints, and the extent to which they can be manipulated, all the colors that are available should be tried out at some time.

The point of this is that once the visual experience of mixing colors has taken place it will remain as a guide for future reference. Once seen, never forgotten. The more mixing that is done now, the more confident will be the results later. The results of these experiments should be kept, at least for a time, as a reminder.

COLOR MIXING
Exercise 1—light to dark
The very first experience with

mixing can be with just white and black, before trying out the other colors. It is slightly easier to judge tones and tints of gray than the

tones and tints of primaries and secondaries. This exercise is basic to all the color mixing exercises. It will incorporate mixing, applying, and experiencing the visual impact of tone, tint, and hue.

Mixtures should be well integrated, on the palette, with a knife, and with enough fluidity to allow the brush to make a good, clean stroke.

For the kind of grid that will suit this exercise best, use six squares, about ½ in. (1 cm) in size, which can be conveniently filled with variegated tones of paint from light to dark, and from dark to light. Method 1. Add black to white, to make a series of grays, from the palest to the darkest tints, in six steps. The gray of medium strength should occur in the center of the scale. Method 2. Reverse the process by adding white to black.

This exercise can now be repeated with all the colors, one by one, included in the palette, utilising

Method 1 to make tones, and Method 2 to make tints. Points to remember, observe and develop:

1. These exercises are fundamental. There is no need to paint them carefully, if your natural inclination is to paint them freely. The practice should be as enjoyable as possible. The only proviso is that care should be taken in the mixing of the paint, so that each change of tone, in its respective square, is as clear as possible.

2. There are no rules; and no end product to cause worry. The main point is, that when trying any new color, do it this way before using it for whatever purpose you have in mind.

LEFT The grid with seperate tones.

ABOVE The horizontal and vertical grid.

3. The aim of this exercise is to sharpen sensitivity, and give valuable experience not only in mixing color, but to see what the color looks like when mixed.

4. The exercises can be carried out in any order; size is optional, but for the best results, white paper

or card (cardboard) is recommended, primed or unprimed. For a primed white surface one thin coat is sufficient.

5. The grid may be varied to accommodate more tones and tints, and more colors. As a variation, the tones and tints may be further mixed horizontally as well as vertically.

6. As an alternative exercise the mixing may be carried out without using white. The colors can be lightened by the addition of water to make them more transparent. This is the same technique as is used in painting with watercolors. It is a useful exercise, but needs more care than in using opaque acrylic, as the washes are more difficult to control. However, whatever result is obtained, practice in using color this way is valuable, if only to experience the differences between using opaque and transparent color. As a further experiment the exercise can be carried out on different surfaces (as with watercolor) with both primed and unprimed paper.

7. Painting can be done with knife or brush. Try experimenting with them all, at some time or other, and become familiar with them at every available opportunity. This is the true meaning of practice.

8. Once confidence in mixing is acquired, any other acrylic color may be tried out—the umbers, siennas, ochers, as well as the cadmiums, blues and greens mentioned earlier.

WHITE PAINT

White plays a most important role in painting and you will need more of it than any of the other colors. If possible buy the larger quantities.

Large tubes will be less troublesome than small tubes which will run out very quickly. There is no good reason that I can fathom why one cannot use acrylic primer, if one does run short, as it is made of the same pigment, titanium white, and acrylic binder, as the tubed titanium white.

Titanium white is the only white pigment used, at the moment, for acrylic white paint, and is very powerful. A little goes a long way. So one has to be careful when mixing to add the white sparingly, or strong colors will be reduced to tints surprisingly quickly.

With jars of white, be very careful to keep the tops of the containers clear of dry paint, or the water will evaporate and the paint harden. A good tip is to sprinkle a few drops of water on the white to ensure that it doesn't, before putting the lid back on.

BLACK PAINT

Mars black, which is absolutely permanent, is manufactured from artificial oxides of iron and is rather powerful so that, like white, it should be mixed sparingly with other colors. Although its use is suggested in the exercises, tones can be produced with many other combinations of color—red and green, for example, make very good gray-blacks, as do blue and umber. Black is nevertheless a good utilitarian standby and an ideal color for beginning the mixing of tones without too many problems.

Exercise 2—direct vision

As mentioned before, learning about mixing and applying colors can be done directly from nature,

but the process can be confusing to those unused to the practice. As a bridge from mixing colors on a systematic chart basis as in Exercise 1 to the full examination of color in nature which will lead to the painting of pictures, the following method is a simple and easy step in that direction.

Color mixing and application are exactly as in Exercise 1.

1. Thin, opaque paint.
2. Primed or unprimed paper or card (cardboard), size optional but not bigger than 33 X 22 in. (84 X 56 cm).
3. The choice of brushes is again optional.
4. Black and white paint are mandatory.
5. Three primaries only to begin with: red, yellow, and blue; other colors can be added later for further experiments.

The aim of this exercise is to examine one color at a time in all its variety, subtlety, and visual impact by observing directly a group of objects all of the same color.

To carry out this exercise, select a number of objects of the same color: red, yellow, or blue (omit green for the moment). Though only one of these colors is to be used at a time, the more varied the shades, the surfaces, and the size that can be assembled the better.

If a particular color is chosen, say red, to begin the experiment with, it will be immediately noticed that reds vary enormously. Some are warmer, others colder. Shiny reds will appear quite different from matt, some will be darker than the others and so on.

As an aid to selecting objects use this framework as a guide:
1. Size: large, small, cylindrical, cubic, round, triangular, or concave.
2. Surfaces: smooth, rough, shiny, matt, textured, patterned.
3. Tone: light, dark, brilliant, faint, harsh, soft.

As a general rule three objects on a similar color background are sufficient to begin with, arranged so as to make the maximum effect of the color obvious.

The painting can be done either freely, in broad brush strokes or flatly, in simple plain-colored areas.

The object of this exercise, whichever way it is painted, is to mix different tones and tints of the same observed color. The experience of Exercise I will be of great help here, and the painted charts can be referred to constantly if need be. The exercise will be helpful in making the eyes color-sensitive to the gradations and variations of tones and tints that make color so fascinating and elusive to control. This particular way of observing color will enable you to grasp the essentials of manipulating color.

The suggested method of painting to adopt is as follows:
1. Establish the large areas of color first: this is usually the background, but if there isn't a great deal showing, begin with the largest shapes instead.
2. Use the brush to make deliberate marks of paint. Let the brush do the work. Avoid strain and above all avoid scrubbing. Load the brush with as much paint as can be held comfortably, and when exhausted replenish with fresh paint. Don't ever scrub with a dry brush. It will ruin the hairs, and make an unpleasant mark. Let the brush flow freely.
3. Build up the shapes of tone with crisp dabs of paint. Make no effort to make the painting look "real." Aim instead to examine the different areas of color, and try to state them as approximately as possible. Don't strain to make a picture, let the paint and the color dominate instead.

This exercise should be repeated using all the primaries. It can then be followed by exploring the secondaries: green, orange, and violet.

BELOW A similar complementary chart to the one below, incorporating intermediate tones and tints.

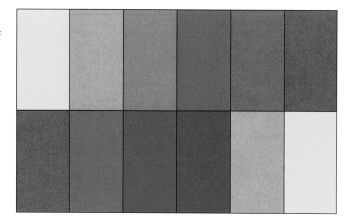

Variations on this theme can be made by:
1 changing the background to a different color from the objects
2 introducing one object of an entirely different color
3 introducing a white and black object to create a contrast
4 introducing two different colored objects
5 painting on a colored support
6 changing the background to black
7 changing the background to white.

COMPLEMENTARY CONTRAST
Complementary colors are those that lie opposite one another in the color circle. As a follow up to the last exercises, and for further variations on color combinations, here is the way in which complementaries work in contrast with one another. They make an interesting point about the way we respond to groupings of colors, and it is absolutely essential for designers to know what they consist of for future use.

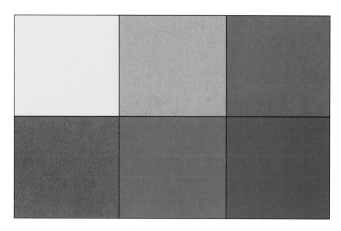

ABOVE This chart shows the primary colors, yellow, blue, and red with their contrasting complementaries, violet, orange, and green, respectively.

Examples of primaries and secondaries consists of: yellow, violet, blue, orange, red, green. And in all these pairs, primaries are always apparent—hence the necessity of mixing them together to make secondaries in the early stages. One gets to understand them better by doing so.

These colors are opposite yet require each other: they produce a vividness when adjacent, yet annihilate each other when mixed to produce a dark gray (useful as the basis for a neutral background, or underpainting to work on).

Another useful peculiarity of contrasting complementaries is that, though opposite, they have the remarkable ability to appear perfectly harmonious. This makes using them an agreeable pictorial device for enhancing both paintings and designs. By utilizing the complementary chart, you have the beginnings of ready-made color schemes that can easily be carried out with acrylic.

COLORED SURFACES
Colored surfaces and supports fall into two distinct categories: naturally colored materials, such as wood, unglazed ceramic, metal, linen, hardboard etc; artificially colored materials, like pastel papers, mounting card, plastic, dyed fabric etc.

Possibly the best surfaces of all are those you prepare yourself. Ready-made surfaces are rarely as versatile or satisfactory enough to suit all requirements. Those you prepare, moreover, have the advantages of better control of the work from its inception. The appropriate colored surface will aid judgment of the tone of the color

—which a white or, for that matter, black, surface will rarely do. The reason for this is not difficult to find when considering tone. The addition of white or black to a primary or secondary color works within a tonal scale that has white at one end and black at the other. This is in accordance with one way the natural world is seen: as gradations of dark and light. This tonal scale moves in a series of progressions from one end of the scale to the other. To find the right balance within it is more difficult to judge, if we are forced to work from one end or the other. If instead we begin in the middle and work outward, the result will be more successful, more visually effective and, more important, will be much more enjoyable to do.

IMPASTOS
Impastos are thick, heavy strokes of paint made with brush or painting knife, and commonly associated with oil paint. With acrylic they can be achieved

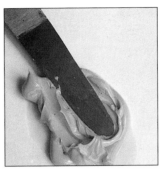

1 The artist uses the knife to mix the paint on the palette. He then spreads it thickly in broad, textured ridges.

2 A heavy impasto may be sculpted to produce swirls and ridges.

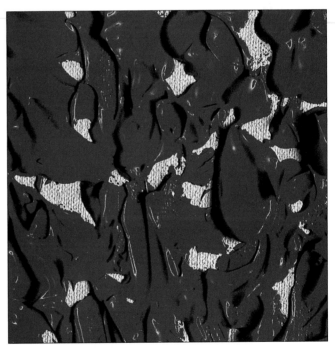

1 Use undiluted acrylic paint from the tube, or mix tube color with an equal proportion of gel medium.

2 Use a knife or a stiff bristle brush to spread the paint on the canvas.

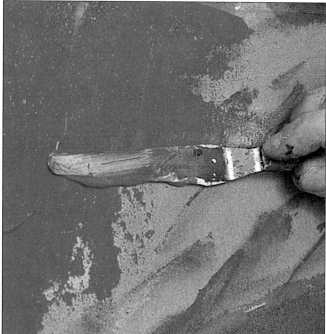

ABOVE When applying impasto with a brush, mix the paint to a fairly stiff consistency. Dab the paint onto the support. Spread and shape it as required. The brushmarks will form part of the composition.

ABOVE An alternative method of applying impasto is to use a small palette knife. Scoop up some paint and lay it on the support. Spread and shape the impasto.

straight from the tube, like oil paint, and by the addition of either of two mediums, gel and texture or modeling paste, can be made as thickly as desired—something that can only be done with difficulty with oil paint, as oil paint dries slowly and cannot be thickened beyond a certain point without damage to its inherent and visual appeal.

Impastos have a direct, spontaneous visual impact, and are attractive to look at, and for many painters are easier to handle than thin paint, especially with a knife. But though attractive and pleasant to do, impastos can easily become an indulgence and so lose their initial charm unless something is done about extending their capabilities by experiment and experience. Therefore they should be tried not only straight from the tube, but with gel and texture paste, and with a knife and brush separately and in combination. Impastos are intensified and conversely made more subtle when glazed.

KNIFE AND BRUSH
The painting knife on its own has an important role to play especially for those unused to a brush. But essentially what gives impastos their value is the directness with which they are done. Mess them about by too much overpainting and the vitality is severely reduced: you end with tinted mud.

The knife is probably less liable to mess, in spite of being clumsier than a brush. The flat blade of the knife constructed for mixing merely remixes the paint when applied to painting, whereas the brush being less able to mix, will only stir the paint up. Brushing paint should therefore be very deliberate, and if the sweeps and swirls fail to delight for whatever reason, scrape it off with a knife before it dries too hard, and start again.

A glaze will bring out the unique features of impasto if applied carefully. But glazes can do a number of other things equally well. And because of the special qualities of acrylic mediums, they can do the job quicker and more effectively than oil paint, and may be used frequently without any bother, as the normal process of using acrylics.

TEXTURAL IDEAS

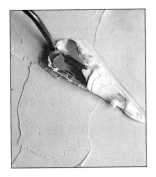

A B O V E A thick layer of acrylic mixed with modeling paste is applied with a painting knife and smoothed out.

A B O V E A kitchen fork is pressed into the wet paint to produce a pattern of grooves and ridges.

A B O V E An adhesive tool is used here. By twisting and turning it, many different patterns may be made.

GLAZES

If impastos are the thickest paint used with acrylic, then glazes are the thinnest— thinner even than the washes. Briefly, glazes are a mixture of medium and transparent pigment which is applied over dried underpaintings. The color of the underpainting blends with that of the transparent glaze, and because it is not mixed with it, has an optical effect which is more vital than if it had been.

Glazes are, in effect, transparent colored windows, and behave not unlike sunglasses —reducing the amount of light, and slightly changing the color. Of course with colored glazes, one tries to enhance, rather than reduce the color, but to take the example of sunglasses further, glazes can and do have the power to unify the tones and tints of a work by reducing the color, much as sunglasses do. Many a discordant work has been harmonized by placing a dark glaze over the whole of it.

A B O V E To make this glaze, mix a small amount of color with a lot of medium. Apply with a soft brush and allow to dry.

A B O V E A more transparent glaze can be made by adding extra matt medium to the pigment.

ABOVE A transparent scumble is made by mixing a lot of matt medium and water with the color to produce delicate scumbles. Further scumbles can be built up in layers to give greater effect.

Exercise in glazing

For the exercise only, a small piece of card (cardboard) or paper is necessary. But to get the most out of it, both plain and primed supports should be tried. Glazes should be as thin as possible, which makes them fragile, because the binders are weakened. Therefore the addition of a medium (in this instance the binder itself is absolutely vital. Also the medium gives body to the glaze, which the pigment fails to give. As a beginning, to get used to the feel and visual impact of glazing, use the acrylic medium alone. If it feels too thick, add a few drops of water—the cardinal rule.

The exercise can be repeated with gel medium, both with brush and knife. Glazes can take on a different quality with a knife, and so should be tried.

The diagrams describe

RIGHT Use short, irregular strokes to produce an area of broken, scumbled color.

visually what takes place. On a grid of twelve squares, a layer of glaze is placed and allowed to dry. Another layer of glaze of a different color is placed across it. Where the two glazes intersect, a third color will be apparent. The rest of the grid can now be completed with further layers of glaze.

As you can see, the permutations of this principle are numerous:
1. Thin glazes over thin opaque paint,
2. Thin glazes over thin transparent paint,
3. Thin glazes over thick paint,
4. Thick glazes over thin paint,
5. Light glazes over light glazes, and so on and so on. All these variations are fascinating to try out and will produce some very exciting effects.

SCUMBLING

The brush mark that combines some of the transparent qualities of a glaze with the exuberant spontaneity of impasto is a scumble. Scumbling is a somewhat vague term for applying a thin coating of color vigorously brushed over the entire work or parts of it

to soften the effect, but the real point of a scumble is to create a free or broken brush mark which will allow the under-painting to show through to animate the color and the surface at the same time.

Unlike a glaze, a scumble may be applied without any additional medium, and be either semi-transparent or opaque. Provided the underpainting is perfectly dry, the scumble may be dragged, scrubbed, dabbed, or brushed in any fashion suitable for covering the entire work, or parts of it, quickly and spontaneously.

Scumbling is cruder than glazing, which implies carefully controlled transparent layers over selected parts of the work. Scumbling by its very nature is more hit-and-miss, and will delight

SCUMBLING

Yellow and green are scumbled together but not blended.

Scumbles must be applied thinly so that previous applied layers show through.

those who go for textural effects, the particular transitions of broken brush work and changes of mind, and will give a great deal of pleasure, both doing it and looking at it afterwards.

Scumbling, as its name seems to imply, breaks all the accepted rules for the methodical application of paint. Dry paint, hitherto discouraged as being bad for brushes and palette, is looked upon with favor. "Dry paint"—a term artists often use when referring to applying a scumble—is a stiff rather than thick paint, so that when it is dragged across a surface —underpainting or canvas–—it will leave a pleasant broken effect. Consequently instead of throwing away old, worn out brushes you find that they are ideal for the job of creating textural effects, used with dry paint, and with the scrubbing and rubbing that characterizes scumbling. And when these old brushes finally collapse, use a wad of tissue paper and dab with that to get the kind of effect you want.

Scumbling is particularly effective for dragging light paint over a dark ground and vice versa, or dragging one complementary color over another. It is the perfect foil to flat, carefully done painting, and should be resorted to from time to time, not only for the experience of creating broken color effects, but as an exercise in improvisation. As an experiment, try scumbling over any discarded paintings, and observe how a once-rejected work takes on a new life when scumbled over.

WHITING OUT

Perhaps the opposite of the glaze and the scumble, despite its overlaying similarity, is the process I call "whiting-out," or more accurately repriming, which is exactly what it is. The method I devised is ideally suited for acrylic, for it enables a painting to be continued indefinitely, or at least until you are satisfied with the result, without the repainted surface showing that it has been reworked in any way whatsoever.

Repriming is something that can be done without any difficulty with acrylic because of the quick drying and versatile textural qualities of rough or smooth, transparent or opaque. It cannot be done successfully with gouache or oil paint, because gouache picks up and oil paint is too thick and dries too slowly to make the operation worthwhile. But It is worthwhile, as paintings frequently "go wrong."

SOME OTHER TECHNIQUES

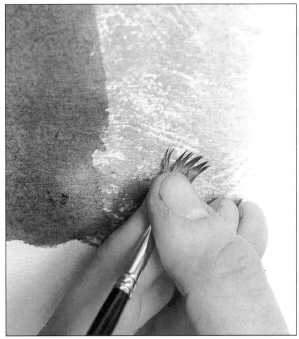

ABOVE Using a dry brush, pick up color on the brush and move it lightly across the support. The dry brush technique is used to blend or paint areas of finely broken color.

ABOVE Scratching. Any sharp tool can be used to etch lines and texture into acrylic paint while it is still wet. Here a paint brush handle is being used.

They don't, in fact, go wrong, they go astray, or outgrow their original intention. Nevertheless, however natural this feature may be, it can cause frustration, helplessness, and despair when you are faced with it. To circumvent or anaesthetize the pain it can cause, whiting out or repriming will remove some of the sting. Moreover this can be repeated until the work adjusts itself and begins to flower again.

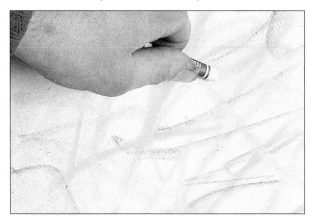 

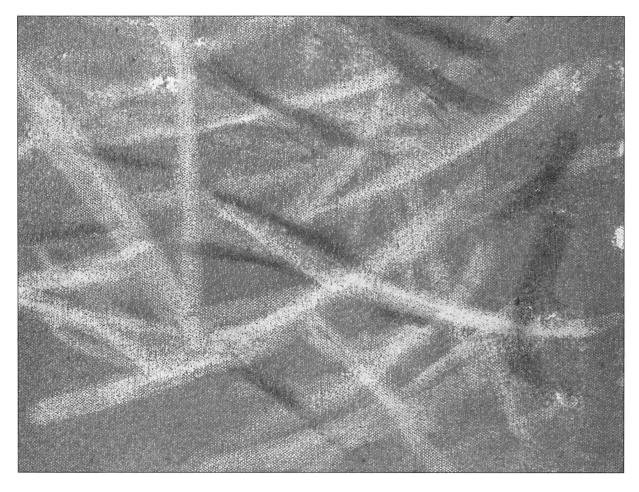

MIXED MEDIA

TOP LEFT Wax resist. Wax crayon is applied to the support. Candles or any fatty, waxy material will do.

TOP RIGHT The next step is to paint acrylic over the crayon.

ABOVE The wax resists the paint, allowing a textured pattern to show through.

Only two conditions need be observed for this method to work properly.

1. The surface of the paint must be smooth. Any impastos or texturing will interfere with the successful application of the new paint.

2. The white paint (or tinted paint) must be semitransparent.

Whenever part of a painting needs correcting or changing, or loses its freshness, or the whole of the painting needs altering, dilute some white priming or tube white with water to make a thin semitransparent wash, and white-out the part or parts to be repainted. The density of the paint must be gauged by eye, just so long as the underpainting isn't completely blotted out.

Whiting-out can be done over an entire work. Repainting on still-discernible shapes can begin and whiting out can be done as often as necessary. With this method, the whiting-out is done with a painting knife. The white paint is gently spread over the work and allows the old work to show through better than if done with a brush, as it can be spread really thin with the blade of a knife.

Another way of using this method is to use it not only as a corrective device but as an actual technique of building up a work from the start. The design or drawing is painted on unprimed white card (cardboard), or paper, with monochrome washes, and then whited-out over the entire work, letting the drawing or design show through.

As a variation on the white tone, the paint can be tinted with a color. Experiment will tell whether a particular color is suitable for whiting-out in this way, but umbers and ochers are good colors to begin with, rather than the primaries (though I have used blue tints with a great deal of success). The best advice I can give is to try them all. The permutations are many, as with most things connected with acrylic. The advantage of white as a reprimer is that it is ideal for transparent rather than opaque application of color. The sparkle of transparent washes will be more easily retained with repriming with white. A tinted white would not be of much help here, and, though some of the effects may be quite startling, white is probably the safest tone to use if you want to be certain of the results.

ABOVE To lay a flat wash, prepare plenty of paint. Use a wide, flat brush and run the strokes in one direction only. Each stroke should slightly overlap the one before.

WASHES

Washes used in watercolor painting are perhaps the most difficult to control, and are probably one of the most difficult processes to master. Controlling them is a never-failing source of anxiety for some watercolorists, because if a wash goes wrong it cannot be put right, and so the work loses its point and purpose. Washes, even with acrylic, can be ruined, but because of the nature of the paint itself, you can use whiting-out and put it right again.

Although acrylic can be used like watercolor, it must be clearly understood that acrylic washes function differently from watercolor washes. The main difference is the paint composition itself, for though the pigments may be identical, the binders are not. Watercolors can be diluted so thinly that they have hardly any body at all. The gum binders are capable of holding the pigments together despite overthinning. Acrylic, on the other hand, has a binder that imparts weight and substance to the paint which must be considered, especially when overthinning the paint, and it cannot be ignored without breaking down its inherent qualities. A useful measure to adopt is always to add a good few drops of the acrylic medium when diluting acrylic paint for washes, as a precaution. It will keep the wash from looking thin and lifeless, and will add a sparkle that ordinary watercolor sometimes lacks.

Acrylic washes can be varied in a number of ways not unlike watercolor, but happily because the particular characteristic of the medium is to impart bulk to a paint once thinned, it is easier to manage. A simple trial with watercolor will prove this quite conclusively. Watercolor occasionally behaves in a capricious way that some painters find almost impossible to control. By comparison, acrylic, by the very nature of its medium, is less temperamental, always provided that additional medium is reintroduced into the wash and can be manipulated by even the most inexperienced with relatively little skill.

There is perhaps only one rule to observe, that like pure watercolor, once a wash is applied, leave it alone.

Acrylic washes can be formed by:
1. flooding one wash into another
2. adding fresh color to an already applied wash
3. adding color to moistened paper
4. gradated tones from dark to light
5. flat
6. animated by brush strokes 7. overlay
8. allowing the surface to play its part
9. allowing the wash to run freely, without any control whatsoever.

The following experiments should give a great deal of experience. They should be tried on paper, card (cardboard), and even canvas, with and without priming. Vary them by using both smooth and textured surfaces. The addition of the water tension breaker or wetting agent will make sure that washes will flow and absorb well on to the support. It is important to experiment in the following ways occasionally, so that you become familiar with the effect each method has.

Sables are traditionally more suitable for washes than hog's-hair brushes, and should be as large as possible (Nos. 7 or 8). Hog's-hair may be tried but are less flexible for gradating and spreading a wash smoothly. As long as you recognize this, they can be tried as a means for creating variations of the basic wash technique.

Experiment 1—flat wash
• Squeeze out ½ in. (1 cm) of paint into a clean container.

A B O V E Experiment 2. To achieve a gradated effect, work quickly, adding water to the paint in increasing quantities with each successive band of color.

A B O V E Experiment 4. To produce this wet-in-wet, the artist began with a graded wash of cobalt blue and added a graded wash of lemon yellow.

A B O V E Experiment 3. Single color wet-in-wet wash, made by covering the support with a layer of water and allowing a wash of color to flood into it.

• Add water to dilute, mix well to make sure that there are no lumps of undissolved paint as this will ruin a wash.
• Add some acrylic medium last— about a teaspoon will do.
• With a large brush spread the wash down the paper or card (cardboard), working from the top, to make a flat wash. Whatever

OVERLAY

ABOVE Lay the palest colors first, so that the light reflects off the white paper.

ABOVE It is vital to allow one color to dry completely before applying the next one.

ABOVE The artist applies a thin wash of Hooker's green over the first color. Where the two washes cross, a third hue is produced.

RIGHT The use of animated strokes with a hog's-hair brush produces a very active texture.

happens, do not touch the wash once it has been applied. Let the color find its own level.
• The application can be carried out upright or on the flat. If upright the wash will run down rather quickly.

Experiment 2—gradated tones
Exactly the same as Experiment 1, only in this experiment instead of painting the wash completely in one color, halfway through continue with clean water only and let the color blend into it. This is easy to do with pure acrylic color, provided there is plenty of medium in the wash, and water tension breaker (wetting agent) in the water.

Experiment 3—moistened paper
First cover the paper or card (cardboard) completely with water. Then, before it has properly dried, flood a wash into it as above.

Experiment 4—adding color
This experiment can combine any or all of Experiments 2 and 3. Proceed as above, and before the color has dried flood another color into the wet surface. Often known as wet-in-wet.

Experiment 5—overlay
This is exactly like glazing. Proceed as above, but let the color dry out thoroughly. Then apply further washes over the dried paint. In pure watercolor, the paint may pick up, but with acrylic this can never happen.

Experiment 6—animated brush strokes
For this experiment, use an ample amount of acrylic medium with the paint and, when well mixed, the wash can be applied, letting the brush play its part by animating the wash with brush strokes. Hog's-hairs can be used for this experiment with profit.

Washes are one kind of effect that looks well without under- or overpainting, hence their popularity for immediate statements, especially for figurative work like landscape painting where, being outdoors in all kinds of weather, speed and spontaneity are vital.

Immediacy and fluency, however, are easily lost if these washes are overworked, which may be the reason why flooding and merging of one color into another is not really possible with opaque or more solid paint which depend on their effects by overpainting in layers.

Washes can, of course be overpainted, which, as has been pointed out, is similar to glazing, but unlike glazing—which can be carried out on all kinds of surfaces, underpaintings and impastos— overpainting washes is always better on a white

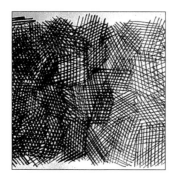

ABOVE Hatching using ink. By varying the density of the lines, a wide variety of tones is achieved. Freely drawn lines look more lively than perfectly straight, mechanical lines.

RIGHT An old, splayed brush was used to create this slightly rough, hatched texture in acrylic. The underlying color glows through overpainting to great effect.

surface. This ensures the retention of the transparency and sparkle so typical of watercolor.

HATCHING

Hatching is a very old and basic means for gradating tones on white paper with something as dense and impenetrable as pen and ink. Gradating tones with a pencil is much easier, as most of us will have experienced before now, and painted washes are perhaps one of the simplest and best means of achieving it in the most subtle and effective way. When painting expanded from simple washes to the more complex paints like gouache, tempera, and fresco, the technique that was adopted was that of hatching, which reached its full development in the 14th and 15th centuries, before the introduction

of oil paint rendered it obsolete. Oil paint could render gradated tones so much more realistically than hatching with tempera—but at a cost. The qualities of texture and color that hatching brought were sorely missed, until renewed interest in water-based painting revived the method. Acrylic, being one of these, is ideally suited to hatching.

Hatching consists of the criss-crossing of hundreds of small lines over each other to produce a rich variegated tone. The more these fine lines are hatched the more dense the tone becomes. Many drawings by the old masters were done this way, and so inevitably became the basis of the way they painted. When one examines a 14th- or 15th-century tempera panel, it will be seen to be made up of hundreds of tiny strokes of

color, sometimes going around the forms, to accentuate the solidity, sometimes across the forms to show the play of light and dark.

In painting with a hatching technique, the open network of lines means that not only are the tones gradated, but the underpainting can filter through as well, thus enhancing both tone and color at the same time—another reason why, perhaps, tempera painting has a brilliance that oil painting seems to lack over the centuries.

Hatching with acrylic will involve small sable brushes (0, 00, or 1) as well as thin paint, which can be either transparent or opaque, or even a mixture of both. But it must not be too thick, or the hatching will lose its delicacy, and be more difficult to manipulate.

Hatching is a delicate and

painstaking operation, but with patience can produce remarkable and effective results that are well worth the trouble they involve.

Experiment in hatching

Draw a small grid of 1 in. (2.5 cm) squares. About four will suffice. Try filling them with a variety of hatching as follows:

1. cross hatching with one color,
2. cross hatching from dark to light,
3. cross hatching from the center outward,
4. cross hatching from the outside inward.

Vary the hatching with both transparent and opaque lines, and short and long, thick and thin strokes, to create as much variety of texture as possible.

STIPPLING

Stippling is somewhat like hatching in that it is the building up of tone with hundreds of tiny marks. But with hatching, the marks are strokes of the brush—long, short, thin, or thick—whereas with stippling, dabs are made with the point or end of the brush.

If sables are used for stippling, it is wiser to use the older, more worn out brushes, as stippling can be very hard on them unless used with a very gentle kind of stipple, which is not easy to do as the dabbing action is a forceful one. As with hatching, the process is a painstaking one. The overpainting of hundreds of tiny dots one on the other gives a pleasing effect, and the tonal gradations are even more delicate than with hatching. However it is unnecessary to cover the work completely with stippling. You can confine it to the parts with

a more telling effect.

Georges Seurat, the pointillist painter, who took Impressionism one stage further, stippled his tones and tints of pure color, without mixing them, throughout the painting. The intention was to let the eye do the mixing. Unfortunately his paintings were not carried out in acrylic, as they hadn't been invented at that time—but there is no reason why acrylics shouldn't be tried in this manner, provided the stippling has some kind of color system as a foundation for the design, or that the stippling is consistent in its marks throughout the work.

Experiment with stippling in the same way as hatching. The paint can be thicker than with hatching, if desired, and stippling can also be carried out with materials other than brushes: sponges, wads of paper, toothbrushes, even fingertips will do as an alternative.

LEFT Stippling with a brush is carried out by holding the brush at right angles to the painting surface, and repeatedly touching the tip to the surface.

BELOW The effect is an area of colors that appears lighter and brighter than the equivalent color applied in a flat wash.

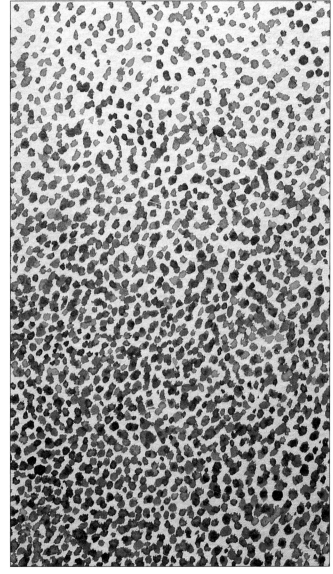

CHAPTER FOUR
The Projects

Painting is about looking and seeing and translating
what you see in the three-dimensional world around
you, through selective and imaginative processes, into
pictures. Visual source material for your paintings is
everywhere around you, on your table, in your room,
through a window, or even in your mirror. Look at
your everyday surroundings with new eyes for a
subject and you will find plenty of inspiration.

SWIMMERS IN HONG KONG

Waterside pictures are popular subjects for artists, not only because they conjure up holidays, but also because they offer at least three quite separate elements to work on, the water, the landscape, and the sky. This picture was painted essentially as a landscape and then brought alive by the addition of figures, buildings, and other points of human interest.

The artist used the photographs as starting points only, identifying major features in them, particularly the vegetation, the mountains, and the water, before creating his own imaginary landscape. The form of the trees will be treated with adjacent areas of light and shadow while the hazy distant mountains will be emphasized by the use of colors, mainly white and blue.

1 Two photographs of the city provide the artist with basic ideas for his picture. He will "sandwich" these with other images in his own mind to compose the scene he wishes to paint.

2 The artist fills the water in primarily with phthalocyanine blue with titanium white which effectively reflect the colors of the sky and background landscape. The trees are strengthened with Hooker's green and the hills given more weight and bulk with medium magenta.

4

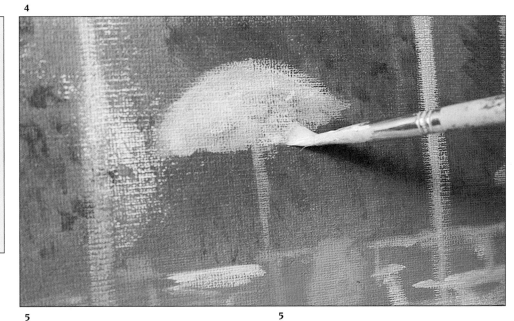

MATERIALS USED

SUPPORT: prepared, acrylic-primed canvas board, measuring 36 X 25 in. (92 X 64 cm).
COLORS: Hooker's green, ivory black, phthalocyanine green, medium magenta, titanium white, cobalt blue, phthalocyanine blue, and raw sienna.
BRUSHES: Nos. 2 and 5 round bristle and synthetic, Nos. 2, 4, 6, and 11 flat bristle and synthetic.

3 The sky is brought on further with cobalt blue which is also added to the water to deepen and brighten its color.

4 Detail in the foreground is now developed, with the correct emphasis on form retained, in keeping with the overall picture.

5 Although the figures are very much in the foreground detail would have been impossible here, as the perspective of the composition, with mountains and tall skyscrapers in the background, requires that they be fairly small.

6 The trees are darkened with Hooker's green and highlighted with phthalocyanine green, again in broad brush strokes.

5

5

6

7

8

7 The skyscrapers are blocked in with strong, simple brush strokes and are set off against each other with varying mixtures of blues and white.

8 The figures have plenty of movement and definition as a result of the careful combination of different colors and tones.

9 The finished painting is very successful and owes much of its success to the way in which the brush strokes were applied to the canvas. The texture of the canvas itself has also been used to advantage to give depth to the picture and to convey the steamy atmosphere characteristic of Hong Kong.

SWIMMERS IN HONG KONG

9

The almost impressionistic finish was achieved by the use of soft, carefully directed brush strokes and reinforces the relaxed holiday atmosphere which is the central theme of the painting.

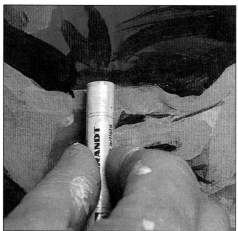

1

YOUNG MAN IN A STRIPED SHIRT

This is effectively a rapidly-done sketch on a large scale. It could have been taken much farther, but the bold and quick brush strokes, and the scale, allow it to work as a vigorous and lively piece already. The spontaneous use of color, to catch the most significant elements in the composition, was more important than filling in all the finer details.

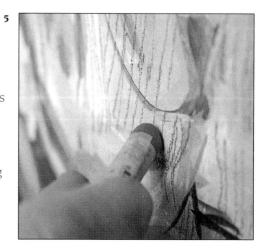

2

3

MATERIALS USED

SUPPORT: prepared board, measuring
24 X 20 in. (60 X 50 cm).
COLORS: ivory black, titanium white, chrome oxide, naphthol red, yellow ocher, and cerulean blue.
BRUSHES: Nos. 6 and 10 round bristle. No. 4 flat bristle.
OTHER MATERIALS: oil pastel, soft pastel, and pencil.

4

Try painting quickly as it is a useful discipline that will teach you to structure and compose the whole picture and stop you from becoming too distracted by less important minor details.

5

YOUNG MAN IN STRIPED SHIRT

6

1 The artist will attempt to work as quickly as possible as the model is sitting up fairly straight, quite a tiring position to maintain for any length of time.

2 The artist paints directly onto the support without bothering to make any rough drawing or outline sketch. The shadow tones of the head and torso are blocked at first.

3 The main blocks of color, the hair, the trousers, the arms, and the face are built up quickly with relaxed brush strokes, and then the shirt with a mixture of all the colors.

4 A soft pastel is used to give extra life and color to the flesh tones; the texture of the pastel allows the artist to obtain a firm edge on the arms and hands.

5 The combination of different mediums such as soft pastel, oil pastel, and pencil injects variety of texture into the picture.

6 The finished picture has a delightful informal sketch-like quality and shows just what can be achieved by working quickly and confidently without dwelling too much on relatively unimportant superficial details.

FOOD ON THE FARM

Still-life is one of the simplest and most accessible of painting subjects. Unlike landscapes, for example, still-lifes give you the opportunity to choose and arrange objects in any way you like. There is no need to stage an elaborate arrangement of objects, either, especially if time is pressing. In this painting the artist has chosen as his subject the remains of a simple rustic meal left on the table. An arrangement such as this can have great appeal, because somehow it captures a moment in time: it isn't merely a collection of lifeless objects.

In keeping with the earthy simplicity of the subject, the artist used a painting knife to give a rough-textured surface to the painting. Acrylic paint has a thick, buttery consistency, and can be "sculpted" to create interesting surface effects that lend character to the painting. A knife can not only pile on thick paint successfully, it can also be used for scraping out unwanted passages. You must work quickly, though, due to the fast drying time of acrylic paint.

Another interesting point about this picture is that it was painted, not onto a white support, but over another painting beneath. This was an unfinished painting which the artist had rejected. Because the original work had not reached an advanced stage it was an easy matter to overpaint it, especially since acrylics have such

4

5

6

1

2

3

1 Simple and uncontrived, this still life group nevertheless contains an interesting variety of shapes and textures.

2 Working over an old painting, the artist begins by blocking in the main color areas with loose brush strokes.

3 The forms of the still life are drawn in with a brush and diluted paint. Parts of the old painting still show through in places.

4 Now the image is beginning to take shape.

5 This detail shows the various textures that can be achieved with a painting knife, from the

good covering power. Rather than paint out the original image, however, the artist chose to work directly onto it, so that faint lines and shapes showed through the blocks of color as the new work progressed. This method has one great advantage: it alleviates the problem of facing a glaring white canvas and being afraid of "spoiling" it. Having shapes and colors already there on the canvas is much less inhibiting.

7

MATERIALS USED

SUPPORT: prepared board primed with acrylic, measuring 24 X 20 in. (60 X 50 cm).
COLORS: burnt umber, yellow ocher, cadmium red medium, ultramarine, ivory black, titanium white.
BRUSHES: Nos. 7 flat hog's-hair, Nos. 2, 4, and 6 round sable, Nos. 3 and 5 synthetic fiber.

FOOD ON THE FARM

8

smoothness of a knife blade to the rough, stippled texture of a crumbled brown loaf.
6 The paint is used thickly, often being mixed directly on the canvas instead of on the palette. Note the rough-hewn texture created by the knife.

7 This close-up of the earthenware jar shows how the artist has used the painting knife to partially mix the colors and build up a textured impasto.
8 The finished painting shows how bold and direct a knife can be. The artist has

deliberately left the paint surface rough and unfinished, preserving a lively spontaneity that is entirely in keeping with the rustic simplicity of the subject.

STILL LIFE WITH BOTTLE, FRUITS, AND VEGETABLES

For this still life painting, the artist has used an intriguing combination of a modern medium —acrylic—and a traditional oil painting technique dating back to the days of the Old Masters: namely, that of developing a detailed underpainting over which transparent glazes of color are applied, layer upon layer, to achieve a translucent and shimmering surface.

Hundreds of years later, the miraculous effects achieved by the Masters still fill us with admiration and awe. However, the technique which they used was a slow and laborious one, since each layer of paint had to be left for several days to dry out before the next one could be applied. If a layer of oil paint is applied over an underlayer that is not completely dry, cracking ensues and the painting can be ruined in a very short time.

With the advent of acrylic paints in the 1950s, this problem was at last solved. Like oil paint, acrylics can be used thickly or in thin washes; but, unlike oils, they dry very quickly and repeated layers of color can be built up without any danger of cracking.

Acrylics, then, can achieve all that oil paint can, but much more quickly and with less risk.

Following the traditional method, the artist has here worked on a tinted ground, painting from dark to light with very thin layers of color. Before starting to paint, the artist drew a detailed sketch of the still life. This, coupled with the quick-drying properties of the acrylic paints, allowed him to complete the painting rapidly once

1

2

3

1 For this still life, the artist chose objects whose soft colors and shiny textures would lend themselves well to the glazing technique. **2** The first step is to tone the canvas with a thin wash of burnt umber, well diluted with water. This sets the tone for the whole painting, and softens the stark white of the canvas. the still life objects are then indicated with thin black paint and a No. 2 brush.

4

5

6

begun, as all preliminary planning and decision-making had been finished beforehand.

7

8

9

STILL LIFE WITH BOTTLE, FRUITS, AND VEGETABLES

3 Next the artist blocks in the lightest areas of the painting with thin white paint and a No. 10 brush, blending them with a rag.

4 Working over the entire surface, the artist blocks in the strong highlight areas with a No. 4 brush and pure white paint, used a little more thickly this time.

5 With a No.2 sable brush, the artist redraws the outlines of the subject in black thinned with water.

6 A dilute mixture of cadmium yellow and white is used for the onions. Then the shadow areas around the onions and the table are strengthened with thin washes of ivory black.

7 A cool tone of white and yellow ocher is now applied with a No. 10 brush and worked well into the surface. Note how the warm underlayer still shines through.

8 With a fine brush and white paint, the artist develops the highlights and reflections in the bottle and the onions.

9 The completed painting has all the vigor of an *alla prima* painting, yet it also has a subtlety and delicacy. The dark underpainting ensures a unity in the painting as it permeates all subsequent layers of paint giving an overall warmth.

> **MATERIALS USED**
>
> SUPPORT: prepared canvas board, measuring
> 16 X 20 in. (40 X 50 cm).
> COLORS: ivory black, burnt umber, cadmium yellow light, yellow ocher and titanium white.
> BRUSHES: Nos. 2, 4, and 10 sable round oil brushes.

INTERIOR

7

INTERIOR

You don't need to travel far and wide in order to find a suitable subject to paint; often the most interesting pictures are those which feature familiar objects and ordinary places. An interior scene, for example—perhaps the very room you are sitting in now—can provide an endless source of inspiration for the creative artist.

As with still lifes, you can arrange the objects in an interior, and also control the lighting, to express a particular mood or to make a personal statement. In this painting, for example, the artist has created a spare, almost abstract composition which captures the melancholy mood of a large, bare room on a cold winter's day. Through the window we catch a glimpse of the gray, wintry landscape beyond. The shadow of the window slants across the cold, empty wall. And in the corner stands a grand piano, half-hidden by a shroud-like dust sheet. Altogether, an atmospheric and thought-provoking composition.

To capture the mood of the scene, it was essential to work quickly before the light changed, and this is where the fast-drying properties of acrylics saved the day. The artist worked with a limited palette of neutral colors, and applied the paint directly onto the canvas with broad, flat washes.

1 The artist begins by making an outline drawing of the subject on the support, using a B pencil.

2 The pale tones of the wall are established first, using yellow ocher

mixed with white, and lemon yellow in the lightest parts.

3 Using a No. 4 flat brush, the artist paints in the lines of the window frame, and its shadow cast on the wall, with raw sienna.

4 Now the dark tones of the foreground are blocked in with burnt umber darkened with black.

5 The artist paints "negatively," working the dark tones around the white shape of the dust sheet covering the piano. The folds in the dust sheet are indicated with strokes of burnt umber.

6 The shadows on the background wall and on the dust sheet are now built up using Payne's gray, cobalt blue, yellow ocher, and titanium white.

7 Finally, the scene outside the window is painted in, using Payne's gray, Mars black, burnt umber, and titanium white. Subtle, neutral colors have been used throughout, and this contributes to the quiet, introspective mood of the painting.

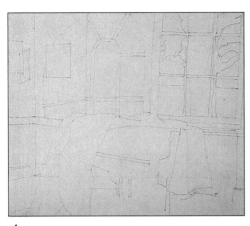
1

2

3

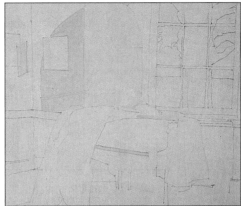
4

5

6

MATERIALS USED

SUPPORT: gesso primed hardboard, measuring 10 X 12 in. (25 X 30 cm).
COLORS: raw sienna, yellow ocher, Payne's gray, Mars black, titanium white, burnt umber, and cobalt blue.
BRUSHES: Nos. 4 and 7 flat synthetic hair.

IRISES IN A GREEN VASE

A still life subject such as a vase of flowers may seem like a simple one, but it is nevertheless very important to plan the composition carefully in order to create a pleasing image.

Because this vase of irises was such a symmetrical shape, it could have produced a stiff, boring picture. But the artist has avoided this problem by lighting the subject from one side to create interesting elongated shadows. He also arranged the subject on the canvas in an interesting way. Rather than place the vase of flowers in the center of the canvas, which would have been the most obvious solution, he chose to place it off-center, where it interacts with the rectangles created by the shelf and the side of an alcove.

Part of the appeal of this painting is in its crisp, clean edges. The artist used masking tape as a stencil in order to achieve the clear-cut characteristics of the highlights and shadows on the vase and the leaves.

1 The tall, elegant irises are placed against a cool, gray background which complements the cold blues and greens in the arrangement.

1

2

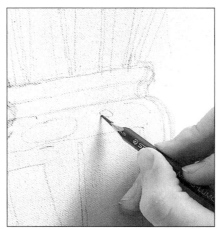

3

4

5

6

2 The artist places the subject off-center, to create an interesting visual tension with the surrounding space.

3 Because the artist intends to build up the picture systematically, the drawing is detailed enough to act as an accurate guide to the placement of each area of tone and color.

7

8

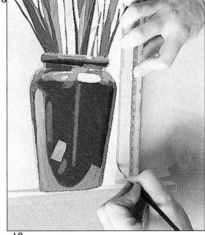

4 The artist begins by painting the flowers. A purple-blue is mixed from ultramarine, white, black, and a little crimson.

5 The irises are developed from light to dark, each tone being completed in flat patches of color.

9

10

11

12

6 The leaves are painted in three tones of green mixed form chromium oxide, ultramarine, and white. Cadmium yellow is also added to the irses.

7 The vase is painted with a mixture of emerald, chromium oxide, and raw umber. The artist uses white and yellow ocher for the shiny highlights..

8 The shadow area is painted with a mixture of Payne's gray and ultramarine.

9 Unlike the background, a slightly darker tone of gray is used for the shadows of the flowers, which are softened and blurred at the edges.

10 The shelf is painted next, using a mixture of raw sienna and white.

13

14

15

11 The final details of the flowers are completed in oil paint because the color is slow-drying and easier to manipulate. The darks in the flowers are mixed from ultramarine, alizarin crimson, and a touch of white.

12 When the paint is dry, the artist begins work on the crisp shapes of light and shadow on the leaves. He uses masking tape as a stencil, sticking it firmly to the canvas so that no paint can seep under the edges.

13 The delicate shapes are cut out with a sharp scalpel or blade, being careful not to cut the canvas. These shapes are then peeled away.

14 Thick oil paint is used to paint the shapes which have been cut out of the stencils.

15 When the paint is thoroughly dry, the masking tape is gently peeled off the canvas, revealing the sharp, clean lines of color on the leaves.

16

IRISES IN A GREEN VASE

17

16 Because the style of the picture is so graphic, the artist decides to add texture to the flat background color using a soft pencil.

17 The finished painting has a pleasing sense of harmony and balance. The square canvas is divided into three geometric shapes, whose straight lines provide a contrasting setting for the organic flower forms and their soft shadows cast upon the wall behind. The loose pencil strokes are in complete contrast to the tight composition and precise shapes.

LANDSCAPE WITH SHED

Acrylic is without doubt one of the most versatile painting mediums to date. This landscape demonstrates how techniques and methods borrowed from other mediums can be effectively and harmoniously combined in one picture. For example, the artist has used a sheet of stretched heavy white paper, as one would with watercolor, but has begun the painting using the traditional oil technique of underpainting.

The artist continued to develop the picture using both watercolor and oil techniques. For example, thick paint has been scumbled and dragged in places, in the manner of oil paint. In other areas, the wash, a traditional watercolor technique, is used to exploit the underpainting and create a light, subtle tone which complements the heavier, opaque passages. All of which goes to show that there are few rules in acrylic painting, and that a wide range of expressive techniques can be used to get the most out of your subject.

MATERIALS USED

SUPPORT: stretched heavy white drawing paper, measuring 20 X 23 in. (50 X 58 cm).
COLORS: alizarin crimson, ivory black, burnt sienna, cadmium red medium, cerulean, chrome green, yellow ocher, and titanium white.
BRUSHES: Nos. 4 and 6 synthetic fiber.

1

2

3

4

5

1 Working on stretched and dampened paper, the artist begins by lightly sketching in the subject with a pencil. Then he starts to block in the shed wih washes of alizarin crimson and burnt sienna.

2 The main shapes and outlines are further developed with very wet washes of burnt sienna. In places the tip of the brush is used to "draw" the outlines.

3 The roof color is put in next, using a mixture of burnt sienna and cadmium red. The darker grass and shrub colors are flicked in with pure chrome green.

LANDSCAPE WITH SHED

6

4 Now the painting is taking shape. A thin wash of cerulean blue is used for the sky, with pale scumbles of alizarin crimson for the clouds. The light and dark tones of the foliage are developed with mixtures of chrome green and white.

5 A light green tone is used for the highlights in the foliage and grass. A wash of burnt sienna is brushed into the foreground area.

6 The artist now covers the foreground with a light green tone of dryish consistency, allowing the brown underpainting to show through. With a No. 4 synthetic brush, the artist works over the painting putting in the final details, such as tiles on the roof. Notice how the artist weaves warm reds and cool greens through the painting to create a vibrant color harmony.

BOATS ON THE BEACH

Often the most difficult stage in the painting process is that of actually getting started. A sheet of stark white canvas can be quite intimidating—one is nervous of applying the first brush stroke for fear of making a mistake.

The application of a toned ground can help by providing a more sympathetic color upon which to begin work. Traditionally used in oil painting, a toned ground is a thin wash of color which is brushed over the entire canvas prior to commencing the painting.

A toned ground serves two purposes: firstly, it provides a more neutral color than that of the canvas itself and makes it easier to judge the relative intensity of the color mixtures which are applied over it. Secondly, if the toned ground is allowed to show through the overpainting in places it acts as a harmonizing element, tying all the other colors in the painting together.

Traditionally, a toned ground is a neutral or earth color, or it can give a generalized idea of the overall color scheme of the subject. In this painting, for example, the artist uses a warm, earthy tone which harmonizes with the colors laid over it.

TONED GROUND

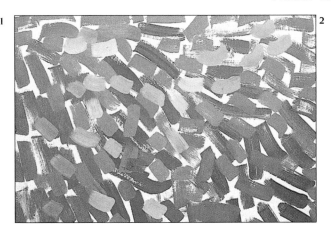

1 Generally, the color for a toned ground is mixed on the palette and applied to the support with smooth, even strokes. Here, however, the artist begins by applying the color in loose strokes which will be blended together on the canvas. Cadmium red, yellow ocher, and white, well diuted with water, are freely and loosely painted over the white surface.

2 When the canvas is well covered, and thoroughly dry, a thin wash of white paint is scumbled over it. The result is a medium-to-light toned surface in which the brush strokes are only partially blended. The colors blend in the viewer's eye, however, and the effect is more vibrant than a flat wash of color mixed on the palette.

5

3 Several charcoal pencil studies were made of individual elements and used as a basis for the final composition. This preparatory sketch concentrates on the beached boats.

4 A key drawing is made from the sketches, which will be traced onto the painting at a later stage.

6

5 Toned ground now dry, the artist blocks in the sky area with a very pale wash of white and ultramarine, toned down with a touch of burnt umber, foreground is brushed in with burnt umber, yellow ocher and white.

6 The artist now adjusts the tones in the scene, darkening the sea with ultramarine and lightening the foreground with pale washes of white, yellow ocher, and ultramarine.

7 The line of surf is painted with pure white. The key line drawing is traced onto the painting and outlined in burnt umber with the tip of a No. 2 sable brush.

MATERIALS USED

SUPPORT: prepared board primed with acrylic, measuring 24 X 20 in. (60 X 50 cm).
COLORS: burnt umber, yellow ocher, cadmium red medium, ultramarine, ivory black, and titanium white.
BRUSHES: No. 7 flat hog's-hair, Nos. 2, 4, and 6 round sable, Nos. 3 and 5 synthetic fiber.

7

BOATS ON A BEACH

8 The outlines of the figures and the boats are filled in with color, using burnt umber, ivory black, ttanium white, and ultramarine. Stippled dots of yellow ocher mixed with white are used to create the texture of shingle on the foreshore. The charm of this picture lies in its simple, "naive" style. The fishing boats and the figures are composed and arranged in such a way as to lead the viewer's eye from the foreground to background.

A CORNFIELD IN SUMMER

Acrylic paint is extremely versatile, having many of the advantages of other mediums but few of the disadvantages. In this landscape composition the artist has combined a number of different painting techniques, from thin washes and glazes to thick impasto. Since acrylic paint dries in minutes, the artist was able to build up succeeding layers of paint very rapidly. In addition, the efficient covering power of acrylic means that light colors can be painted over dark ones without any danger of the underlying color showing through. This gives the artist considerable freedom to experiment and make alterations to the composition and colors as the painting progresses.

Many landscape artists work out of doors on small pencil or watercolor sketches of the subject and return to the studio, using the drawings as reference material for larger paintings. This is far more convenient than carrying cumbersome equipment from place to place—especially if the weather is unreliable. It also allows the artist to observe the subject more closely and gather a great deal of information on form, color changing light, textural details, and so on.

Simple sketches are also an invaluable way of "editing out" superfluous details and helping to capture the essence of the subject; painting in the field, it is all too easy to become overwhelmed by the complexity of the scene. Working from sketches, back at the studio, also allows the artist to use his or her imagination to play about with the subject and get closer to the original experience.

1

2

3

1 A common practice with landscape artists is to make rough sketches, which often include written notes on colors, lighting, and so on. The painting demonstration that follows is based upon this sketch.

2 The artist starts with a broad underpainting of thinly diluted paint. The basic forms of the landscape are indicated with a mixture of gold ocher and raw umber, applied with a No. 8 bristle brush.

3 A thin glaze of warm orange is applied to the foreground, and olive green over the distant hills. A thicker layer of lemon yellow is applied across the center.

4 The forms of the hills are further developed with a mixture of chromium green and yellow ocher. The foreground color is warmed with a bright orange mixed from vermillion and yellow.

5 The artist applies thinly diluted cobalt blue over the sky area, spreading the color with a rag. The foreground is further developed with a vivid green made of chrome green and lemon yellow.

6 The artist develops foreground details with a variety of greens and grays, working with thin glazes of color and thick dabs of opaque paint.

7 Background details are added with a No. 3 bristle brush and a thick mixture of chrome green and black. The foreground is lightened by adding small patches of light green and white.

8 The artist lightens the tone of the sky and links it with a pale blue-green in the foreground. A mixture of light orange and white is used to intensify the color of the distant cornfield.

9 The tone of the central field is brightened with a smooth layer of creamy yellow mixed from gold ocher, white, and a touch of green.

10 The finished painting. The artist has exploited both the opacity and the transparency of acrylic to build up a variety of subtle textures and forms.

LIGHTHOUSE

Although acrylic paints are a relatively new arrival in the painting world, their use has spread rapidly, since they are flexible enough to accommodate traditional styles of painting as well as modern styles. For example, their fast drying time and ability to be thinned to the consistency of watercolor make them ideal for the classical approach of building up layers of color one upon the other: a technique known as glazing.

In the past, almost all paintings were done this way. Many of the Old Masters spent a great deal of time developing the underpainting, which was then finished off with thin glazes of color through which much of the underpainting remained visible. What we see when we look at a Velasquez or a Rubens are simply the last steps the artists took to complete the picture, hiding much of the underpainting below the surface.

For this painting of a seascape at dusk, the artist chose to use a reddish underpainting which would give the whole picture a warm tone. He has also used the traditional method of working from dark to light, and building up slowly from general forms to more specific details.

MATERIALS USED

SUPPORT: prepared canvas board, measuring
24 X 26 in. (60 X 65 cm).
COLORS: alizarin crimson, burnt sienna, burnt umber, cadmium green, cadmium red light, cadmium yellow, cobalt blue, phthalo blue, ultramarine, and titanium white.
BRUSHES: No. 3 synthetic fiber brush, Nos. 2, 3, and 4 bristle brushes and Nos. 4 and 5 sable rounds.

1

2

3

4

5

LIGHTHOUSE

6

1 The artist mixes burnt sienna with water to a thin consistency and applies it quickly and loosely with a broad brush, blocking in the main areas of the composition.

2 The sky tone is a thin wash of alizarin crimson, again brushed in loosely. The lighthouse is painted with a thin wash of burnt sienna, and the ground is covered with a darker, more opaque tone.

3 A thin wash of ultramarine is brushed into the sky area. Small patches of grass are indicated with chrome green and cadmium yellow medium. When this is dry, the foreground is lightened with vertical strokes of yellow ocher and white.

4 A very thin wash of phthalo blue is put in for the sea, and highlights are redefined with yellow ocher and white.

5 The artist mixes alizarin crimson and burnt sienna and carefully puts in the lighthouse stripes with a small sable brush.

6 In the finished painting, you can see how the reddish tone of the underpainting glows up through the succeeding layers of color, imparting an overall warmth that enhances the peaceful mood of seascape at dusk.

VIEW ACROSS THE ROOFTOPS

These days, many of us dwell in towns and cities, and are often far removed from the traditional subjects of the landscape painter: hills, valleys, rivers, coastlines, and so on. The city does, however, offer exciting opportunities for those artists who are prepared to seek out more unusual subjects.

One of the most accessible subjects we have is the view from our own window. A high window, in particular, offers an excellent vantage point and can be just as exhilarating as looking at a view from a mountain top. The geometric shapes of buildings and rooftops, for example, can afford the opportunity to create bold, dynamic compositions in which shapes, colors, and patterns are emphasized.

The particular view illustrated in this painting is a fine example of how an artist with a searching eye can find a certain beauty in even the most commonplace subject. Out of a cluttered jumble of buildings and rooftops, he has created a calm and ordered composition in which roughly half the canvas is given to empty sky and the other half to lively geometric patterns.

1

2

3

4

5

1 The subject is complicated, and the artist starts by making a drawing in which he simplifies the tones and colors.

2 A fairly detailed outline drawing is made on the support. The artist begins by blocking in the darkest areas using a mixture of black and raw umber, well diluted.

3 The middle tones are blocked in next, using Payne's gray and a No. 3 sable brush.

4 The artist now begins to add colors over the original dark tones, using mixtures of white, yellow ocher, cadmium red, and burnt sienna.

5 The painting is now developing into an interesting pattern of abstract shapes and colors.

6 This detail reveals the thinness of the paint, and how simply the blocks of color are applied.

6

VIEW ACROSS THE ROOFTOPS

7 The artist adds details using rich reds and beiges mixed from Payne's gray, yellow ocher, and white.

8 In the final painting the sky has been added with a flat wash of cerulean blue mixed with titanium white, toned down with a thin glaze of raw umber. The artist has resisted the temptation to fill the picture with too much detail; the large, empty space of the sky provides an exciting contrast with the clutter of roofs beneath.

MATERIALS USED

SUPPORT: hardboard primed with emulsion, measuring 22 X 26 in. (56 X 66 cm).
COLORS: Payne's gray, ivory black, cadmium yellow, cadmium red, burnt sienna, raw umber, and titanium white.
BRUSHES: No. 6 sable and a No. 10 synthetic fiber.

FRUIT TREES

The central theme of this picture is the brightly colored fruit trees sparkling in the sunshine, contrasted against the slanting shadows of the street below.

The painting is based on a small sketch, rapidly executed while the artist was on holiday in the Mediterranean. Over the years he has amassed a large collection of sketches like these, which he does not regard as "finished drawings" but rather as records of interesting scenes or objects, which can be used later, either as foundations for complete paintings done later in the studio, or as fragments to be inserted into other compositions.

The habit of always carrying a sketchbook is an invaluable one, particularly when traveling abroad. You may be just "passing through" a place, and yet a scene or objects presents itself as an ideal subject for a painting. A sketch can be done in minutes, and provides enough

information about the subject to allow you to make a painting at a later date. A photograph may also help, but with a sketch you can make a more personal statement, isolating and emphasizing those elements which particularly appeal to you. A photograph is much less selective, and besides, there is no guarantee that it will turn out as you expected!

1

2

3

4
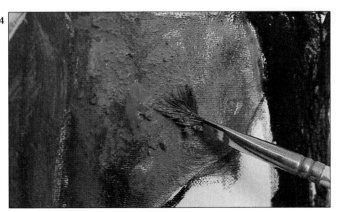

1 This small sketch was made several months prior to the painting, yet it gives the artist enough to kindle his imagination and memory because it includes written color notes and details about the play of light and shadow.

2 The artist begins by transferring the image onto a primed canvas in black paint applied with a sable brush.

3 Changing to a bristle brush, the artist blocks in the dark tones of the tree trunk and leaves.

4 The artist mixes ordinary builder's sand with the paint to capture the rough, sandy texture of the wall. Only a little sand is neccessary, otherwise the effect can look too crude and there is a danger of overloading the paint.

5

Because acrylic is adhesive, the paint can be mixed with other substances such as sand or grit and thus interesting textural effects can be obtained. In this painting the artist has mixed ordinary builder's sand with the paint in order to capture the rough sandy surface of the stone wall.

5 Color is laid on in small, thick dabs to create a lively surface texture. The artist moves across the whole canvas, building up the image bit by bit.

6 Tones of warm brown are worked into the black tree trunks. Because acrylic dries to an opaque finish, light tones can be laid over darker ones without any danger of the darker color showing through.

6

MATERIALS USED

SUPPORT: hardboard primed with emulsion, measuring 22 X 26 in. (56 X 66 cm).
COLORS: Payne's gray, ivory black, cadmium yellow, cadmium red, burnt sienna, raw umber, and titanium white.
BRUSHES: No. 6 sable and a No. 10 synthetic fiber.

7 The painting is now almost complete. The paint is applied directly, in the *alla prima* technique, in keeping with the liveliness of the scene. The colors, too, are selected for their suitability to the bright, sunny nature of the subject.

7

FRUIT TREES

8

8 The artist has created a highly personal interpretation of the scene, which is much more exciting than a mere photographic copy. Because the scene is viewed from the shade of a pavement café, there is a frame of shadow around the picture which helps to focus the eye upon the brilliantly sunlit street. Although the colors are bright, they are nevertheless harmonious; yellows, greens, and earth colors have been skilfully woven throughout.

THE THAMES AT RICHMOND

This leafy river scene is one which is very familiar to the artist who painted it, since it lies directly beneath the window of his studio. It provides an endless source of inspiration to the artist, as the colors change with the passing of the seasons.

The success of this picture lies in its simplicity, which captures the tranquil calm of a summer's day. Acrylic paint can be diluted with water or medium to the consistency of watercolor, allowing delicate, translucent effects to be obtained. For this painting, the artist chose to work in the manner of a watercolor. Without any preparatory drawing or underpainting, he applied his colors directly onto a sheet of stretched paper. Working from light to dark, in the traditional watercolor manner, the artist applied the colors in thin, transparent glazes which allow light to reflect off the white of the paper and up through the colors, giving them a luminous quality.

1 A photograph of the view from the artist's window. Compare this to the finished painting, and notice how the artist has simplified much of the detail to arrive at the essence of the scene.

2 Without any preliminary underdrawing, the artist begins by blocking in the main areas of the composition with pale tints of Payne's gray and raw umber.

3 While the first tones are still damp, washes of Hooker's green mixed with a litle raw umber in the shaded areas, are worked into the trees and foreground.

4 The quiet ripples on the water's surface are indicated with pale lines of Payne's gray and raw umber.

5 The artist uses sable brushes throughout the painting process, to achieve the softness of form and delicacy of detail neccessary.

1

2

3

4

5
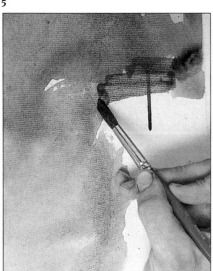

6

THE THAMES AT RICHMOND

8

6 The artist strengthens the tones in the painting by applying glazes of color, one on top of the other. The glazes are very thin and transparent, allowing the underlayer to glow up through the overlayer and create the luminous effect of a watercolor painting.

7 Opaque white is used to redefine complicated edges such as the leaves on the trees. The paint is not used thickly but is still watery in texture.

8 The completed painting has all the freshness and sparkle of a watercolor. The artist has resisted the temptation to overwork the washes or to build up the paint in opaque layers. In addition, he has cut out much of the detail in the scene and presented us with his own personal interpretation of a much-loved subject.

7

MATERIALS USED

SUPPORT: stretched Bockingford watercolor paper, measuring 16 X 12 in. (40 X 30 cm).
COLORS: Payne's gray, ivory black, Hooker's green, yellow ocher, raw umber, burnt sienna, and titanium white.
BRUSHES: No. 4, 6, and 10 sable.

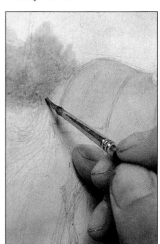

1 One of the drawings that became the basis of the horse in the painting—though in reverse.

2 The artist makes a detailed drawing of the subject with a 3H pencil. He then applies a very dilute wash of burnt sienna over all the parts of the horse which will be brown.

3 Background and foreground are washed in with very pale tints of blue and green.

SUFFOLK PUNCH

Acrylic is a popular painting medium with animal artists. Its rapid drying time means that artists do not have to struggle home with a wet canvas after a day's work in the field. In addition, its versatility means that it can be used to render a wide range of textures, from the softness of fur to the clean, sharp lines of a bird's feathers.

The artist has been painting animals all his life and so has an extensive knowledge of their anatomy, appearance, and characteristics. This painting was developed from two separate drawings of the horse and the dog, made at different times and then combined into a picture that derives as much from imagination as from fact. It is a good idea to keep a sketchbook with you at all times, so you can make drawings of things that interest you and which can later be incorporated into your paintings.

As is often the practice with acrylics, the artist has here used a combination of transparent and opaque techniques. This combination of thin washes and opaque color creates a range of textures which reflect the quality of the surfaces they describe.

MATERIALS USED

SUPPORT: cartridge paper, measuring 11 X 15 in. (28 X 38 cm).
COLORS: raw umber, burnt sienna, bright green, cadmium yellow, cadmium red, cobalt blue, ivory black, and titanium white.
BRUSHES: No. 6 sable.

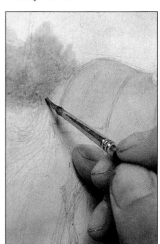

8

9

10

4 To create an impression of mistiness in the foliage, the artist wets the paper in that area and allows the colors—raw umber and bright green—to blend so that they diffuse with soft edges.

5 The trees are treated in a similar way, but more opaque paint is added for the fir trees. When the background washes are dry the artist continues to work on the body of the horse, using a series of transparent washes of burnt sienna.

6 The artist works on one of the trees,

stippling opaque color over a pale underwash to build up texture and form in the foliage.

7 With the broader areas now established, the artist starts on the finer details. Here he is using a fine brush and thick white paint for the horse's mane.

8 For the grass the artist uses bright green and a No. 6 sable brush, adding raw umber and white in the shadow areas.

9 This detail shows how the artist works around the shape of the dog.

10 The final painting. Only in the latter stages does the artist add the finer details. The dog's coat, and the characteristic plumes of hair on the horse's legs, are added using thin white paint, and then the harness and chains are added with black, red, yellow and white.

Adding detail in the final stages and working from large to small, and from light to dark, is the ideal way to control a painting.

1 The painting evolved from these sketches made at the zoo.

2 The artist begins by making an accurate drawing of the subject on the canvas with a B pencil.

CHIMPANZEE

Apes resemble humans in many ways, except that they have a good deal more charm. Chimpanzees are particularly endearing, with their bright, curious eyes and their impish behavior—qualities which are captured in this delightful "portrait."

This painting was developed from sketches made at the zoo, supplemented by photographic reference in natural history books. The artist's approach, however, is not merely to make a slavish copy of the subject; rather, he aims to capture something of the character of the animal, to reach farther than just surface appearance. A great

deal of imagination is brought into play, and the artist allows the medium itself to play its part in translating the essential character of the subject.

Another important aspect of painting is choosing the format and viewpoint that best express what you want to say. In this painting, for example, the artist has chosen a landscape format, rather than a portrait shape which might seem more obvious, given the shape of the subject. The chimpanzee is placed low down in the picture, and this somehow communicates a clownish, comical air which is entirely in keeping with the subject of the painting.

6

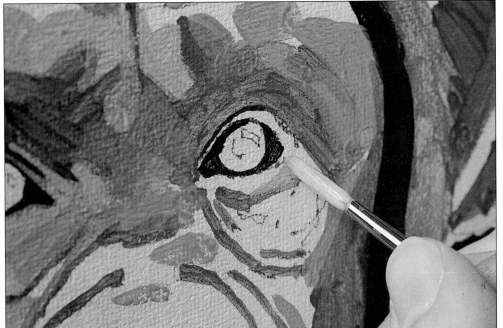

MATERIALS USED

SUPPORT: prepared canvas
panel, measuring
20 X 24 in. (50 X 60 cm).
COLORS: raw umber, burnt
sienna, Payne's gray, ivory black,
cerulean blue, yellow ocher,
cadmium yellow, sap green,
cadmium red, and titanium
white.
BRUSHES: No. 2 sable, No. 7
synthetic and a No. 6 bristle.

8

7

3 The main shapes of the body are blocked in with broad strokes of raw umber, burnt sienna, ivory black, and Payne's gray.

4 The sky is blocked in with a mixture of cerulean blue and titanium white.

5 The artist now begins work on the chimpanzee's face—the most important part of the composition. He starts by laying in the darkest tones using a mixture of yellow ocher, raw umber, ivory black and cadmium red. The color is thinly diluted with turpentine and applied with a No.7 Dalon brush, with a No. 2 sable brush for the finer lines.

6 The artist lightens the mixture used for the face by adding more white and yellow ocher and starts to lay in the middle tones.

CHIMPANZEE

7 Because all the large areas have been dealt with the painting builds up very quickly. This is useful, because it gives the artist something against which to judge subsequent tones and color.

8 The lightest tones in the face are now added, by adding cadmium yellow and more white to the original mixture. When the paint is thoroughly dry the artist scratches into it with a craft knife, making fine marks which indicate the whiskers on the chimp's chin.

9 Using mixtures of sap green and ivory black, the artist indicates the trees in the background. When the first paint layer is dry the artist puts in the lighter foliage, created by adding white and yellow ocher to the original green mixture.

10 Using masking tape to protect the surrounding areas, the artist blocks in the gray background with Payne's gray, yellow ocher and titanium white. The finished painting has a charm and directness which is perfectly matched to the character of the subject. The way the subject is placed within the edges of the support creates a series of simple shapes which are an important feature of the composition.

I

1 One of the many charcoal sketches which the artist made, using photographs as reference. The end of a thin stick of willow charcoal is used to achieve crisp lines, while tone and modeling are achieved by smudging and smearing the charcoal.

2 Before starting to paint, the artist makes a simple charcoal drawing on the canvas to fix the position of the subject and outline the main features.

3 The loose particles of charcoal are flicked off the canvas with a duster to prevent them from contaminating subsequent paint layers. The artist

TIGER

Painting an animal involves much the same sort of challenge as painting a human portrait: we must aim not only to capture a likeness of our subject but also to convey something of their character and personality. In this painting of a tiger the artist has used his skill to portray the animal's strength, intelligence, and awesome beauty.

The power and directness of this painting belies the fact that the artist worked entirely from photographic reference. He did not merely copy the photographs, however; instead, he used them as a starting point for the study. His

own imagination, and his feeling for the subject, provided the spark of inspiration that turns what could have been an ordinary painting into something more meaningful.

Another point to bear in mind is that the artist did not begin painting straight away. Instead, he made many pencil studies of his subject, in which he investigated the facial markings, the structure of the head, the proportions of the body, and so on. This process can be compared to a dancer learning steps, or a musician practising scales: all the sweat and labor of the preliminary work is what, in the end, will lead to success.

2

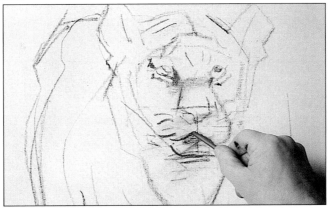

deliberately chose a long, narrow canvas which emphasizes the lean power of the tiger's body.

4 The artist starts to lay in broad strokes of color immediately, without any underpainting. The paint, raw sienna and cadium yellow deep, is applied with a 1 in decorator's brush to encourage a free, spontaneous approach.

3

4

5

6

6 With the main areas established, the artist begins work on the details of the tiger's features. Here a No. 12 ox-hair brush is being used to paint the striped markings on the face.

7 The artist continues to apply color all over the painting, often stepping back from the picture to assess its progress.

8 In this detail we see just how exciting the paint surface is. The broad, loose marks create a dynamic force which animates the picture and makes us feel as though the tiger is about to pounce.

9 The finished painting demonstrates how a fast, vigorous, *alla prima* technique creates an impression of a subject such as a wild animal. Acrylic paint dries quickly, allowing the artist to work fast and keep the paint surface fresh and lively.

7

8

5 The artist now blocks in the background with vigorous brush strokes, using the same decorator's brush and sap green diluted with water. Notice how the brush strokes remain visible, adding drama and movement to the image of the tiger.

MATERIALS USED

SUPPORT: ready-primed flax canvas, measuring
30 X 20 in. (76 X 50 cm).
COLORS: raw sienna, cadmium red, cadmium yellow, cadmium yellow deep, sap green, ivory black, and titanium white.
BRUSHES: 1 in. (2.5 cm) decorator's brush, No. 12 round ox-hair, No. 8 sable round and a No. 4 bristle round.

TIGER

9

The image of the tiger emerges convincingly from the vigorous brush work, the separate areas of bright color merging in the viewer's eyes. Note also how the artist deliberately confines the subject within the narrow limits of the picture's boundaries, giving the impression that the tiger is about to burst from the painting.

LANNER FALCON

The subject of this painting is a Lanner falcon, a native of the Mediterranean and North Africa. This particular bird, posing regally on its Arab-style perch, belongs to the artist. Falcons are his special love, and he knows the subject so well that he is able to paint the details and wing patterns of these birds virtually with his eyes closed!

What we can learn from the artist is that the better you know your subject, the more likely that you will be able to do justice to it. If you really want to succeed, it isn't enough to paint a subject just once and then forget it. The more you practise the more skillful you become.

MATERIALS USED

SUPPORT: ready-primed flax canvas, measuring 30 X 20 in. (76 X 50 cm).
COLORS: raw sienna, cadmium red, cadmium yellow, cadmium yellow deep, sap green, ivory black, and titanium white.
BRUSHES: 1 in. (2.5 cm) decorator's brush, No. 12 round ox-hair, No. 8 sable round and a No. 4 bristle round.

1 The subject of this painting was the artist's own falcon on an Arab-style perch.

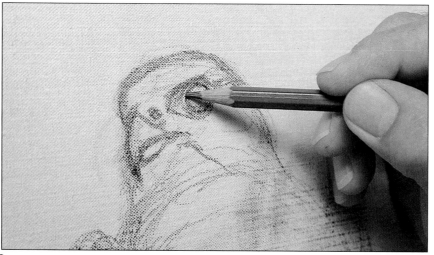

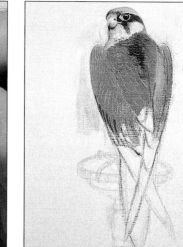

2 The artist begins by making a drawing on paper. He transfers this to the canvas by covering the back of the drawing with charcoal powder and tracing over the lines of the drawing with a 4B pencil.
3 The artist starts the painting with the head because the eye and the beak are important in capturing the personality of the subject. If he gets these right, the painting will succeed.
4 Now the artist blocks in the body of the bird with a mixture of Payne's gray and raw umber. He then draws the scalelike shapes of the feathers with a small brush and light gray paint.

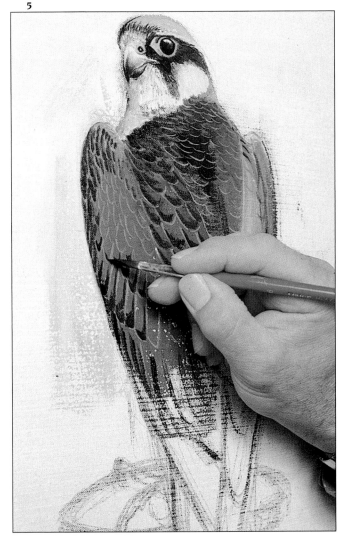

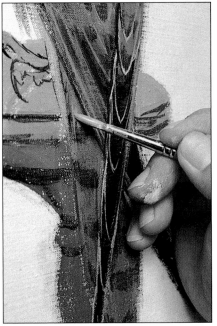

5 He then develops the shading on the feathers with tiny hatched brush strokes of raw umber and black, applied with a No. 2 brush.

6 The artist develops the details on the neck of the bird with white paint, smudging it with his finger to give a soft texture. He then continues working over the plummage, and lightly blocks in the background with loose strokes of white and yellow ocher.

7 The artist highlights the tips of the wings with light gray, then gently smudges the paint with his finger to create a soft, feathery edge.

LANNER FALCON

9

8 The background is darkened with a mixture of burnt sienna and yellow ocher, applied with a No. 5 bristle brush. The artist is not happy with this, however, as he feels it detracts from the main subject.

9 In the finished painting, we can see how the artist has overlaid the dark background with a pale, neutral one which gives much greater force and power to the image of the falcon. The removal of the dark background was easily accomplished thanks to the efficient covering power of acrylic paint; even the

darkest color will not show through a light one laid over it. Also, acrylic paint dries to a hard, impermeable finish which means that a fresh layer of paint cannot "pick up" the color underneath and cause muddiness, as sometimes happens with other, less versatile painting media.

SELF-PORTRAIT

If you are looking for a convenient model for a portrait painting—someone who is inexpensive, reliable, and available at times that suit you—then there is no better subject than yourself. Painting a self-portrait also has the added advantage that you don't have to worry about flattering your sitter!

Acrylic paints are an especially suitable medium for selfportraits. Their consistency can be varied to suit a whole range of styles, from loose and impressionistic to tight and realistic, depending on the mood you wish to convey.

Strangely, it is usually difficult to 'see' ourselves proper y. You may think you know your own face extremely well, but when it comes to painting a portrait it is essential to study your features as if for the very first time. If necessary, make a series of sketches before you begin the actual painting.

1 The artist begins by making an outline drawing of himself on the canvas., using a B pencil. He then blocks in the main light and shadow areas on the face with broad strokes of burnt sienna, diluted with water for the light areas.

2 Now the dark tones of the hair, beard, and moustach are put in with burnt sienna darkened with cobalt blue.

3 This close-up reveals how the artist is building up the broad masses and planes of the face with washes of color which indicate the light, medium, and dark tones.

4 The artist continues to model the face using various tones of earth colors such as burnt sienna, burnt umber, Turner's yellow, brilliant orange, and raw sienna. The eyes are painted with Payne's gray and black, and the mouth with red ocher.

5

6

7

8

MATERIALS USED

SUPPORT: gesso-primed hardboard, measuring 20 X 16 in. (50 X 40 cm).
COLORS: burnt sienna, cobalt blue, Turner's yellow, yellow ocher, brilliant orange, cadmium red medium, ultramarine, Payne's gray, and titanium white.
BRUSHES: Nos. 4 and 7 synthetic brush and a 1 in. (2.5 cm) bristle brush.

5 Now the cast shadow on the wall is brushed in with a 1 in. (2.5 cm) bristle brush and a weak solution of Payne's gray, white, and yellow ocher.

6 The details of the shirt and tie are painted with a No. 3 sable brush and cadmium red medium and brilliant orange.

7 Washes of ultramarine blue complete the coloring of the shirt. These bright, vibrant colors are deliberately chosen to bring a touch of vitality to the otherwise somber composition.

8 The artist now completes the modeling of the head and the facial features. The highlights in the skin tones are added with thin washes of Turner's yellow and white, and white highlights indicate the reflections on the mouth and eyes.

9 The finished portrait. Notice how the unique placement of the figure and the use of clean, white space around it force the viewer's eye into the face of the subject. The strong colors of the shirt and tie contrast boldly with the white of the paper and create a dynamic visual tension.

SELF PORTRAIT

9

1 Before starting to paint, the artist made sure that the model was sitting comfortably and in a relaxed position.

2 Working with black, white, vermillion, and burnt sienna, the artist blocks in an overall impression of the figure. The colors are loosely applied with thin paint to allow for correction as the painting develops.

WOMAN IN A SPOTTED DRESS

Painting a portrait makes more demands on an artist than any other subject. In creating a likeness, every feature of the head and face must be carefully analyzed in terms of color, shape, and tone. Because the character of the image is dependent upon this detailed analysis, small adjustments at any stage of the painting can make all the difference between success and failure.

The sympathetic nature of acrylic paints can help to overcome some of the problems of portrait painting. Unlike watercolors, which are difficult to control, and oils, which are slow-drying, acrylics allow you to work at a comfortable pace, building up the colors layer upon layer. In addition, the opacity of acrylics allows you to make adjustments or cover up mistakes without any danger of the colors turning muddy.

MATERIALS USED

SUPPORT: stretched and primed cotton duck canvas, measuring 20 X 18 in. (50 X 45 cm).
COLORS: burnt sienna, burnt umber, cadmium yellow, cobalt blue, vermillion, yellow ocher, ivory black, and titanium white.
BRUSHES: Nos. 6 flat bristle and a No. 4 round sable.

4 The background color is applied with a mixture of cobalt blue, yellow ocher, black, and white. A thin glaze of black is then applied over the model's dress.

3 The light flesh tones of the face are applied. Cobalt blue is added to the basic flesh tone mixture for the cool shadow areas. When these are dry, rich reds and browns are used to define the mouth. Deep shadows on the underside of the chin and nose are painted as precise, shapes of cool, gray purple.

WOMAN IN A SPOTTED DRESS

8

5 The artist adopts an unusual technique to paint the small colored spots on the model's dress. Using a piece of perforated scrap metal as a stencil, he stipples the opaque paint into the holes with a bristle brush.

6 The stenciled dots are now strengthened with a small sable brush,

using white, cadmium yellow, and vermillion.

7 The artist continues to build up the pattern on the dress. Larger spots are painted freehand.

8 The finished painting. By starting with broad strokes and thin paint, the artist

was able to establish the pose and the correct proportions of the model in the early stages, without building up a thick, dense layer of paint. Working from this firm foundation, he was able to work quickly and confidently when applying the finer details. The completed portrait retains some of the lively, spontaneous strokes made in the early stages of the painting.

CHAPTER FIVE

Designing with Acrylics

A book of this kind can only touch briefly on design.

Such a subject would need a book of its own to do it

justice. So I have confined myself to highlighting

some of the more obvious things that

acrylic is capable of doing.

I try to define design and design methods as exactly as possible.

However, the result will inevitably take on a personal note. As someone who has worked as a painter and designer for many years, I have naturally come to a number of conclusions, some of which are very personal. One conclusion is that all the disciplines—painting, drawing, design and sculpture—have a great deal in common, and relate closely to each other.

I prefer to think of drawing not as a separate activity, but as the base connecting painting and design, for drawing serves them both equally. Therefore if you draw, you are directly concerned with painting and designing, even though the ends to which they are put may differ appreciably.

Without going too deeply into the philosophy of the visual arts, I have taken the view that design has, basically, a decorative function, which confines itself to environment, objects, and communication media, and does this principally by the use of color, shape and form, pattern and texture, and imagery.

Painting, however, though using the same elements of color and form, is more concerned with expressing an individual point of view. Moreover it may incorporate research of an aesthetic or philosophical nature quite outside the province of design, though design itself may be indirectly related to these researches in no small way. Drawing spans both activities and can be research and communication, decorative and creative, all at the same time.

That painting has influenced design over the centuries is obvious. A great many innovations in posters, furniture, textiles, and interiors can be more or less traced to the experiments of painters during this century. Many of these painters were also sculptors and became, in turn, designers themselves, of no mean achievement. Picasso and Braque spring readily to mind as two important artists who left their imprint on design as much as on painting. In many instances the public will reject an artist's researches out of hand, but accept them eagerly when transformed into design. Those who intend to design should bear this in mind and recognize that research is important to all areas of art, and that drawing is perhaps the best form of it.

It is also interesting to note that in French and Italian the word for drawing is the same for design.

Acrylic is also an ideal medium for research and experiment because, like drawing, it is immediate, and research depends on spontaneity and the quick grasp of ideas. Acrylic can offer extended opportunities for going over the same ground until something exciting emerges. In addition it is able to do things that other mediums cannot attempt.

ABOVE Acrylic medium can be used for collaging. Cut the canvas shape and paint one side with medium.

ABOVE Press the shape onto stretched canvas. Rub it down with a clean, dry brush.

ABOVE Collage can also be done using the adhesive qualities of acrylic paint.

COLLAGE

The word collage comes from the French *coller* to stick—an apt description for a picture or design that is made up from pieces of paper, cloth, or other material and stuck to a firm support.

MODELING AND SURFACE TEXTURES

Adhesion is only one of the many attributes of acrylic modeling or texture paste. Another is its modeling ability and the way it may be used to make exciting surface textures, with or without the addition of paint. With the simplest of modeling techniques, surfaces can be transformed simply by using this paste.

Sawdust can be added to the acrylic paste to give it more bulk and texture, also a little white primer to give it more body. It can then be thoroughly mixed and spread on to a piece of card (cardboard). Pattern effects can be made by impressing various shapes or edges into the drying surface. Alternatively the paste could be mixed with a little sand, white primer, and umber to darken it. Lines can be scratched into it very freely with the back of a brush to create a relief effect. It may then be further stained with color, and the surplus wiped off.

As another variation, some cellulose filler can be added and some blue to give it a little color. Lines could be incised on the surface with a comb. When dry this surface could be stained with umber and wiped off before nearly dry. The mixing of the paste with sawdust, sand, and cellulose filler, as well as white primer and a little tube color, gives the paste that is formed an entirely different texture each time. The addition of the white primer to the other aggregates changes the qualities of the paste, for without it the paste dries somewhat transparent.

These few variations give unlimited scope for experiment and if pursued farther, would aid an interior designer or stage designer in discovering interesting surfaces by trying out the paste on models or on pieces of card (cardboard), and then lighting them from various angles.

Another method for creating surface textures of a completely different kind is to embed small regular or irregular fragments of objects into a smooth paste. Make up a smooth texture paste of cellulose filler with a touch of white primer, and experiment with all kinds of materials— buttons, hairpins, tacks, or staples for regular shaped objects, and peas, lentils, seeds, or macaroni for irregular ones.

TEXTURES WITH GEL

A B O V E Equal proportions of gel and paint are mixed. The thickened color should be used immediately, as it dries quickly.

A B O V E A painting knife is used to mix the gel and paint.

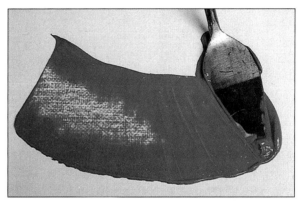

A B O V E The result is a paint with a stiff buttery consistency which retains the shape of knife marks.

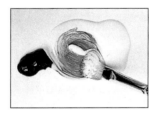

A B O V E Alternatively, a brush may be used to mix the gel and paint in equal quantities.

A B O V E Used with a stiff brush, gel lends itself to rugged brush work which retains the impression of the bristles.

A B O V E The mixture is then applied to the support with direct, spontaneous strokes.

TEXTURE WITH OIL

Modeling paste is spread evenly over the support.

A piece of crumpled foil is pressed into the paste while it is still wet.

The modeling paste takes on the texture of the foil.

When the paste is dry, it is ready to be overpainted.

The rougher texture creates broken color where the paint is applied. The finer texture on the right produces mottled patches of color.

TEXTURE PASTE

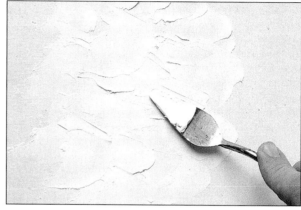

ABOVE Texture paint is applied directly to the support with a knife.

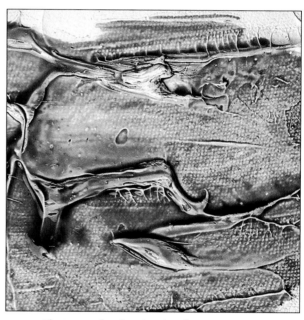

ABOVE The textured surface is painted over to create a delicate glaze.

Three other ways of using acrylic which are ideal for designing purposes are staining, spraying, and taping.

STAINING

Because acrylic is quick drying and water-resistant, and can be used thick or thin with equal ease it can be painted on unprimed cloth, and not only is it perfectly safe, but if it is thin enough, it soaks into the fibers of the material without any loss of brilliance, with remarkable affinities to dyeing and screen printing. This opens up a wealth of possibilities for painting and fabric designing.

Thin colors can be sprayed, dribbled, or splashed on to various kinds of cloths to produce a diversity of effects quickly without the bother of any kind of printing process to intervene.

STAINING

ABOVE To stain a support, mix the tube color with a medium to produce a thin fluid consistency.

ABOVE Work the color into the weave of the support using a decorator's brush or a sponge.

When you try the staining technique, add some water tension breaker (wetting agent) to the water diluting the paint, as this will increase the surface wetting and penetration properties of the colors. The addition of a few drops of matt medium will make sure that the thinned color will flow well, dry matt, and retain the binding properties of the medium.

SPRAYING

Thin acrylic paint can also be sprayed from an airbrush or spray-gun. The mixture can be as transparent or opaque as you like. The dilution can be as great as 50/50 water to acrylic or as little as 25% water to 75% paint. The addition of either gloss or matt medium is recommended to make sure maximum adhesion of the paint. Spraying can be carried out on any kind of surface as recommended in Chapter 1. Spray-guns are delicate instruments and the makers' directions regarding the application of the paint and cleaning should be followed scrupulously.

The results of spraying can vary from gently gradated tones to more brilliant effects. Spraying is a flexible way of creating realistic and decorative effects, and to carry it out numerous masks and stencils are needed. One way to protect parts of the work from undue spraying is to apply masking tape to them.

TAPING

The use of masking tape to protect parts of the work not to be damaged or painted accidentally has given rise to a number of techniques which can be used for certain kinds of painting.

For example, if the work is to be very flat, and very precise in its form, masking tape placed at the edges of the area to be painted, will protect that edge, and make sure that a good flat paint can be produced without the fear of going over the edges. The masking tape will give a good hard edge to the areas of paint.

The paint can be brushed over the masking tape with complete confidence. When the paint is thoroughly dry, the masking tape can be removed leaving behind a crisp, flatly painted area with hard edges.

However, it is advisable to make

STAINING

ABOVE Use the spray-gun with masking tape to create a pattern.

ABOVE When the masking fluid has dried, spray a layer of paint over it.

sure that the masking tape is carefully stuck down, and that there are no bubbles in it. Also the density of the paint should not be too thin. For the best results, the paint should be really opaque, if necessary applied in a thick layer. The addition of a matt or gloss medium or water tension breaker (wetting agent) will make sure that the paint flows well.

MASKING

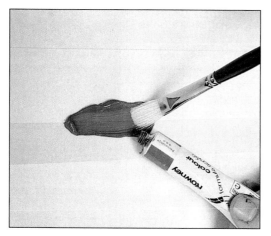

A B O V E Masking tape is placed across the support in the appropriate place. The artist works with color from the tube, spreading it across the tape with a small brush.

A B O V E The artist continues to spread the paint, working away from the masked area.

A B O V E When the paint is dry, the tape is removed. The underlying support has been protected and a hard line of paint is produced.

MURAL PAINTING

In all my experience as a mural designer, I have found acrylic to be the best all-round paint for painting on walls. Wall painting is at best an arduous task which can be made unnecessarily difficult if the paint used is unsympathetic to work with.

Problems with murals arise because you never know how the walls will be deployed from site to site. Sometimes they can be ideal—the right height, good light, easy access, plenty of room to work in. In such circumstances the problems of the paint are not so imperative.

But very often the walls will be high, the light poor, or changeable, and so work has to be carried out on steps or scaffolding, which means that the mixing table might be elsewhere, and the paint carried to the wall for application. If the mix is wrong, the whole operation has to be repeated: mixing in one place, and painting in another, which can be very tedious to say the least. I find acrylic easy to mix, store, and transport up and down ladders, and it is easily brushed on to the wall, and you know that the paint film is tough enough to withstand the wear and tear a wall painting has to endure.

When I used acrylic for the first time on a mural, I devised a completely new method to deal with it. First the walls were primed with acrylic primer, which was a delightful surface to draw on, and when completed the drawing was covered over with a semi-transparent wash of pale ocher, umber, and white.

The intention was to create a neutral tone over the whole work so that the lighter and the darker tones would relate properly with each other.

When the underpainting was dry the major areas of the mural were filled in carefully, including some of the detail. Because of the neutral tone covering the whole work, this could be done with confidence, whereas if it had been attempted on a white ground all kinds of problems would have ensued.

The method adopted here was to become the foundation of the whited-out method discussed earlier. Though it wasn't used in this instance, it was used in later works of this kind.

As will be seen in the color reproduction, the colors are rich and bright, the detail sharp and clear. This could not have been achieved so successfully with other paints, as they do not possess the quick-drying properties and translucency of acrylic, therefore the overpainting method cannot work as well.

As will be observed in the almost completed wall, large areas of the underpainting have been left untouched, and remain as they

were originally painted with the free brush work contrasting with the clear-cut shapes of the design.

Acrylic is ideally suited to murals and wall decoration, not only as paint, but as a means of creating textures, and surface variation so that the light can play its part as well. For those unused to painting on a wall, who would like to try some of the methods suggested in this section, if the work cannot be carried out directly on the wall, it can be done on sheets of card (cardboard) or hardboard first, and placed into position afterward. This means that if the work is not immediately successful, it can be removed easily, and a new section put in its place.

Of course, the real satisfaction of mural painting is to paint or work in situ, but working on removable panels is a good introduction to

seeing if the design is effective without harm to the wall.

DRAWING AND ILLUSTRATION

Though drawings and illustrations can be adequately carried out in most other mediums, acrylic offers tremendous scope for the further exploration of tones, shapes, textures and color, which would be of inestimable value in both areas.

Black and white drawings can be enhanced by the addition of washes of transparent or semi-opaque acrylic color, provided a few conditions are observed. Charcoal, charcoal pencils, conté crayon, carbon pencils, chalks, and pastels will tend either to run or be picked up by any washes or overpainting, and unless this particular quality is especially needed, it is advisable to fix the drawing first. The ordinary type of fixative is not

recommended as it might impair the adhesive qualities of the acrylic, therefore some acrylic gloss or acrylic matt medium can be sprayed with safety over the drawing with a spray diffuser and will hold the drawing in place.

Alternatively the drawing can begin with washes and then be drawn over with pen, charcoal pencil, crayon, and so on. Ordinary pencils smudge less and pick up less than carbon pencils and can be painted over quite easily.

Pure charcoal, however, is prone to smudging and picking up as it does not contain any binder whatsoever. And though most other drawing mediums contain a little binder, it is safer to fix them as a precaution.

MELISSA

CHAPTER SIX
Epilogue

Acrylic—as I hope I have amply demonstrated—is a wonderful paint. In fact, a magic paint that can do everything other paints can do, and in many instances far better—more transparent than watercolor, more opaque than gouache, and thicker than oil paint. It dries quicker, is more resilient to damage, and more versatile than any known paint today.

OPPOSITE This portrait of a young girl was painted on primed hardboard using as reference a color photograph blown up to life size.

To make acrylic produce wonders is not the province of the manufacturers, but of the user. The magic, alas, won't happen by itself.

Technique will enable acrylic to go some of the way to fulfil its potential, but the magic needs imagination. Whereas oil paint demands years of discipline to allow any magic to come through, acrylic can accommodate lots of imagination to let it happen sooner. You can experiment with acrylic in a way that would seem presumptuous with other mediums. There are no rules you break at your peril, only a few simple conditions that should be observed, to get the magic working. They can be summarized thus: Use plenty of clean water. Keep brushes clean by washing immediately after use. Mix the paint well. Don't be cautious about adding extra acrylic medium to mixtures; additional medium always makes paint flow better. To produce the maximum visual qualities of acrylic in a subtle and arresting way, let the painting show on its surface the effect of the layers beneath. Vary the layers and allow each one to show through. Starting with lean paint, and finishing with thick is better than starting with thick paint, because once acrylic is dry it is almost impossible to remove. Allow washes to show the white surface through the transparent layers. Unlike glazes which can cover any surface or underpainting, both thick and thin, washes depend on the white surface to give the sparkle needed When in doubt white it out. Enjoy the process.

Whoever said, "Paints were invented solely for enjoyment. . ." made a good point. They undoubtedly are, and acrylic paints even more so. But to enjoy them fully a number of conditions have to be considered. Some are familiar; others might be somewhat strange. But they are all relevant, as much to the amateur, as to the professional.

Briefly they are: Liking what we do, rather than doing what we like. Accepting that means are more important than ends. Letting the ends take care of themselves. It is the process that matters. An attitude of optimism. Aim to be natural, and not to strive too hard. Cultivate patience. Allow progress to develop at its own pace. Decide and act. Practice constantly.

Liking what we do means accepting our own efforts as valid—even if they don't come up to our own expectations—because they are our own and not somebody else's. Of course it is natural to admire the achievements of others, and wish to do likewise, but this kind of ambition will only lead to disappointment. Equally we may like to impress others with what we do, and because it fails to excite the admiration we would like, we will tend to become discouraged. And when this happens, enjoyment flies quickly out of the window.

ABOVE David Hockney, *Mr and Mrs Clark and Percy*. The artist achieved the fine translucent finish of the vase and flowers and general even tone by using paint in a carefully controlled manner.

LANYON QUOIT

ABOVE An understated composition, subdued colors and restricted tonal contrast are masterfully combined in this painting to create this somber and overcast scene.

WINTRY LANDSAPE

ABOVE An advantage with acrylic is that
light colors can be laid on top of dark.
Here, the warm, dark undertones provide
a contrasting base to the cold, light tones
of the snow and sky.

BOTTLE, FRUITS, AND VEGETABLES

ABOVE Acrylics were chosen for this still life because of the bold color scheme of the subject. The aim of the artist was to create a composition using the classical triangle, with the bottle as the focal point.

The ends we choose will have a direct bearing on the way we enjoy our work—hence means being more important than ends. If we enjoy the means the ends will take care of themselves.

This is not to say that ends are not without value and that aims, ambitions, or intentions are unnecessary. Far from it. In their proper context, they can be the motive or spur for what is to be done; moreover they can provide the excitement that goes toward the creating of significant work. But for the successful realization of these goals, each stage of the process must be given due attention and not be rushed or skimped (hence the need for patience), or despaired over (hence the need for optimism).

Whatever the personal target, working toward it should be enjoyable. For if we enjoy what we do, the enjoyment becomes part of the work and will be seen and enjoyed by others in turn. What we should realize is that our work is like an open book, available for all to dip into and read. What we put into it, someone else can take out.

Painting and designing are processes that need constant practice. This is the secret: only practice will encourage skills to grow, understanding to ripen, and allow work to develop and, above all, for enjoyment to increase.

Practice *is* everything. It is the center of an artist's working life and, consequently, looked forward to, if only for an hour a day.

Of course "mistakes" will be made, but they should be seen as part of the process. Making errors of judgment is the only way to develop, make us more critically aware, and so build up confidence in what we are doing.

If making mistakes is a persistent worry remember that "those who never make mistakes, never make anything ... " and take heart.

The methods that I have described in this book take all this into consideration. The suggested painting exercises and experiences will do a great deal to forestall many of the major difficulties that may occur when using acrylic for the first time. This is because the exercises bring into play natural abilities. There is no need to learn any special way of doing things as one would when learning a performing art. These exercises can and should be adapted to suit the individual personality of the user. They can be played by the book or turned upside down if need be, without harm. The information is there to be used, and how it is done is a personal matter, whether you are an amateur dabbler or an aspiring professional.

Expertise should be acquired slowly on your own terms. The principle to follow is to do things gradually and deliberately at your own pace, in your own way.

If I were asked to sum up this book in one word, it would be action. Painting is an immediate activity that takes place only in the present. In short, it happens now. To enable this to happen, the best procedure to adopt is to decide and act. The secret is to make up your mind as clearly and firmly as possible and then, without any hesitation, act. For whatever is decided —and this is the point— will be correct. The success of the outcome depends not on what is decided, but on the act of decision itself.

ABOVE This composition deliberately contrasts hot and cold colors, The use of complementary colors is heightened by small touches of shadow.

WALLFLOWERS AND FORGET-ME-NOTS

ABOVE This micro-landscape, painted
out-of-doors from life, has no formal
composition of focal point. The use of thin
paint on a good quality stretched paper
produced the watercolor effect.

PLOWED FIELDS

ABOVE The furrows in this plowed field
were painted using the wet-into-wet
technique. This avoids a hard line and
achieves instead, a soft, blurred image.

THE LIGHTHOUSE

ABOVE What makes this painting
interesting is the artist's use of graphic
technique to produce bold lines, and his
creation of different textures.

Painting
in
Oils

Introduction...
...Why Oils

In recent decades there has been an amazing proliferation of new materials for the artists and designers, so much so that a visit to one of the larger artist's suppliers can leave an uninitiated person feeling confused and bewildered. There are pencils, pens, crayons and pastels in every color of the rainbow; there are acrylic paints, both in tubes and in pots; there are watercolors in tubes, pans and boxes; there are gouaches and poster paints; there are even special paints for fabrics and ceramics. Indeed, special materials are now available for almost any surface that could conceivably be painted or decorated. and, often tucked away unobtrusively in one corner, there are oil paints.

In recent decades there has been an amazing proliferation of new materials for artists and designers, so much so that a visit to one of the larger artists' suppliers can leave an uninitiated person feeling confused and bewildered. There are pencils, pens, crayons, and pastels in every color of the rainbow; there are acrylic paints, both in tubes and in pots; there are watercolors in tubes, pans, and boxes; there are gouaches and poster paints; there are even special paints for fabrics and ceramics. Indeed, special materials are now available for almost any surface that could conceivably be painted or decorated. And, often tucked away unobtrusively in one corner, there are oil paints.

Why, then, are oil paints still so popular with professional artists and "Sunday painters" alike? There are two main reasons for this, the first being that oil paint is the most versatile of all the painting media, and can be used in any number of ways to suit all styles, subjects and sizes of work. The second is that it is the easiest medium for a beginner to use. Which is not to say, of course, that a novice will automatically be able to create a masterpiece at first try—that is most unlikely. But because oil paint can be manipulated, scraped off, and overpainted, built up and then scraped down once again, it enables you to learn by trial and error, uninhibited by the thought of having "to start all over again," or waste expensive materials. This is not true of any other medium: acrylic, for example, cannot be moved at all once it has been laid down, and watercolor—a lovely medium but a tricky one—quickly loses all its qualities of freshness and translucence if overworked. Of course, an overworked oil painting will not be a perfect picture, but it may at least be a creditable one, if only because of the knowledge gained in painting it.

OIL PAINT IN THE PAST

Oil paint, though regarded as a "traditional" painting medium, is actually quite young in terms of art history. In Europe, before the invention of oil paint in the 15th century, artists painted with tempera, which is color pigment bound with egg yolk. This was a difficult medium to use as it dried very fast, and thus called for a deliberate and meticulous approach.

The Flemish painter Jan van Eyck (c.1390–1441) was the first to experiment with raw pigments bound with an

LEFT *Self Portrait* by Rembrandt van Rijn (1606–69). Rembrandt shocked many of his contemporaries by his bold use of paint, which produced thick, textured surfaces. The popular Dutch paintings of the time were characterized by a very smooth finish, with no visible brushstrokes, while in Rembrandt's later work brushstrokes and the paint itself are used to suggest texture, the paint being used almost as a modeling medium in places.

FAR LEFT *Old Woman with a Rosary* by Paul Cézanne (1839–1906). By Cézanne's time, the techniques of oil painting had been largely freed from the earlier restrictions and prejudices. The brushstrokes are an integral part of this dramatic composition, as are the areas of broken color, while the face itself has been treated in a bold, broad manner as a series of planes.

BELOW *Man in a Turban* by Jan van Eyck (active 1422–41). In his oil paintings, van Eyck used much the same methods as previously used for tempera work, building up thin layers of paint, one over another, the technique known as glazing. However, oil paint used in this way gives a depth and luminosity of effect which cannot be achieved with tempera.

oil mixture, when he found that one of his tempera paintings had split while drying in the sun. Not only did the oil paints dry without cracking, but, as van Eyck discovered, they could be applied in thin, transparent layers which gave the colors a depth and luminosity hitherto unknown.

The- early painters in oil, like van Eyck, used the paint thinly, with delicate brushstrokes that are almost invisible to the eye. But the full potential of oil paint was not really exploited until it was taken up by the Italian painters of the 15th and 16th centuries, notably Giorgione (1475–1510) and Titian (*c.*1487–1576).

In Titian's hands, and later in those of the great Dutch painter Rembrandt (1606–69), oil paint was at last used with a feeling for its own inherent qualities. Both artists combined delicately painted areas of glazing (thin paint applied in layers over one another) with thick brushstrokes in which the actual marks of the brush became a feature rather than something to be disguised. Rembrandt's later paintings must have seemed quite shocking to a public accustomed to the smooth, satin finish of other contemporary Dutch paintings—a common complaint was that they looked unfinished.

The English landscape painter John Constable (1776–1837), and the French Impressionists later in the 19th century, took the freedom of painting to even greater lengths by using oil as a quick sketching medium, often working out of doors. In Constable's day the camera had yet to be invented, and artists had of necessity to make a great many sketches as references for their finished works. Constable's wonderful sky and landscape studies, made rapidly, often on scraps of paper and cardboard, were never intended as finished works of art; but to our eyes they are much more pleasing, and infinitely more exciting, than his large polished studio paintings, because they have the quality of immediacy that landscape painting seems to demand.

The Impressionists, who drew inspiration from Constable, applied their paint in thick dabs and strokes of broken color to depict what was their main preoccupation —the ever-changing effects of light on the landscape. Vincent van Gogh (1853–90), who was not an Impressionist but is sometimes grouped with them because he was working at much the same time, used both the color and the texture of the paint to express his emotions and to define forms, treating the paint almost as a modeling medium. We are so familiar with van Gogh's paintings through countless reproductions that it is hard to appreciate how strange, indeed even offensive, those great, thick, swirling brushstrokes must have looked to his contemporaries (van Gogh sold only one painting during his entire lifetime).

The very diversity of painting techniques in the past has had the effect of freeing us from any preconceptions about the medium. It is what you want it to be; there is no "right" or "wrong" way of doing an oil painting. Today's painters use oil paint in so many different ways that it is often hard to believe that the same medium has been

used. Interestingly, the art of tempera painting is now undergoing a revival, and some artists working in oil use a similar technique, applying thin layers of transparent glazes to produce a luminous, light-filled quality. Other artists apply paint thickly with a knife, building it up on the surface of the canvas so that it resembles a relief sculpture.

New painting mediums—oils, varnishes, and extenders—are constantly being developed in recognition of these different needs; for example, you can choose one type of medium if you want to build up delicate glazes, another if you want to achieve a thick, textured surface using the impasto technique.

OPPOSITE TOP LEFT *Autumn at Argenteuil* by Claude Monet (1840–1926). The French Impressionists were very much influenced by Constable's landscape paintings, and Monet in particular took the preoccupation with the effects of light almost to the point of an obsession. He frequently worked out of doors, and would paint several versions of the same scene in different lights, building up the paint in thick impastos to achieve the everchanging effects suggestive of motion which he sought.

FAR LEFT *Olive Trees* by Vincent van Gogh (1853–90). The Impressionists' use of paint was free and daring by the academic standards of the day, but van Gogh's was the most innovative by far, and even those accustomed to the newer styles found his paintings perplexing and even shocking. No one had hitherto dared to represent the sky or foliage as a series of thickly-painted swirls, as in this painting, or the ground as broken lines of bright, unblended color.

LEFT *Chain Pier, Brighton* by John Constable (1776–1837). Constable was among the first artists to use oil paint as a sketching medium, and his small studies, often on pieces of paper or primed cardboard, are infinitely fresher and more spontaneous than his large studio canvases. This tiny sketch, no more than 10 in. (25 cm) high, makes a complete statement about light and color, as well as recording all the important details of the scene.

Gordon Bennett

CHAPTER ONE

Materials and Equipment

Materials for oil painting can be costly; so it is advisable to work out your "starter kit" carefully. Begin by buying the minimum and adding extra colors, brushes, and so on when you have progressed to the stage of understanding your particular requirements. For example, someone who intends to specialize in flower painting will need a different range of colors from someone whose chosen theme is seascapes, while a person working on a miniature scale will use brushes quite unlike those needed for largescale paintings.

CHOOSING PAINTS

Oil paints are divided into two main categories: artists' and students' colors. The latter are cheaper because they contain less pure pigment and more fillers and extenders, but in general they are a false economy for that very reason; they cannot provide the same intensity of color as the more expensive range. However, students' colors are fine for practising with, and it is possible to combine the two types using the students' colors for browns and other colors where intensity is not a prime requirement and artists' for the pure colors such as red, yellow, and blue. A large size tube of white works out most economical, since white is used more than most other colors.

Paints in the artists' range are not all the same price—a trap for the unwary. They are classified in series, usually from 1 to 7 (different manufacturers have different methods of classification), series 7 being extremely expensive. The price differences reflect the expense and/or scarcity of the pigment used. Nowadays, because there are so many excellent chemical pigments, it is seldom necessary to use the very expensive colors, such as vermilion, except in very special cases.

It is often said that all colors can be mixed from the three primaries, red, yellow, and blue. To some extent this is true, but they will certainly not provide a subtle or exciting range, and in any case there are a great many different versions of red, yellow, and blue. The illustration shows a suggested "starter palette," which should provide an adequate mix of colors for most purposes. In general you will need, as well as white, a warm and a cool version of each of the primaries, plus a brown and a green and perhaps a violet or purple. Strictly speaking, greens are not essential as they can be mixed from blue and yellow, but it takes time and experience to arrive at the right hue, and there really is not much point in spending more time in mixing than you need. Vividian is a good choice, since it mixes well with any color. Other useful additions to your palette are rose madder in the red group; a lemon yellow such as Winsor or cadmium lemon in the yellow group; cerulean blue and Antwerp or cobalt blue in the blue group; and sap green and chrome green in the greens. Good

ABOVE A suggested "starter palette." From right to left: white (above), yellow ocher, cadmium yellow, cadmium red, alizarin crimson, cobalt violet, ultramarine, Prussian blue, and viridian.

The palette chosen depends very much on the subject to be painted: for instance, violet might not be needed at all, cobalt blue might be used instead of the other two blues, an additional green, such as chrome oxide, added, and a different yellow chosen.

The photograph shows the colors mixed with varying amounts of white.

browns and grays are burnt sienna, burnt umber, and Payne's gray. Flake white dries quickly and is resistant to cracking, but it contains poisonous lead; for this reason some artists prefer to use titanium white, which is non-toxic. The use of black is often frowned upon, and many artists never use it as it can have a deadening effect, but it can be mixed with yellow to produce a rich olive green, and many landscape artists use it for this purpose.

PAINTING MEDIUMS

Oil paint can be used just as it comes from the tube, or it can be a combination of oil and a thinner (what artists call a *medium*). If you try to apply undiluted paint accurately in a small area, you will see why such mediums are necessary; without them the paint is not easily malleable.

The most popular medium is the traditional blend of linseed oil and turpentine or white spirit, usually in a ratio of 60% oil and 40% thinner. Linseed oil dries to a glossy finish which is resistant to cracking—but be sure to buy either purified or cold-pressed linseed oil, which dry without yellowing. Boiled linseed oil—the sort found in DIY shops—contains impurities which cause rapid yellowing.

Linseed oil is slow to dry, which may not suit your way of working and can produce a rather churned-up paint surface. There are several faster-drying mediums available, such as drying linseed oil, drying poppy oil, stand oil (which also makes the paint flow well and disguises brushstrokes), and an alkyd-based medium sold under the name of *Liquin*.

Turpentine is the most commonly used artist's thinner, though in fact white spirit is just as good and is less likely to cause the headaches and allergic reactions which artists sometimes complain of when using turpentine. White spirit also has less odor, and stores without deteriorating.

Special ready-mixed painting mediums are sold for specific purposes. Linseed oil, for instance, is not suitable for glazing (see p. 271) as it will dribble down the surface of the canvas, but Liquin is excellent for this purpose. Another alkyd medium, *Oleopasto*, has been developed specially for impasto work (see p. 271). It is designed to extend the paint and add body to it so thaf it can be applied in thick layers, with the brush or knife marks clearly visible.

BRUSHES AND KNIVES

Paint brushes for oil painting come in a wide range of

shapes, sizes, and materials. Good-quality brushes cost more, but are worth the initial outlay as they last longer and hold their shape better. For oils, unlike for watercolors, you need more than just one or two brushes, otherwise you will be forever cleaning them between applying one color and the next. The ideal is to have one brush for each color, but a selection of six should be enough to start off with.

The illustration shows the main shapes and types of brush:

Flats have long bristles with square ends. They hold a lot of paint and can be used flat, for broad areas, or on edge for fine lines.

Brights have shorter bristles than flats and produce strongly textured strokes. They are ideal for applying thick paint for impasto effects.

Rounds have long bristles, tapered at the ends. Like flats, they produce a wide variety of strokes, but they give a softer effect which is excellent for backgrounds, skies, and portraits.

Filberts are fuller in shape than flats, with slightly rounded ends that make soft, tapered strokes.

Of the four types of brush, rounds and flats are the most useful to begin with. Brights and filberts can be added later, should you require them.

Each type of brush comes in a range of up to 12 sizes; so choose the size that best suits the style and scale of your paintings.

Hog's-hair bristles and sable hair are the traditional materials for oil-painting brushes; hog's hair is fairly stiff and holds the paint well, while sable gives a much smoother and less obvious brushstroke. Sables are very expensive indeed, but there are now several synthetic versions of the softer type of brush, and also mixtures of sable and synthetic. In the case of the soft brushes, you may need several or none at all, according to the way in which you work; some artists use nothing but soft nylon brushes and others nothing but hog's hair.

Palette knives, made of flexible steel, are used for cleaning the palette and mixing paint, while painting knives are designed specifically for painting. The latter are unlikely to be needed by a beginner unless you have a particular desire to experiment with this kind of painting, but an ordinary straight-bladed palette knife should form part of your "starter kit."

LEFT A selection of oil-painting brushes in both hog's hair and synthetic fiber. The four white (hog's-hair) brushes are the basic shapes: from left to right, flat, filbert, round, and bright.

RIGHT A selection of palette and painting knives. Second from the left is the standard palette knife, which is designed mainly for cleaning the palette and mixing paint, but can also be used for applying paint to the support. The others are all specifically designed for painting. As with brushes, some experimentation is needed to find out which shape suits which individual; some artists never use painting knives at all.

PALETTES

Palettes come in a variety of shapes, sizes, and materials, designed to suit your individual requirements. Thumbhole palettes are designed for easel painting. They have a thumbhole and indentation for the fingers, and the palette is supported on the forearm. Before buying a palette, try out different sizes and shapes to see which feels the most comfortable.

New wooden palettes should be treated by rubbing with linseed oil to prevent them absorbing the oil in the paint. You can even improvize your own palette, from any non-absorbent surface, making it any size and color you like. An old white dinner plate might do, or a sheet of glass with white or neutral-colored paper underneath it. Disposable palettes made of oilproof paper are a boon for outdoor work, and remove the necessity for cleaning.

PAINTBOXES

Theoretically, any old cardboard box will do to keep paints, brushes, and media in, but if you are intending to carry paints around with you it is worth investing in a proper box with separate compartments for paints and brushes. Most of these are wooden, with a carrying handle, and are sold with their own palette which fits into the lid.

Alternatively you can improvize you own paintbox from a toolbox or fishing tackle box, which are less expensive and lighter to carry.

OIL PAINTING ACCESSORIES

Other essential items include dippers for your painting medium, which can be attached to the palette; jam jars or tin cans to hold white spirit for cleaning brushes; and of course a large supply of rags or kitchen paper (oil paint is very messy and needs to be cleaned up frequently). Another useful painting aid is a mahl stick, which steadies your hand when you are painting small details or fine lines. For anyone who intends to do a lot of outdoor work, a pair of canvas separators is very useful.

SUPPORTS

This is the term given to whatever surface is used to paint on, whether stretched canvas, hardboard, or cardboard, paper—even a wall. The most commonly used support for oil painting is canvas, usually made of linen or cotton, and stretched to make it taut, but many other surfaces can be used, and each one has its own individual characteristics. Canvas provides a sympathetic surface and holds the paint well, while primed hardboard, favored by some artists, is unyielding and holds the paint much less well, so that it tends to slip about. This can be an advantage for someone who paints with thinned—and thus quicker-drying—paint, and makes use of finely drawn detail, but is less suitable for thickly applied paint, as each successive layer will disturb the one below. You will certainly have to try several different supports before you can be sure which one suits you best, and even then you will probably find that different paintings call for different supports.

Canvas

Canvases can be bought stretched and ready for use, but they are very expensive and it is much cheaper to stretch and prepare (prime) your own. Unprimed canvas can be bought by the meter in artists' suppliers, as can stretchers, which are sold in pairs so that any size can be made up. The illustration shows some different types of canvas, ranging from fine weave to very coarse. Generally, a coarse weave is suitable for broad, heavy brushwork, while a finely woven texture is best for finely detailed work. Linen canvas, which is undoubtedly the nicest surface to work on, is expensive and could be an unwise choice for a first attempt. Cotton canvas is much cheaper, and perfectly adequate. Cotton duck, in particular, stretches well because it has a tighter weave.

Stretching canvas

Stretching canvas is not at all difficult, and will save you money. To stretch a canvas you will need four wooden stretcher pieces—one for each side of the frame. In addition you will need ½-in. (12-mm) carpet tacks to attach the canvas to the frame, a hammer, and a pair of sharp scissors.

Boards and paper

Hardboard is an inexpensive, strong, yet lightweight support which you can buy from any timber yard or

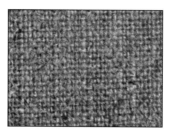
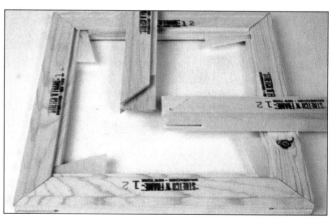

ABOVE Stretchers can be bought in a wide variety of sizes. They are sold in pairs, which are then fitted together to form rectangles.

TOP Types of canvas. From left to right, top row: inexpensive cotton; good-quality cotton, which is similar to linen. MIDDLE ROW: hessian, very coarse and thus unsuitable for thinly applied paint or fine work, and linen. BOTTOM ROW: a different weave of linen and a ready-primed linen, suitable for most work and available from the larger artists' suppliers.

builders' suppliers. Either the smooth or the rough side can be used, the latter being suitable only for those who like to use their paint thick. Its disadvantage, which applies also to the canvas-covered hardboard described above, is that it warps, but if you are framing your work it can be straightened out at this stage by battening the back (sizing both sides of the board also helps to reduce warping). For a large painting, the hardboard can be battened first by either sticking or screwing two pieces of hardwood battening across the back. (If using screws, take care they do not come through to the front, as hardboard is quite thin.)

Prepared canvas boards can be bought from artists' suppliers in a variety of different surfaces, the more expensive ones being the best. The cheaper ones tend to have a rather coarse and greasy surface, but are probably adequate for a first attempt. Such boards are also prone to warping.

Paper and cardboard make perfectly satisfactory supports for oil painting as long as they are primed (see *Sizing and priming*). They are excellent for small, quick sketches, as the paper, being slightly absorbent, allows the paint to dry quite quickly. If using paper, buy a good-quality, heavy watercolor paper, as a thin paper will buckle when primed. Specially prepared paper, called oil sketching paper, can be bought, usually in pads. Some people get on well with this, but others find its surface greasy and unpleasant to work on, like that of the cheaper painting boards.

Sizing and priming

The conventional method of priming all supports is first to apply a coat of the animal-skin size described above, and when dry to apply a coat (or sometimes two) of oil-based primer. You can use ordinary household undercoat for this, but special oil primers are sold by artists' suppliers for the purpose, and are probably the wisest choice. However, oil primers do take a fairly long time to dry. An alternative is to use emulsion paint, which dries quickly, or the acrylic primer sold under the (incorrect) name of gesso, which is compatible with oil paint. Acrylic primer should always be applied direct to the canvas, without the preliminary coat of size, and two coats will usually be needed.

The purpose of sizing and priming is to provide a protective layer between the canvas and the oil paint. Some contemporary artists, among them the English artist Francis Bacon (b.1910), do paint on unprimed canvas in order to achieve special effects, but this should never be a general practice. The oil paint will eventually rot the canvas or other support, and the paint itself will dry out and flake off as all the oil will have been absorbed.

Easels

An easel is a necessity. You may manage to produce one small painting by propping up your canvas on a table or shelf, but you will very soon find out how unsatisfactory this is. Without an easel you cannot adjust the height of your work—essential if you are doing a painting of a reasonable size, as you must be able to reach different areas of it easily and comfortably—and you cannot tilt the work, which you often need to do either to avoid light reflecting on its surface or to catch the best light for working.

There are several different types of easel on the market, from huge, sturdy studio easels to small sketching easels that are light and easily portable. Your choice will be dictated by the space in which you are working, whether you intend to work mostly inside or outside, and by the size of your work and the type of painting you are doing. If you intend to work out of doors frequently you will need a sketching easel (though small sketches can be done by propping the canvas or board against the open lid of a paintbox). If, on the other hand, you know you are unlikely to paint anywhere but indoors, the heavier radial easel could be a good choice, but this cannot easily be dismantled and put away, so you might choose a portable easel for space reasons.

There are three main types of sketching easel, the box easel, the wooden sketching easel, and the aluminum sketching easel. The first type combines an easel and a paintbox, and can be folded up into a case for carrying. These were at one time very expensive, and the best ones still are, but cheaper versions are now appearing on the market, and for an outdoor painter they are a good choice, as everything can be carried in one piece of luggage.

Wooden sketching easels are inexpensive, but are not recommended, as the blocks which slide up and down in slots to enable you to adjust the height of the work tend to become warped, so that they either do not slide at all or are impossible to fix in position. There is nothing more infuriating than having to fight your easel, which often involves knocking it over, just when you want to work particularly fast

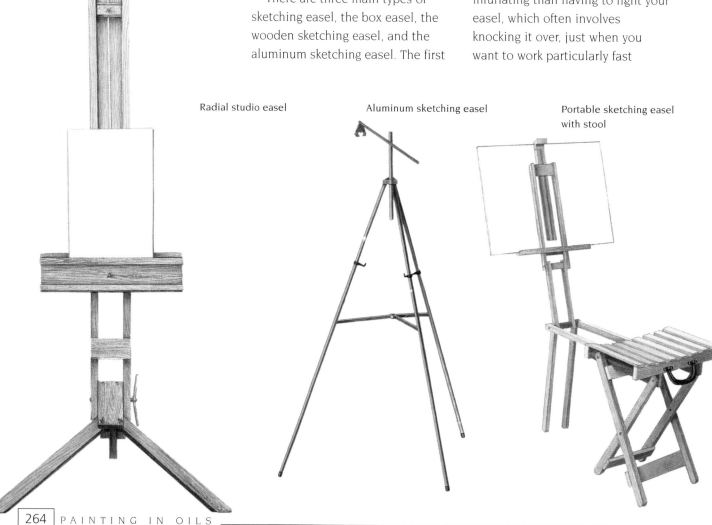

Radial studio easel

Aluminum sketching easel

Portable sketching easel with stool

because the light is changing.

The metal sketching easel, on the other hand, is excellent, and suffers from none of these disadvantages because metal cannot warp. It is easy to adjust, holds the work firmly, and has the additional advantage of being adjustable to a horizontal position for watercolors (you may find that you want to experiment with other media from time to time). It is also quite adequate for indoor work, providing you are not working on a vast scale, and can be tucked away unobtrusively in a corner when not in use.

The problem with all sketching easels except the heavier version of the box type is that because they are light, and thus easy to carry, they are also vulnerable to gusts of wind, the canvas or board acting as

Box easel

a most effective sail! Some artists manage to anchor their easel by pushing tent pegs into the ground and tying the easel legs to them, or by hanging a heavy stone from the center of the easel.

The working space
Few non-professional painters are fortunate enough to have access to a studio; nor indeed are all professional ones. Most people have to make do with a small, under-equipped room or just a corner of a room used by other people for other purposes. This can create problems, but these are surmountable with a little organization.

One problem is that oil paint is a messy medium and has an almost magical way of appearing on objects that seemed to be nowhere near it when you were painting. You get it on your hands without noticing, then you go and make a cup of coffee and it will be on the kettle, the mug, the spoon, and so on, ad infinitum. If you are working in a corner of a room, clean up as often as you can, including wiping your hands, never wander about with a loaded paintbrush, and cover the equipment table with plenty of newspaper.

A more serious problem is lighting. The best light for painting is, of course, daylight, but daylight is unpredictable and changes all the time, not only in variable weather conditions but also according to the time of day. If you have a north-facing window you are

lucky, as north light (or south light if you live in the southern hemisphere) changes much less, but many rooms face east or west, in which case you will sometimes have the sun shining directly on to the work and reflecting off the paint surface, while at other times you will have almost no light at all.

Always try to position your easel so that the light source is behind you and coming over your left shoulder if you are right-handed.

Good light is vitally important: if you look in a good light at a painting done in a poor one you will see why. What were intended to be subtle gradations of color and tone now appear as crude mixtures of bright colors and dingy ones, while what you thought of as nicely-blended, unobtrusive brushwork is actually quite clumsy and obvious.

One way of coping with this problem is to use artificial lighting which, while not as perfect as northerly daylight, is at least constant. The best lights for painting are the fluorescent "daylight" ones, which can be bought either as ceiling lights or as lamps which can be fitted on to a shelf, table, or windowsill. Look carefully at what is available before buying, as mistakes are expensive, and work out where the light source should be placed so that it does not reflect off the paint. One method is to fix a lamp over the window so that it boosts the available light, but a certain amount of trial and error may be involved before you arrive at a satisfactory solution.

CHAPTER TWO

The Mechanics of Painting

Although there are really no hard-and-fast rules in oil painting, it is helpful to have an idea of the various ways in which artists go about things so that you can experiment with different techniques, color schemes, and compositions as you evolve your own particular style. Rules are often useful in a negative way: once you know a rule you can break it for reasons of your own, or "bend" it, as many artists have done with the rules of perspective. Constable and the French Impressionists broke the rules of their times, thus freeing painting from the very rigid set of procedures to which artists had previously been forced to adhere, but their knowledge of all the theories of painting was very thorough indeed.

TOP, ABOVE AND RIGHT This painting was begun with a monochrome underpainting in dilute cobalt blue, an unusual but deliberate choice of color, as the blue is repeated throughout the picture. The flowers and drapery were then built up in thicker paint, the method known as "fat over lean," the background and foliage being left quite thin.

GENERAL PAINTING TECHNIQUES

If you are painting a very simple subject, such as an empty landscape with a wide expanse of sky, there is often no need for an underdrawing or underpainting, except perhaps a line or two to delineate the horizon. However, for a more complex subject such as a figure study, or perhaps a landscape including people or buildings, a preliminary drawing on the canvas is usually advisable. This enables you to work out the composition and the position of the main elements within it, and to plan the balance of dark colors and light ones. For a portrait or figure painting you will need to establish how you want to place the figure in relation to the background, and you will need to get the proportions of the figure right. If you start an ambitious painting with inadequate drawing you will be forever altering parts of it, which will not only spoil your enjoyment, but will also produce a labored and overworked painting. Careful planning at the start enables you to be more spontaneous later.

Underdrawings can be done either in pencil or charcoal, the latter being preferable, as it is a broad medium, easier to use freely. To avoid loose charcoal mixing with the paint and muddying it, brush it down lightly with a rag before starting to paint—you will still retain the main lines of the drawing.

Underpainting—another form of drawing but done with a brush—can be made either in monochrome or an understated version of the finished color scheme, in both cases using paint well thinned with turpentine. If you find a blank canvas somewhat intimidating, you will find that an underpainting overcomes the problem by providing a "stepping-stone" from which you can build up the succeeding layers of color with confidence.

A monochrome underpainting should concentrate on the main masses of light and shade, as in the example illustrated, and a colored one should avoid bright and light colors, as you will want to build up to these as the painting progresses. Nowadays artists often use acrylic paint for underpainting, as this dries much faster than even thinned oil paint, enabling the next stage to proceed immediately.

A good general rule for oil painting—and a very old one—is to work "fat over lean." This simply means that in the initial stages the paint should be used fairly thin (diluted with turpentine only) becoming thicker and oilier as the painting progresses. Working in this way reduces the risk of the paint cracking as it dries out. If, however, "lean" paint is brushed over a layer of "fat" paint (containing a greater proportion of oil) what happens is that the lean layer dries first, and when the fat layer beneath it eventually starts to dry it contracts, causing the dry layer on top to crack.

Not all paintings, however, are done in stages in this way; many are completed at one sitting, with a minimum of drawing or underpainting or even none at all. This is known as *alla prima* painting, and is much used for landscape or quick portrait studies where the painter wants to record his impressions rapidly in a free and spontaneous manner. The paint is used thickly, with each color laid down more or less as it will finally appear. When oil paints are used in this way, the colors blend into each other, particularly when one is laid on top of another. This is a feature of *alla prima* painting, known as working "wet into wet," and was much exploited by the Impressionists, particularly Claude Monet (1840–1926) in his outdoor paintings. For anyone who has not used oils before, alla prima is a good way of starting, as it will give you an immediate "feel" for the medium and force you to work fast without being over-conscious of each brushstroke.

SPECIAL PAINTING TECHNIQUES

As has been mentioned, there are many different ways of applying oil paint to create particular effects. Some of these are used almost unconsciously, when the painting seems to demand a particular approach, while others are the result of careful planning.

The method called *scumbling* comes into the first

ABOVE This small painting was done by the *alla prima* method, with the paint used quite thickly and put down rapidly with little subsequent alteration.

The photograph (RIGHT) shows colors being blended into one another by working wet into wet. ABOVE a thin layer of transparent red paint is being laid over a dry layer of yellow. This is the technique called glazing, which gives an effect quite unlike that of one layer of thicker paint, as the color below reflects back through the glaze, giving additional brilliance.

FAR LEFT The paint surface here is an important part of the painting, the broken patches and restless texture of the thickly applied color enhancing the vividness of the subject. The paint was applied with a knife alone, and the detail, (LEFT), clearly shows how different is the effect from that of traditional brush painting.

LEFT Rembrandt used both glazing and impasto in his paintings. In *Woman Bathing*, the delicately glazed areas of flesh contrast with the bold brushstrokes and thick paint of the garment.

RIGHT Here scumbling was used to suggest the texture of the chalk cliffs. The paint was scrubbed on with a brush over dry paint below, and in places was worked in with the fingers. The foreground was put on rather dry.

category and simply means applying semi-opaque paint on top of another dry or semi-dry area of color in an irregular way. Part of the layer below will show through, so that a "broken" color and texture is created. This can be very effective for particular parts of a painting, such as skies, rocks, tree trunks, fabric and so on. Anything can be used for putting on scumbled paint —stiff brushes, a rag, or even the fingers—and the paint can be dragged, smudged or stippled.

Areas of irregular texture can be made by laying a flat area of color in opaque paint and then "blotting" it, when semi-dry, with non-absorbent paper such as pages from a glossy magazine. As you peel back the paper, it drags at the surface layer of paint and creates a stippled texture. This technique is called frottage.

A way of creating another kind of texture is impasto, in which the paint is laid on thickly, often with a palette knife. In the past, artists such as Rembrandt combined impasto with areas of delicate brushwork, pointing up the differences in texture between, for example, flesh and clothing. Today many artists use impasto as a

technique on its own, building up heavy layers of paint to make a raised and densely-textured surface. Special painting mediums are available which increase the bulk of the paint (see p. 259), and some artists even mix paint with sand for a rough, grainy surface.

Interesting effects can be achieved by drawing or scratching into a layer of wet oil paint to reveal another color beneath or sometimes the white ground of the canvas, as in the example illustrated. The implement used can be anything pointed, such as the end of the brush handle or a

knitting needle. This method is called *sgraffito*.

A technique that comes into the deliberate planning category is *glazing*, in which thin, transparent paint is laid over an area of already dry paint. Layers of glazes can be built up one over the other to create effects akin to the deep glow of wood that has been lovingly polished—but glazing is not a quick method as each layer must dry before the next is applied. Many of the rich, glowing colors used by artists of the past, such as Titian, were produced by laying thin glazes of brilliant color over an underpainting, and the luminous quality of the landscapes painted by J. W. M. Turner (1775–1851) are the result of layers of glazing over thick, pale impastos.

COMPOSING A PICTURE

The word "composition" has a slightly alarming ring to it—it sounds as though it might be an intellectual exercise quite beyond the capabilities of the ordinary person. This really is not so: composing a painting is mainly a question of selecting, arranging and rearranging, just as you might do when deciding on the decor for a room or when taking a photograph. A large, complex

These thumbnail sketches, of female figures in various poses against different backgrounds, illustrate the way in which some artists try out possible compositions for paintings. Such drawings,which can be done quite quickly and need be little more than scribbles, are an excellent means of working out the arrangement of the main shapes and the balance of lights and darks.

painting with numerous people and objects in it does, of course, need some thought; otherwise there may be too much activity in one part of the picture and not enough in another. But even here, it is less a matter of following a prescribed set of rules than of working out the balance of the various shapes, as in the case of planning a room—no one would put all the furniture crowded together on one side and leave the rest empty.

A "good composition" is one in which there is no jarring note, the colors and shapes are well-balanced, and the picture as a whole seems to sit easily within its frame or outer borders. Even a simple head-and-shoulders portrait is composed, and a vital part of composition is selection—what you put in and what you leave out. In the case of a portrait you will need to establish whether the person should be seated, and if so on what, whether you want to include the chair, whether you want the hands to form part of the composition, and

whether you want to use something in the background, for example part of a window frame, to balance the figure.

If you are painting a landscape you may think composition is not involved, that you are just painting what you see, but you will have chosen a particular view, just as you would when taking a photograph, and in choosing it you will have gone at least some way toward composing it. You may then find that you want to exaggerate or re-arrange some feature in the foreground, such as a rock or a tree, to provide extra interest, or alter the bend of a path to lead the eye into the picture.

There are some basic errors which should be avoided if possible. In general it is not a good idea to divide a landscape horizontally into two equal halves—the land and the sky—as the result will usually be monotonous. A line, such as a path or fence, should not lead directly out of the picture unless balanced by another line which leads the eye back into it. A still-life or portrait should not be divided in half vertically, while a flower painting is unlikely to be pleasing to the eye if the flower arrange-ment is placed too far down in the picture area, too far to one side, or very small in the middle, with a large expanse of featureless background.

In the case of interiors, portraits, still-lifes, and flowers, backgrounds can be used as a device to balance the main elements of the composition. Use part of a piece of furniture behind a seated figure, for example, or a subtly patterned wallpaper which echoes or contrasts with the main shapes and colors in the figure. In landscape painting the sky is a vital part of the composition, and should always be given as much care and thought as the rest of the painting.

Even if you are working quickly, it is often helpful to make some drawings, known as thumbnail sketches (though they need not be small) before you start on the painting. These may consist of just a few roughly drawn lines to establish how the main shapes can be placed, or they may help you to work out the tonal pattern of the composition.

A viewing frame is equally useful, particularly for landscapes painted on the spot. When faced with a large expanse of land and sky the problem is always how much of it to paint, where to start and finish, and how much of what you see will actually fit on the canvas. Anyone who takes photographs will be familiar with this problem: you raise your camera at a splendid view only to find that the

ABOVE The natural inclination when painting subjects like trees is to try and get everything in, but in this painting the artist has allowed the foreground trees to "bust" out of the frame, giving a stronger and more exciting effect.

polaroid camera; several photographs of the subject taken from different angles and with different backgrounds will give you an idea of how you can best approach the painting, and they will also help you to work out the balance of colors and tones.

RIGHT In this painting the contrast between the dark and light tree trunks has been emphasised by the use of very thin paint. The solid foliage of the evergreens draws attention to the slenderness of the foreground trunks and provides a counterpoint.

small section of it you can see through the viewfinder is quite dull and featureless. A viewing frame is simply a rectangular aperture cut in a piece of card—a good size is about 4½ x 6 in. (11.5 x 15.25 cm)— which you hold up in front of you to frame and isolate the subject. Once you have chosen the particular area of landscape that interests you, you can then decide how you want to treat it and how much re-arranging is needed to make an interesting composition.

A useful aid for indoor work is a

COLOR AND LIGHT

Color can be a very complex subject indeed—whole books have been written on color theory. Such theory is beyond the scope of this book, and in any case would be more likely to be a hindrance than a help to an inexperienced painter, but there are some basic guidelines which will help you to make a picture work, and there are also some terms which you will need to understand.

Color has two main qualities, tone and intensity, the first being the

darkness or lightness of a particular color and the second being its brightness. If you take a black-and-white photograph of a landscape composed entirely of greens, you will see that some appear darker than others—proving that a single color can have dark tones and light tones. In the same landscape, some of the greens will be brighter and more vibrant than others—in other words, more intense.

Colors which are opposite one another on the color wheel, such as red and green, yellow, and violet,

are called *complementary colors*. These can be used in a deliberate way to balance and "spark off" one another; for example, a small area of bright red in a landscape could be used to enhance and intensify a large expanse of green. The Op painters of the 1960s used complementary colors in a highly intellectual way: by juxtaposing complementaries of the same hue and tone they created restless, "jumping" effects.

Colors are basically either "warm" or "cool," and the warm ones will tend to "advance," or push themselves to the front of a painting, while the cool ones will recede. In general, the warm colors are the reds, yellows, bright yellow-greens, and oranges, while cool ones are the blues and colors with blue in them, such as blue-green.

Some blues, however, are warmer than others, and some reds are cooler than others. You can see this by placing ultramarine or cerulean blue (both quite warm) next to Prussian or Antwerp blue (both cool), and alizarin crimson (cool) next to cadmium red (warm).

You can make use of the "advancing" and "retreating" qualities of warm and cool colors in modeling forms and in creating a sense of space and depth. In portrait painting, for example, use warm colors for the prominent areas such as the nose, chin, and cheekbones, and cool colors for receding or shadowed areas such as underneath the chin. In landscapes, use warm colors in the foreground and cool, bluish tones in the background to emphasize the feeling of receding space.

There is no color without light, and the direction, quality, and intensity of light constantly changes and modifies colors. This fact became almost an obsession with the Impressionist painter Claude Monet; he painted many studies of the same subject—a group of haystacks—at different times of the day in order to understand and analyze these changes. You can see the effects very easily for yourself if you look at any scene—the view from a window or a corner of the garden—first on a cloudy morning and then in low evening sunlight. In the evening everything will suddenly become golden and a brick wall which might have appeared a drab brown in the morning may now be a bright hue of orange or pink.

Light is vital to a painting,

whether a landscape or a still-life or portrait study, and the way it falls defines the shape of objects and determines their color. Both photographers and painters of landscape know that the high midday sun is their enemy, as it creates dense patches of shadow and drains the landscape of color and definition. A portrait or still-life can also look flat, dead and colorless if lit directly from above, while a side light can suddenly bring it to life, creating exciting shadow areas of purple or green and vivid, sparkling highlights.

AERIAL PERSPECTIVE

This is a way of using color and tone to give a sense of space in a painting, and to indicate recession. It is particularly important in landscape painting. If you look at an expanse of landscape, such as one with fields and trees in the foreground and distant hills or mountains beyond, you will see that the colors become paler and cooler in the distance, with details barely visible. The objects in the foreground will be brighter and have much clearer areas of contrast, or tonal differences, which will become smaller in the middle distance and may disappear altogether in the far distance, so that the hills or mountains appear as pure areas of pale blue. It takes

some experience to use aerial perspective successfully; if you accidentally mix a rather warm blue on your palette and try to use it for the distant hills you will find that they seem almost to jump forward to the front of the picture. The same applies if you combine a pale color with a much darker one; there will then be a greater tonal difference than is actually present and the background will begin to vie with the foreground.

Aerial perspective can, of course, be either exploited or ignored. Sometimes, for instance, you might be more interested in creating a flat pattern or you might want simply to use areas of vivid color.

BELOW A scene such as this relies on some understanding of the laws of perspective or the effect of the high-perched buildings would be lost. When sketching out of doors, it is often helpful to mark in a horizon line so that the angles can be related to it; the eye alone cannot always judge such angles truthfully.

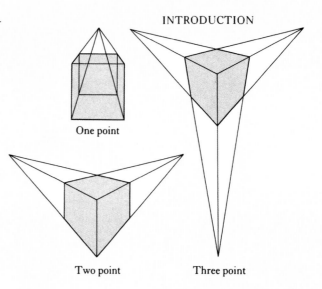

RIGHT One-, two-, and three-point perspective. In the first, only two planes can be seen, and thus the parallel lines have the same vanishing point. When three planes are visible, two separate vanishing points are needed, and if the same cube is seen from above or below the horizon the sides will also converge at a third vanishing point.

INTRODUCTION

One point

Two point

Three point

horizon line

LINEAR PERSPECTIVE

This, like color theory, can be a very complex subject, almost a science. During the Renaissance, when the laws of perspective were first being formulated in a systematic way, artists vied with one another to produce more and more elaborate perspective drawings; for example Paolo Uccello (*c.*1396–1475) made a study of a chalice broken down into a series of separate receding surfaces which is quite breathtaking in its intricacy. However, unless your particular interest is architecture—you might perhaps want to make a series of detailed studies of the interiors of churches, for instance—it is most unlikely that you will need to understand more than the most basic rules, which are helpful when faced with

the problem of how to make buildings look solid or how to indicate that they are being viewed from above.

The primary rule, which many people learn at school, is that all receding parallel lines meet at a vanishing point, which is on the horizon. It is easy enough to learn such rules, but far less easy to apply them. A single building has several different planes, or sets of parallel lines, and a group of buildings, such as a farmhouse with barns and outhouses, has even more, as the buildings are often set at random angles to one another. Where, you may ask yourself, is this horizon at which they will all meet, and how is it determined? This is dependent on your chosen viewpoint. If you are high up, on a

cliff or hilltop, the horizon will be level with you, so that you have very little sky and a large expanse of land or sea. You will be looking down at the group of buildings, and the parallel lines receding from you will slope up to the horizon. If you are at a low angle, perhaps sitting on the ground, the horizon, still at eye-level, will also be low, giving a large expanse of sky. The buildings will be above the horizon and the receding parallels will slope down to it.

In the case of parallels running directly away from you, the vanishing point would be within the picture area, but for different planes at angles to them it will be a hypothetical one which can be some way outside the picture area to the right or left.

CHAPTER THREE

Starting to Paint

If you have never painted at all, or if you have not used a particular medium before, the idea of making a start can be quite daunting. If you are intending to go to a painting class, it is less alarming, as you will be painting what is put in front of you to paint, and a teacher will be on hand to advise, but if you are working at home there will be a great many decisions to make. For instance, what will you paint, what size will you work, and how will you actually begin? This chapter provides some suggestions and guidelines to help build up your confidence and so increase your enjoyment of painting.

CHOOSING A SUBJECT

Many people seem to feel that, just as there are "proper" ways of going about a painting, there are also "proper" subjects. This is quite untrue; as we have seen, there is no way of applying oil paint that is more correct than another, nor is there any one subject that makes a better painting than another. Nudes, still-lifes, flowers, and landscapes are all types of painting hallowed by long tradition, but many artists have made fine paintings of just the corner of a room, a wall with a few flowers against it, or a single tree. Vincent van Gogh made deeply moving and expressive still-lifes from such subjects as a pair of peasant's boots or a pile of books on a table.

Still-life did not exist as a painting subject until the Dutch artists of the 17th century "invented" it. Nor was landscape, except as a background to a figure or group of figures, acceptable until the late 18th and early 19th centuries. In the past, the subject of a painting was largely dictated by the demands of patrons, but we have no such restrictions.

It should be said, however, that some subjects are more difficult than others, and it can be discouraging to find you have set yourself a task which your experience is not equal to. Portraits, for example, are particularly difficult. You have to cope with so many problems: how to render the color of flesh, the texture of hair and clothing, the way the light falls on the planes of the face and, finally, how to "get a likeness." If your interests do lie in this direction, you could start with a self-portrait, as in this way you will have total control over your "sitter" and can work at your own speed without feeling rushed and flustered. You will know your own face well already.

Still-lifes, flowers, and landscapes all provide good starting points, depending on your particular interests. Subjects for still-lifes can be found in most people's homes or the nearest vegetable or flower shop, and you can choose your own arrangement, light it in any way you want and take your time over it. In the case of landscape, if the weather is not suitable for outdoor painting, or if you feel shy about it, you could start by working from a photograph (but beware of trying to "copy" it in exact detail) or you could paint the view from a window.

CHOOSING A SHAPE AND SIZE

This may seem trivial, but in fact both shape and size have an important part to play in the composition and

ABOVE AND RIGHT
Domestic interiors have been a favorite subject with artists since the Dutch 17th-century masters. These two paintings, Van Gogh's *Yellow Chair* and Gwen John's A

Corner of the Artist's Room in Paris, although totally different in their treatment and handing of color and paint, both give a strong feeling of serenity, just as the Dutching paintings did.

treatment of a painting. A panoramic landscape, for instance, may suggest a wide horizontal shape which will enable you to show the broad sweep of the land as well as giving a sense of peace and tranquility. A single tree might call for a narrow vertical painting, while a still-life with a lot of objects in it could suggest a rather square one.

Size is a very personal matter: some artists work on vast canvases too big to fit in most living-rooms, while others produce tiny, detailed work on supports no larger than the average photograph. If you are working at home you are unlikely to want to work on a very large scale, and it is not usually a good idea to

Lighting plays a vital part in the arrangement of a still life, flower painting or portrait, and a subject can change quite dramatically according to the way it is lit. Back lighting (TOP LEFT) can be very effective for flowers, as the light will shine through the petals in places, giving a brilliant sparkle, with the front foliage and vase appearing very dark. Front lighting (ABOVE LEFT) tends to make any subject seem flat and dull, while side or diagonal lighting (TOP AND ABOVE RIGHT) will define the forms more clearly.

start very small. A good starting size is about 20 x 16 in. (51 x 40.6 cm), a standard one in which you can buy both boards and canvases.

Painting is rather like handwriting—people with large writing feel constricted if for any reason they are forced to write small, and if your "natural size" for painting is much larger than the support you have chosen you will soon find out, as your painting will seem to spread of its own volition beyond the edges. Until you have established a size which suits you, it is wise to use an inexpensive support, such as a piece of primed paper or cardboard, oil sketching paper or "canvas board." Hardboard is not recommended for early attempts as it has a slippery surface which can give a messy and unmanageable paint surface.

AVOIDING DISCOURAGEMENT

If your painting goes wrong at an early stage you are bound to feel depressed and discouraged. Various suggestions are given here which will help you to avoid or overcome the more common problems.

Tinting the ground

Starting to paint on a glaring expanse of white canvas can be quite daunting, but even more important is the fact that a white surface is also "dishonest," as it prevents you from judging the tones and colors correctly. There is very little pure white in nature, as white, like any other color, is always modified by the light or shadow falling on it. Also, no color exists in a particular way except in relation to the colors surrounding it. Thus, if you start a flower painting by putting down a bold brushstroke of pure cadmium red on a white canvas it will almost certainly be wrong, as the red you are seeing is actually given its quality by its relationship to the background, which may be neutral or even dark.

A method often used by artists is to tint the canvas in a neutral color, usually a warm brown or gray, before starting the painting. This can be done either by mixing pigment in with the primer or by putting a wash of oil paint, such as raw umber, heavily diluted with turpentine, over the white ground. Acrylic paint can also be used for this since it dries much faster than oil paint, and you could buy a single tube just for this purpose. But remember that acrylic paint should not be used over an oil ground; oil can be used over acrylic, but acrylic cannot be used over oil.

Preparation

Always start with an adequate drawing or under-painting in order to place the main design elements in the way you want them. Even a simple subject such as bowl of fruit can go very wrong if you fail to judge correctly the size of the fruit in relation to the bowl, or the bowl in relation to the table it is

A B O V E Although still-life and flower arrangements need not be elaborate, some thought is needed in the initial setting up if the foreground and background are not to become dull and featureless. Thumbnail sketches and polaroid photographs are useful aids in setting up an arrangement.

A B O V E The subject of this simple still-life was the artist's collection of assorted bottles, with the fruit used as a balance to the colors and texture of the glass. The lighting was entirely natural, simply the side-light coming in through a window, but the objects were set up with care so that the shadows fell pleasingly.

  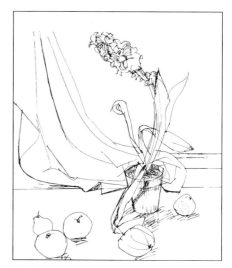

ABOVE These drawings show the different elements of a still-life arranged in a variety of ways. A symmetrical arrangement (LEFT) tends to be monotonous, but the arrangement, with the flat plane of the table angled away from the eye and a more varied grouping of the fruit (CENTER), has considerably more visual interest. The drawing of the flower and fruit with draperies (RIGHT) provides more linear contrast and a busier background.

standing on. You may be impatient to start on the real business—the laying on of paint—but it does pay to take your time at this stage, for it will avoid a lot of frustration later.

Keeping the picture moving

Try to avoid working in detail on one part of the painting at the expense of others. This approach can lead to a disjointed-looking painting, since you are more likely to tire of it half-way through. Generally, it is better to work on all parts of the canvas at once, so that you have a better idea of how one part relates to another in color, tone and texture.

Some artists, such as the English painter Stanley Spencer (1891–1959), successfully reversed this process by starting with a careful and detailed pencil drawing and then painting area by area.

There is theoretically nothing wrong with working in this way, but an inexperienced painter is unlikely to have the very clear vision of the finished painting which is required for such an approach.

In general, it is easiest to build up oil paint light over dark, as white is the most opaque color; so keep to dark and middle tones in the early stages, working up gradually to the light and bright tones and colors. Always try to see the background as part of the painting, not just as an unimportant area; even a plain white wall has colors in it, and a totally flat background can be used as a shape, to form part of the composition. Avoid getting bogged down in detail too early; fine lines, such as the stems of flowers or small facial details in a portrait, are best left until last.

Problem-solving

Even paintings by professionals go wrong, but the beauty of oil paint is that they can so easily be altered. If you suddenly notice that your drawing is incorrect and that you have quite misunderstood a shape or color, the best course is not to try to overpaint, but to scrape off the area with a palette knife and then repaint it. You may even decide to scrape down the whole painting and start more or less from scratch—this is often more satisfactory than trying to become so overloaded with paint that you are just churning it up by continuing to add layers, there is a useful method, invented by a painting teacher called Henry Tonks and named *tonking* after him. This is by laying a sheet of absorbent paper, such as newspaper, over the painting, rubbing it gently and

Different artists have different methods of making sketches, according to their individual style and what particular aspect of a scene they want to note and remember. Some do detailed wings in pen and ink or pen and wash, some make rough pencil sketches with color notes, while others use oil paint, which is an excellent sketching medium because it can be applied so quickly.

removing it; this takes off the top layer of paint, and leaves you with something similar to a colored underpainting.

USING REFERENCE MATERIAL

Painting is about looking at things—a good painter is constantly assessing objects and scenes with a view to translating them into paintings. This kind of analytical vision is largely a matter of habit and training—the more interested in painting you are the closer you will look and the more you will see—but few people have perfect visual memories, and for this reason artists often make visual references to use later on. Normally these take the form of sketches, and art students are always urged to carry sketchbooks at all times. Even a small, rough pencil sketch, sometimes with

notes made about the quality of the light and the colors in the scene, can be turned into a complete landscape painting, or sometimes several sketches are made for different parts of a planned painting. For instance, a view of boats in a harbor might call for a rough overall sketch and some additional, more detailed drawings of individual boats.

It is certainly a good idea to carry a sketchbook— it is good practice if nothing else—but it takes some degree of skill to produce drawings which are good enough to provide all the information you may need and it takes experience to know what it is you actually want to make such "notes" about. Photographs are now much used for this purpose, either as alternatives to sketches or as additions to them, and some

artists even use picture postcards, either to suggest a theme for a painting or to remind them of some forgotten detail. One advantage of photographs is that they can record fleeting impressions, such as the sparkle of light on water, or a dramatic purple-gray sky just before a storm. They are also very useful for portrait painting, since few people are able to stay in one position long enough for a complete painting to be done.

However, photographs should be used with caution, and treated as aids to painting rather than models to copy. Straight copies of photographs, either of landscapes or people, can look very dull and dead, missing either the sparkle of the original scene or the character of the person.

CHAPTER FOUR

Outdoor Subjects

All the paintings on the following pages, although very different from one another, fall into the broad category of landscape, a term which can really be used to describe any subject that is located outside the walls of the studio or home, even if it is a painting of a building or a single tree. Outdoor subjects such as these need not actually be painted out of doors—indeed many fine landscapes are painted in a studio—but at some stage in the inspiration and evolution of a good landscape, close observation of the outdoor world is vital. Outdoor subjects thus present challenges and problems very different from those of still-lifes or portraits: the painter of landscapes cannot arrange the subject and lighting as he chooses; he can only decide on a scene and then select what he wants to show and what he will leave out. One painter, for instance, may be particularly interested in the way the light falls on a particular scene, or in the ever-changing shapes and colors of the clouds, while another will ignore these aspects in favor of shapes or flat patterns.

A FARMHOUSE IN DERBYSHIRE

This painting was done from one of several sketches made on the spot. As you can see, the sketch is quite a rough one, but it provides all the necessary information as the subject is fairly simple and has been treated broadly, with little detail. When doing sketches specifically for paintings, rather than just sketching for its own sake, it is necessary to have some idea of how the finished painting will look, or you may find you have not made the "notes" you will need. For example, if the artist had intended to treat the buildings in a much more precise and detailed way he probably would have needed to make more sketches of particular aspects of the building.

The composition has been somewhat altered in the painting, to make the path more central, and the gatepost has been exaggerated to create a sense of space between it and the farmhouse. The composition is simple and effective, with the curves of the lane and fence leading the eye in to the buildings, which are the focal point of the picture. This compositional device of a curve leading in to a central point is much used by landscape painters. The horizon is quite high, with the sky broken up into a rough triangle by the lines of the trees descending on each side of the building, and the sky itself echoes the line of trees on the right.

The painting was done very quickly, almost as it might have been if done on the spot, and the hardboard used as the support was first tinted with thinned acrylic paint in a shade of yellow ocher. This colored ground has been allowed to show through in places in the finished painting, giving it a warm glow. This could not have been done on a white ground, as patches of white showing would be distracting and would throw all the colors off balance. Yellow ocher was chosen in this case because the painting was planned in shades of yellow and warm green, but for a different subject, a cool seascape, for example, a blue or gray ground might be used.

A charcoal underdrawing was done first to establish the main lines of the composition, after which thinned paint was used to block in the main areas. The paint became thicker as the painting progressed, with each area being worked on at the same time, so that the picture quickly began to emerge as a whole rather than as a series of bits—sky, foreground, middle distance, and so on. When painting the buildings, the artist applied

1

2

TOP 1 A rough underdrawing was done with charcoal to establish the main lines. Pencil could have been used instead, or similar lines drawn with a brush and diluted paint, but pencil tends to mix with and muddy the paint, while a brush drawing takes a while to dry sufficiently to enable the first layer of paint to be put on. Charcoal can either be sprayed with fixative before the paint is applied or "knocked back" by gently flicking with a rag to remove the surplus.

paint that was only roughly mixed on the palette, so that each brushstroke actually contained several colors. (Buildings can look flat and unreal if painted in too regular a way.) In the case of the trees, wet paint was applied on top of another still-wet layer (known as "wet into wet"), thus modifying the colors and giving an impression of leafy texture. Quite a limited palette was used: three greens, three yellow-browns, and one blue, plus black and white. Some artists disapprove of black and do not use it at all, but it is useful in landscape painting as it can be mixed with yellow to produce particularly rich greens.

BELOW OPPOSITE **2** and RIGHT **3** The main areas of color were quickly blocked in with thinned paint and a medium-sized flat brush. This shape of brush should not be used for scrubbing on paint—a round one is best for this—but for more sweeping strokes.

BELOW **4** The picture began to emerge as a whole entity, as paint was applied loosely all over the surface at the same time. The colors used became slightly modified and defined as the painting progressed, but the basic balance of lights and darks was established at this stage.

3

4

ABOVE **5** and RIGHT **6** The paint was used more thickly as the painting progressed, the steps at the side of the house being put in last with thick paint and a small brush. Details such as this, and the fence and gatepost, were left until the final stages, and add a crisp definition to the painting. Note how the yellow ground has been allowed to show through the loosely applied paint behind the house, echoing the golden color of the path and giving a unity to the whole picture.

5

6

MATERIALS USED

SUPPORT: hardboard 24 x 36 in. (60.7 x 91.4 cm) primed with acrylic primer ad tinted with acrylic yellow ocher
BRUSHES: flats and brights, numbers 5, 7, and 10
COLORS: ivory black, titanium white, permanent green, sap green, chrome green, yellow ocher, raw sienna, burnt sienna, and ultramarine

THE HEADLAND

This painting shows oil paint being used in a way more often associated with watercolor—in very thin washes. The paint was diluted so much that it was virtually transparent, and each wash was allowed to dry before the next was applied. Since oil paint mixed with a medium such as linseed oil can take a very long time to dry, turpentine was used in combination with the fast-drying alkyd medium, Liquin, which binds the pigment as well as thinning it; if turpentine had been used alone the paint would simply have dribbled down the surface.

If you look at the photograph of the scene you may see why the painter has chosen to work in this way; it is an extremely linear and angular subject, with the group of trees starkly defined against the sky and the very distinct lines of the cliffs converging at the bottom. Using paint thickly, in a more conventional manner, would have given an effect much softer than the one created in this picture.

Using oil paint in this way requires a rather deliberate approach—again much more like a watercolor technique—and the painting was begun with a very careful drawing in pencil. The color scheme is deliberately somber, with only six colors being used in all, but although the palette is so limited the colors are neither dull nor muddy, with the blue of the sea appearing quite bright in the context of the surrounding grays and greens. The sky, which the photograph shows as containing two distinct areas of tone, has been painted almost, but not quite, as a flat area, thus allowing the eye to concentrate on what is really important —the cliff itself. Painting the clouds as they actually appeared would have detracted from the effect rather than enhancing it. This kind of selection and rejection of elements is an important part of landscape painting.

The support chosen for the painting was a tall, narrow one, which suits the vertical emphasis of the subject. The surface of the canvas board shows through in places, and additional texture has been introduced by drawing with a pencil on top of the paint to define the lines of the cliffs, by scratching into the paint with a scalpel and by spattering thinned paint on to the board to suggest the appearance of the shingle beach.

A B O V E **1** A detailed and precise underdrawing was made with a sharp 3B pencil, after which the first diluted wash of olive green paint was carefully laid down on the area at the top of the cliff.

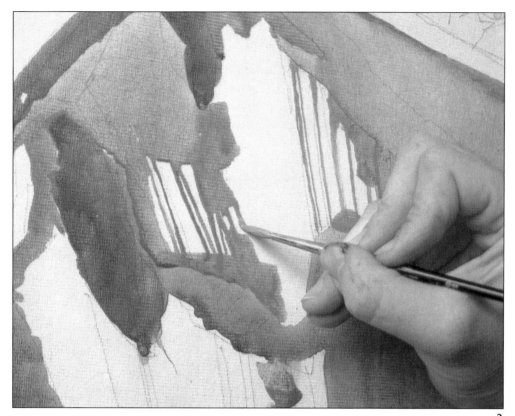

LEFT **2** More thinned paint was applied with a fine, soft brush, with areas of white being left uncovered. The lines were painted very carefully as this technique does not allow changes to be made. The pencil lines of the original drawing show through the thin paint, but this is not a disadvantage as in this case it adds to the effect.

BELOW RIGHT **4** The same pencil used for the original drawing was now used to draw into the paint to create the effect of the rocky fissures in the cliff face. As the paint is so thin the pencil marks in thicker paint would create indentations similar to those made by scratching with a knife.

2

4

LEFT **3** The trees and the wall below them were painted almost as flat areas with a fine sable brush. The painter could safely rest his hand on the painting while doing this detailed work as the paint in that area was already dry.

3

5

6

7

MATERIALS USED

SUPPORT: finegrained,
readyprimed canvas board
30 x 20 in. (76.2 x 50.8 cm)
BRUSHES: number 6 sable
and a number 6 soft synthetic
as well as two flat bristle
brushes, numbers 4 and 7
COLORS: titanium white, ivory
black, cobalt blue, Payne's
gray and yellow ocher,
thinned with turpentine and
Liquin

8

9

TOP LEFT **5** The support
has now been fully covered, but
areas of white have been left
unpainted, to be treated in a
different way in the final stages.
The edges which separate each
area of color from the next are
sharp and clearly defined at this
stage; no blending has yet been
done.

The detail (TOP RIGHT **6**)
shows wet paint being applied to
the dark area below the cliff. A
crumpled tissue was used to
create texture.

CENTER RIGHT **7** To suggest
the shingled beach, diluted
paint was spattered on to the
support with a stiff brush.

ABOVE LEFT **8** A scalpel
was used to scratch into the
paint, allowing fine lines of white
to show through, a technique
known as *sgraffito*.

ABOVE **9** This detail shows
thicker paint in a mixture of white
and Payne's gray being used for
highlights. The paint was then
blended with the finger.

IN THE GARDEN

This painting of a corner of a town garden, while falling within the general category of landscape, is actually more of an "outdoor still-life," and it illustrates very well the statement made earlier that subjects for paintings can be found virtually anywhere. If you put two or three people into the same garden and told them to do a painting of some aspect of it, they would probably all choose quite different ones, depending on their particular interest and way of looking at things. This particular artist chose a subject which was literally under his feet, because he was attracted to the colors and patterns of the flagstones, the lines of the pot and stakes, and the texture of the foliage.

The painting was done out of doors in circumstances of some difficulty—the weather, and therefore the light, was changeable—and the painting had to be completed under an umbrella. A comparison of the finished painting with the photograph shows two things: firstly how the camera flattens out both color and perspective, and secondly how various selections, rejections, and adjustments have been made by the artist in order to make a satisfying composition. The foliage in the background, for instance, has been reduced to a few telling brushstrokes (if treated in more detail they could have detracted from the foreground); the colors of the flagstones have been altered and lightened to allow the foreground foliage to stand out, and the line of the stake has been altered so that it neither cuts the pot in half nor conflicts with the lines of the flagstones.

The painting had to be done quickly as the weather was so unpredictable, and the composition was established rapidly by blocking in the main areas in thinned paint. This degree of certainty about the way a finished painting should look is largely the result of years of observation and practice, but even professional artists sometimes change their minds, and as the painting progressed it became necessary to make some alterations. In the first detail you can see that the line of the stake ran exactly parallel to the line of the flagstone on the right, and led the eye of the viewer out of the picture, which should always be avoided. Thus the artist decided to change it, bringing the stake further over. Once this alteration was done, the paint was built up more thickly over the original thinned color—in one place it was even smudged on with the fingers—and the paint

I

ABOVE I No drawing was done on the support as time was so limited, and the main areas were blocked in quickly with diluted paint. It became obvious very soon that the line of the stake would have to be changed, and this was done with masking tape, a useful addition to the painter's tools. Two parallel lines of tape were laid down to define the new line, and color was applied rapidly right over it. The tape was then removed, leaving a clear, well-defined line.

surface in the finished picture is richly textured, particularly in the foreground area, where the brushstrokes have been used in a directional way to suggest individual leaves.

Paint surface is extremely important and plays a more vital part than many people realize in the finished effect

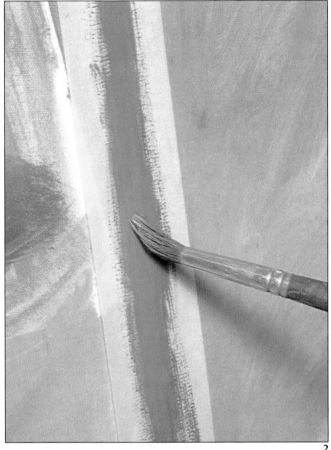

2

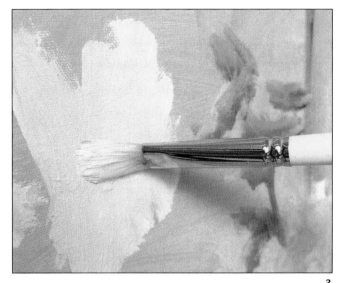

3

LEFT Once the underpainting was complete, the picture was built up with thicker paint, and more colors were introduced. The photograph (ABOVE) **3** shows a thick mixture of yellow and white being used for one of the flagstones over an underlayer of pinkish-brown. Other flagstones were painted in shades of blue and muted gray.

Thick paint is being applied (BELOW LEFT) **4** to define the rim of the pot, and the foliage is being built up (BELOW) **5** with areas of scumbled paint and thick brushstrokes of yellow-green.

4

5

of a painting; however well-chosen the colors and however good the drawing and composition may be, an unpleasant, slimy or churned-up paint surface will detract from the picture and may even make it impossible to see its virtues.

6

ABOVE **6** This detail of the foreground foliage illustrates the way in which paint and particular brushes can be used to create texture. The leaves here are suggested by short, curving brushstrokes, using thick paint over a still-wet layer beneath it so that the color does not go on totally flat but is modified by the one beneath. No attempt has been made to define all the leaves, and some areas have been left quite loosely painted, adding to the spontaneous and free effect.

RIGHT **7** The artist uses his fingers to smudge in highlights.

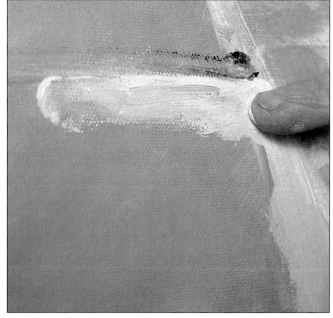

7

SEASCAPE OFF CRETE

His painting provides a contrast to that on page 295, as in this case the paint was used thickly on a very coarse-grained type of canvas called scrim. This is too flimsy to be stretched in the conventional way; so it was stuck down on a piece of hardboard with glue size.

The inspiration for the painting came from some photographs taken on holiday in Crete in blustery fall weather. The painting set out to recapture the look of a harbor in late evening in far from tranquil weather, and the way the paint has been used gives an added drama and immediacy, so that it looks as though it could have actually been painted quickly on the spot. The particular photograph used as a reference is quite dull, but the painter has drawn on his own recollections for the color scheme and composition.

The composition is a simple one, with the sea, the foreground and the background all being similar wedge shapes, relieved by repeated horizontal lines at irregular intervals. The buildings; little more than suggested shapes treated broadly and boldly, provide interest without in any way detracting from the focal point, which is the sea, shining with the reflected evening light.

Because scrim is such a coarse surface, it absorbs a good deal of the paint, which has to be applied thickly to cover it. Also, the paint covers such a surface unevenly, catching on some parts and sinking into others, effects which have been exploited in this painting to create an interesting, lively paint surface. Other effects have been used too: when painting the sea the artist squeezed white paint on to the support direct from the tube and then used yellow oil pastel in blobs on top of a layer of blue paint. The buildings were defined by drawing on to dry paint with a pencil, and some of the paint in the foreground area was wiped on with a rag. This is an excellent demonstration of the way in which different techniques and media can be combined to good effect. Some people feel inhibited about mixing media, believing that it is not "proper" painting, but it is a mistake to feel restricted to the contents of your paint box—if you want to mix paint with sand and apply it with your fingers, and it seems to work, then do so.

1

ABOVE **1** Paint was applied thickly with a loaded brush and scrubbed into the surface. The color used here was a mixture of white and cerulean blue, and the way in which the warm color of the ground has been allowed to show through in places enhances it, whereas if the ground had been white it might have detracted from the effect of the blue.

BELOW **2** The basic composition of the picture— interlocking wedge shapes—can be seen very clearly at this stage, when the hills in the background have not yet been painted. The sea has been blocked in roughly, with a modified version of the same color repeated in the sky.

2

3

4

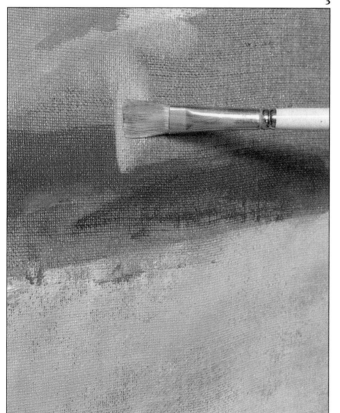

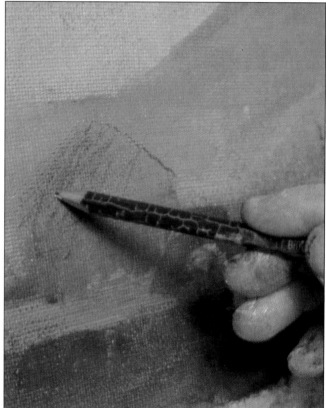

5

6

TOP LEFT **3** This detail shows yellow oil pastel being dabbed into the blue of the sea. This enhances the blue, since blue and yellow are complementary colors, as does the golden color of the ground showing through.

TOP RIGHT **4** For the foreground, a mixture of black and raw umber was applied with a rag in broad sweeps. Here, too, the golden color of the ground has been allowed to show through in places, modifying the darker layer of paint.

BELOW LEFT **5** The artist has allowed the color of the support to show through the blue for the sky by applying the paint quite thinly.

ABOVE **6** In the detail a pencil is being used to redefine the buildings, which had become rather amorphous in shape. The pencil also modifies and darkens the colors beneath, in the same way as would applying a dark glaze to a lighter color beneath.

7

ABOVE 7 The details show
white paint being squeezed on
to the support straight from the
tube and then smeared with the
fingers to blend it into the
surrounding areas.

FALL MISTS

This painting, done on the spot on a gray fall day, has a quiet harmony that captures the quality of both the type of landscape and the lighting. The light on days like this tends to have a flattening effect as there is no sunlight to cast shadows and create dramatic tonal contrasts, and distant objects look nearer for this reason—on a bright day this particular landscape would have had a totally different appearance. A gray sky and muted light can, however, provide a subtle but glowing range of colors, which have been fully exploited here; even the background was painted in pure, clear blues.

When painting out of doors, you may be tempted to ignore composition or think it is irrelevant—you are just "painting what you see," after all. This is not really the case, as composition is always important; indeed you will find you are almost subconsciously composing as soon as you start to put a line on the canvas, by selecting some elements, exaggerating others, placing the horizon in a particular position, and so on. Here the composition is simple but effective, and was established at the outset by a sketchy line drawing. The curves of the path, dividing the foreground into a series of triangular sections, lead the eye to the strong horizontal line at the base of the tall tree, and from this point the main lines are the vertical ones of the trees reaching up to the sky. All the compositional elements are important: the tree on the left, going out of the frame at the top, is balanced by the one on the right, while the gentle diagonal at the base of the right-hand tree breaks up the broad horizontals elsewhere in the painting. An interesting exercise is to block out one part of a picture and note how it alters the whole balance. If, for instance, you block out the right-hand tree with your finger you will see that it results in an unbalanced, uneasy composition, where the eye has "nowhere to go."

The painting was done rapidly, the main areas being initially blocked in in shades of ocher and gray to establish the middle tones. Quite a small range of colors was used—one green, one blue, one bright yellow, and four browns and ochers as well as white, as this subject did not require a great range. When working out of doors, it is a good idea to restrict your palette in this way, as otherwise you will be tempted to use too many colors, which can often spoil the unity of a painting.

1

LEFT **1** The broad outlines
were drawn in with a fine sable
brush and cobalt blue paint
very much thinned. This type
of painting does not require a
detailed underdrawing, but it is
essential to establish the main
elements of the composition.

BELOW **2** As the effect of the
painting depends on the
relationship of the various
broad masses of color, the
artist began to apply color
immediately, working all over
the painting and placing the
cool and warm middle tones in
relation to one other. These,
once established, provide a
key against which the darker
and brighter colors could be
assessed.

ABOVE **3** The dark masses of
the trees were painted next,
followed by the relatively vivid
green of the path (RIGHT) **4**,
which was carefully related to
the rich ochers of the rest of the
foreground.

3

2

4

5

SUPPORT: fine-grained canvas 30 in. (76 cm) square, primed with animal-skin size and an oil ground
BRUSHES: numbers 2 to 8 in both flats and rounds, with a number 4 sable for the initial drawing and the final details
COLORS: titanium white, lemon yellow, yellow ocher, burnt sienna, raw umber, alizarin crimson, cobalt blue, and viridian

ABOVE **5** The colors of the background were modified and "cooled" to increase the sense of space by making the background appear to recede.

RIGHT Finally, a small sable brush was used to paint the details of the distant trees, and the area at the base of the right-hand tree was darkened and defined.

GREEK VILLAGE

This painting was not done on the spot, but it is the result of much sketching and observation of a particular part of Greece, where the painter frequently spends holidays, and it captures the sun-soaked Mediterranean atmosphere very successfully. A series of drawings was made for the painting, together with color notes and photographs, so that the composition and color scheme could be planned and worked out from a wide range of reference material.

The painting shows a view from a window, a subject which often makes an interesting composition as the viewpoint is higher than the usual street-level one and tends to include more varied elements. In this case, the bird's-eye view of the rooftops provides an attractive contrast to the smaller rectangles of window frames and doors, and the straight lines of the buildings are balanced and enhanced by the curves of the trees, foliage-covered walls, and the vegetable patch in the foreground, which lead the eye into the picture. The taut diagonals of the two rows of steps give an effect of movement and rhythm to the whole composition, which is full of interest and detail without being in any way fussy—even the small figures and the chairs and tubs on the balcony play a part in the scene, but are never allowed to dominate it. The balance of lights and darks is particularly important in this painting, as the artist wanted to capture the effect of the bright Mediterranean light, which creates strong tonal contrasts.

The painting was completed in one day. The paint was used quite thinly to begin with and built up to a thicker and richer surface as the work progressed (this is the classic oil painting method known as working "fat over lean"). The quality of the brushstrokes is an integral part of the painting, and has been used in places to create textures and suggest forms, such as in the tree and the vegetable patch in the foreground.

The support was a fine-grained canvas, particularly suitable for a painting with areas of small detail and sharp straight lines, which would be more difficult to achieve on a very coarse canvas.

1

ABOVE **1** An underdrawing was done on the support using a small brush and cobalt blue paint heavily diluted with turpentine. Although the drawing itself was not very detailed, the painting had already been carefully planned, a necessary preliminary for a subject as complex as this one with its many contrasting shapes and tones. The artist then proceeded to block in the mid-tones, using thinned paint. Once these were established they provided a key for the lighter and darker tones. Another artist might have worked in a quite different way, doing a monochrome underpainting or charcoal drawing to establish the lights and darks first.

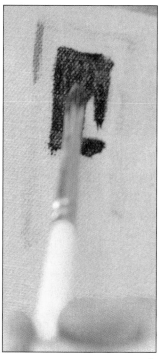

2

ABOVE **2** With the mid-tones established, together with the main lines of the drawing, the architectural details could be drawn in with dark paint.

RIGHT **5** The areas of foliage were then developed using viridian and raw umber for the dark tones and lemon yellow and cobalt blue for the lighter ones.

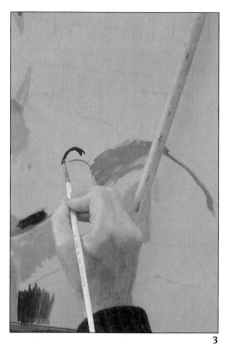

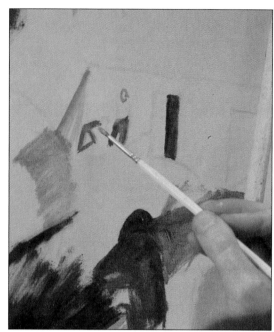

FAR LEFT **3** The artist rests his hand on a mahl stick to steady it while he draws a precise curve. The mahl stick is held in the non-painting hand with the cushioned end resting on a dry part of the canvas, or on the edge of it if the paint is wet. In a painting like this, careful drawing is essential—an inaccurately placed window frame or a crooked roofline would have a jarring effect, and spoil the overall harmony of the picture.

LEFT **4** A small round bristle brush was used to paint in the figures, giving detail without being over-meticulous.

3   4

5

6

ABOVE **6** and RIGHT At this
stage, with all the main tones and
colors established, the painting
has emerged as a complete
entity, whereas previously it had
been a series of disparate
elements. The feeling of warmth
in the grays and shadow areas
was achieved by mixing alizarin
crimson into the cooler colors,
while mixtures of white, yellow
ocher, Naples yellow, and burnt
sienna were used for the warm
browns and yellows. The colors
were then modified and some
areas developed and clarified,
with the paint applied more
thickly, and the final details such
as the chairs on the balcony were
added.

LANDSCAPE WITH PALM TREES

A photograph provided the main reference for this painting, and in this case it was quite adequate, as the shapes are all quite bold and clearly defined. However, the photograph is noticeably dull in comparison with the painting, which reflects the artist's interests and ideas in a highly personal way. The paint has been used in a way which creates its own excitement and drama, enhancing the spikiness of the trees in the foreground and the angularity of the cypresses.

One of the most striking features of the painting is the sense of depth and recession which the artist has managed to convey through the use of aerial perspective (see page276). The mountain in the background is painted in pale shades of gray with rather thin paint, while the foreground has much more tonal contrast, and the paint has been applied very boldly, with vigorous brushstrokes. Another device used to increase the feeling of space was to allow the main vertical shapes, the palm trees, to go out of the frame at the top and bottom of the picture, thus bringing them forward so that they exist on what is usually referred to as the "picture plane," while the cypresses are clearly further back in space, in the middle distance.

The composition itself has departed from that in the photograph in seemingly minor, but actually vitally important, ways. The uncomfortable central placing of the two trees in the photograph has been changed to place the tall tree slightly further to the right, with the front tree to the left so that it balances the cypresses, while the tree at the far right has been brought just far enough into the picture for it to read as a tree rather than as an anonymous and rather dull shape. The detail of the middle distance has been considerably simplified, and the foliage at the top left given a more definite and pleasing overall shape. When working from photographs, always allow yourself to change the composition in whatever ways you feel will benefit the painting, even if you have taken the photograph specially with a particular painting in mind.

The paint itself has been applied in a way which creates an interesting surface, an important aspect of any painting. A variety of brushes was used to create a range of textural effects; thick paint was drawn into with the handle of a brush and scraped into with a knife (the technique known as *sgraffito*); and paint was flicked on with a painting knife to suggest foliage and the bark of the palm tree in the foreground. The palette itself was limited to only six colors plus white.

1

2

TOP LEFT **1** A rough pencil drawing was done on the canvas, after which the painting was begun with very diluted paint, each area being developed at the same time. Using paint thinned with turpentine and just a little linseed oil enabled the main shapes to be blocked in quite quickly. At this stage all the main areas had been blocked in and the canvas was completely covered, but the shapes were as yet treated only as broad, flat areas, and the foliage at the top right-hand side had not been treated at all.

BELOW LEFT **2** The foliage was added when the paint for the sky was fairly dry, and a painting knife was used to flick on the paint. This gave an effect unlike any that could be achieved with a brush. It needs a sure hand to use a painting knife with confidence.

3

LEFT **3** The side of the painting knife was used to put on thick paint over a thinner layer below in a way that suggests the texture of the bark of the tree. Techniques such as this give a feeling of drama and excitement to a painting as well as creating areas of decorative texture. The thickly applied paint representing the trunk of the tall tree was drawn into with the handle of a brush (BELOW) **4** to suggest the spiky palm fronds,

4

5

6

LEFT **5** Paint was smudged
on with the fingers and a
small piece of rag in places
where a soft effect was
desired. The foliage was
further defined by using a soft
brush to work thick paint on
top of the still wet layer
below. This is called "working
wet into wet;" the top layer
will pick up some of the paint
from the layer below, an effect
which is exploited deliberately
in paintings such as this.

BELOW **6** Texture was added
to the tall tree and the
mountain was defined with
cool, pale grays to increase
the sense of space (cool
colors recede, while warm
ones come forward). The
cypress trees just in front of
the mountain were added,
being just suggested with one
brushstroke each, working wet
into wet so that the green was
modified by being allowed to
pick up some of the
underlying gray.

DERELICT PIER

This subject is an ambitious one in which accuracy of drawing is particularly important; so several careful pen-and-ink studies were made before the painting was begun. (Rain came before the one illustrated was completed—hence the splashes.) The main lines of the pier, with its railings, seats, lamp-posts, and buildings, were then drawn on to the support with charcoal. Note the diagonal line running through the tops of the lamp-posts, enabling the perspective to be plotted correctly. The drawing was tightened up and emphasized in places with thinned black paint and a small brush, after which the main color areas were blocked in with gray, green, and yellow ocher. The paint was initially used quite thinly, and applied with flat bristle brushes. Patches of the white support were allowed to show through in places, but the paint became thicker as the painting progressed, finally being built up into a rich scumbled surface which is extremely satisfying to the eye.

The composition is based on the relationship of the diagonal and vertical lines, with those of the railings leading in to the strong vertical formed by the outer edge of the building and then up to the opposing diagonal of the eave of the roof, which takes the eye back to the center again. The curves—of the arches, lampposts and seat arms—act as a counterpoint to the taut, angular shapes.

The color range is quite limited, but the colors nevertheless glow and shimmer with life, partly because of the way the paint has been physically applied and partly because of the way the colors themselves are

ABOVE RIGHT **I** The main lines were drawn on to the support with willow charcoal. This was then dusted off and the lines were strengthened with thinned black paint applied with a fine synthetic brush. (RIGHT) **2** The lines of black have been overpainted very little, so that they are still visible as an integral part of the finished work. The artist worked from several sketches, but developed the painting further, so that it is not identical to any of them.

LEFT 3 and BELOW 4 The sea was laid in first as a flat area of green, which was then given warmth and a feeling of light and movement by cross-hatching with brushstrokes of burnt sienna, white and red. There is a strong element of perspective in this painting, and the artist has used the railings against the large blocks of color as a visual device to lead the eye of the viewer straight into the picture. The brushstrokes are very much part of the composition, and have been used in a directional way to strengthen the effect; those on the seat follow and accentuate the form (BOTTOM LEFT) 5 and those on the railings are worked round rather than along the forms. This has also helped to suggest the texture of the old metal.

3

4

juxtaposed. The building on the right, for example, could have been treated simply as an area of flat gray, but here rich color has been introduced, with relatively bright patches of blue and yellow inside the arch, while blues and yellows recur on the front of the building, echoing the greens of the sea and the rich ochers of the pier top. Even the lampposts and seat arms have been warmed and enlivened by touches of muted yellow, which occur again in a stronger form in the area at the bottom of the railings, representing the reflected light from the sea.

5

6

MATERIALS USED

SUPPORT: smooth side of a
piece of hardboard 24 X 30 in.
(60 X 75 cm), which had been
sanded down before priming
to remove the shine. Some of
the sanding dust was left on
the board to provide texture,
and it was then primed with
white gesso primer
BRUSHES: Dalon synthetics
numbers 4 to 11, which the
artist liked because they are
less soft than nylon and give a
good, fine point for detailed
work
COLORS: titanium white,
yellow ocher, light red, burnt
sienna, ultramarine, sap
green, cadmium green, and
lamp black, which is warmer
than ivory black and gives
deep, rich tones when mixed
with ultramarine

ABOVE **6** The brushstrokes on
the building are straight, following
the vertical plane, and they have
not been blended or worked
together, so as to leave the paint
surface clean and fresh. Although
quite bright colors have been
introduced here, they have been
very carefully related to each
other so that no one color jumps
forward or assumes undue
importance. This is much more
difficult than it looks.

RIGHT The final touches
involved more work on the
building and the addition of a
scumbled texture over the whole
painting, heightening the
impression of old, crumbling
metal.

CHAPTER FIVE

Indoor Subjects

All the paintings on the following pages, whether portraits, figure studies, still-lifes or flower paintings, have one thing in common—they have all been done under conditions which are in the control of the artists themselves. A portrait or still-life can be set up in whatever way you want—you can usually dictate what your model should wear and what the background will consist of, and you can decide what objects you want in your still-life or flower painting.

All this can be an advantage, as it means you need not feel rushed, but it can also be a disadvantage, as that very sense or urgency you feel when confronted with a subject that must be captured quickly can often produce a more interesting painting. One way of artificially creating this sense of urgency, and thus not allowing yourself to fall prey to the temptation of niggling away at a picture, is to set yourself a time limit. Take as long as you like over arranging and lighting a still-life or doing preliminary drawings for a portrait, but when you start the painting, decide that you will complete it in one or two sessions.

The only drawing for the portrait consisted of a few lines and outlines made with a number 3 bristle brush and thinned paint, **1** after which yellows, blues, and warm red-browns were laid on, to be modified and defined later **2**. A rag was used to wipe off some paint from the forehead, cheeks and chin, **3** thus lightening, the highlight areas. It was also used to smooth the previously roughly-applied paint in the background, removing some of the excess. **4** and **5** Shadows and highlights were built up in the face and

PORTRAIT OF A MAN WITH A BEARD

This portrait was done quite quickly, in only two sessions, and has a fresh and spontaneous quality. Portraits often have to be completed in less time than the painter would perhaps consider ideal, since few sitters have either the time or the inclination to sit in one position for long periods of time. This particular portrait was actually done mainly from the photograph, which was freely adapted to convey the artist's own impression of the subject's coloring and character rather than being used as a "copy" to be reproduced in paint. He could, of course, have taken much longer over the painting since he was not working from a live model, but he preferred to simulate the conditions of working from life in order

hair, the paint being blended with a bristle brush and short, dabbing strokes. Because the painting was done on hardboard, which is not very absorbent, only turpentine was used as the medium at this stage, as the addition of oil would have made the paint too sloppy and caused it to dry too slowly. **6** Even so, by the sixth stage the paint had now become too thick and wet to work on satisfactorily, so the whole surface was blotted with newspaper, which removed the excess layer while still leaving a quite distinct image.

1

2

3

4

5

6

RIGHT **7** A piece of newspaper was applied, pressed lightly and lifted off, to remove some of the surplus paint. Blotting paper or toweling can also be used for this purpose.

BELOW **8** A rag was used to clean up the area on the face where the paint had become too thick.

7

8

to avoid an overworked, tired painting. It is often a good idea to set yourself a time limit in this way, both with portraits and landscapes, and to try to rely on your original impressions of a face or scene rather than peering at a photograph and trying to find the exact shade or line you seem to see in it.

The painting was begun with an underdrawing in neutral browns and blues, using thinned paint, after which layers of thicker paint were built up. The facial features were left quite undefined in the early stages, emerging only gradually from the broadly treated planes of the face, and the scarf was added later almost as an afterthought. All areas of the painting were worked on at the same time, the whole canvas being covered almost immediately, so that the relationship of the tones and colors could be assessed, balanced and altered where necessary. When the head was

reasonably complete the artist decided to lighten the colors of the background, which also gave him an opportunity to correct and redefine the outline of the face. The tones and colors of the flesh were then adjusted in relation to the new background, and the relatively bright colors of the scarf blocked in to balance them. In oil painting, almost any such alterations can be made, but it is easier to work light over dark because white is the most opaque color. If the painting had started with a light background, an attempt to change it to a dark one would probably have been unsatisfactory.

Because the painting was done quickly, there was no time to allow the paint to dry between stages, so a rag or a piece of newspaper was used from time to time to lightly blot the surface, removing the excess paint. A rag was also used to spread the paint in the background areas and to lighten

the highlights in the early stages. Such techniques are particularly useful when working on a non-absorbent surface such as hardboard, which can easily become so overloaded with paint that successive layers stir it up and muddy it.

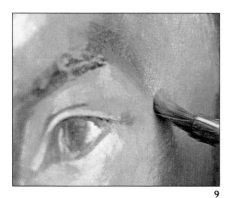

9

ABOVE **9** and RIGHT **10** Using a small brush, the artist begins to work on the more detailed areas of the painting to define the hitherto vague facial features.

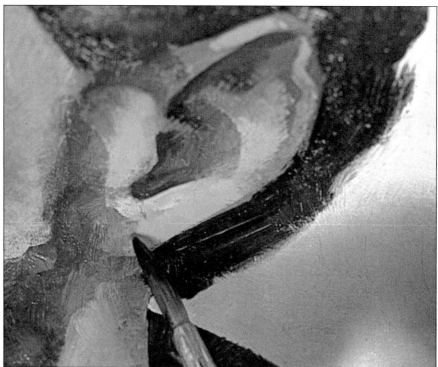

10

MATERIALS USED
───────────────

SUPPORT: primed hardboard 18 x 12 in. (45 x 30 cm)
BRUSHES: number 3 flat bristle and a number 5 round sable for the fine details
COLORS: titanium white, ivory black, cadmium yellow, yellow ocher, vandyke brown, cobalt blue, ultramarine, chrome oxide, and vermilion, and the painting mediums were turpentine and linseed oil

11

12

ABOVE **11** and **12** When the painting was almost finished it became clear to the artist that it needed to be lightened in tone; so he overpainted. the background, taking the opportunity to correct the outline of the face at the same time, and then adjusted the colors and tones of the flesh, blending the paint with light brushstrokes. He then altered the righthand side of the background again, so that from being the darker side it became the lighter one—almost white. The scarf, seen in the finished painting, was not originally planned as part of the composition, but the heightened tones and colors seemed to need a balance, and it was added as a final touch. This portrait provides an excellent example of the way in which oil paintings can be altered again and again without loss of quality.

OPPOSITE Earlier stages involved covering the face with a reddish glaze, giving a warmth and glow to the flesh. The effect of this is clearly visible in both the detail of the brow area and in the finished painting.

ANITA IN MINIATURE

This is a particularly interesting portrait because, although the treatment is bold and free, with clearly visible brushstrokes, the painting is very small, almost the same size as reproduced here. As this artist usually works on quite a large scale, producing a portrait as small as this presented something of a challenge, but she has met it with considerable success. It can be rather disturbing suddenly to change scale from a size which seems natural to one which does not, and this sometimes results in a different style being used, which the painter is not really at home with. In this case, however, the artist has managed to reduce the scale without detriment to her normal colorful and bold style.

As the portrait had to be completed quickly, a piece of cardboard was used for mixing the colors instead of the conventional palette, which had the effect of absorbing some of the oil and letting the paint dry more rapidly. Turpentine, used as the medium, also speeded the drying and provided a matt surface, which this artist prefers. Sable brushes were used in place of the more usual bristle ones in order to apply the paint carefully in small blocks, which were then blended lightly into one another. The colors have been considerably heightened and exaggerated, with the background appearing as an area of clear, bright blue and the face itself composed of separate, though related, patches of pure color. This type of color is known as high key, as opposed to low key, where all the colors are more somber. An artist sometimes makes a deliberate choice to paint a particular subject in a particular key, but often it is more or less an instinctive thing. Some artists always paint in a low key, even when the subject is colorful, and others automatically heighten all the colors. The brightness of this painting was deliberate, and is enhanced by the use of a pure white support, with no underpainting; the white is reflected back through the paint, giving the colors extra sparkle and translucency.

1

ABOVE 1 A careful pencil drawing was done first, and was particularly necessary in this case, since for such a small painting inaccurate drawing or a clumsy placing of the head in relation to the background could be disastrous. As you can see by comparing the finished painting with the photograph, the area of the pink blouse has been reduced to just two small triangles; these balance the bright colors of the flesh and lips. The area of background is greater on the left side of the face than the right, thus avoiding monotony. Even in a head-only portrait compositon this is important and should be planned at the outset.

OPPOSITE 2 The pencil lines, which were quite dense were rubbed down lightly with a rag before the paint was applied, to prevent the graphite dust mixing with and muddying the colors. The first flesh tints, mixed from a wide variety of pure colors, were then applied, and the planes of light and shade began to emerge. Note how the strip of cool, pale color down the side of the face—the reflected light visible in the photograph—prevents the similar tones of the background and the shadow area of the face from merging together. The area of blue was blocked in at an early stage so that the flesh tones could be related to the color of the background, and the artist put dabs of color and tone on to the unpainted side of the face to help offset the effect of the glaring white canvas.

RIGHT **3** and BELOW **4** The areas of pale flesh tones, mainly mixed from red, yellow ocher, and white are being applied to the neck and taken right up to the background. The paint was used fairly thickly so that it was opaque enough to cover the blue and give a clearly defined line. The bright pink area around the eye, applied with a small brush, reflects the bright rose of the blouse, as does the shadow under the chin.

3

RIGHT **5** The only parts left to be painted at this stage were the lips, the headscarf, and the hair over the forehead, with the hair being treated quite broadly and with little detail.

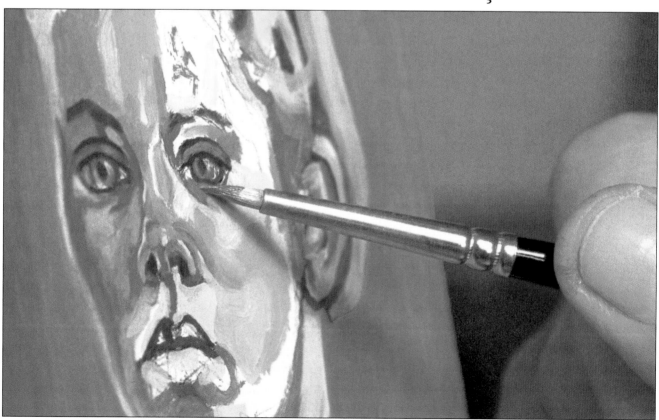

4

5

RIGHT **6** The lips were painted next, and then the patterned scarf, in which each color was carefully related to those in the face itself. When painting in such a high color key, much care and thought is needed to relate the colors to each other, otherwise there will be unpleasant discords. The hair was then modified in color so as to emphasize the bright colors of the scarf, and the fringe was defined with free, bold brushstrokes.

OPPOSITE Note how the whole portrait is "lifted" by the patterned scarf and red lips—all the colors suddenly appear brighter and the entire image is crisper.

MATERIALS USED

SUPPORT: primed hardboard about 6 x 5 in. (15.5 x 12.5 cm)
BRUSHES: round sable numbers 2, 3, 5, and 8, and the paint was thinned with turpentine alone
COLORS: titanium white, yellow ocher, Naples yellow, cadmium yellow, cadmium red, alizarin crimson, Rowney rose, violet, cobalt blue, ultramarine, cerulean blue, and terre verte

6

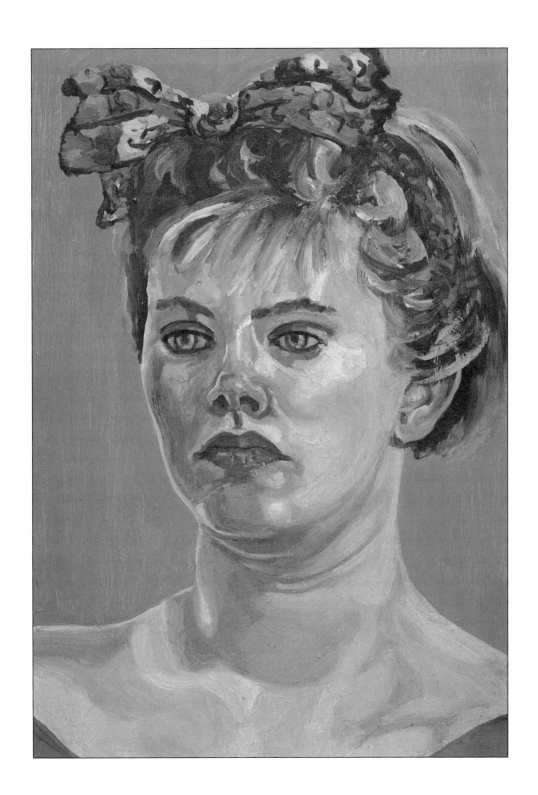

GIRL IN PROFILE

This painting was done in a quite different technique from that used in the other two portraits; the paint here is used very thinly, so that the early stages resemble a watercolor. The colors are also much less vivid, the emphasis being on the contrasts of lights and darks.

A profile is a difficult subject, and profile portraits are not often done, the three-quarter view being the preferred one. This is partly because a profile can look rather boring and unsubtle, and partly because, of course, it does not allow the eyes, the usual focal point of a portrait, to show. Here, an interesting composition has been made by placing the head to one side so that the back and top are cut off, with the line of the hair creating a bold curve to break up what would otherwise have been a stark vertical at the edge of the canvas. The artist has given the space around the head an importance of its own by painting it flat and allowing it to occupy almost as much of the total picture area as the profile itself. The picture can thus be seen as two interlocking areas (this is particularly noticeable if you look at it upside down). This concept is sometimes called "negative space," and can form a very important part in a composition, the "negative" space being used to balance the "positive" image.

The luminous quality of the shadow area of the face has been achieved by *glazing*, a technique of applying thinned paint in layers, one over the other. Glazing is a slow process, as each layer must be dry before the next is applied, but it is a particularly suitable technique for painting flesh, and was much used by the early painters in oil, such as Jan van Eyck. In this case, linseed oil with a very little turpentine was used to thin the paint for the glazes, but linseed oil is not actually the best medium for this technique. A special alkyd medium called Liquin is now manufactured and sold specifically for the purpose; it dries fast and binds the pigment so that the glaze, however thin, will stay where it is put, instead of dribbling down the surface of the support, as can happen with linseed oil.

2

3

LEFT 1 A simple but accurate line drawing was done of the profile, including indications of the shapes of the highlights on the cheekbone, nose, and chin. The background area was then blocked in with a thin wash of gray paint applied with a number 4 flat bristle brush, and a wash of burnt umber was used for the shadow under the brow.

TOP RIGHT 2 The warm tones were established next, using a mixture of yellow ocher and white for the hair, and burnt umber, cadmium red, and titanium white for the face.

ABOVE 3 The shadows around the eyes were painted with a smaller bristle brush, a number 2, each separate block of color and tone being carefully delineated.

1

BELOW **4** The skin tones were developed more fully by applying diluted paint in very thin glazes which allow light to bounce off the canvas and back through the colors. This produces a luminous glow which cannot be achieved with opaque paint. Glazes can also be laid over a layer of thick, impasted paint to modify the underlying color, a method used by both Rembrandt and Turner. Here, however, all the layers are thin; in the detail the texture of the canvas is quite clearly visible through the paint.

OPPOSITE As a final touch, fine strands of hair were added above the forehead and beside the cheek and chin, using a very fine brush and a mixture of titanium white and yellow ocher. Note how these few lines "lift" the whole portrait, hinting at the quality of the fine hair and breaking up the large area of background while allowing it still to exist as a definite shape.

4

MATERIALS USED

SUPPORT: small, fine-grained canvas board bought ready-primed, 15 x 12 in. (37.5 x 30 cm)
BRUSHES: flat bristle, with a small sable for the fine lines
COLORS: titanium white, ivory black, burnt sienna, burnt umber, yellow ocher, cadmium red medium, scarlet lake, and ultramarine. The mediums were linseed oil and turpentine, with a much higher proportion of linseed oil used for the glazing

1

2

3

NUDE AND SUNLIGHT

Figure painting, like portraiture, presents a great many problems, not the least being that of getting the drawing right. When faced with a complex subject such as this, you will find your task much easier if you make the most important decisions before you start work. First, decide which aspect of the subject you are actually interested in and then how you intend to treat it. Some artists will be most concerned with attempting to convey the sheer beauty of the human body and the marvellous and varied colors of flesh and hair, while others will be interested in the pattern that might be created by a figure against a background. Another artist might not be concerned with either color or pattern, and will aim at conveying the dynamic and sculptural qualities of the body, and the way the various planes and shapes relate to one another. Part of this decision will, of course, depend on the model. Some artists' models are beautiful, and cry out to be painted simply as lovely natural forms, while others are less conventionally beautiful but are interesting to a painter in more subtle ways.

ABOVE LEFT **1** A careful drawing was made with a sharp HB pencil, after which the shadow areas and outlines were strengthened with thinned black paint applied with a small brush. It is important to start with a good underdrawing or underpainting to establish the composition to your satisfaction. At this stage, you need to have a firm idea about how much of the figure you want to show, how it should be placed in relation to the background, and so on. It can also be helpful to make some small thumbnail

This painting shows one particular approach to the subject; here the artist's main interest was not in the body as such, or the colors of the flesh, but in the interplay of shapes and the relationship of lights and darks. While being quite distinctly a "figure painting," it is quite abstract in feeling, with the figure seen as just one element in the composition. The shadows—both that cast by the figure on the background and that cast on the figure by the window bars—have been given considerable importance, as have the shapes in the back-ground. Another artist, whose preoccupations were different, might have played down these elements, or even excluded some of them, softening the shadows

sketches first, before you start to draw on the canvas, as this is often the best way of working out a composition. **2** As the prime concern of the artist was the relationship of light and dark shapes, he painted in the dark areas first so that they provided a "key" for the rest of the painting, leaving the lighter and brighter areas white at this stage. **3** The shadow areas across the body were painted (with burnt sienna) before the flesh was blocked in, and all the other areas were then related to these.

and painting the background as an area of space.

The painting was begun with a careful drawing in pencil, in which the figure was drawn in outline. This is not a method recommended for a beginner, as a drawing such as this, although it looks simple, is the result of years of practice and observation. But a good underdrawing in pencil, charcoal, or thinned paint is important in a complicated subject, as without it you will find yourself having to make endless corrections, which may ruin the composition you were aiming at as well as giving you a clogged and overworked paint surface.

The dark side of the figure was then outlined more distinctly with black paint and a small brush.

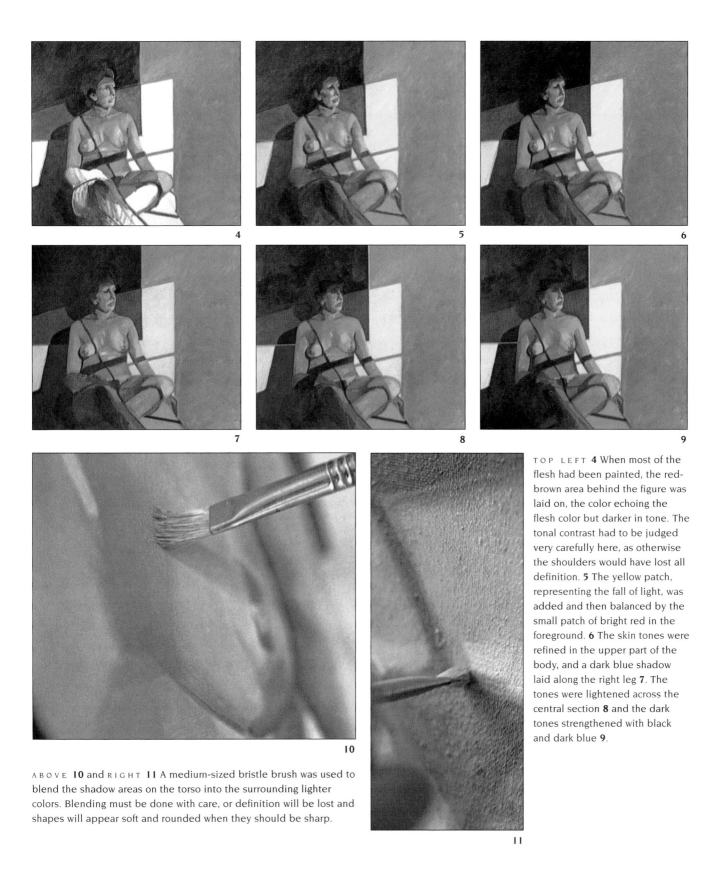

4

5

6

7

8

9

10

11

TOP LEFT **4** When most of the flesh had been painted, the red-brown area behind the figure was laid on, the color echoing the flesh color but darker in tone. The tonal contrast had to be judged very carefully here, as otherwise the shoulders would have lost all definition. **5** The yellow patch, representing the fall of light, was added and then balanced by the small patch of bright red in the foreground. **6** The skin tones were refined in the upper part of the body, and a dark blue shadow laid along the right leg **7**. The tones were lightened across the central section **8** and the dark tones strengthened with black and dark blue **9**.

ABOVE **10** and RIGHT **11** A medium-sized bristle brush was used to blend the shadow areas on the torso into the surrounding lighter colors. Blending must be done with care, or definition will be lost and shapes will appear soft and rounded when they should be sharp.

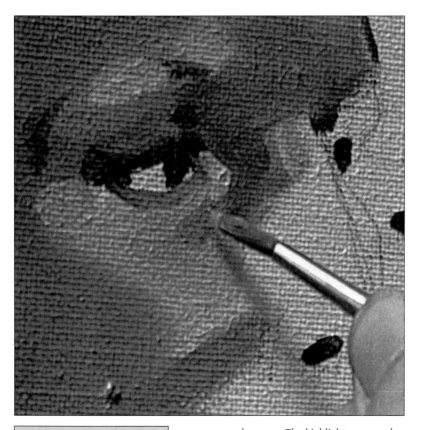

SUPPORT: cotton duck, stretched and primed, 36 x 20 in. (90 x 76 cm)
BRUSHES: two number 6 bristle flats, a number 6 round sable and a 1-in. (2.5-cm) housepainter's brush for the background areas
COLORS: ivory black, titanium white, burnt sienna, raw sienna, raw umber, burnt umber, cadmium yellow, yellow ocher, ultramarine, and vermilion. The medium was turpentine alone

ABOVE and RIGHT The highlight areas and facial details were painted with a fine sable brush and a mid-tone was blended between the shadow and highlight areas. Facial details should be left to a late stage in a figure painting, when you are quite sure no alterations have to be made to the drawing and composition.

DIANA

This full-length portrait, or "clothed figure study," was done partly from life and partly from the photograph. A comparison of the finished painting with the photograph is particularly interesting in this case as it shows how much the artist has simplified the subject in order to deal with what he personally found interesting—the figure itself and the richly glowing blues, violets, and orangey-browns. Another artist painting the same subject might have treated it in a quite different way, perhaps including the view through the window, the pattern on the sitter's blouse, and the details on the cupboard, thus making a much busier composition, but here all the emphasis is on the figure itself, with the background areas treated very sketchily so that they do not compete with the main image.

Color is the dominant aspect of this painting, and the artist has started to place the colors immediately, with only the minimum of underdrawing, using thinned paint in shades of violet and cobalt blue. With the vivid violet of the blouse established, the canvas was then completely covered with thin paint, the color of the background being more or less that which appears in the finished painting. The background paint was left thin, but the figure itself was built up in thicker paint, and in places the *sgraffito* technique—drawing or scratching into the paint with a knife or brush handle— was used to remove paint from the highlight areas, allowing the white ground to show through.

The composition is a simple one, as befits the subject, with the figure itself placed centrally but made to appear less symmetrical by the placing of the unequal shapes on left and right—the window and cupboard. The image has been given movement and interest by the diagonals formed by the bottom of the window frame, the skirting board, and the top and bottom of the cupboard, the latter two leading the eye in to the figure. The angles literally point to the figure so that its central position, which might have resulted in an unfocused or flat painting, is quite acceptable. The bottom corner of the window and the top corner of the cupboard form a triangle with the light reflected from the top of the jeans, providing depth. If the background had been on a flat plane with the skirting board as a horizontal the effect might have been monotonous.

FAR LEFT **1** The artist began to lay the color on immediately, using paint very much diluted with turpentine so that it would dry quickly. Marking in the vertical and horizontal lines for the cupboard and background helped him to position the figure correctly.

LEFT **2** As soon as the whole canvas was covered with paint the artist began to work on the highlights to define and sharpen the forms.

2

RIGHT **3** Here a painting knife is being used to scrape back to the white surface of the canvas.

BELOW RIGHT **4** The arm has now been more fully modeled, with a dark line of shadow down the outside, and a brush handle is being used to draw into it. Some of the purple color of the blouse has been repeated on the inside of the arm and then scraped away, leaving just enough to suggest the reflected color in the shadow.

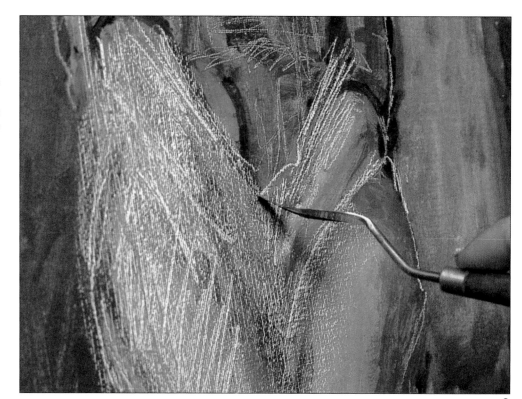

3

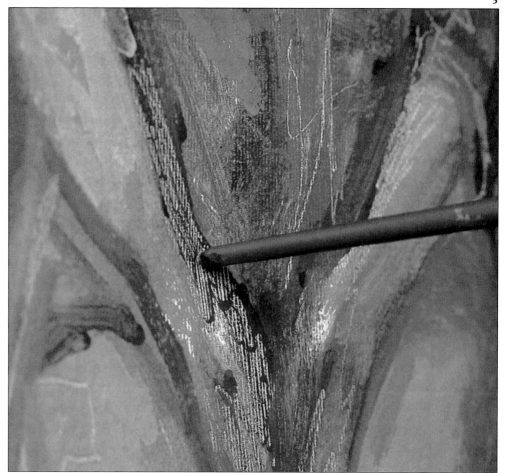

4

5

6

LEFT **5** The color of the blouse and jeans is vitally important to this painting, and the artist has chosen to simplify by ignoring the pattern on the blouse (visible in the photograph) so that it stands as an area of vibrant blue. However, it was not applied asjust one color; mid and dark purple were used for the shadow areas and bright blue for the highlights.

BELOW LEFT **6** Shadows nearly always have a color of their own rather than being simply a darker shade of the highlight color.

RIGHT **7** The face, like the clothing, has been built up in thick paint, freely but carefully applied so that the features are distinct but not over-meticulous. Little blending has been done, but because the artist is working wet into wet the colors are modified by the process of laying one on top of another. The line of blue on the right, representing the reflection from the blouse, has been left quite distinct.

OPPOSITE The finished painting shows how the figure has been given solidity by the use of thick paint and strong tonal contrasts, while the background has been left as areas of quite thin and transparent paint. Although there is little detail in the background, it is not flat and uninteresting; different colors have been used to echo and harmonize with those of the figure itself.

MATERIALS USED

SUPPORT: bought, ready-primed canvas 24 x 18 in. (61 x 46 cm)
BRUSHES: a selection of bristle and synthetic, a flat bristle being used for the background and small, round synthetics for the face and details of the clothing
COLORS: titanium white, cobalt blue, cerulean blue, cobalt violet, light red, alizarin crimson, yellow ocher, burnt sienna and raw umber. No medium was used except in the early stages, where the paint was thinned with turpentine

TEA-CADDY ON A WINDOW SILL

This small, quietly harmonious painting, with its limited range of colours and simple subject, provides a contrast with the one on page 356, where the approach is quite different. It also illustrates the way in which color and composition can be used quite deliberately to create mood: here there are no jarring compositional elements and no bright or discordant colors, but the effect is far from dull—just pleasantly peaceful.

Most people have one or two items about their homes that seem to suggest an idea for a painting, and in this case the artist was attracted to the swelling curves of the pot and its decorative motif. In order to highlight these qualities, he chose to make the composition a geometric one, in which the horizontals and verticals of the window frame and shutter act as a foil for the curved and rounded shapes. The composition is very carefully balanced, with the strip of blue-gray in the foreground just slightly narrower than the window sill above, and the rectangle on the right large enough to be "read" as the view through the window but not so large as to dominate the painting. The verticals of the window frame have been carefully planned so that they do not interfere with the dominant shapes of the pot and bowl, and the slanting shadows on the left, which appear in the photograph as very distinct areas of tone, are merely hinted at by a very slightly darker color at the top left.

The paint has been applied very carefully and meticulously, with sable brushes used to build up thin layers, and the support, a fine-grained canvas, was chosen as particularly suitable for this kind of painting. For a picture like this it is important that the straight lines should really be straight—an accidentally slanting vertical line, for example, would provide just the jarring element the artist has been at pains to avoid—so masking tape was used to aid the process. At one time such techniques were considered rather "mechanical," and frowned upon, but it is extremely difficult to draw a straight line freehand, let alone paint one with a brush, and there is no reason why masking tape or rulers should not be used.

The range of colors used was deliberately very small— just two blues, a green, gray, black, and yellow. It can be a useful discipline to limit your colors in this way, choosing just one or two colors and their complementaries (blue and yellow, as here, or red and green) plus grays and

TOP 1 and ABOVE 2 As the composition is so somple, no underdrawing was necessary. Instead, the main elements were quickly blocked in, using thin paint and a sable brush, in more or less the colors that appear in the finished painting.

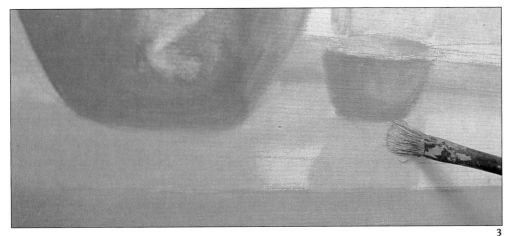

LEFT **3** At this stage a bristle brush was used, as the paint was rather thicker (though still relatively thin). The blue of the pot was built up using a mixture of ultramarine and white, with white and Payne's gray used for the window sill. Payne's gray is a useful and versatile color, with a slight mauvish tinge. Here it appears quite warm in relation to the deep blue. A mixture of black and white would have given a much less "alive" quality.

3

LEFT **4** Masking tape was applied to the line which separates the edge of the window frame from the little rectangle of landscape beyond. This allowed the paint to be applied quite freely on the window-frame area.

BELOW LEFT **5** The tape was then lifted off, leaving a clean, straight edge. To use this method successfully the paint must be quite thin and at least semi-dry; otherwise the tape, when lifted off, will take the top layer of paint with it.

4

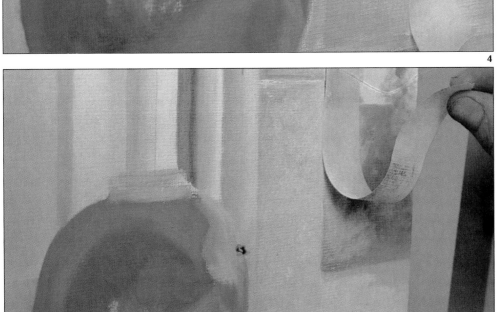

browns. It may cut down your choices, but this can also be an advantage as you will have fewer to make, and you may find that your painting achieves a harmony and unity that it might not have had with a whole range of colors at your disposal. It will also teach you far more about mixing colors than reading a, whole book on the subject.

5

RIGHT **6** and BELOW RIGHT
7 At this stage, several thin
layers of paint had been built up
one over the other, but the
details, which give a crisp
definition to the finished
painting, had not been added. In
the detail (RIGHT) a small sable
brush is being used to paint the
fine lines and small cracks at the
bottom of the shutter. If you look
at the finished painting you will
see that this delicate diagonal
line is actually vital to the
composition, leading the eye to
the pot and bowl, which are the
focal points.

OPPOSITE The brickwork was
painted in a mixture of Payne's
gray, yellow ocher, and white,
with viridian and white used for
the mini-landscape through the
window. Great care must be
taken with an area such as this; if
the tonal contrast were too great
or the colors too bright the
landscape would "jump" forward,
assuming too much visual
importance and conflicting with
the foreground. Viridian, being a
cool, rather blue green, is useful
for receding backgrounds.

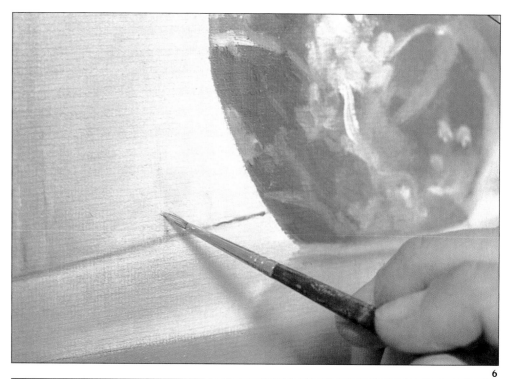

6

7

MATERIALS USED

SUPPORT: small, ready-
primed, fine-grained canvas
only 12 x 10 in. (30.5 x 25.4 cm)
BRUSHES: small sable and a
number 8 round bristle
COLORS: titanium white, ivory
black, Payne's gray, yellow
ocher, cadmium yellow pale,
viridian, ultramarine, and
Prussian blue

STILL-LIFE WITH WATERMELON

This still-life, while very different from the one shown on page 349 in its use of thick paint and bright colors, has a rather similar atmosphere of simple, quiet harmony. One of the most difficult aspects of still-life painting is deciding on the initial arrangement; it is only too easy to buy up a greengrocer's entire stock and then find yourself unable to arrive at a satisfactory way of arranging the different elements, or to rush around the house collecting bowls, plates, and vases which, when placed together, don't seem to add up to anything you want to paint. Here, as can be seen in the photograph, the artist has chosen a simple arrangement, but one in which the shapes are balanced very carefully.

The composition of the painting is based on a triangle with the point at the top left, and the circular shapes of the plate and half melon intersecting at different angles. The smaller piece of melon echoes the triangle, while the strawberries in the foreground both break up the area of white space and give a feeling of solidity by establishing the plane on which they rest. If you mask them out with your finger you can see how drastically the composition would be weakened and how the main elements would then appear to float in space. The artist has chosen to ignore the line created by the back edge of the table, treating the table top and background as a flat area of "negative space;" treating the table and wall as separate planes would have detracted from the composition and reduced the importance of the main shapes, which appear almost as though "carved out" of the space.

A variety of painting techniques has been used to create an interesting paint surface, the first step being a colored underpainting in very washy paint, after which areas were built up and defined in much thicker paint. The watermelon was given texture by spattering paint on to the surface from a stiff-haired brush; a pencil was used to draw into the fruit; and the white background is very slightly textured with just-visible brushstrokes.

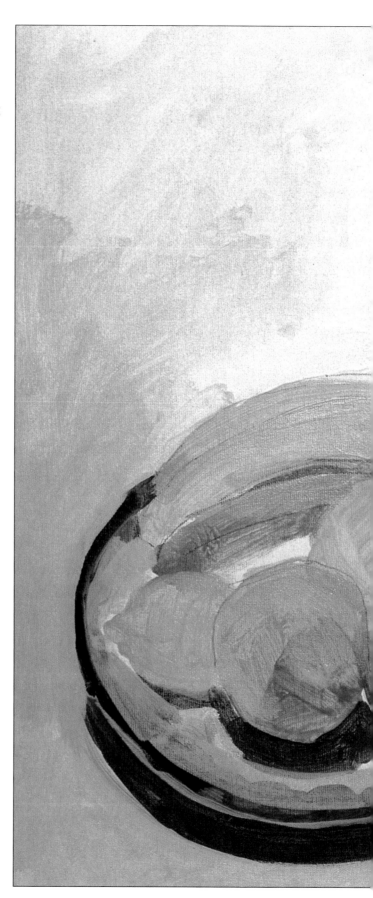

RIGHT **I** A faint underdrawing was done with pencil to position the main elements of the composition, which were then blocked in with heavily-diluted paint.

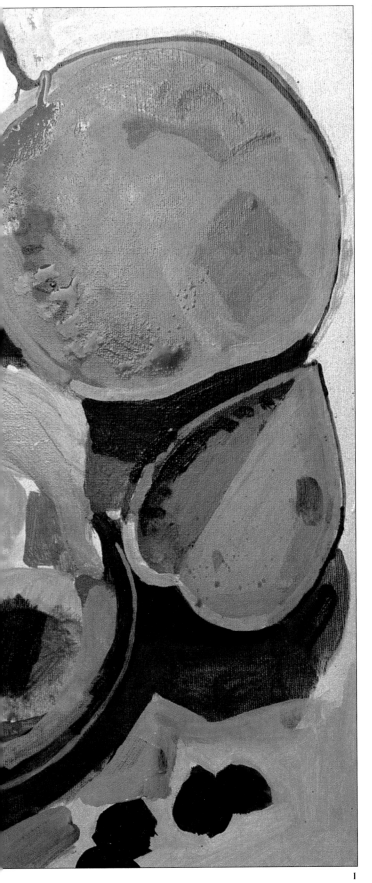

1

2

3

TOP RIGHT **2** and ABOVE **3**
As soon as the underpainting
was dry the artist began to
define the separate pieces of
fruit, building up the highlights
in thick, juicy paint.

The artist then drew into the dry paint with a pencil, OPPOSITE 4 a technique which has a dual function in this case as it gives texture and visual interest to the fruit as well as taking down the tones without the necessity for overpainting.

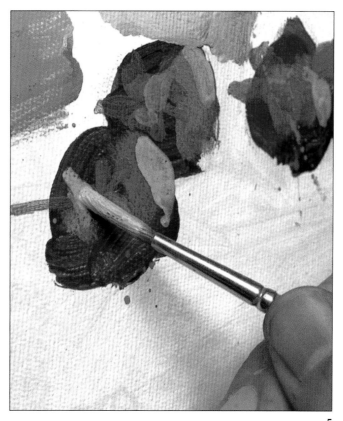

5

LEFT 5 Until now the strawberries had been left as just bold brushstrokes of dark red, but here the artist has given them shape and form, painting the highlights in a light pink and the leaves and stems in bright green.

BELOW 6 The final touch was to modify the shapes by working back into them with white paint and to paint the shadows in blue-gray, clearly outlined on the white background and establishing the plane of the table top.

6

RIGHT **7** The watermelon required special treatment, as the texture is an important element of the painting. The artist has chosen a technique he frequently uses—spattering paint from a stiff-haired brush (a toothbrush is often used for this purpose). In order not to splash paint on the rest of the painting he has cut a mask from newspaper, leaving exposed only those areas to be textured. Two tones were used for the spattering, one lighter and one darker than the mid-tone of the underpainting, the paler one echoing the highlights on the strawberries.

BELOW RIGHT **8** The tones and colors were chosen with great care as they had to be light or dark enough to show up, but not so sharply contrasting as to "jump" off the surface.

7

OPPOSITE In the finished painting the pencil drawing is still just visible on the banana and the apple, and the same technique has been used on the smaller piece of watermelon and on small areas of the shadow under it and the plate. It is touches such as these that give a painting that special "something," creating extra interest and liveliness; but they should never be allowed to become too important— special techniques are tools, not ends in themselves.

MATERIALS USED

SUPPORT: bought, ready-primed canvas board 20 x 16 in. (51 x 40 cm)
BRUSHES: number 12 white bristle and a number 4 hog's hair, with a 1-in. (2.5-cm) housepainting brush used for the spattering
COLORS: titanium white, yellow ocher, vermilion, cadmium red, cadmium yellow, sap green, cobalt blue and Payne's gray, a range consisting almost entirely of good, strong primaries

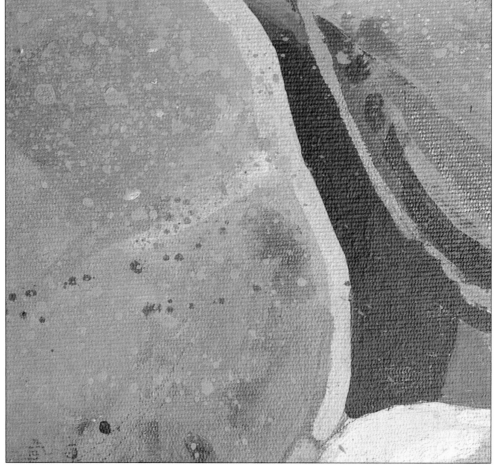

8

FLOWERS ON A WINDOW SILL

Although you would not think it from looking at the painting, this is actually a very difficult subject, presenting a good many problems. The main one is how to deal with the picture planes—the foreground and the space beyond it—in such a way as to create a feeling of space and recession while still retaining the unity of composition which is the hallmark of a successful painting. If the background is allowed to recede too much it will run the risk of becoming dull, but if it comes forward too much it will overwhelm the foreground. The foreground itself has to be given much thought too; otherwise the vase of flowers, which is the focal point, could assume too little importance, and not be strong enough to balance the landscape beyond. Here the artist has solved all the problems very cleverly; the foreground has been given extra importance and interest by the inclusion of the window blind and curtain on one side and the top of a chair on the other, so that an interesting composition exists even without the buildings in the background. The hill, village, and mountains beyond have been allowed to recede just a little so that they read as a separate and more distant picture plane, but they are still very definitely part of the painting, a landscape in themselves, neatly framed by the verticals of the window. The artist has been lucky, as the hilly terrain has provided a landscape that fits the window; a flatter view would have necessitated a quite different treatment in terms of composition.

The colors used for the landscape echo the deep blues of the vase and cushion, but are slightly nearer one another in tone so that they do not come forward and fight with the foreground. As he worked, the artist had frequently to half-close his eyes, which makes it easier to assess tonal contrasts, and to make small adjustments. Although the colors are vivid and the tonal contrasts bold, the paint itself has been used fairly thinly, in a technique akin to that of watercolor, with small areas of unpainted white canvas left showing in the finished picture. This has given the painting a fresh, sparkling appearance, unlike that achieved by areas of applied white (though there are such areas too). This lively, spontaneous effect is enhanced by the quite rough and sketchy treatment of the window frame and sill, and it is interesting to compare this with the painting on pages 346 to 349, in which the window frame has been treated in a very much more detailed and deliberate fashion.

1

2

TOP **1** This is a complex subject, in which the correct placing of the verticals and horizontals is just as important as the bowl of flowers and the chair top; so a preliminary pencil drawing was made on the canvas to position all the elements in relation to each other. The main shapes were then blocked in in thin color, the window frame being laid down first, with the bowl and chair painted over the resulting grid. This simple device of overlapping also serves to create depth. At this stage the background has been left as an undefined area of gray-blue in a midtone which will act as a key for the more specific tones and colors to be added later The dark greens of the leaves (ABOVE) **2** provide the key for the darker tones of the foreground.

3

LEFT **3** Once the tones of the foreground were established, the artist began to work on the buildings in the landscape, carefully relating the shapes and colors to those in the foreground.

Here yellow ocher is being applied thinly to the roofs, and the row of cypress trees has already been painted, echoing and balancing the leaves on the flowers.

4

5

ABOVE **4** and RIGHT **5** Now the artist works on the flowers, deepening the greens, heightening the reds and yellows, and at the same time deepening the blue of the vase. Small areas of the white canvas hae been left unpainted, giving a sparkling effect to the leaves and flowers.

RIGHT **6** This detail of the flowers and leaves against the background buildings shows the way the greater tonal contrasts make the flowers stand out just enough to be read as being on a nearer plane. White paint has been applied to the tops of the flowers where they catch the light.

OPPOSITE The artist worked over all the areas of the painting at the same time, moving from foreground to background and constantly making small adjustments. The final touches were the fine lines of white to indicate the fold of the curtain on the left, and the addition of a cushion to the chair. This forms a triangle just intersecting the horizontal of the window sill.

MATERIALS USED

SUPPORT: bought canvas board 20 x 16 in. (51 x 40 cm)
BRUSHES: bristle, number 12 flat and number 6 filbert. Turpentine was used to dilute the paint in the early stages
COLORS: titanium white, vermilion, cadmium red, cobalt violet, raw umber, Indian red, yellow ocher, chrome green, oxide of chromium, ultramarine blue, and cerulean blue. (Vermilion is a very expensive color, but is occasionally necessary for a subject like this, which relies on vivid and pure colors)

GERANIUM IN A POT

Some people regard flower painting as a rather limited branch of art, but there is no reason for this attitude, as there are almost as many ways of treating a flower painting as there are of treating a landscape or portrait. Flowers can be painted outdoors as part of a landscape, indoors as part of a still-life, or simply by themselves, like the illustrations to natural history books. In the previous painting, the flowers were only one element in a busy composition, while here one simple bloom in an undecorated pot forms the whole painting.

The problem with flowers is the same as with still-life—how to make an interesting and well-balanced arrangement that you can translate into paint without getting too bogged down in the minute details. Artists of the past, particularly the Dutch 17th-century masters, tended toward very elaborate arrangements with many different blooms, often in intricate and beautiful porcelain vases, which were really exercises in the minute depiction of fine detail, but this painting demonstrates how a simple subject can make an exciting painting.

As can be seen from the photograph, the artist has considerably exaggerated the angle of the flower head and the length of the stalk in order to give a diagonal emphasis to the subject, and has strengthened this by means of the slightly curving diagonal lines in the background and on the slanting edge of the skirting board. Placing the pot below eye-level has allowed the rim to be shown as a definite curve and the shadow to assume importance as part of the composition. The result is simple but pleasing; like most good paintings, this one looks deceptively easy.

The paint here has been used thickly, unlike that in the previous painting. Parts of the background were applied with a palette knife, with the side of the knife used to make sharply defined lines on the leaves. The flower heads were built up in thick impasto; in some places the brushstrokes themselves form the petals and in other places paint has been squeezed on direct from the tube, so that the painting has an interesting and varied surface. This is particularly important in a subject as stark as this, which might have looked rather dull and lifeless. A good artist plans the paint surface as carefully as the composition, so that it forms an integral part of the whole, rather than just letting it happen, but

1

ABOVE **1** A few lines made with a sharp pencil served to place the main shapes, which were then quickly blocked in with bright colors. Even at this stage the paint was used quite thickly, as can be seen on the flower pot and the leaves at the top.

accidental effects can often be used to advantage also, and can frequently give rise to a new technique that can be put to use in a subsequent painting.

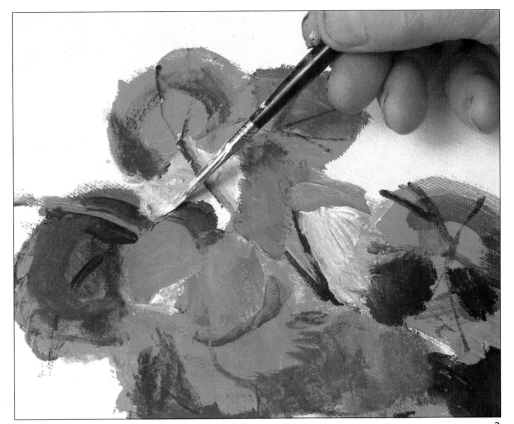

2

3

4

LEFT **2** and ABOVE **3** The diagonal line for the edge of the skirting board was painted in next, together with an area of color around the pot (ABOVE), acting as a key for the other colors. The photograph (LEFT) shows thick white paint being applied with a small brush to sharpen and define the edges of the leaves and stems.

LEFT **4** Here a medium-sized round brush is being used to apply thick paint to the flower heads so that the brushstrokes themselves form the shapes of the petals, and a special impasto medium was mixed with the paint to give it extra body. This is a good example of using particular brushes to create particular effects; a flat brush would not have been suitable for this purpose.

RIGHT **5** Here the flat of the painting knife has been used to apply thick white paint to an area of the background, giving a lively, rough-textured effect.

5

RIGHT **6** This detail shows the way the paint has been built up quite thickly on the highlight areas of the leaves so that they stand out from the areas of thinner, darker paint. The lines of dark green radiating from the centers of the leaves were made with the edge of a painting knife.

OPPOSITE The final touches involved more work on the background, foreground, and shadow areas, so that the background is now perceived as an uneven piece of white fabric with folds and creases. There is just enough texture and detail to give interest to the painting without in any way detracting from the plant itself. The floor in front of the pot, previously painted flat, has now been broken up with short, stabbing brushstrokes, indicating an uneven fall of light.

6

INTERIOR WITH BROOM

This kind of painting, of familiar objects in a domestic setting, has always been popular with artists, and has its roots in the lovely, tranquil interiors of the Dutch painters of the 17th century. Probably the most famous of all such paintings in more modern times is Van Gogh's *Yellow Chair*, but the French artists Edouard Vuillard (1868–1940) and Pierre Bonnard (1867–1947), among others, also painted many exquisite interiors. Looking at such paintings, one often has the feeling that the artists were fortunate in having rooms that look so much more attractive than our own. This is, of course, sometimes well justified, since few people live in houses with fine views or with large shuttered windows, but this painting demonstrates what can be done with seemingly quite unpromising material—just a corner with a broom and a hat hanging on the wall. The artist has aimed at creating a feeling of quiet domestic intimacy by the choice of a subject in which there is no drama and no main focal point.

Here the artist had a very clear vision of how the painting was to look, and went about organizing it with this vision in mind. It is basically abstract in feeling, with no bright colors; so only a small palette was used. The main lines are vertical, with the diagonals at the bottom of the wall and door forming a zigzag line from left to right. What the artist had to consider was the balance of the lines and shapes and that of the lights and darks, all of which were planned with great care. Any change in the composition—for example, reducing the width of the door, removing the hat, or making the area of black floor larger—would upset the balance quite seriously.

Because the subject is such a stark and goemetric one, the artist has chosen to use his paint fairly thinly, to emphasize these qualities, and has created small areas of texture by drawing with a pencil and spattering the paint in places. He has also used masking tape to ensure that the vertical and diagonal lines are really straight and true, with clean, hard edges. In a painting like this, any deviation from a true parallel, however small, would completely destroy the effect.

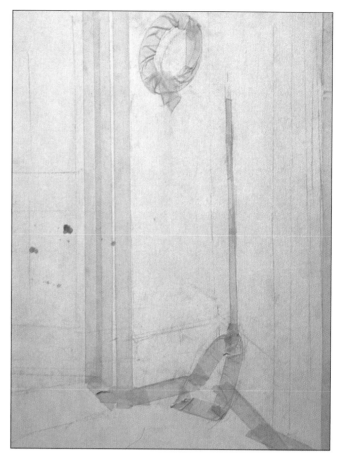

ABOVE **1** The first step was to make a very careful drawing, using a sharp pencil, a ruler and a set square. Masking tape was then placed over all the edges, so that the preliminary stage of this painting looks quite unlike the more conventional drawing or underpainting.

LEFT **2** and OPPOSITE TOP LEFT **3** Paint was applied quite freely over the masking tape with a medium-sized flat bristle brush.

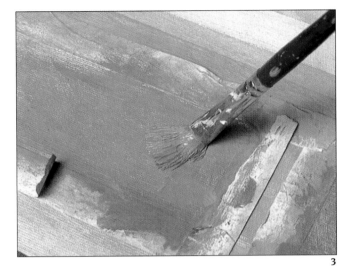

ABOVE **4** As soon as the tape was dry it was lifted, giv ing sharp, clean edges. Care must be taken when using this technique not to use the paint too thinly or it will seep under the tape.

ABOVE **5** The large area of the walls was covered with quite thick paint, a mixture of titanium white modified with small quantities of Payne's gray, raw sienna, and cobalt blue.

LEFT **6** The underpainting was now complete, and the paint sufficiently dry to work on. Here the artist is using a small sable brush to paint small details of the hat and ribbon.

MATERIALS USED

SUPPORT: fine-grained canvas board 20 x 16 in. (51 x 40 cm) (a surface particularly well-suited to this type of "hard-edge" painting)
BRUSHES: medium-sized flat bristle and a number 6 sable
COLORS: titanium white, Payne's gray, raw sienna, burnt umber, cobalt blue, viridian, and cadmium red

FAR LEFT **7** By this stage all the canvas had been covered and the main areas were more or less complete, but the focus of interest, the broom, needed further definition and texture.

LEFT **8** The artist re-tapes the edges of the broom and places newspaper over the rest of the painting to protect it, leaving exposed the small area of base board around the broom. He then loads a bristle brush with thinned paint and spatters it with his finger.

7

8

9

10

ABOVE LEFT **9** and ABOVE RIGHT **10** The bristles of the broom are suggested by firstly drawing into the thin, dry paint with a pencil and then by scratching the paint away with the handle of a brush.

OPPOSITE A comparison of the finished painting with the earlier stage clearly shows how important the final touches were. The eye is now drawn to the textured broom and spattered area of base board,

whereas previously the painting had rather the appearance of a stage set waiting for something to happen, without a "focal point." The colors are muted, the atmosphere is calm.

Painting
the
Nude

Introduction

The portrayal of the human figure has been an abiding
concern of artists from the earliest times to the present
day. Despite the trend toward abstraction, their
fascination with the figure has not diminished in the
20th century, and the nude continues to occupy a
central place in contemporary art. Alexander Pope's
statement that "The proper study of mankind is man" is
as true today as it was for earlier societies.

Naturally enough, in visual terms the human form has performed a large variety of different functions through the centuries. The scientific study of the nude—and of anatomy—is essentially an innovation of the Renaissance. Nonetheless, without acute observational skills prehistoric artists would not have been able to depict running and hunting figures with such eloquence. For them, function—the magical power over prey—dictated style (if they depicted a speared antelope, such would be the outcome of their hunting). The famous Willendorf Venus shows a rotund female form with large breasts, and was a symbol of fertility. In the exotic art of India the hips and breasts are exaggerated.

Art is created out of that tension between the natural (retinal) appearance of things and society's needs and influences, as well as

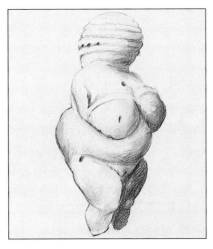

A B O V E A pencil study of the *Venus of Willendorf*, one of the earliest known pieces of prehistoric sculpture: a small fertility image of Palaeolithic origin dating from around 30,000-25,000 BC. At first sight it appears over-simplified and stylized, but in drawing it one realizes just how well the form has been observed. It repays study to make copies of works of art of all periods.

B E L O W Egyptian art existed to glorify the pharoahs and the noble classes. Their highly stylized paintings were governed by strict rules, ensuring that every feature was shown to the best advantage.

from the artists' feelings and emotions, and is frequently a complex mixture of all three. in earlier societies the artists' personality tends to be less obvious, and it is perhaps only since Renaissance times that the artist assumes increasing importance. We have a story of changing ideas and requirements.

In Ancient Egypt a strict formal imagery was imposed upon artists in describing daily life, and the way of death and after-life. Their art would not work, however, without a strong observational base and, as art historian E. H. Gombrich suggests, their figures are presented to us with each element shown to best advantage and from its most characteristic angle: the head in profile but with a full face, the shoulders and chest from the front; the stomach, legs, and feet from the side.

Greek art displays a much more naturalistic ideal of beauty, based on a sound knowledge of human form, but it is nonetheless an ideal and in that sense formalized. it was here, and later with the Romans, that some of the formal archetypes (e.g. the Capitoline Venus and the Three Graces) appear and re-appear throughout the history of art. The Romans, the Etruscans and the wall-paintings of Pompeii show a real grasp of form and space.

Observational skills lay dormant throughout most of the Middle Ages, but pictorial storytelling flourished at the behest of the

church. imagery became transcendental and hierarchical. Much expressive and highly charged work appeared during the later Gothic period, and the figure was used in a way that emerged again in 20th-century Expressionist art.

With the growth of humanism and the re-awakening of people's interest in their life on earth, with St Francis's reverence for things physical and earthly, and the emergence of a real scientific interest in man and his world we reach the Renaissance. The great classical traditions come alive again, and in the space of 250 years we move from the monumental form and space of Giotto (1266?–1337) and Masaccio (1401–28), through Leonardo da Vinci (1452–1519) and Michelangelo (1475–1564), to the riotous extravagance

ABOVE *The Three Graces* is of Greek origin and was copied by the Romans. A Pompeilan wall-painting of the Ist century AD depicts them. In the l8th century Antonio Canova (1757–1822) produced his famous group, and in the 20th century the sculptor Maillol has used the theme. Rubens was one of many painters to employ this archetype in his work and this charcoal drawing by the author is based on a small sepia oil sketch by Rubens.

of the Baroque and Rococo periods in the 17th and early 18th centuries. The great religious themes of the Crucifixion and Deposition, where human beings gather round the dead Christ, attain increasing realism.

These religious and mythological themes and classical archetypes find their northern expression with Peter Paul Rubens (1577–1640). He is further recorded as having made notes on color theory, and the subtle rainbow colors in his treatment of flesh find a later flowering in the work of Eugene Delacroix (1798–1863) and Auguste Renoir (1841–1919). Arguably, work of the deepest humanity is found in Rubens's contemporary, Rembrandt van Rijn (1606–69), who made constant use of models in his work. One of the most tangible, authoritative and real nudes in Western painting appears in his *Bathsheba with King David's Letter*.

ABOVE Correggio, a contemporary of Titian, was a masterly painter of light flowing over soft and graceful form, as can be seen in his *Jupiter and Antiope* (c. 1531). Equally at home with religious or mythological subjects, he makes his Antiope as seductive as possible under the approaching Jupiter.

BELOW Goya painted the *Naked Maia* (*Maja Desnuda*—the Spanish *maja* meaning "a flirt") around 1798, the subject being the Duchess of Alba, a close friend and by all accounts the mistress of the artist. There Is, of course, an equally famous version of Her Grace clothed.

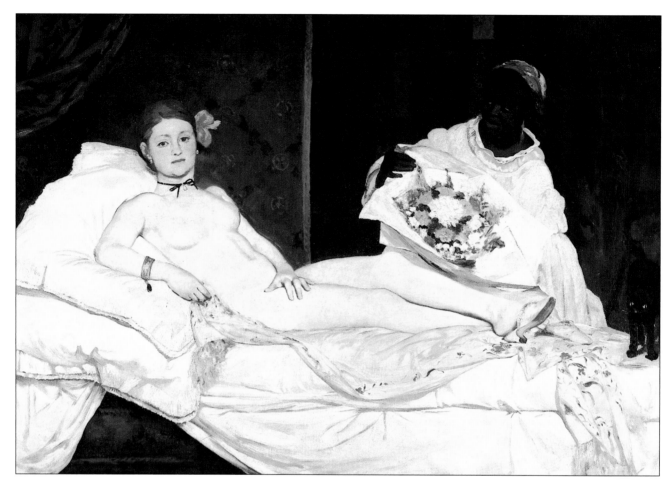

The female form is celebrated by Giorgione (1478–1510) and Titian (1485?–1576) in the 15th and 16th centuries, with their classically posed and sumptuous Venuses, and frequently by Correggio (1489?–1534) within a framework of classical subject matter. But perhaps it is only with Francisco Goya (1746–1828) and his *Naked Maja* that the nude stares at us, unabashed, and in the 19th century, *Olympia* by Edouard Manet (1832–83) faces us with her implacable look, coolly gazing at the observer from her huge satin bed.

The life room, where artists and students gathered to study formally the male and female figures, is a relatively recent phenomenon, dating back to the 18th century, and a rich tradition has developed from it. Many 20th-century artists have broken the mold of classical representation.

ABOVE Both Manet's *Olympia* (1863), illustrated here, and Goya's *Maja Desnuda* on page 373 are variations on the theme of the Renaissance classical model. Manet's model comes at the end of a long line of Venuses. The classical reclining nude rediscovered by Giorgione and Titian was brought right up to date in Manet's avowedly realist approach, which employed a real model in a situation that scandalized people at the time.

From the intimate domestic settings of Pierre Bonnard (1867–1947), the light and color of the "odalisques" of Henri Matisse (1869–1954) to the inventive and authoritative forms of Picasso, the figure has been an unending source of inspiration and variety. Northern artists, meanwhile Edvard Munch (1863–1944), Max Beckmann (1884–1950) or the German Expressionists, for example—have used the figure to reflect and comment upon the human condition.

In the work of Balthus (*b* 1908), Alberto Giacometti (1901–66), Richard Diebenkorn (*b* 1922) and Francis Bacon (1909–92) we find artists of the late 20th century continuing the great figurative tradition. With the nude as a central element in their art, they produce images for our time.

CHAPTER ONE

General Information on Oils and Watercolors

The wonderful colors that we use are made from pigments held together by a binding vehicle. In the case of oil paints the vehicle is cold-pressed or refined linseed oil, or sometimes poppy oil. The water-based fresco painting of southern Italy suffered badly in more northern climes and gradually oil painting came into its own for artistic purposes around the early 15th century in Northern Europe and shortly after that in Venice. During the following 200 years it gained gradual acceptance, especially among the later Italian painters, and by the 17th century its use had become common.

Watercolour employs almost all the same dry pigment colors as oil paint, but they are ground in gum arabic, which is water soluble. Watercolor painting as a distinct technique was not employed much before the 18th century, when the English school firmly established its practice. Watercolor paintings dry by evaporation (of the water), leaving the pigment stuck to the paper by the gum. Oil paints, on the other hand, "saponify:" the air causes the oil to undergo a chemical change, gradually becoming more "soapy" and ultimately becoming a tough paint film.

It is not true that watercolors fade more quickly than oils because of their relatively thin film of color. Kept away from direct and bright light, they have as long a life as oil paintings, which in any case should also be displayed away from bright light.

Students'or artists' quality?

There is a choice between students' quality and artists' quality paint. There is only one possible reason for buying students' quality, and that is an economic one. These paints are characterized by a uniformly low price. Consequently the more expensive pigments (such as cadmiums) will be replaced by substitute approximations and labeled cadmium red (hue). They often contain extenders, neutral-colored substances that bulk out the paint, whereas artists' quality paints contain pure pigment.

Obviously if you are starting out and need to buy a large number of colors, it is a help financially to buy students' quality paints, but you should replace them with artists' quality as soon as you can afford to. Ultimately it is a false economy to buy students' quality as you will use far more paint trying to achieve the brilliance that you can get with a small amount of artists' quality, just as a good-quality brush outlasts several cheaper ones.

Students' quality paints often have a brand name as well as the manufacturer's name, and will all be the same price, Artists' quality paints must be labeled A*rtists' oil color* or A*rtists' watercolor*, and the price will vary with the pigment. Earth colors will be cheapest, cadmiums and cobalts the most expensive. (Beware one paint firm that states on its students' quality paints O*il color for artists*—this is *not* artists' oil color.)

Now we come to the palette—not the one on which we mix our colors (more of that later), but meaning the range of colors we use. A bewildering number of colors are available, but many are unnecessary except in the case of individual needs or preferences, which come with experience Picasso said, "Actually, you work with only a few colors, but they seem like a lot more when each is in the right place." Rembrandt used yellow, warm browns and reds, a blue pigment called smalt, an occasional green, black and white.

L E F T A competent pianist does not have to search for the notes on the keyboard and no more should we have to search for our colors. A system that makes sense is based on the color circle (see page 449). Starting at the top right and moving anticlockwise: violet, French ultramarine, cobalt blue, cerulean blue, Prussian blue, cobalt green, viridian green, raw umber, cadmium lemon, cadmium yellow mid, yellow ocher, burnt sienna, cadmium red, mars red, alizarin crimson, and titanium white. There are one or two optional extra coiors here: cobalt green, burnt sienna, and mars red, and they have been given a relevant position on the palette. The colors move from violet into warm (i.e. violet) blues, into cold (i.e. green) blues and green, then cold yellows, becoming warmer and moving through yellow ocher to hot yellows and red and finally through cold red (crimson) back round to violet.

Rubens and Titian used very few more and Monet, that great painter of light, used a palette restricted to white, emerald green, cobalt blue, *garance toncée* (burnt madder), and chrome yellow.

MATERIALS FOR OIL PAINTING

The following is a basic recommended list of oil colors French ultramarine, cobalt blue, cerulean or manganese blue, (phthalo or Prussian blue), (cobalt green), viridian green, raw umber, cadmium lemon or cadmium pale, cadmium yellow mid, yellow ocher, (raw sienna), (light red), cadmium red, alizarin crimson, violet, and titanium white.

A violet is useful, but in artists' quality cobalt violet is extremely expensive, so look for a substitute. The colors in parenthesis are useful but not essential. Black has been omitted at this stage because when used to darken colors it usually only makes them dirty.

The basic shape of the palette is unimportant. What is important is to have a system for laying out colors. Firstly they should be placed around the edges of the palette to allow maximum space for mixing and to facilitate cleaning afterward, leaving unused paint around the edge. There is nothing worse than a palette with paint randomly squeezed all over it with no sequence at all. Painting is demanding enough without adding to the problem.

Brushes

Brushes for oil should be hog-hair, and come in a range of shapes and sizes. It is a false economy to purchase cheap brushes; they lose their shape quickly and become

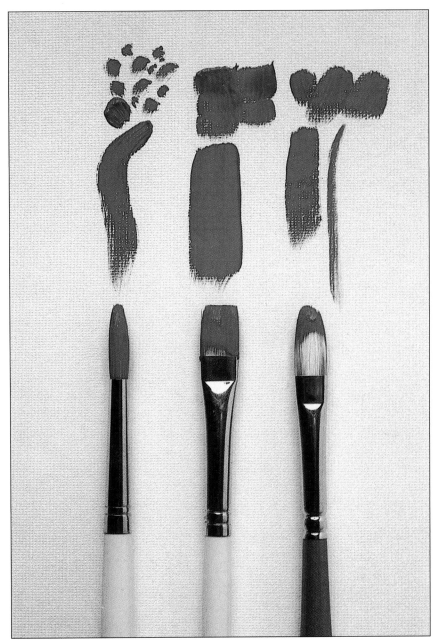

ABOVE The three basic shapes of brush used for painting in oils and the marks they make.

limp. There are three basic shapes—round, square, and filbert. I would recommend the filbert as the best all-purpose brush. It can be used flat to cover large areas, on its edge for linear work, or its point for fine detail. A small round brush is a help for linear work. Long-handled sables can be useful for

very fine detail. Basically a no. 5 and a no. 8 filbert are versatile enough for most occasions.

Palette

A palette can be purchased ready made, and the strip-off disposable types are also useful. However, it is recommended that you make your own simply by giving the smooth side of a piece of hardboard or composition board a coat of clear varnish and allowing it to dry overnight.

Mediums

White spirit for cleaning brushes as you proceed, and genuine turpentine for mixing with the paint, are all that you need. You should purchase these from a general or hardware/DIY store as they are the same as the more expensive versions sold in art stores. Refined linseed oil for mixing with the paint in the later stages of a picture must be purchased from art stores. A useful all-purpose painting medium is a 50/50 mixture of genuine turpentine and linseed oil.

Supports

Wood Plywood tends to warp and separate. Blockboard is solid, but heavy. Hardboard can generally be recommended, but use the smooth side. The textured side does not approximate to canvas—it blots up the paint and ruins the brushes. Some hardboard now produced is smooth on both sides. Larger pieces will need a batten support at the back. MDF (medium density fiber board) is one of the best and most inert surfaces now available and comes in various thicknesses.

Oil painting paper and canvas boards These are very convenient, but the priming tends to be unpleasant and slippery to paint on.

Canvas Ready-made canvases are expensive, and it is worth the time and effort to make your own. Cotton should be avoided as it is very susceptible to changes of humidity. It slackens and tightens constantly and disturbs the ground and paint film. Linen is best, and the various grades for artistic purposes are usually available from specialist sail and canvas suppliers.

LEFT A variety of painting surfaces for oils.

Stretching a canvas

Canvas is normally sold by the yard or meter in large widths. Its thickness is defined by weight, i.e. 15 oz (510 gsm) canvas is thicker than 12 oz (410 gsm). To stretch the canvas you require stretcher bars, which can be purchased in various sizes or ordered to your own requirements from specialist woodworkers.

Priming

Boards and canvases must be primed before working in oils. It is especially true in the case of canvas, because oil in contact with bare canvas will rot it. Acrylic primers are available which do not require any prior sizing. They are adequate for boards or even paper (a good quality matt white emulsion paint is also adequate). To produce the best surface, however, you should first size the board or canvas, and then prime it with an oil-based or tempera primer.

Glue size should be purchased from good art stores. Rabbit-skin glue is the best type available. Take approximately 1 oz (25 g) dry weight and add it to 1 pt (600 ml) of cold water. Leave it to soak overnight, Using a double-boiler or one saucepan inside another, warm up the mixture until the glue is thoroughly dispersed. Never apply direct heat or allow the glue to boil. When the size has reached blood temperature apply it to the board or canvas with gentle, even strokes. Do not overbrush and create bubbles. In the case of canvas, the moisture will further stretch the canvas on drying, and this is why it is important that the canvas is not too tight in the first place. Wedges

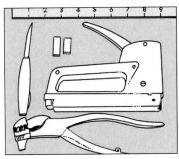

1 The tools required are a ruler, a knife, a staple gun, and staples (or tacks if you prefer) and a pair of canvas pliers.

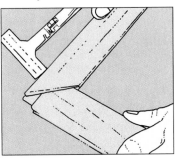

2 Fit the corners of the stretcher firmly together. Give each a sharp tap to be certain it is secure.

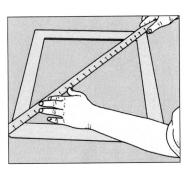

3 Check that the stretcher is square by measuring the diagonals.

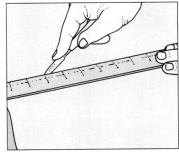

4 Cut the canvas to size using a ruler and a knife. Allow a 1½ in. (3.75 cm) overlap all round.

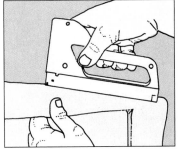

5 Lay the stretcher on the canvas. Fold the canvas over at one end and insert a staple in the outer edge of the stretcher.

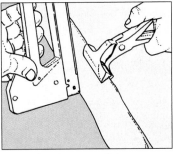

6 Use the pliers to pull the canvas tight at the opposite end and insert a staple. Pull the other sides tight and staple.

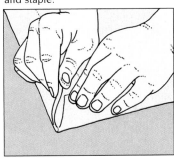

7 Insert staples at 3 in. (7½ cm) intervals all round, to within 2 in. (5 cm) of the corners. Fold in the first corner tightly.

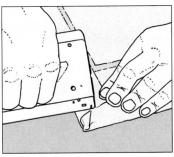

8 Secure the corner with two staples and repeat the process for the three other corners.

should never be inserted into the stretcher corners initially, but should be used to take up slack when the picture is finished.

Allow this coat of size to dry, ideally overnight, and the board or canvas is ready for priming. An oil-based, commercially prepared primer can be used. Alternatively, use the recipe below for a universal tempera primer for canvas, board, or paper; it has proved very durable.

Add an equal quantity of water and again beat thoroughly. The quantities therefore are: one part egg, one part linseed oil, and two parts water. The order in which they are mixed is crucial. The egg is an emulsifying agent, allowing oil and water to mix.

Now take some titanium white dry pigment and add it into the mixture gradually, stirring thoroughly with a spatula. The

resulting mixture should have a buttery consistency and, when spread out flat with the spatula, should glisten slightly. Finally take a very few drops of warm glue size and add it to the mixture until it is of a brushable consistency. Now prime your canvas or board with it. The result will be a technically sound priming. It is slightly absorbent, which is an excellent property for the first layers of paint.

MATERIALS FOR WATERCOLOR

Any list of watercolors approximates to that of oils. Colors sometimes vary from firm to firm, and in the list below cobalt green dark and light and *stil de grain* pink are Schmincke, whereas aureolin and alizarin crimson are from Winsor and Newton. Only trial and error will enable you to find the exact colors you like. A comprehensive list of watercolors would include

French ultramarine, cobalt blue, cerulean blue/ manganese blue, or equivalent, phthalo blue or Prussian blue, cobalt green dark, cobalt green light, viridian green, *stil de grain* pink or aureolin, cadmium lemon or pale, cadmium yellow mid, cadmium red light, alizarin crimson, and ultramarine violet. If you are painting with a pure watercolor technique there is no need for Chinese white.

Whether to purchase tubes or pans is largely a personal question. Pans enable you to work with greater immediacy without the nuisance of opening tubes. Tubes are useful when a large quantity of one color is needed, or when laying down a wash. You can purchase empty watercolor boxes and fill them with the colors of your choice.

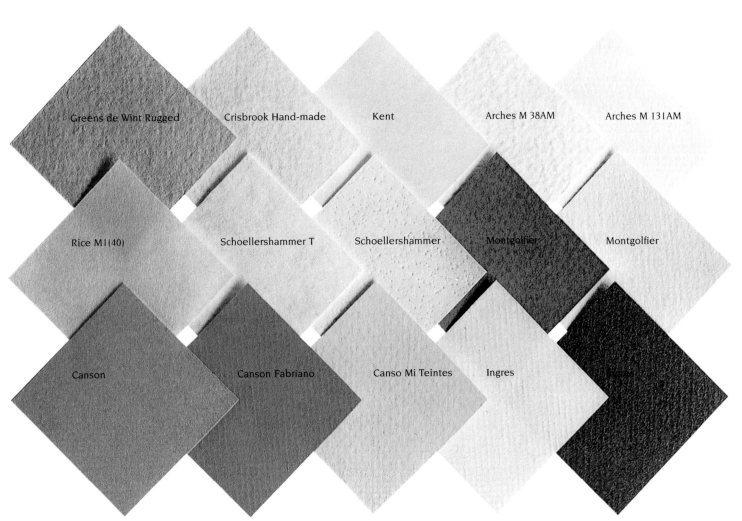

Greens de Wint Rugged
Crisbrook Hand-made
Kent
Arches M 38AM
Arches M 131AM
Rice M1(40)
Schoellershammer T
Schoellershammer
Montgolfier
Montgolfier
Canson
Canson Fabriano
Canso Mi Teintes
Ingres

Brushes

The same advice applies to watercolor brushes as to oil painting brushes. It is a false economy to purchase cheap brushes. With watercolor, the inadequacies of cheap brushes are even more glaring. There is nothing more frustrating than a flaccid brush that will not make and keep a point. Sable, therefore, should be used if at all possible. There are now quite adequate sable and synthetic fiber mix brushes available that are reasonably inexpensive. Test a brush for its "spring" to see if it is any good. A good brush should have a degree of resistance.

Paper

The three main types of paper in use are classified as: hot-pressed (HP), which is smooth; "not" or cold-pressed (CP), which is lightly textured; and rough, which has a coarse-textured surface. "Not" or cold-pressed is the most popular. Its semi-rough surface takes washes well; a dryish brush dragged quickly across the surface will exploit its texture to good effect, especially at the beginning of a picture.

Paper thickness is expressed by weight. In imperial it is the weight of one ream (500 sheets); in metric, it is the weight in grams of one square meter of paper. The three commonest weights are: 90 lb (185 gsm), moderately thick; 140 lb (300 gsm), thick; 300 lb (640 gsm), almost card.

The best paper has a high rag content, ideally 100% cotton. There are many good cheaper papers available: always look for those described as wood-free.

Papers that are 90 lb (185 gsm) and 140 lb (300 gsm) will need stretching prior to use to avoid cockling, where the paint becomes uneven and can lie in puddles.

LEFT A variety of watercolor brushes. From left to right: large mop brush useful for washes, long thin rigger brush for fine lines, synthetic round hair, mixed fiber round, ox-hair round, squirrel-hair round, sable fan bright, long-handled square sable, sable round, and sable rigger.

ABOVE Some of the many different types of watercolor paper available.

HOW TO STRETCH PAPER

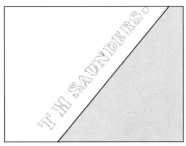

I First check which is the right side of the paper. Hold it to the light so the watermark appears the right way round.

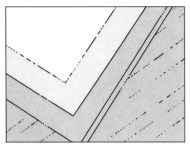

2 Trim the paper to size for the drawing board, leaving a good margin of board so that the gummed tape will adhere.

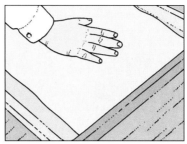

3 Soak the paper in a tray or sink full of clean water. The amount of time needed to soak varies with the type of paper.

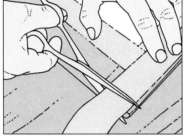

4 Measure out lengths of gummed paper tape to match each side of the drawing board.

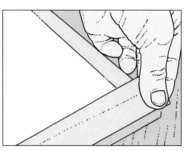

5 Take the paper out of the water and drain it off. Lay it on the board and stick dampened, gummed tape along one side.

6 Stick gum strip along the opposite side of the paper. Tape the other two sides. Keep the paper quite flat throughout.

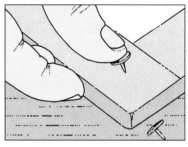

7 To secure the paper, push a thumbtack Into the board at each corner. Let the paper dry naturally or it may split.

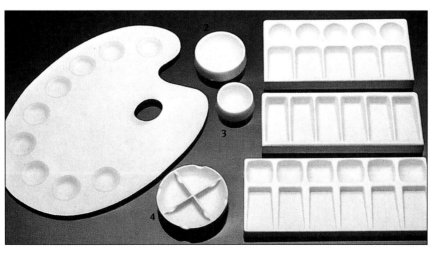

LEFT A selection of some types of palettes you can purchase for watercolors.

CHAPTER TWO

Seeing Things Simply

Beginning to paint means beginning to think like a painter. The brush can move paint around and manipulate form and space, which is not the same as drawing lines and filling them in, or making shapes and coloring them in. With a few strokes the brush can cover large areas of paper or canvas; just one stroke of the brush can describe, say, a whole arm or leg.

It is important to be selective in your approach to a painting. When you are confronted by a jumble of appearances, you need to make some kind of order out of the chaos. Details that might catch the eye are not as important in the early stages of a painting as developing a feeling for the whole.

GIRL SEATED SIDEWAYS

DAVID CARR

Small pieces of board and a minimum palette are used here to make two quick oil studies. The artist's aim is to see and keep things as simple as possible. The palette used consists of French ultramarine, cerulean blue, viridian green, cadmium lemon, cadmium yellow, cadmium red, alizarin crimson, and titanium white, thinned with turpentine in the early stages. The brushes are a no. 5 filbert and a no. 2 round hog-hair. The boards are 10 x 11 in. (25 x 27.5 cm), primed with commercial primer.

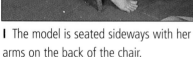

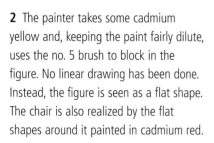

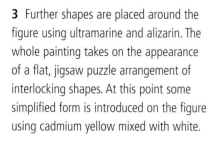

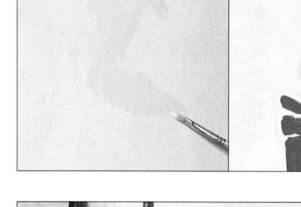

1 The model is seated sideways with her arms on the back of the chair.

2 The painter takes some cadmium yellow and, keeping the paint fairly dilute, uses the no. 5 brush to block in the figure. No linear drawing has been done. Instead, the figure is seen as a flat shape. The chair is also realized by the flat shapes around it painted in cadmium red.

3 Further shapes are placed around the figure using ultramarine and alizarin. The whole painting takes on the appearance of a flat, jigsaw puzzle arrangement of interlocking shapes. At this point some simplified form is introduced on the figure using cadmium yellow mixed with white.

4 Some of the darker tones of the figure are now established using very light touches of light green and blue painted into the wet yellow paint. Note that the defining line down the front of the figure is put in after the main shape of the figure has been established. It was not drawn first and filled in.

5 Depth is now given to the space around the figure through variations in tone, and some of the warmer shadows on the figure, notably under the thigh, are painted in.

6 The space is pushed back and pulled forward using cool and warm colors. Ultramarine is painted into the crimson carpet and shapes adjacent to the figure are defined. The result is a clear, simple statement.

7 Every part of the picture surface has been made to work, and the figure, simply conceived, occupies a credible space.

GIRL SEATED ON ARM OF CHAIR

DAVID CARR

This is a slightly less successful attempt than the preceding example on page 20. Nonetheless it aptly illustrates the point. Here the length of the vertical pose suggests a different-shaped board is required.

1 The model is half-seated sideways on the arm of a chair.

2 Notice again the simple, direct approach of lightly massing in the figure and space with thin paint.

3 The artist gradually develops the shapes around the figure. The axis of the shoulders, breasts, and pelvis is well felt.

Note how the picture evolves through a combination of line and mass and not through an initial line drawing,

subsequently filled in. It is useful to think in terms of an interlocking jigsaw puzzle of shapes.

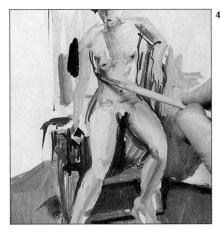

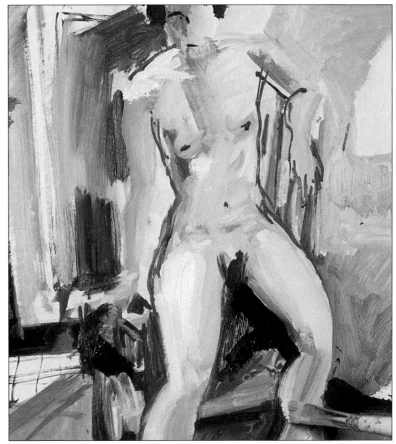

4 Into these simple areas the painter now draws with a fine brush. The figure's right side and left arm are carefully described by the shapes around them.

5 The no. 5 filbert is used again to work back into the figure more broadly. Here much of the cool lemon color of the flesh is stated.

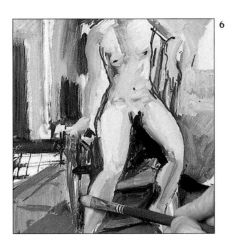

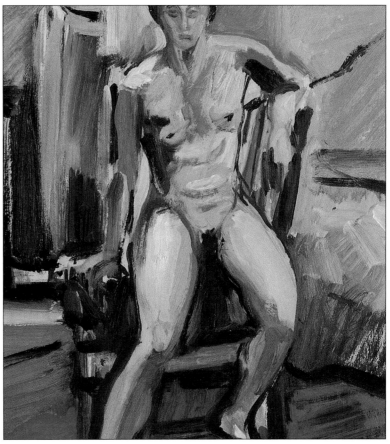

6 The space around the figure is now more thoroughly blocked in and unified.

7 Stronger defining lines are painted boldly around the legs of the figure and the seat of the chair. The head and shoulders are resolved, and although some of the top of the head and the lower foot are lost, this is a most useful preparatory study that could lead to a more finished painting.

WOMAN BY A WINDOW

K A Y   G A L L W E Y

A change of medium to watercolor does not mean a change of approach. The
thinking is the same. Watercolor is an ideal medium for seeing things broadly
and simply. In exploiting the immediate and direct qualities of the medium, detail
is subordinated to a feeling for the whole.
The artist is using a restricted palette of French ultramarine, permanent green, Van
Dyck brown, cadmium yellow, and cadmium red. The paper is a warm buff color,
and the artist is using a no. 2 brush and small pieces of tissue.

I A thin wash of light orange (mixed from
cadmium red and yellow) is laid down for
the figure, and a stronger cadmium red is
used for the cloth against which the figure is
standing. Some strokes of ultramarine into
the wet paint surface give the slightest
suggestion of form. The forms are softened
with a tissue. A tissue can also be used to
remove excess moisture.

2 One or two marks in Van Dyck brown are
placed to define the edges of the form.

3 It is only at this stage that the artist
begins to draw the form with any
definition, using line. Prior to this she was
only concerned with the main masses of
the composition. Both ultramarine and
brown are used in the drawing.

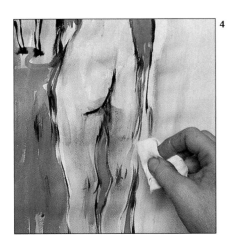

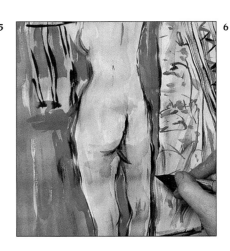

4 Using tissue, the artist is able to control the amount of bleeding and achieve just the right softness of line she requires.

5 The light washes of blue on the legs define the shadow well and throw up the hips and buttocks into the light.

6 Right at the end of the painting the artist introduces pattern into the drapery and carpet, and into the foliage outside.

7 The final picture, which is the result of less than 30 minutes work is a simple, satisfactory statement about the figure and its relationship to the room.

CHAPTER THREE

Composing a Picture

Thinking about things simply, attempting to organize a jumble of appearances, trying to make clear, simple statements, inevitably introduce thoughts about composition. Decisions about the composition of a picture involve choices: what to keep and what to reject, whether to fill the picture space or to place the figure more deeply in space, whether to deal with part of the figure only and so on.

DARK-HAIRED WOMAN IN CHAIR

D A V I D   C A R R

This project is a study in oils which demonstrates the use of a space frame and the value of preparatory studies. These are an invaluable aid in composing a picture. However small, they help in making choices and in familiarizing oneself with the subject. It is important that the studies and the board or canvas on which the final picture is painted should have the same proportions. The process for matching the proportions of the painting board and those of the paper used for the preliminary studies is quite simple.

1 The model is in position and the artist has prepared his palette of French ultramarine, cobalt blue, viridian green, cadmium lemon, cadmium yellow, cadmium red, alizarin crimson, and titanium white. The brushes were no. 5 and no. 8 filbert and no. 3 round hog-hair. It was painted on board prepared with a commercial white ground.

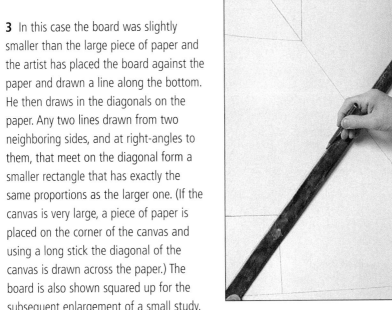

2 A space frame is a useful compositional device. It may be adequate to cut a rectangle out of the middle of a piece of card and hold it up to the subject, but this restricts the shape of the picture. A more flexible device can be made with two L-shaped pieces of card, which can be moved against each other to form a rectangle of varying proportions.

3 In this case the board was slightly smaller than the large piece of paper and the artist has placed the board against the paper and drawn a line along the bottom. He then draws in the diagonals on the paper. Any two lines drawn from two neighboring sides, and at right-angles to them, that meet on the diagonal form a smaller rectangle that has exactly the same proportions as the larger one. (If the canvas is very large, a piece of paper is placed on the corner of the canvas and using a long stick the diagonal of the canvas is drawn across the paper.) The board is also shown squared up for the subsequent enlargement of a small study.

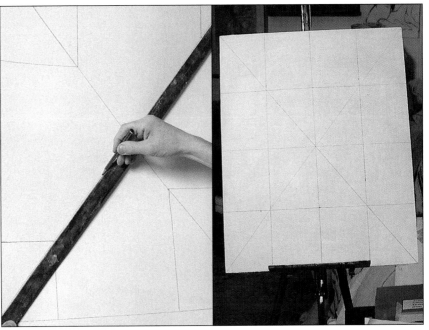

4

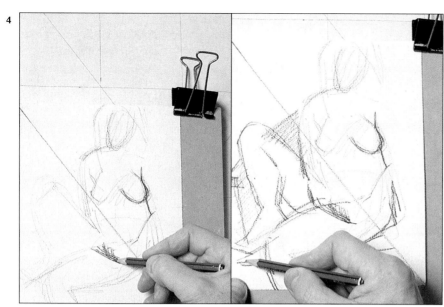

4 Having cut out one of the small paper rectangles which now has the same proportions as the board, the artist begins to make a simple drawing of the figure.

Having used the L-shaped pieces of card, he decides to let the figure fill the space and he is making the study accordingly.

5

5 He makes a further study and manages to lose the head. Consequently he rejects this and decides he will probably use the first drawing.

6 He now squares up the small drawing using the same number of squares as on the larger board, and begins to transfer the drawing very simply using charcoal.

7 He then fixes the drawing.

6

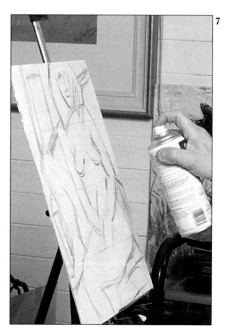

7

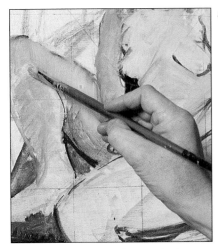

8 Looking at the model again, he begins to paint the flesh tones using a mixture of cadmium red and yellow. He draws the chair cushion in ultramarine, and defines some of the form using the same color.

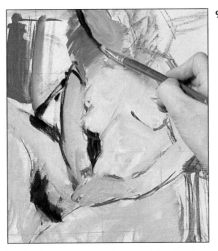

9 His aim is to establish everything firmly and simply. He works color into the flesh and paints strong defining lines into the form. The shapes around the figure are developed.

10 The figure is fully established but sits rather squarely in the chair. The flesh has been painted simply with basic yellows and pinks. The artist now works into this with neutral colors based on blue and green and redraws the figure.

11 Gray/blue is worked into the stomach and under the model's right thigh, and slabs of paint push this leg back diagonally toward the chair back. The hair and face are defined more fully.

12 The point of this whole exercise is to make sure that the artist is in charge of the painting from beginning to end.

PRELIMINARY STUDIES

The importance of making preliminary studies cannot be overstressed. Time and effort spent thinking things out at this stage saves much frustration later on. Painting oneself into trouble takes seconds; painting oneself out of it can take hours.

RIGHT The artist, Jill Mumford, used a sketchbook to make a small gouache color study before starting her painting of the back of a seated nude. She decided to place the figure high on the page and to make something of the large space in the foreground; it occupies almost half the picture. A clear, simple statement has established a composition with due regard for the distribution of shapes around the figure.

BELOW In the finished picture, done in oils, we feel that we are very close to the figure. The head has been cropped and the foot just squeezes into the picture space. The artist has extended the dark tone of the thigh down the whole leg and exploited the slabs of light falling on the back, floor, and bed and the silhouette of the leg, thigh, and breast.

RIGHT For the figure seated in the chair Jill Mumford worked out the relationship of the figure to the floor, wall, and chair in broad terms. The composition was worked out in more or less primary colors in oils, and the forms were seen in simplified terms.

BELOW In the finished picture, in oils, the flesh tones and colors are more subtly modulated from warm to cool. The figure sits satisfactorily in the chair. The dramatic light on the figure clearly comes from a second window to the left, out of the picture.

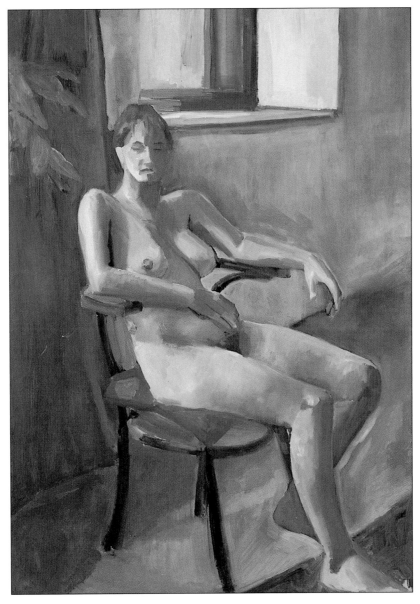

CHAPTER FOUR

Alla Prima Technique

The commonest and most basic oil technique in use today is known as *alla prima*, meaning literally "at the first." The paint is applied in a direct and spontaneous manner and it really came into its own in the 19th century. Instead of building up the paint stage by stage with successive layers of drawing, glazes (thin layers of transparent paint) and scumbles (layers of opaque paint dragged over existing layers of dry paint), the artist lays down each patch of color more or less as it is intended to appear finally.

ALLA PRIMA IN OILS

The invention of the tin paint-tube in the 19th century helped artists to take the paints to the subject and paint it at one sitting. A painter like Van Gogh (1853–90) worked directly onto the canvas with a fully loaded brush, and the evidence is there in the clearly defined brushstrokes.

It is, however, possible to work wet into wet, i.e., to apply paint over or into wet paint on the canvas, and at the same time build up a painting over a short space of time. The golden rule is to work "lean to fat." Any oil painting technique must obey this principle, otherwise the painting will crack

and flake when it dries. Each successive layer of paint must have a little more oil in it. Dilution of the paint with turps at the beginning is a sound technique for initial drawing and early paint layers, but the full tube-paint consistency, with a little linseed oil added, should be used for subsequent layers.

RECLINING WOMAN

J O Y   S T E W A R T

This small *alla prima* oil study was painted in less than an hour. The artist used a restricted palette of yellow ocher, cadmium red light, alizarin crimson, French ultramarine, and titanium white. She is working on board primed with white acrylic, using no. 5 and no. 8 filbert hog-hair brushes.

1 The model in a reclining position as seen by the artist.

2 Without any preliminary charcoal drawing, the artist lays in the figure in terms of mass using a mixture of yellow ocher and cadmium red.

3 She begins to draw into this with alizarin crimson and French ultramarine.

4 The wall is established, and boundary lines and points around the form hold the figure in place.

5 Using white the artist begins to give the frm more volume and to work some blue into the ocher flesh paint to define the darker parts of the form.

6 Using the same palette the artist works into the fabric on the wall and the bed. The plant pot and the plant are painted in simply, introducing an additional lemon yellow mixed with ultramarine.

7 The volume of the figure is strengthened as the artist works wet into wet with light ocher, pinks from the alizarin, and purples from mixing ultramarine and alizarin.

RECLINING WOMAN 2

S U S A N   C A R T E R

This oil painting of the same pose from a different angle illustrates the principle of working from lean to fat. The artist is using much the same palette as in the preceding project, with an additional light red, viridian green, burnt umber, and a mineral violet. She likes to use a painting medium made from about two-thirds turps to one-third oil.

1 The model in pose.

2 The initial drawing has been done with paint thinned with plenty of medium. The artist soon sets about laying down thin masses of color over the whole canvas.

3 The aim is to develop the picture as a whole.

4 The artist paints the flesh using light red, yellow ocher, and white, and draws into it using blues and umber.

5 It is important to keep moving around the canvas, adjusting each part to preserve a credible sense of light throughout.

Touches of warmth are introduced into the cloth. The result is a light and airy study.

6 **6** By continual attention to the whole picture surface the artist has attained a sense of completeness rather than finish.

RAPID ALLA PRIMA STUDY

This small study of the reclining nude against a tartan rug was completed in around an hour and is another example of the use of the *alla prima* technique with oils.

L E F T A standard palette of French ultramarine, cobalt blue, viridian green, cadmium lemon, cadmium yellow, cadmium red, alizarin crimson, and titanium white was used. A small amount of turps has been used to help the paint flow a little. It is painted on board on a white ground. Plenty of warm yellows and light oranges have been used for the light flesh, in contrast with the cooler blues and pinks in the shadows. The brushstrokes follow the direction of the forms.

ALLA PRIMA IN WATERCOLOR

The term *alla prima* is never used in watercolor, as in a sense watercolor is always *alla prima*. It is an immediate medium that does not improve with overworking. Confidence and a sure touch, which can only come from practice, are needed.

A very useful way to train the eye and hand and experiment with watercolor at the same time is to take numerous small pieces of paper cut or torn from a larger sheet and force yourself to work rapidly and simply.

LEFT AND BELOW These small watercolor studies by David Carr probably took less than 10 minutes. First a light wash of warm color was laid down, with the side of the brush following the main direction of the torso, head, and limbs. While the paint was still damp, and using drier paint and the point of the brush, ultramarine and crimson mixed was drawn into this. Thin washes of cooler paint were glazed over the warm areas where the figure is in shadow giving a sense of form and movement.

LINEAR WATERCOLOR SKETCHES

These linear watercolor studies show how effective this technique can be in describing the volume and fluidity of the human body. The ability to work quickly is all-important in achieving this effect.

ABOVE AND LEFT This artist, Kay Gallwey, has taken a more linear approach In her simple watercolor studies of the nude. The stronger lines were added last. She began by taking very watery pinks and light ochers, and followed the main direction of the form, the curve of the spine being crucial. The volume of the thigh was felt and then the langorous line of light umber lapped round the form already suggested. The final marks gave the details of headscarf and hair. She employs the same technique in other work. It is essential to work quickly, and constant practice is necessary to gain this amount of fluidity.

ALLA PRIMA IN OILS USING THICKER PAINT

These three paintings demonstrate the variety of rich and powerful effects that can result from the use of thick paint applied with brushes, palette knives and even with the fingers.

ABOVE Thick oil paint has been used in the study of the reclining nude on the striped bedspread. The problem was to maintain consistent light on the figure and the fabric. White was mixed with most of the colors, but not to the extent of making them chalky. The passage down the form moves from warm to cool continuously. The orange of the arm contrasts with the blue-greens of the torso, and cool pinks play against warmer yellows. Thick oil paint and a palette knife were used throughout.

RIGHT Here the artist, Mike Knowles, has used large brushes, palette knives, and tins of oil paint. The continuous working and re-working of the painting by scraping off and re-stating the forms has built up an encrusted paint surface. Slabs of paint and strong drawing make a powerful final statement, the result of prolonged observation.

ABOVE Some time was spent drawing the figure quite carefully, but once the main forms were established, thick paint was applied very freely. The objective was to describe the figure against the light without loosing the warmth, and raw sienna and alizarin crimson tempered with French ultramarine were used to paint these darker masses. The complementary contrasts have been exploited—the blues behind the figure against the orange blanket cascading onto the floor, the lilacs against the splashes of yellow on the windows and the chaise-longue. Not only were large brushes used here, but fingers dipped in the paint, drawing directly to keep the paint fresh and sparkling. It is said that Titian in later life used his fingers to work in the richer areas of his paintings.

CHAPTER FIVE

Seeing Planes and Structure

The fundamental problem facing the painter is that of dealing with a three-dimensional world of space and volume and of translating that onto a two-dimensional surface. One of the most important steps is to look for planes. A plane is a way of expressing the changes of direction that occur across a form. Outline as such does not exist, and a contour is merely the point at which a plane turns out of sight. It is light that gives the clue to form, and as a form turns we can see the shadow edge, which from another viewpoint would be a contour. This shadow edge is a change of plane.

GIRL LYING ON RUGS

D A V I D   C A R R

In this watercolor the artist is building up a series of planes with thin directional strokes of color. This is painted using a glaze technique (pages 468–475) as well as some wet-into-wet (pages 476–480) on 140 lb (300 gsm)—"not" surface paper. The palette consists of French ultramarine, cerulean blue, cobalt green light, cadmium lemon, cadmium yellow, cadmium red, alizarin crimson, and ultramarine violet.

1 The model is positioned on the floor with the artist standing looking down on the figure.

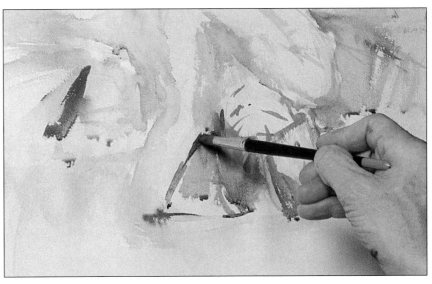

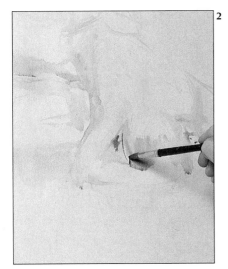

2 The first marks begin to deal with the large triangular plane of the upper chest. The palest dilute alizarin, cadmium red, and cerulean blue have been used here.

3 A much stronger yellow is placed down the side of the torso and the arm. Do not be afraid of watercolor. It dries paler than it looks when it is first applied. Cobalt green and French ultramarine are used to begin defining the floor.

4 The floor is developed, and a dilute cadmium red is used to establish the side plane of the thighs. Some linear work under the thigh and round the hip defines what was first described by planes.

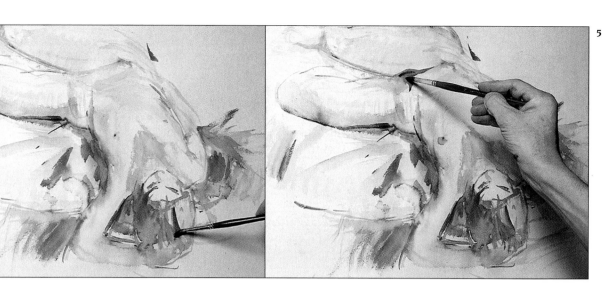

5 Marks follow the direction of the planes felt in the floor. Greater volume is given to the head and body. The planes on the top of the thighs are drawn with line. The painting has been conceived in terms of planes. In other words the planes were found first so that the position of the contours could be located.

6

6 The light and transparent marks follow the direction of the planes and the white of the paper has been used as a positive element.

ESTABLISHING CLEAR STRUCTURAL PLANES

These paintings all show the artists' awareness of strong directional light producing clearly defined planes.

BELOW The artist, Sharon Finmark, has glazed plane upon plane in her watercolor of a reclining nude on a settee. She has used color mainly for the darker tones; for some of the lighter tones she has left the paper white. She used a restricted palette of French ultramarine, cadmium yellow, cadmium red, and alizarin crimson.

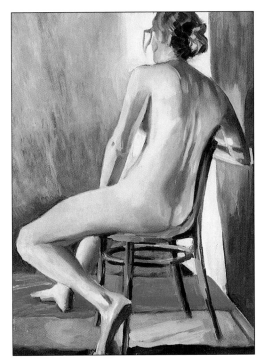

ABOVE The gradation of planes up the back and shoulders is well felt in this oil painting by Jill Mumford. Over a predominantly warm skin tone, the violet and deep crimson planes move up from the base of the spine and follow the curving form of the shoulders. The lighter areas were seen in warm and cold yellows. Note the structural work of the left arm, the shadows cast on the inside of the right arm and the sharply defined planes of the calf and foot.

ABOVE The marks in this tall, thin oil painting follow the direction of each form. Although the figure stood against the light and the bent arm was in silhouette, there was a high light-source from a lightbulb in the room. The figure's weight was thrown forward at the hips, pushing the legs into shadow. There was an almost step-like change of plane at the stomach. Painted over a warm sienna base for the figure, the lighter planes were put in using yellow ocher with touches of blue and yellow. The darker planes were described by strong directional brushmarks of viridian green, and deep purples and blue-grays using a mixture of ultramarine and alizarin crimson.

USING BRUSHMARKS TO FOLLOW THE FORM

The pair of oil studies below, by David Carr, show the same pose under different light conditions. As all four of these paintings demonstrate, whether the picture is a full figure in a complex space or a more intimate portrait, an awareness of planes is important.

ABOVE In the lighter of the two, the planes were knocked in rapidly, using multi-directional strokes. A slab of orange described the upper chest, and then lighter ocher followed the planes of the stomach and pelvis and the inside thigh of the extended leg. The structure was brought together by strong lines of blue-black, which cut into the form to emphasize the direction of the planes.

ABOVE The darker picture was painted under artificial light, hence the harsh tonal jumps and the clear shadow cast by the figure. The lighter parts of the flesh were painted using yellow ocher, cadmium red, and white mixed, and the darker masses with green and blue-grays. Again, strong lines pulled the form together at the end.

LEFT This is a large oil painting 5 x 4 ft. (1.5 x 1.2 m) by David Carr taken to a greater degree of finish than the seated studies. Painted very much in an *alla prima* technique, the palette was cadmium yellow pale, cadmium yellow mid, yellow ocher, cadmium red, alizarin crimson, French ultramarine, and titanium white. The final drawing of the figure was done in thick, dark lines, over which the directional brushmarks followed the planes. Light blues and violets were used to describe the darker form, which was generally high-keyed. Around the cheek and neck, this cooler color is sharply contrasted with the highlight on the cheekbone. Strong, light pink ochers (yellow ocher, cadmium red, and white) start above the breasts and follow the form of the stomach, thighs, and shins. Note the slab of paint traveling across the right shin below the knee. The artist was standing while painting this, and felt the importance of establishing the feet firmly and giving the feeling of looking down onto the top of a plane.

LEFT The artist, David Carr, was very aware of the way the planes flowed round the head in this small oil study of a friend. Again done *alla prima*, a warmer initial layer of paint comprising cadmium red and yellow ocher was worked into, using directional strokes of light yellow ocher. The brush moved round the forehead, almost skipping over the color beneath. The plane of the side of the face and cheek was strongly established and a few strokes of light blue bring round the jaw.

CHAPTER SIX

Anatomy

The preceding sections have been concerned with thinking in painterly terms, with seeing things simply and being selective in making decisions about composition. After the problems of representing a three-dimensional world on a flat surface have been considered, the figure itself needs to be looked at in greater depth. Confidence in painting the figure comes from knowing something of the "vocabulary" of the figure—its anatomy. A great depth of anatomical knowledge is not essential—only that known as "superficial anatomy," which concerns itself with the way certain bones, muscles, and tendons affect the surface form needs to be understood.

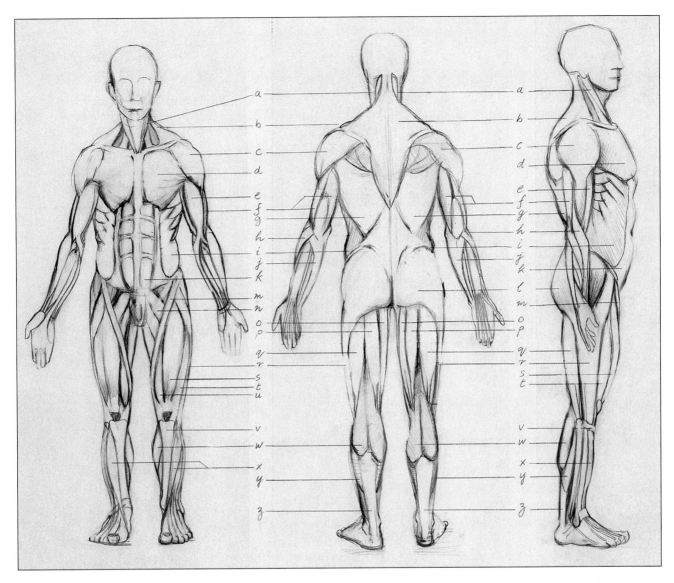

ABOVE These three drawings of the figure from different positions show all the main muscles of the body.

Here is an ABC of the figure—26 important points to help in a confident and authoritative approach. The standing figure shows off the muscles to good advantage. Whatever position the figure takes, these same muscles can be found, either tensed or at rest.

The somewhat complex names of some muscles make sense when analysed. Frequently they describe the progress of the muscle. The *sterno-mastoid* (a) travels from the sternum (breast-bone) to the mastoid process behind the ear. The *rectus femoris* (r) originates in the rectal area and attaches to the end of the femur (thigh-bone).

Around the head, neck and shoulders the main muscles are the *sterno-mastoid* (a) and the almost diamond- or trapezoid-shaped *trapezius* (b). The *trapezius* begins at the base of the skull, travels far down the back, attaches itself to the shoulder-blades at the side and continues over the shoulders to connect with the collar-bone (clavicle) at the front. it is this muscle that gives the characteristic slope to the shoulders. This is dealt with in greater depth on page 418.

The *latissimus dorsi* (g)—there is one on each side of the back—laps round the ribs and tucks up underneath the armpits, attaching to the upper arm-bone (humerus) at the top. At the front, the large *pectoral* muscles (d) move from the breast-bone (sternum) up to the collarbones and out to the upper ends of the arms. The long, flat muscle down the front of the body is known as the *rectus abdominis* (k) and is divided into four main parts, which are more or less clearly seen depending on the muscularity of the person. The *external obliques* (i) move out from the *rectus abdominis*, round the waist area and up to the *latissimus dorsi*.

The shape of the shoulders is completed by the *deltoid* (c). Viewed from the side it is like an inverted triangle (the sign for delta in the Greek alphabet is a triangle). It covers the arm joint rather like a raglan sleeve in shape. It moves down the arm and tucks in between the biceps (e) and the triceps (f).

Much of the characteristic shape of the outside of the lower arm or fore-arm is created by the supinator *longus* (h)—supinate means to turn—together with the long *radial extensor* of the wrist immediately below it. On the inner side are the group of muscles that move the fingers and cause the inner bulge. The outermost of these is the *ulnar flexor* (j) of the wrist, seen most clearly from the back.

At the front of the legs the *sartorius* (m), a long, thin muscle, travels from the pelvis, in and across the leg, down to the top of the lower leg and attaches to the tibia (main lower-leg or shin-bone). It is essential to look for this muscle in defining the leg. The three large muscles—the *rectus femoris* (s), the *outer vastus* (t) and *inner vastus* (u)—although clearly defined, especially when tensed, are really part of one large muscle, which has a common tendon connecting it to the kneecap ((patella). On the inner side

of the thigh, moving into the pubic area, is a group of muscles known as *adductors* (n).

At the back, the *gluteus maximus* (1) and the *gluteus medius* form the buttocks. It is important to note how these muscles are attached by a strong tendon to the *ilio-tibial band* (r), which flattens the outside of the thigh and travels right down to the top of the *tibia* (v).

The back of the thigh is composed of the three long flexor muscles of the knee —the *biceps* (q) and the grandly named *semi-membranosus* (o) and *semi-tendinous* (p). They originate from the pelvis and are covered at the top by the buttocks. They produce the fullness of the back of the thigh. when the knee is bent they stand out as prominent chords and are often referred to as the hamstrings.

The most pronounced muscle down the front of the lower leg, just at the side of the shin, is the *tibialis anticus* (x), and at the back the calf is made up of two main muscles. The underlying and flatter one, not unlike a flat fish in form, is aptly called the *soleus* (y), and the predominant muscle is called the *gastrocnemius* (Latin for the belly of a toad). It has two heads, the inside one being lower than the outer. Lastly, but not least, as it is the largest tendon in the body, the *Achilles tendon* (z) connects the *soleus* and *gastrocnemius* to the heel.

Of necessity, these are anatomical diagrams and are idealized in form, but it is an important practice to draw from anatomy books. Often, well-illustrated medical books are most useful. Above all, an understanding of the mechanics of the human body is crucial for a painter's progress.

CONTRAPPOSTO

From classical times a standing pose known as *contrapposto* has been one of the archetypes that have appeared and reappeared. It is an ideal state of equilibrium created by contrary movements of the body. Whatever position the figure takes, there is a push and pull of opposing forces enabling it to stand. *Contrapposto* illustrates welll how these forces and balances operate.

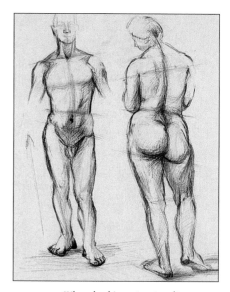

A B O V E   When looking at a standing figure, it is important to note which leg is bearing the weight —it is seldom equally distributed except on a parade-ground. Here, one leg clearly carries the weight and there is a pronounced change of plane at the great trochanter, which is the bony protuberance at the top of the thigh (from the femur or thigh-bone). There is a clear diagonal axis across the top of the pelvis. This becomes slightly less pronounced at the waist. The spine curves away, dropping the shoulder above the weight-bearing leg. The diagonal axis therefore changes dramatically at the pectoral muscles and shoulder-blades, and the shoulders balance the opposing movement of the pelvis.

ABOVE This standing nude, painted in oils, by the author involved the *contrapposto* pose quite unconsciously on the part of the model. It also happens to be *contro luce* or *contre Jour*—against the light. She was leaning against a chair with her arms behind her back. Her left leg is clearly carrying the weight, as the right leg is bent. Notice the axes of the pelvis, the waist, breasts, and shoulders moving in opposite directions. It is broadly painted, and much of the room is done with a palette knife and impasto (paint applied very thickly). A great deal of white was used in the space to give a shimmer of light. The base color of the figure is raw sienna into which slabs of indigo, alizarin crimson, and some cadmium red follow the direction of the planes.

BALANCE AND WEIGHT

This series of watercolors by David Carr explores the problem of balancing the figure and describing the forces at work. Each painting is done from a slightly different angle.

ABOVE In this standing nude with the arms raised above the head, the weight is on the left leg, and the enormous change of direction at the waist bears this out. Looking carefully at the watercolor, you will see that the mass of the figure was first established with a warm yellow (aureolin) and the drawing with French ultramarine into the damp paint followed. A brush loaded with ultramarine was taken up the torso with just a touch of alizarin crimson. Three primaries have been used to express the "idea" of standing.

ABOVE In this little watercolor, the figure turns and takes the weight off the right leg, transferring it to the left. Again painted with minimal means, a dark violet (French ultramarine and alizarin crimson) was drawn into a warmer wash. Note the slight bleeding of the color, which helps to give a sense of form.

ABOVE In this, more of the back was visible. A pale, flat yellow established the shape of the figure. A strong red line was placed down the leg carrying the weight, over which a glaze of French ultramarine put the whole leg in shadow, creating a powerful change of plane at the hip.

ABOVE Here, the artist moved around to the front to see more of the stomach and the bent leg. Again cadmium red was worked into aureolin. Extremely dense lines were painted into that with a mixture of French ultramarine and cadmium red, which gives almost black. This is most noticeable in the hair, but it also helps to give tension to the weight-bearing leg. The cast shadow from the legs helps to give a sense of direction to the plane of the floor.

CHAPTER SEVEN

Head, Neck, and Shoulders

When you come to paint the head and shoulders, it is of the utmost importance to understand the basic structure of this area. Here is a brilliant piece of engineering, allowing the head to rock backward and forward on the first vertebra (the atlas), while turning from side to side on the second (the axis).

So often the head is conceived as if it were a football stuck on top of a pole, when a rudimentary knowledge of this crucial area would inform and articulate the painting so much more.

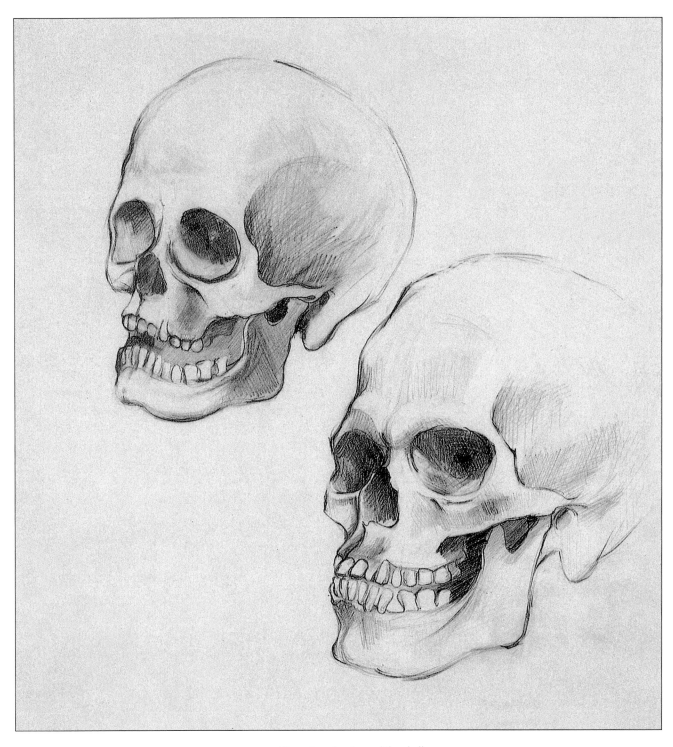

Looking at the skull, you can see the differences between the male and the female. The male tends to be a little squarer, and the brow is more prominent. The male forehead tends to slope backward, whereas the female is more vertical. The jawbone is larger in the male. The angle at the back of the female jaw

A B O V E These two drawings of the skull show the basic differences between the mate and the female—the lower of the two is the male.

is much gentler. Note the cheek-bone (malar), which moves right up the side of the eye, and how it is joined to the side of the skull by a slender bone known as the zygomatic arch. The skull is made up of a series of bones fused immovably together, and the only moving bone is the lower jaw or mandible.

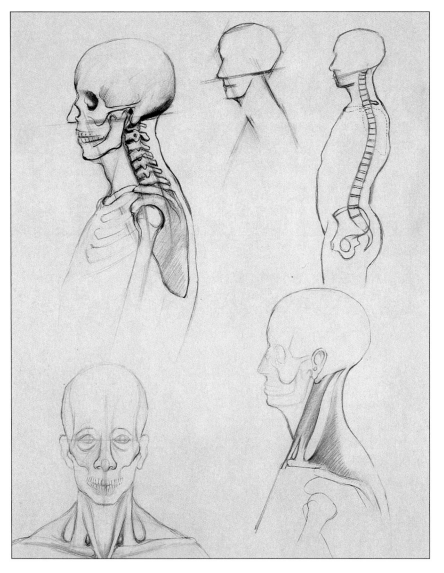

This illustrates three important points. Firstly, the back of the skull is much higher than the base of the jaw-bone or chin. This may be obscured by the hair, in which case the base of the skull is often placed too low. Secondly, the spine does not enter the head vertically, but at an angle. It then proceeds to describe a shallow S from shoulder to waist to pelvis. And thirdly —the most important point—the mastoid process, a lump (process) of bone, can be found immediately below and behind the ear. Even if the hair obscures it, you know where it is if you note the position of the ear, and this gives you the base of the skull.

From this point comes the sterno-mastoid muscle, so important in giving the neck its characteristic form. It starts at the mastoid process and then divides, one part being attached to the top of the sternum or breast-bone, the other to the inner end of the clavicle or collar-bone, The windpipe and throat move forward at an opposing angle from behind the breast-bone, moving up between the sterno-mastoid muscles into the jaw.

The other main muscle involved is the trapezius, which travels from the back of the head down to the scapula or shoulder-blade, forming the ridge that gives the shoulder its slope. Note how the sterno-mastoid and the trapezius tense and relax as the head moves from side to side. If you look in a mirror and hunch your shoulders forward, note the pits that appear between the muscles and the collar-bones.

ABOVE LEFT Drawing to show the relative positions of the skull, spine and sterno-mastoid muscle.

LEFT Drawing which demonstrates the action of the sterno-mastoid muscle.

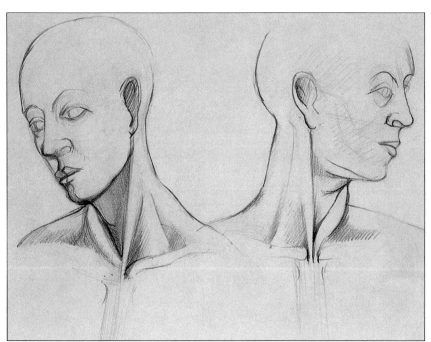

PORTRAIT HEAD

D A V I D   C A R R

When painting this portrait the author took care over the points described earlier in this chapter.
It is important to feel the volume of the skull under the skin and to see that the hair follows
this volume and is not added as if it is a wig. It is sometimes a good idea to ask a female sitter to put
her hair up so you can observe the base of the skull at the back more clearly.
The palette for this was French ultramarine, cobalt blue, cerulean blue, cobalt green, viridian green,
raw umber, cadmium lemon, cadmium yellow, yellow ocher, cadmium red, alizarin crimson, and
titanium white. The brushes used were no. 8 filbert, no. 3 round hog-hair, and no. 8 sable-nylon mix.
It was painted on canvas primed with an egg tempera ground.

1 The model in position with the light coming from the left.

2 The initial drawing was done very lightly using a minimum amount of charcoal and mainly with a very dilute mixture of raw umber and ultramarine. The light was coming from the left. The lighter parts of the face, head, and shoulder were established with a mixture of cadmium yellow, cadmium red, and yellow ocher plus white. Then ultramarine, raw umber, and cadmium red were used to define the darker parts. The artist was very aware of the volume of the skull and its height at the back beneath the hair. The sterno-mastoid has been very clearly painted in, as has the zygomatic arch leading from the cheek to the ear.

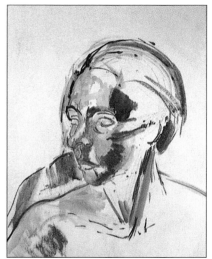

3 Cobalt blue and green, viridian green, cadmium lemon, and alizarin crimson were being used. To paint the wall behind the figure the artist used largely viridian and cobalt blue with some white and yellow ocher.

4 The back of the chair on one side has been defined very strongly. These slabs of color will be important in establishing the profile. Note the continued attention to the underlying form.

5 The trapezius muscle has now been established and therefore the shoulders, and the structure of the neck has been further clarified, showing that the throat comes out between the sterno-mastoid muscles. The hair should always follow the form of the skull.

6 The chair and wall have been further defined. The artist drew into the head with an ultramarine/raw umber mixture, constructing the eye more clearly and defining the hair traveling round the head.

7 The artist was aware of some reflected light from the body under the chin.

8 The artist noted a rhythm of shadow down the forehead, cheek, and neck and in establishing this flattened the face too much and lost some of its volume. Consequently the actual likeness has gone to an extent.

9 Note in the detail, however, that the planes around the eye and down the side of the nose have been developed. The forehead needs to be broader and the cheek bone re-defined. The chin is also weak.

10 This reworking has been done using a light flesh tone of cadmium yellow and cadmium red with white and some yellow ocher. The way the hair flows round the head has been emphasized. The lips are fuller, as is the chin.

11 Adjustments have also been made to the head and neck and the artist has built up the planes on the shoulders and upper chest using the same flesh tones but modulated with a little ultramarine and alizarin crimson.

12 Some warmth has been introduced into the nostril to bring the nose round, and a light plane has been introduced just under the eye to bring the lower lid around the eyeball. It is important that eyelids follow the volume of the eyeball underneath. A light blue-gray has been used to establish the whites of the eyes. The use of pure white should be avoided as it is usually tonally too sharp and jumps out.

13 Some violet in the wall behind the head and neck helps to give the flesh a sense of light by reacting with the yellow. The green (both the dark patch on the left and the light green-yellow under the violet) acts against the warmer areas of red in the figure.

14 The picture underwent several changes and at one point was almost lost. The successful conclusion shows the importance of constant reference to structure in rescuing form.

CHAPTER EIGHT

The Face and its Features

We should now look more closely at the head, and in particular the face. There are quite a number of muscles involved in the many subtle facial expressions that people make. Do not be alarmed, however, as we only need to look at those muscles beneath the skin that give the face its characteristic form.

The whole of the skull is covered by a thin film of muscle. A muscle at the side of the skull —the *temporal muscle* (a)—travels down behind the *zygomatic arch* (b) onto the jaw-bone This together with the *masseter* (g), that large muscle traveling from the cheek-bone to the jaw, is involved in opening and closing the mouth. You will often see the masseter flexing when someone grits their teeth in determination.

Coming from the inside top of the nose, muscles travel down each side of the nose to the inside edges of the nostrils and the corners of the upper lip. These are the *elevators* of the upper lip and nostrils (d). They raise the corners of the mouth and the nostrils and cause the characteristic furrow between the nose and the cheeks, especially pronounced in the male.

Other muscles move away from each corner of the mouth, notably the *buccinator* If), which can pull the side of the mouth back and expel air between the teeth and the cheek. The *zygomaticus major* (e) and *minor* (c) similarly lift the corner of the mouth and upper lip, especially if one sneers.

The sling-like *depressors* (h) of the lower lip and angle of the mouth pull the jaw open and lower the corners of the mouth. It should be noted that a ring of muscle encircles the entire mouth, and it is with this that we close the mouth firmly and purse our lips. It is known as the *orbicularis oris*, and the surrounding muscles (buccinator, depressors, and elevators) interlace with it to enable us to move our mouth in any way we wish.

The eye is similarly surrounded by a circular muscle—the *orbicularis oculi*. This is involved in squinting and closing the eye. The most important point here is that the amount of the eye that we see is only a small proportion of its total size. It is spherical and slightly egg-shaped and goes back deep into the skull.

We should be most particular to note that the eyelids follow its spherical shape. Neither is the eye an almond shape pointed at each corner. The tear-duct, not unlike a tear-drop itself, occupies the corner near the nose. At the outer corner the upper lid always crosses the lower lid.

The nose is about two-thirds gristle or cartilage (the shaded area), and it is only at the top that there is a bone (see the skull). If you are unfortunate enough to acquire a broken nose it is this small bone that is broken.

The ear is also almost all cartilage, except for the fleshy lobe. It consists of two bowls—the outer, flatter one forming most of the flap of the ear, the inner bowl being deeper and leads into the ear-hole. This is bounded in front by a little flap. There is a great variety of ear shapes and the best way to become familiar with this complex little structure is to stand in front of a mirror and practise drawing your own ears.

LEFT In this self-portrait in oils by the painter John Arnold there is a terrific sense of the volume of the skull, and the hair and beard have a structure that follows the form of the head and the facial muscles. The initial paintwork was quite broad, but the final paint layers were applied with smaller brushes in an almost cross-hatched technique. A build-up of planes has been preserved throughout. Note the deep furrow down the side of the nose and the side of the mouth, caused by the elevator muscle. The large masseter muscle can be felt under the beard. The structure around the eye, with the emphasis on the brow and cheek-bone, is beautifully described, and the eyelids perfectly follow the form of the eyeball. The ear is clearly and simply defined. The cartilaginous nature of the nose is very noticeable and here reflected light has been used to good advantage.

CHAPTER NINE

Arms, Hands, and Feet

The arm is a remarkable structure, especially the forearm. The radius bone can revolve around the ulna, which is hinged to the upper arm-bone, or humerus, and turn the hand almost 360°. To help your understanding of this complex series of muscles, extend the left arm with the palm uppermost and place the fingers of the other hand on the crest of the ulna and the thumb in the hollow of the elbow. That group or bunch of muscles now held by the hand are the ones involved in bending the fingers in a gripping action. The group on the outer side of the arm not held are involved in extending the fingers outward as well as twisting and turning the hand.

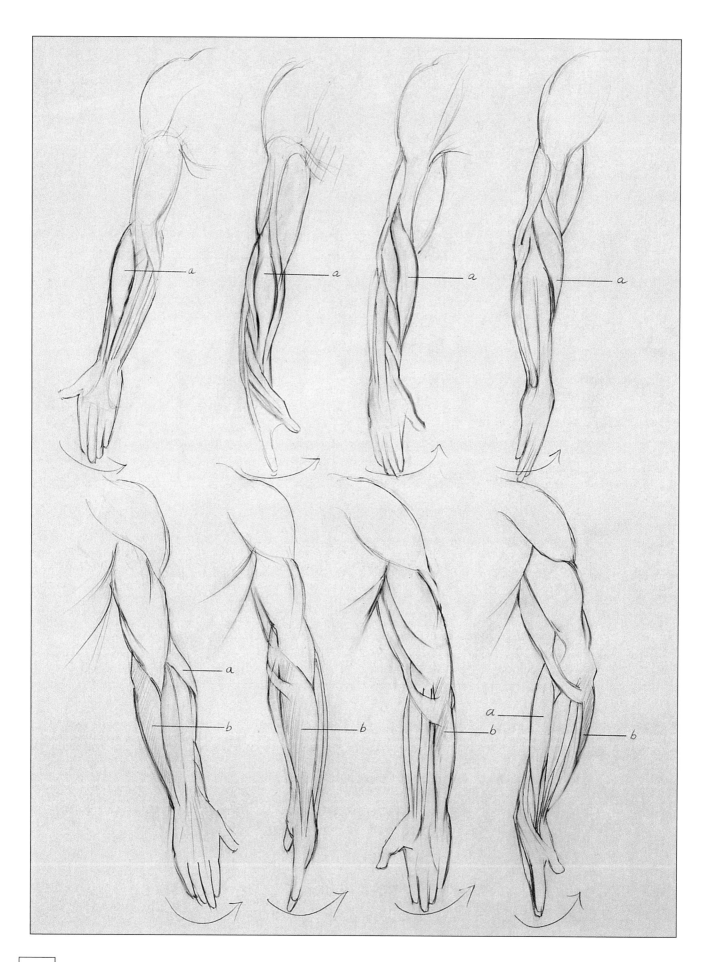

LEFT The technical term for turning is supination: look at the full figure on page 411. The long supinator was shown giving the arm much of its characteristic shape. The top row (left) shows the right arm with the palm open. Twisting the thumb inward, toward the body, in the direction of the arrow, note the position of the supinator (a) as the thumb almost completes a circle. In painting the arm, which of course will assume many positions, it is important to observe and imagine what this muscle is doing in any position. It will be the greatest help in describing the structure of the arm. Looking from the back (bottom row), the muscle giving the characteristic form is the ulnar flexor of the wrist (b), which travels from the elbow to the wrist. Note how this muscle behaves In the turning arm, and also the position of the supinator (a), which is just visible initially but reappears prominently when the arm has turned fully.

BELOW Hands and feet often frighten the beginner as well. Here the most important thing is to simplify the problem by concentrating on planes. Trying to describe a hand, finger by finger, is asking for trouble, and often results in a bunch of bananas. Firstly note a triangular plane that is made by the back of the hand, the first knuckle and the joint of the thumb. This is known as the digital triangle (a). Then it Is useful to think across the knuckles, a line called the transverse arch (b). See the back of the hand as another plane (c) and take a line across each of the finger joints to give fundamental planes (d) and (e).

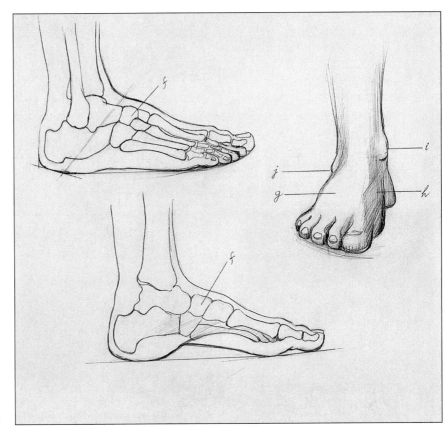

ABOVE The commonest fault when painting the foot is to make it too much of an L shape with a sharp angle from the leg to the top of the foot. In fact the top of the foot comprises a mass of seven bones called tarsals (f)— they correspond to the eight carpals in the wrist —and a flat triangular plane (g) falls away from the ridge caused by this group, down to the toes and outer side of the foot. By contrast the inner side of the foot is an almost vertical flat plane (h). The protuberance of the ankle on the inside caused by the tibia (i) is higher than that on the outside caused by the fibula (j).

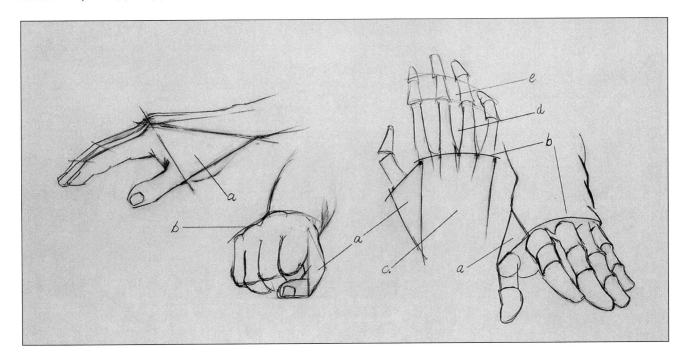

A PAIR OF HANDS

D A V I D   C A R R

The more practice you have at drawing and painting hands and feet, the better.
You'll have no shortage of sitters if you use a mirror, and continual study will be
repaid handsomely. This study was done in oils. The palette included French
ultramarine, viridian green, cadmium lemon, yellow ocher, alizarin crimson, and
titanium white.

1 The model's hands were placed so that
the light sources clearly illuminated the
planes.

2 In this study the hand is established
very simply in terms of planes. The digital
triangle is there and the fingers have been
treated as a. series of hinged planes. The
colors used are yellow ocher and white,
ultramarine, and alizarin crimson. Some
viridian is introduced to paint the table.

3 The second hand is included and the
table top painted more warmly. The plane
at the wrist is made clear and smaller
planes within the fingers are defined with
smaller brushstrokes. Cooler color is laid
into the darker areas of skin.

4 The basic aim is to see the hands as
hinged planar forms and to realize their
structure clearly and boldly in this way.

5 This basic alla prima study sees the brushwork following the directions of the form.

A PAIR OF FEET

D A V I D   C A R R

In this study, the artist decided to use a much thinner paint than in the preceding study and also a different palette which contained French ultramarine, viridian green, yellow ocher, raw sienna, cadmium red, and titanium white.

1 The outside of the form is drawn very simply in charcoal, and then the silhouette of the form is washed in with dilute yellow ocher. Try to be aware of the difference between the plane on top of the foot and that of the side. All other areas are washed in at this stage.

2 Some raw sienna with the slightest touch of ultramarine is scumbled over the yellow ocher for the darker tones. To preserve a clear change of tone at the ridge of the foot, white is added to yellow ocher to make the light planes clearer still.

3 The darkest parts of the feet around the toes and heel and on the leg, have a further layer of ultramarine and sienna scumbled over them. Finally some linear drawing is done around the toes. The technique of lightly scumbling darker, cooler paint over warmer, lighter paint, allowing some of the warmer paint to show through, gives a good sense of light on the flesh.

4 Note the strong sense of directional
light from left to right which just catches
the leg of the jeans and casts a shadow
over the ankle.

CHAPTER TEN

Skin Color and Tone

Paint manufacturers have produced a color that should be avoided at all costs. Its name is "flesh pink," and it is sometimes called "flesh tint." Its appearance is more akin to that of a cosmetic or dermatological cream, and it has no use whatsoever in the rendering of the luminosity of human skin. in the wide spectrum of skin colous, from the whitest of northern skins to the blackest of African skins, from Middle Eastern hues to the porcelain tones of the Far East, nowhere is this color found except in the circus.

Many different factors are at work creating skin color and tone. Not only is skin color affected by the ambient light, but very much by the surrounding colors, and particularly clothing. Its variety results from racial origin, and degree of exposure to the sun and weather. It varies from one part of the body to another. Look at the flesh painted by the contemporary painter Lucian Freud. Ruddier skin is caused by the closeness of the blood vessels and capillaries to the skin's surface. In very pale-skinned people, the blue veins can sometimes be observed just below the surface.

There is a great variety of cool and warm skin colors and tones, and it is important to use warm and cool colors to the full when painting. Warm primaries include cadmium yellow, cadmium red, and French ultramarine, and cool primaries lemon yellow, alizarin crimson, and cobalt blue. Earth colors, used carefully, are important. These should include yellow ocher, raw sienna, raw umber, and light red.

Careful use of warm and cool colors is a help in modeling the form, as cool colors tend to recede and warmer colors to come forward.

It is also necessary to expect the interaction of complementaries to give a sense of light on and in the skin. Glazing darker colors over light and vice versa can give a real sense of luminosity. The scumbling of darker paint over light, allowing just a little of the underlying color to show through, gives a sense of light in the shadows. Renaissance artists frequently used a cool under-painting of green, gray, or violet, over which they placed warm complementary colors. Very early Italian paintings often display this green appearance where the upper layers of paint have worn away.

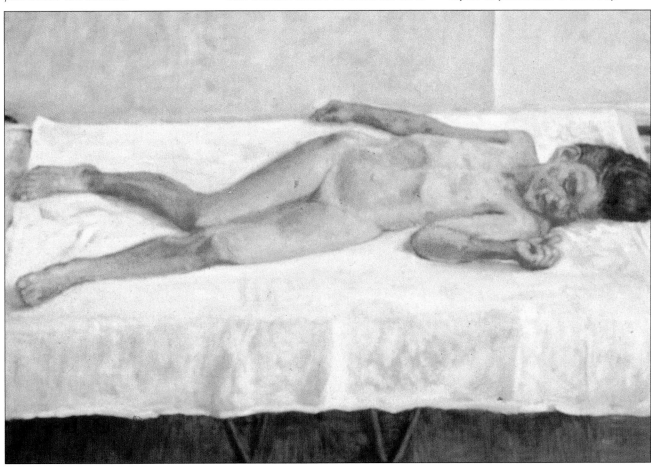

ABOVE In Victor Willis's painting of a young girl asleep a very restricted palette has been used. The medium was oil and the palette consisted of light red, yellow ocher, raw sienna, raw umber, and just a touch of cobalt blue and French ultramarine. Flake white was used throughout. It was executed over a period of several weeks. The overall skin tone was painted using Indian red and yellow ocher mixed with flake white. Darker tones were achieved with a light scumbling of delicate blue and raw umber. The consistency of light was maintained by the same treatment on the wall and sheet. Note how warmer Indian red mixed with raw sienna was used on the more exposed parts of the figure such as the lower legs and arms.

SKIN TONES ON THE FACE AND BODY

These six paintings demonstrate how the colou of skin can vary dramatically, depending on the light. Facial skin can be quite different from the skin on the body. In each painting the use of complementary colors is important in creating the form of the figure or face.

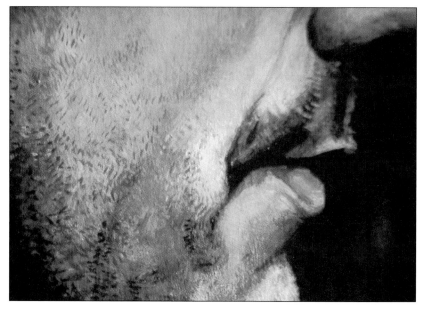

ABOVE LEFT John Arnold's portrait in oils uses more of a glaze technique. The artist began with an underpainting of strong colors, which were gradually muted by lighter glazes of subtle yellows, pinks, grays, and blues. The glazing medium was a 50/50 mixture of damar varnish and turps. He used warm and cold primaries, bright red, winsor yellow, cadmium yellow deep, yellow ocher, and French ultramarine being warm and rose madder, lemon chrome, winsor blue, cold.

ABOVE RIGHT AND RIGHT This dramatic portrait in oils by John Arnold uses the same palette. This was not glazed at all, but painstakingly built up using thin impasto, with careful attention to the planes and color modulations. It was mostly painted using hog-hair brushes, but fine detail was achieved with small sables.

LEFT There's an altogether different approach in Kay Gallwey's oil painting of the back with raised arms. The artist used rags and fingers to paint with, as much as brushes, and we can see how her marks flow round the forms. Working on a warm-toned ground and with lots of turps as a medium, she has established most of the flesh with raw sienna and umbers, into which she has introduced cool pinks and reds and complementary green for the darker tones.

BELOW LEFT AND RIGHT Kay Gallwey adopts a similar approach in her watercolors, and in both pictures of the girl in the black hat she uses large brushes to modulate warm yellows to cooler pinks, defining and re-defining the form with sepia. Notice how she likes to place her figures within an interesting setting. The busy textures and patterns and strong colous act as a foil to the simpler areas of flesh.

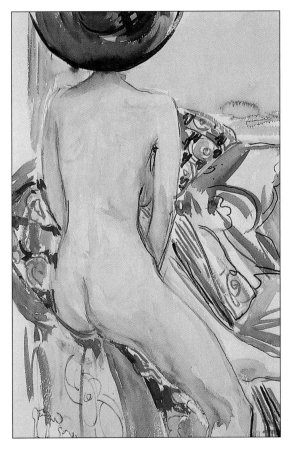

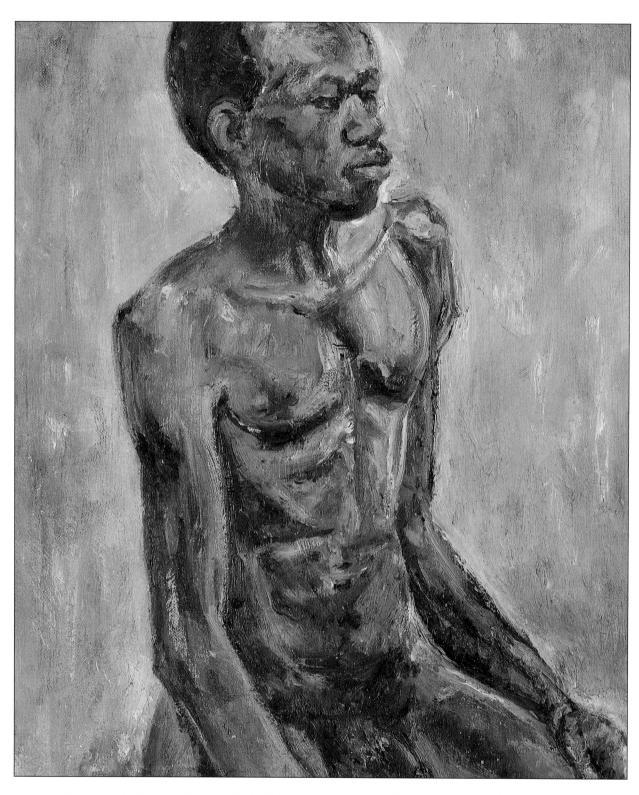

ABOVE In this portrait in oils, the artist, Irene Lightbody, began on a warm-toned ground with an underpainting of dark colors—raw sienna, alizarin crimson ,and French ultramarine. The dark pigmentation of black skin means reflected light is much more noticeable and this can be cool and bluish or warm and yellow. Within the skin itself there is a wide variety of colors—a mixture of Van Dyck brown and yellow ocher simply doesn't work. Strong blue and green accents have been seen and stated boldly, and these work effectively with the golden yellow and warm reds. The blue paint scumbled over the warm ground behind the figure provides an effective contrast.

CONTRASTING SKIN TYPES

There are three very different types of skin represented in these paintings. Even within a relatively small area of skin, there are many subtle changes of color.

ABOVE This oil painting of a reclining figure by the author was completed at one sitting. It is *alla prima* throughout. Beginning with a simple base of warm color using cadmium yellow, cadmium red, yellow ocher, and white over a strong linear drawing of French ultramarine and raw umber, the artist worked into it using thicker paint and a loaded brush. Alizarin crimson, ultramarine, and some viridian green are applied freely into the wet paint to give darker, cooler tones. The large areas of dark cloth and the black socks contrast well with the flesh, and the dramatic orange of the upper arm modified by blues and greens acts against the slab of blue paint on the floor. Some of the later paint was applied with a palette knife.

LEFT This portrait head in oils by Judith Symons is of special interest as earth colors formed the predominant part of the palette, plus a little cadmium lemon and mineral violet. The palette consisted of oxide of chromium (a dull green), Van Dyck brown, raw sienna, Venetian red, cadmium lemon, mineral violet, and titanium white. The artist shows how many subtle changes of color can occur within a relatively small area of skin. It was painstakingly painted with a careful, analytical approach. She used small, square sable brushes with a thin impasto, using a little turps to make the paint flow, but taking care to let her brushmarks stand. This gives clarity to the planes and a good sense of structure to the head.

CHAPTER ELEVEN

Two Approaches to Painting the Figure

It is worth studying two contrasting approaches to the figure. One shows the painter concerned solely with the image of the figure. There is little interest in the figure's relationship to space, and the figure usually fills most of the canvas. This approach was generally followed by Amedeo Modigliani (1884–1920) and might loosely be termed the "Modigliani syndrome." The other convention might be called the "Giacometti syndrome." Alberto Giacometti was an Italian-Swiss painter, whose work is characterized by an obsessive interest in the figure placed in space and its relationship to the position of the painter and the surrounding objects.

THE FIGURE FILLS THE PICTURE

Modigliani's early work was very much influenced by Cubism, which led to his characteristic image of the elongated neck and the graceful long oval forms of his later work. His paintings of the nude fill the whole picture area, often spilling out so that only the head, torso, and pelvis fit the frame. There is no great depth and the simple forms behind the figure suggest a very shallow picture space.

ABOVE The massive forms loom large in *Seated Nude* (1917) by Modigliani, as if the artist was very close to the model.

ABOVE A large and energetic, reclining nude in oils by Kay Gallwey.

This large nude in oils by Kay Gallwey is a good example of the Modigliani approach. The figure is flung backward over the couch and out of the picture. Recessional space is unimportant. The artist's working method is worth noting. She uses a standard palette of hot and cold reds, blues, and yellows with a permanent green and viridian green. She uses very little earth color.

Usually she will be working on a primed white canvas. Her medium is a 50/50 mixture of genuine turpentine and refined linseed oil. much of the painting has been done using soft cotton rags wrapped around the end of the finger. In this way she can maintain a bravura approach and infuse the picture with energy.

Firstly she dips the rag in the

medium and mixes it with warm yellows and reds, and lightly masses in the main areas with quite fluid paint. She is able to wipe off this paint easily in order to create transparency and let the white canvas impart luminosity. She is careful not to lay down any warm colors where there may be a need for cold areas (i.e. patches of blue). She adds more paint using the rag, modeling the form in a very direct way as if the fingers were touching the flesh itself. Lighter

BELOW This technique can be seen to very good advantage in her picture of the back of a girl arranging her hair. Again the paint is applied freely with finger and rags. Although there is more concern for space, as the figure is reflected in the mirror beyond, nonetheless there is a strong sense of a flat jig-saw pattern of shapes dividing up the picture surface. Note again the use of muted green and crimson in the flesh, and the effective contrast of the warm yellow-brown arm against the gray-violet of the reflection.

areas are achieved by rubbing out. More sumptuous color is reserved for the drapery. Note the touches of green shadow in the flesh around the ribs and under the breasts. This is particularly effective against the complementary red of the cloth. Cooler viridian green and alizarin crimson are applied under the thigh.

Brushes are used in the final stages of the painting—notably in the strong pattern of the foreground cloth and finer lines under the breast and around the thighs.

THE FIGURE AND SPACE

For Alberto Giacometti the figure's real existence in light and space is crucial. Most of his working life as an artist was spent trying to bring his image alive. He called it making it "like"—not a copy or likeness—but reaching that moment when the painting or sculpture jumped into life for a split second. It was this search that led him to the elongated and narrow forms of his sculpture, to seemingly incomplete forms. He felt that as he "finished" a figure, it lost its spark of life.

Working on a flat canvas, he did everything he could to create a sense of real space inhabited by a real form. His paintings are more a record of this search than a finished statement.

Giacometti's portrait of Annette (1954) is typical. He is really trying to see the figure "appearance" size, not larger or smaller, and this involves placing the figure in space precisely at its actual distance from the painter. This problem of size and distance drove him to distraction. "An arm is as vast as the Milky Way, and this phrase has nothing mystical about it. The distance between one wing of the nose and the other is like the Sahara, without end, nothing to fix one's gaze upon, everything escapes," he said.

ABOVE In *Annette Assise* (1954) by Giacometti the figure is set back in space, pushed there by the illusory painted borders like multiple window-frames. His whole working process can be seen on the canvas—marks are painted in and out, and all the time relationships between figure and space are established by actual lines of black, gray, white, and ocher moving between the objects through the space. At the heart of this space is the central core of compressed form—the head.

The figure here, painted in oils by the author, is sitting in a light-filled room. Various colored curtains change the color of the light coming through the windows. At the top of the picture in the far corner of the room cooler daylight streams through. The figure traces a diagonal from corner to corner. The predominant colors in the triangle above this are cool, cerulean blues, lemon yellows, cool pinks, and lilac. The lower triangle comprises rich velvety oranges, warm violets, and reds. The figure against the blue areas tends to be orange and the thigh against the warm chair and floor is a very cool light lemon and cerulean. Consciously or otherwise, all these relationships have to play a positive part in creating the sense of a light-filled space.

In technical terms, the initial drawing involved an awareness of all the points of intersection of the space and the figure. In other words, just where did the carpet intersect with the knee? Where did the lines of the windows, floor, and walls, if extended, pass through the figure? This is another way of setting up relationships.

The palette was quite extensive: French ultramarine, cobalt blue, cerulean blue, viridian green, raw umber, cadmium lemon, yellow ocher, cadmium yellow, cadmium red light, and alizarin crimson. Thinner underpainting in base colors is built on wet into wet with progressively thicker paint, until much of the final layer is scumbled and scratched over the surface, allowing previous layers of color to shine through.

BELOW The large studio space was exploited here in this oil painting of a seated figure.

CHAPTER TWELVE
Tonal Painting

On several occasions in this book the term "restricted palette" has been used. It is important to realize how much can be achieved with economical means. A restricted palette can mean anything from three or four colors—for example, titanium white, yellow ocher, raw umber, and French ultramarine, which would be ideal for tonal studies—to earth colors enlivened by one or two primaries, to the three primary colors, or any other combination where the decision has been made to keep the color strictly limited.

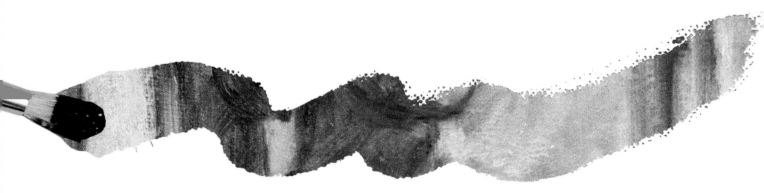

RESTRICTED PALETTE STUDIES

Painting with a restricted palette is often a useful economy but, as these paintings demonstrate, it can also be a good discipline. It requires the artist to concentrate on establishing the right differences in tone, from light to dark, without the freedom of a full range of colors.

ABOVE Mike Knowles's restricted palette used for these two portrait beads in oils was raw umber, raw sienna, Indian red, cobalt blue, Prussian blue, and black. The paintings were worked on weekly a number of times and scraped back between each session. They were each completed finally in one session *alla prima*. A restricted palette can be extended, and In this case some virldian green, cadmium red, yellow, and lemon were used sparingly. The blue/green of the wall behind the head acts as a foil to the flesh, which was painted using various combinations of light red, raw sienna, and white. In the portrait with the tilted head, touches of cadmium red on the forehead and cobalt blue down the side of the nose and forehead push the form around and there is a terrific unity in the painting achieved by the positive brushwork over the whole surface. The second picture has bold planes of light raw sienna down the side of the forehead, on the cheek-bone and down the side of the nose, with a deeper sienna used for the rest of the face. The darker tones under the eyes and around the chin are made with black and cobalt blue with touches of sienna. There are warmer accents on the ear and lip.

ABOVE This seated figure, in oils, is a good example of tonal painting using a restricted palette. Painted on a warm ground, yellow ocher and white depict the brightest and warmest light, and pure yellow ocher the next tone down—the hair, part of the hip, and the model's right foot. Then raw umber lowers the tone further with touches of French ultramarine, notably on her right arm and inside left thigh. More ultramarine was introduced for the darkest areas. Taking this approach, the artist has made decisions involving simplified forms and planes, and at what tone and temperature to pitch each part on a scale from the lightest, warmest ocher to the cooler, darker tones.

SEATED WOMAN

J O Y   S T E W A R T

The restricted palette for this sequence is yellow ocher, cadmium red light,
alizarin crimson, French ultramarine, and titanium white, plus an occasional
cooler lemon yellow.

1 Initially the figure is massed in with thin alizarin crimson, into which are worked mixtures of cadmium red, yellow ocher, and white.

2 This is drawn into with lines of pure ultramarine and alizarin crimson.

3 The form is built up, establishing the strong light plane of the torso with more yellow ocher and red, and placing accents of light yellow ocher on the breast. The darker areas are built up with a light scumble of ultramarine, which is particularly effective around the side of the face. Some reflected light is observed on the breasts, and is picked out with ultramarine and white. A strong form has been achieved with great economy of means. The light works well. There is some very fluid drawing around the arms, and the clear, directional brushwork in the torso makes for a convincing study.

4 A solid and imposing result, using a restricted palette.

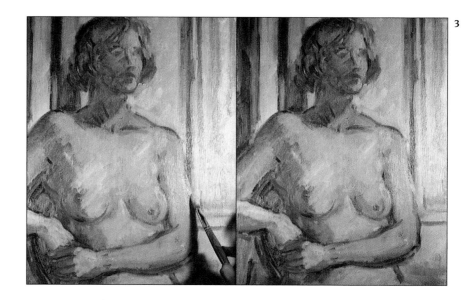

CHAPTER THIRTEEN
Light and Color

"Light cannot be reproduced, but must be represented by something else, color. I was very pleased with myself when I found this out." This simple but crucial statement was made by one of the pivotal figures of late 19th- and early 20th-century painting, Paul Cézanne (1839–1906). Although painters of the 19th century were increasingly interested in the growing scientific research into the field of color, artists have always known that a sense of light is created by a juxtaposition of colors. There are Pompeian wall-paintings full of golden light and lavender shadow; green shadows complement the warm carnation of the flesh in early Italian painting; yellow and violet are used as primary components of color chords in medieval glass.

Sir Isaac Newton's experiments with the prism and demonstration of the components of white light (the spectrum) were to increase this awareness of color and its properties. Eugene Delacroix, in the early 19th century, said his starting point as a colorist came from observing the rainbow and looking at the flesh of Rubens's Nereids in *Marie de Medici landing at Marseilles* in the Louvre, Paris. In his *Massacre at Scios* he introduces hatchings of pink, orange-yellow, and pale blue into some of the flesh. His

experiences in North Africa in 1832 and the impressions of light and color he received there were a crucial influence on his later work, just as they were for Henri Matisse in the early 20th century.

In the same year (1832) the French chemist Eugène Chevreul published a paper on color theory which asserted that "any color in isolation is surrounded by an aureole of its complementary." Among many notable achievements, he invented margarine and lived to the age of 103. In 1824 he was

appointed director of the dyeing department at the Gobelins tapestry factory in Paris and in 1839 produced his most influential book, *Of the Law of the Simultaneous Contrast of Colours and the Assortment of Coloured Objects.*

From Delacroix onward, the influence of scientific color theory allied to the artist's natural observational skills is clear. Impressionism, Post-Impressionism and Fauvism all relied heavily on the behavior of complementary colors.

COLOR WHEEL

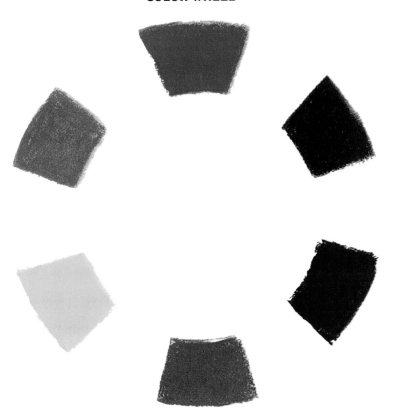

ABOVE At the top of the circle is a primary red. Immediately we encounter the vexed question as to what constitutes a primary red, or any other primary color for that matter. There have been many attempts to fix the primaries, but suffice it to say that primary red must come somewhere midway between orange on the one hand and violet on the other. The three primary

colors are red, yellow, and blue. They are called primary because they cannot be made by taking any other colors and mixing them. The primary colors can be warm or cold. Red is not automatically a warm color—it can be cool as it moves toward violet (e.g., alizarin crimson) or warm as it moves toward orange (e.g., cadmium red light). A cool yellow would be

lemon, and a warm one cadmium yellow deep. Cerulean blue is cool as it moves toward green, and French ultramarine warm as it moves toward violet. The colors between the primaries are called secondaries and each is produced by mixing two primaries. The secondary colors are green, violet, and orange. The fun really begins with complementaries.

ABOVE The complementary of any primary color is the result of mixing the other two primaries. So, in the column of colors, the complementary of primary red is green (primaries blue and yellow mixed),the complementary of primary yellow is violet (red and blue) and the complementary of primary blue is orange (red and yellow). They are diagonally opposite each other in the color circle.

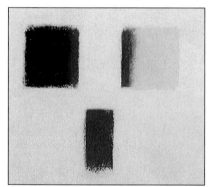

ABOVE The small diagram shows why certain colors, when mixed, give another color. Colored dyes and pigments appear the colors they are because they absorb all color wavelengths except one, which they reflect. The reflected wavelength is perceived as the pigment's color. However, this is a simplification. In the example, blue and yellow each contain a little green. This is not normally noticeable as it is not the dominant color or wavelength. When they are mixed, however, blue absorbs the yellow light, and yellow absorbs the blue and their common denominator, green, now doubled, is given off and picked up by the eye.

Thinking again about light we realize, as Cézanne did, that we cannot copy the brilliance of light itself with our relatively dull pigments. Even the strongest colors are inadequate, and if we resort to the addition of white to increase their brilliance we merely tend to make them chalky. It is through the interaction of colors and their juxtapositions that we can begin to create equivalents for light. Only then can we hope to place our figures in situations of convincing light and space and to paint flesh with any kind of luminosity.

To do this we need to know about primary and secondary colors, which for convenience are usually represented in a color circle.

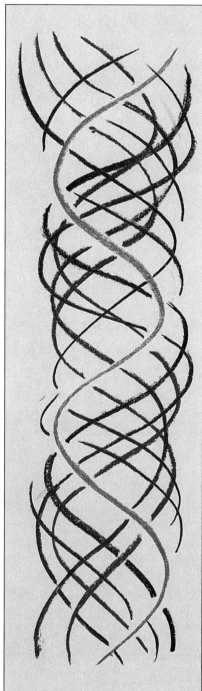

ABOVE In proximity, complementary colors enhance and enliven each other. Another experiment undertaken by Chevreul when he had problems producing a vibrant blue dye for the tapestry industry is illustrated by the "twisted thread." He took several strands of blue (all slightly varied) and introduced a strand of orange —the complementary. The yarn produced had specks of orange in it. The eye perceives the blue as being more intense than it actually is because of the presence of the complementary.

IMPRESSIONIST APPROACH

It is well worth while taking account of these discoveries in your own work. By deliberately trying an Impressionist or Fauvist approach, you can assimilate some of their techniques and enliven your own work in the process. It can help to avoid a tendency to rely too heavily on earth colors when painting flesh, for example, or to resort to brown and black when wishing to make things darker. Instead, you will be able to create shadows that contain light, and play off the figure against its surroundings.

ABOVE In Renoir's painting *Woman's Torso in Sunlight*, the figure is bathed in dappled sunlight. The figure is surrounded by foliage, and we assume that the light is filtering through the leaves and branches above. The face is much warmer than the porcelain-like flesh of the body. This whole effect of light is achieved by exploiting warm and cool complementary color contrasts. Yellows and pinks play off against hints of blue and green over the surface of the flesh itself, and the subtlety of the figure contrasts well with the more boldly painted landscape.

GIRL LEANING ON PILLOWS

K A Y   G A L L O W A Y

This oil painting relies mainly on the delicate contrast of yellow and pale lilacs,
pinks, muted green, warmer yellows, and cool blues.
The palette is French ultramarine, cerulean blue, viridian green, oxide of
chromium, cadmium lemon, cadmium yellow mid, cadmium red, alizarin crimson,
thinned with turpentine.
The brushes used are a no. 5, no. 8 square, a no. 8 round bristle and a
large, round, long-handled hog-hair.

1 The model was seated against a number of cushions.

2 The study painted on a canvas with a warm cream ground. The artist does the preliminary drawing with a fine brush and alizarin crimson. With a rag she works crimson behind the figure and cerulean blue around it, and begins to paint into the figure with cadmium yellow.

3 She supports her arm with a mahl stick rested on the canvas at one end and begins to define the head with violet (alizarin and ultramarine) using the large hair brush. She introduces much stronger accents into the drapery and a striking crimson pink at the figure's shoulder.

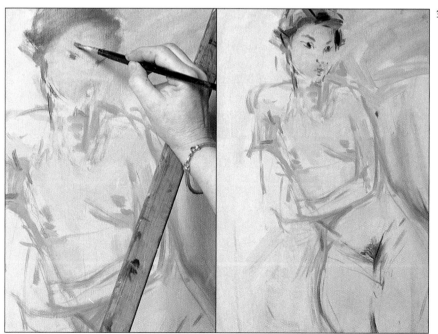

4 The artist takes great care with the axes of the body. There must be a strong sense of the model's right arm bearing the weight and pushing up at the shoulder. She places a clear line at the "hinge" there. She continues to develop the drapery as it will be crucial in creating the rhythmical and fluid contour of the figure. She works more light, warm yellow paint into the body and cooler paint above the breasts.

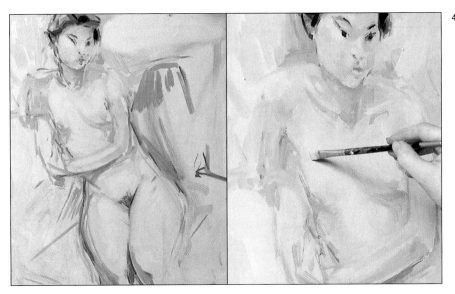

5 She builds up the color in the face and begins to introduce some delicate complementary green to the forehead, around the neck and under the elbow. The green used is oxide of chromium mixed with white.

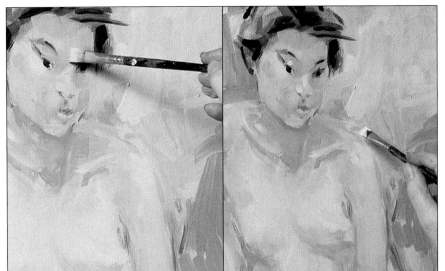

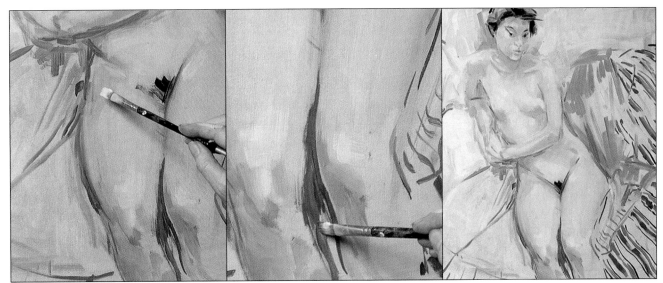

6 She begins to develop the form of the figure further by painting into the shadows. She has wiped away some of the paint with rags and in the detail the cream ground can be seen clearly. It is in fact being used here as a color in the painting. Toned grounds such as this can have a terrific unifying effect within a picture.

7 With the most delicate touches of dull green and violet, she defines the face.

Note the accent of slightly stronger green near the hair line. It is just strong enough

to act effectively with the pink of the cheek.

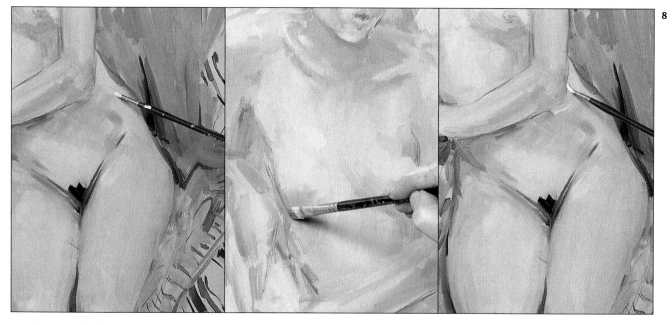

8 Refining work takes place on the body, building up a sense of luminous skin. Subtly modulated strokes of pink and lilac gray play against the predominantly pale yellow flesh.

9 A strong highlight is placed on the shoulder to give an added sense of pressure at this point.

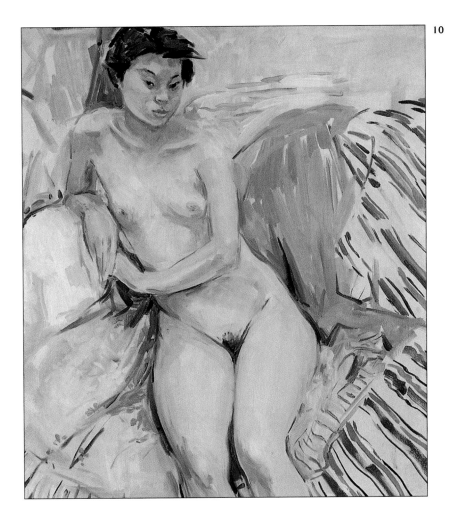

10 The volume of the pink sheet behind the figure becomes more solid, separating the figure from the busy striped cloth on the right. The turquoise cloth is enlivened with touches of pure orange. The drawing of the hand and arm is completed. The feeling of light has been skillfully created by a carefully balanced use of complementaries, delicate green against pink, lilac against yellow, and the warmer yellow against blue.

OIL STUDY USING STRONG COLOUR AND THICK PAINT

In this large painting of a reclining figure by the author much stronger colour has been used. It is 5 x 4 ft. (1.5 x 1.2 m) on canvas. The initial layers of paint were laid in flat with plenty of turps, and were worked into with thick paint of tube consistency. Very little mixing was done on the palette, and many different strokes and swirls of paint were applied with both brush and fingers. The palette is a fairly simple one of titanium white, two blues (French ultramarine and cerulean blue), two yellows (cadmium lemon and cadmium yellow mid), two reds (cadmium red and alizarin crimson), and viridian

green. Blacks have been made with a mixture of alizarin, French ultramarine and viridian green. The flesh is treated more simply than the highly textured paint surface of the drapery. A light cadmium yellow and red mixture has had a variety of colors scrubbed into it—warmer reds

on the lower leg tucked under the body, warmer yellow on the stomach, and cooler lilac and violet touches on the thigh, breasts, and face.

ABOVE **This whole painting has a tapestry-like feeling, with strands of color weaving together to give a sense of light.**

FAUVIST APPROACH

Just as the term Impressionism was culled by a newspaper critic from the title of a painting by Claude Monet, so the Fauves (wild beasts in French) received their name from the critic Louis Vauxcelles at their now-famous exhibition of 1905. Fauvism was a relatively short-lived and loose movement of artists without formal theories or manifestoes that existed during the first years of the 20th century, but it has been profoundly influential.

Color was liberated to operate as a language in its own right, more akin to music. Indeed, the whole business of manipulating color can be likened to striking chords and discords. Matisse was to say later,

"Thus it is that simple colors can act upon the inner feelings with all the more force because they are simple. A blue, for instance, accompanied by the shimmer of its complementaries acts upon the feelings like a sharp gong. The same with red and yellow; and the artist must be able to sound them when he needs to."

WOMAN SEATED BY RED SCREEN

KAY GALLWEY

The model is seated against very bright fabrics to give the artist full play with color. Only a few colors have been used, and the palette comprises French ultramarine, cerulean blue, cadmium lemon, cadmium yellow deep, cadmium red, alizarin crimson, and ivory black. It is painted on white primed canvas tacked to a board

1 The model is seen here surrounded by strong primary colors.

2 Three slabs of color are put down—the stripe of ultramarine along the top, part of the red screen, and cadmium yellow for the body. With a rag dipped in turps, the artist moves the paint around on the canvas.

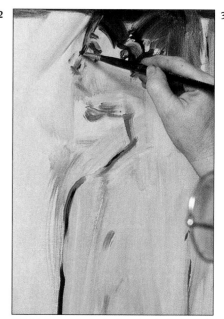

3 With ivory black she lays in the hair, and begins to draw the face, neck, and arms, working into the wet yellow paint and allowing them to mix.

4 More of the body is drawn with black and cadmium yellow deep.

5 The artist works stronger black lines into the hair and has drawn some of the figure in ultramarine. Much stronger, purer color is now applied—a powerful red around the head.

6 The artist extends the red into the cloth to the left of the figure, Then, taking a rag dipped in turps and a mixture of alizarin crimson and ultramarine, she bangs in the fabric.

7 At this point she introduces some fluorescent day-glo paint into the picture to make things really go with a zing. With a no. 5 round bristle brush, she draws multiple contour lines around the form in bright red and green.

8 She uses some of this color in the face, and places some strong accents of a fluorescent blue in the hair, at the same time completing the patterned cloth on the right.

9 The artist makes the cloth darker, and continues to modify the contour with a darker line of deep violet. She paints a lot more lemon yellow, cadmium yellow deep, and light cerulean blue into the flesh of the head, neck, and body.

10 Finally, she works some pure bright green and ultramarine into the head to produce a very jazzy painting.

11 Strong, bold color and rapid execution are the keynotes of this vibrant study.

FAUVIST STUDIES

These two oil studies are both examples of a Fauvist approach. In each case, the resulting painting is a strong statement in bold colors.

LEFT This painting has been achieved with primary colors, only. It is oil on canvas, and the palette is manganese blue (a slightly more powerful and greener blue than cerulean), lemon yellow, cadmium yellow, cadmiumred, and alizarin crimson. The green wall behind the figure contains various mixtures of yellow and blue, the floor mixtures of cadmium red and manganese giving a brownish-violet tinge. White has of course been used in the figure. The base color is cadmium lemon and white, into which slabs of warmer yellow have been worked on the upper chest and the figure's right thigh. Into this stronger drawing, marks have been worked using a deep violet mix to carve out the form.

LEFT Working over a warm ground, the artist, Marie Wylan, has successfully contrasted this monumental figure with the blue wall behind. The warm ground shows through the blue and the base color for the figure is also warm, with colder color applied on top. The palette was French ultramarine, viridian green, cadmium lemon, cadmium yellow, cadmium red, alizarin crimson, and titanium white. The form of the figure has been described with a large, square brush in light alizarin, and over this have been laid strokes of cadmium lemon, tinged with green. Some of the warm cadmium yellow base at the figure's left shoulder, her stomach, and hip bone has been left to give a sense of volume and of light coming into the picture from the right.

RAPID WATERCOLOR STUDIES

These four studies can also be termed Fauvist in approach, with their use of areas of strong color and the clear linear definition of the figure.

LEFT AND BELOW These three small watercolors painted rapidly at one sitting, have a calligraphic quality about them. Strong blocks of pure color have been laid down for the figure and space, and allowed to bleed a little. There is some glazing, but the form is fully defined by dark, sweeping lines of deep violet (alizarin crimson and French ultramarine) or a near black (cadmium red and French ultramarine).

LEFT Similarly, in the small reclining figure by the author, broken washes and glazes of clear, warm, and cold colors gain their definition by drawing in the form.

CHAPTER FOURTEEN

Oil Glaze Technique

The use of oil glazes, layers of thin, transparent paint, is the most traditional of all oil-painting techniques. Unlike *alla prima* or wet-into-wet painting, which is usually completed in the space of a few hours, or days at the most, the glaze technique needs a longer time scale and some careful planning. This considered approach has been used since the time of van Eyck (1390?–1441), and in one form or another is the foundation of the work of painters up to the end of the 19th century. Painters still work in this way today, but it is no longer the norm.

The development of open-air painting, the invention of the oil-painting tube and the desire for the greater immediacy that the Impressionists favored saw the growth of *alla prima* techniques. Van Gogh is a fine example of this bold and direct approach to painting, working with a fully loaded brush and impasto. A late 20th-century painter like Frank Auerbach scrapes off much of the previous day's work and paints the image afresh with luscious and thickly applied paint.

Nonetheless, many contemporary painters feel that the oil-glaze technique satisfies their own particular needs ideally. It is not as complicated or as mysterious as some people think, and is an important addition to the technical repertoire. Even if you do not use it fully, it is a useful introduction to the use of glazes, which can play an important part in any painting in its later stages.

The technique involves an initial drawing in charcoal or an under-painting in neutral colors such as raw umber or the ochers. Some painters used gray, from which comes the term *grisaille*. Titian aptly called this stage of the process—"making the bed of the picture."

When the underpainting is dry, color is glazed over it, layer upon layer, the paint being allowed to dry between each stage. Thicker paint, or impasto, can be applied at any time and allowed to stand in its clarity or further glazed over.

YOUNG MAN LEANING ON WINDOW SILL

M I C H A E L   C H A I T O W

Planning is important. The hgure was seated on a stool against a purple velvet cloth. The artist decided to work from the head and torso and to fill the picture frame with the subject. He was interested in exploiting the dramatic light contrasts of the flesh and the velvet. An oil glaze technique is particularly suited to such dramatic tonal differences.
The palette used is raw umber, cadmium yellow, cadmium red, alizarin crimson, rose madder, winsor violet, and titanium white.

1 The model in position.

2 Working on a white ground, the artist draws in the basic shapes of the figure in charcoal. He has decided to use a waterbased medium, gouache, for the underpainting in order to speed up the process. This is perfectly legitimate as normally he would have to wait for each layer of paint to dry thoroughly. The water-based underpainting will act in exactly the same way as an oil-based one would. If acrylic paint rather than gouache is used it must be kept very dilute. He adds a small amount of acrylic white to the shoulder. He then fixes the drawing.

3 He now begins to strengthen the drawing, giving the figure much greater mass by pushing the charcoal around using both a cloth and his fingers. He uses a putty rubber to pick out some of the form.

4 The figure and its surrounding space are now well established and developed with charcoal, black and white conté, and white acrylic.

5 The artist clarifies the edge of the arm further with black acrylic. We can see how simply but subtly the form has been drawn.

6 Now comes the dramatic part—the application of a glaze. The glazing medium used here is made up as follows: one part stand oil, one part damar varnish, one part genuine turpentine. The pigment in this case is a mixture of alizarin crimson, raw umber, and violet. The artist based this choice partly on the mood of the pose and sitter, and partly on the deep violet velvet cloth behind the figure. The glaze is applied evenly across the picture using a 1½ in. (3.75 cm) brush.

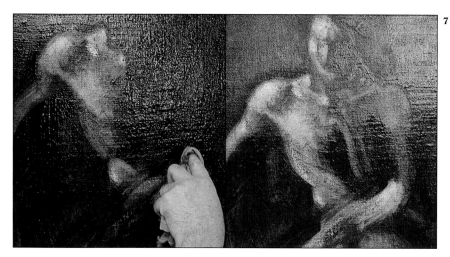

7 Taking a cotton rag, he rediscovers the forms of the figure by gently wiping away the glaze. He constantly refers to the model while doing this as adjustments of form can still be made. We can now see the charcoal drawing and underpainting.

8 Using a flesh tone mixed from cadmium red, cadmium yellow, and white, he begins to paint some of the lighter flesh tones with a thin impasto.

9 The artist uses stronger cadmium red and yellow to paint the warmth around the stomach, and he establishes striking highlights on the model's right shoulder, chest, waist, and wrist.

10 He blends the paint around the model's head and places warmer accents on the forehead, left arm, and hand.

11 The final stage is painted at a laer sitting, once the painting has had time to dry. He gives the painting an all-over glaze, again using a mixture of rose madder and raw umber, and wipes this off with a cotton rag to find the form. He continues to lay in opaque flesh tones. He develops the face and hair further and makes a small alteration to the cloth on the side of the head.

GLAZE UPON GLAZE

These paintings are all examples of the use of oil glazes and they display the richness and depth which can be achieved using this technique.

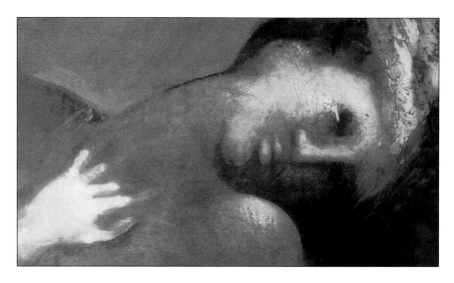

ABOVE In these finished studies by Michael Chaltow the technique can be seen to full advantage. Glaze upon glaze of color mixed with the glazing medium, and carefully wiped off to reveal the form, gives a rich resonance to the pictures. Paint is scumbled over a glaze, over which the artist can glaze again if necessary. Note the impasto around the woman's reclining head in this picture, which has had a further glaze laid on it. Deep, dark areas contrast dramatically with the highly worked lighter forms.

LEFT In this male torso by Michael Chaltow, glazing over the scumbled paint gives a great sense of the underlying power of the turning form.

LEFT In this portrait, cooler glazes over warm give a beautiful sense of light and stillness.

LEFT This painting by Mike Knowles has an underpainting of thin acrylic paint over a white acrylic ground. The model was lit powerfully from the side by an electric light. The basic painting of the flesh was laid In with Indian red and cadmium red, the deep space behind the figure with cerulean blue. Then glazes of Prussian blue and black were applied to the spatial area. The glazing medium is one part stand oil, one part damar varnish and one part genuine turps. The flesh and hair are glazed with thin mixtures of white and cadmium reds and yellows. For the darker areas of the skin, cobalt blue mixed with cadmium red and white has been used to give a grey violet. *Terre verte* (a transparent green) is used In the shadow under the hair.

CHAPTER FIFTEEN

Watercolor Glaze Technique

Watercolor painting is often thought to be very
difficult because once a mark has been made it cannot
be changed. So you must "get it right" first time. To an
extent this is true, but watercolor techniques can in
fact be far more flexible than commonly supposed.
The glaze technique involves building up layers of
light washes, allowing each layer to dry before
applying the next.

WOMAN SITTING BY A WINDOW

S H A R O N   F I N M A R K

This painting demonstrates how a watercolor can be built up with layers of light washes, and how quite large changes can be made during its development. The palette is Prussian blue, French ultramarine, viridian green, lemon yellow, cadmium yellow mid, cadmium red, permanent rose, and alizarin crimson. The brushes used are nos. 10 and 12 sable nylon mix, a no. 3 sable and a (1½ in.) 3.75 cm flat wash brush. A small natural sponge and blotting paper are also used.

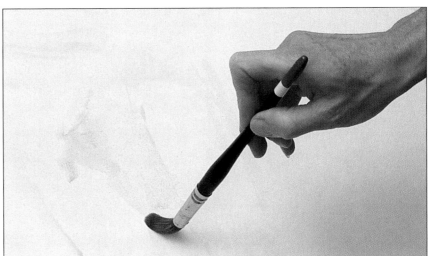

1 The model posed in front of the window.

2 Using a no. 12 brush and keeping the color very thin, the artist uses a dilute mixture of cadmium yellow and permanent rose, and with a combination of line and mass begins to establish the figure. Washes should be kept very light and delicate to allow a gradual build-up of color and form.

3 The artist establishes the shapes around the figure using a neutral color (viridian and rose mixed). Complementaries mixed together always produce interesting neutral tints. Try mixing various reds and greens, blues, and oranges, lemons, and violets.

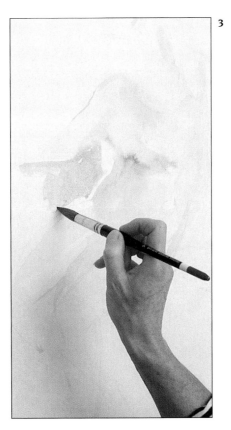

4 The chair and the window behind the model are established lightly, and virician green has been used to describe the cooler shadow on the model's left arm and to define the form of the thighs.

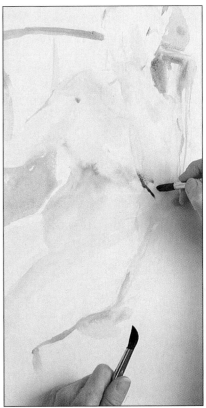

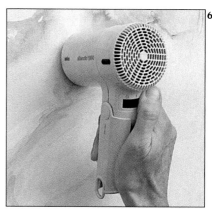

6 In order to control this, she takes a small hairdrier and quickly dries the areas she is changing.

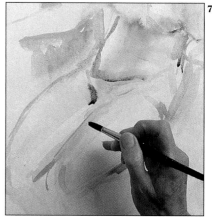

7 Now she can re-draw the figure using French ultramarine and crimson.

5 Now we can see how quite important and necessary changes can be made. The artist feels that the marks down the side of the figure are too strong and impinge too much on the form. The form is defined too strongly in general. She is unhappy also about the position of the figure in the chair and wishes to move it - quite drastic modifications. Taking a small sponge dipped in clear water, she wets the surface and sponges off the colour on each side of the figure.

8 She begins to establish the lower legs and the shape of the chair, and uses some cadmium yellow to bring out the warmth of the chair seat.

9 Note how in the whole scheme of things the lemons and cadmium are acting against the violets and blues.

10 Using a 1½ in. (3.75 cm) flat wash brush, the artist begins to lay the wall and the curtain.

11 Using a large sable mix brush, she lays in the figure more strongly, glazing transparent orange over the completely dry layers beneath.

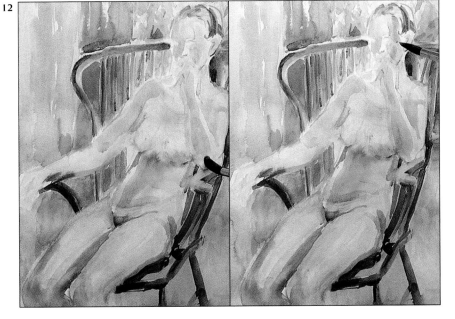

12 Here we see she has warmed up the whole figure as she felt it had become too violet. Note, too, the strong glaze of green along the figure's left thigh, which acts effectively against this warmth.

13 **13** She is unhappy about the strength of the red patch beneath the breasts and takes a brush with clear water to dampen this area and blot it out.

14 The paint has been removed and, with blotting paper in one hand, she takes a fine sable brush and begins to define the face and the breasts.

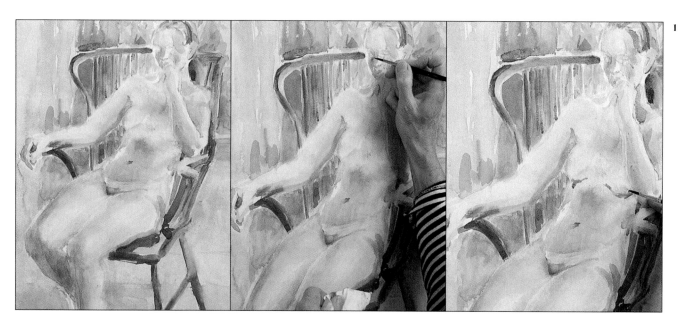

14

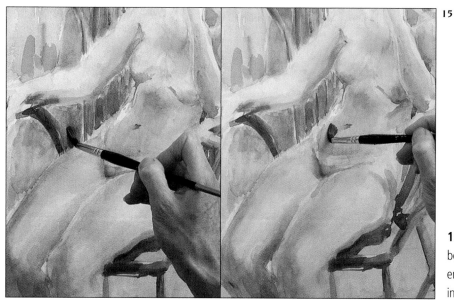

15

15 Finally she strengthens the wall behind the figure with a further glaze and emphasizes the form of the stomach, introducing some green under the breasts.

16 This whole process shows how to build up a watercolor slowly. Let the layers of paint dry thoroughly if you are going to apply a glaze over the top. It is possible by damping, sponging, and blotting to make quite drastic changes to your work.

DIFFERENT EFFECTS USING WATERCOLOR GLAZE

These five paintings are all demonstrations of the use of the watercolor glaze technique, showing how it can be used to achieve very different results.

RIGHT In this watercolor of the back of a seated figure, the artist, Sharon Finmark, used exactly the same technique as in the preceding sequence. A very restricted palette—burnt sienna and cadmium yellow for the warmer areas, and a French ultramarine with a touch of viridian green glazed over thinly to delineate the planes—was used effectively to give a sense of volume.

LEFT In this extravagantly posed nude, the artist, Kay Gallwey, has concentrated on building up the pattern of the drapery with thin glaze marks of different colors on top of each other, allowing the buff paper to unify the whole. In the lower right, a light sepia glaze right across the pattern brings it together. Simple linear drawing in the figure has allowed the use of one or two rhythmical glazes of light crimson along the form, leaving the paper to describe the bulk of the warm flesh.

ABOVE The simplest of means has been used in the two small, rapid studies by the author of a ginger-haired girl. One or two glazes of cool and warm colors describe the form. The smaller of the two shows glazes bleeding into each other, which is not unwelcome.

LEFT Mainly French ultramarine with a touch of alizarin crimson has been glazed over cadmium yellow In this torso by the author. Virtually only two glazes have been used, with a little linear work. Constant rapid experiments with watercolor are necessary to preserve the medium's unique qualities of luminosity.

CHAPTER SIXTEEN

Wet-into-Wet Watercolor

Working wet-into-wet, that is applying new paint while the previous paint is still wet, is an extension of the watercolor glaze technique. It is possible to exploit and to some extent control the behavior of the paint as each new mark bleeds into the next, because the degree of bleeding depends on the dampness of the paper. As the paint dries glazing will occur anyway, and by working rapidly you will build up a rich and lively paint surface.

GIRL SITTING IN A WOODEN CHAIR

DAVID CARR

The palette is French ultramarine, cerulean blue (mountain blue), cobalt green light, cobalt green dark, viridian green, Hooker's green, *stil de grain* vert (green-pink), cadmium yellow light, cadmium yellow deep, pozzouli earth, cadmium red light, cadmium red deep, and ultramarine violet.

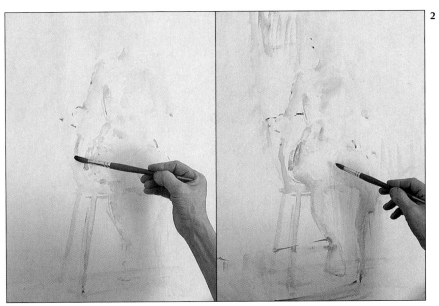

1 This is exactly the same pose as that in the previous sequence on page 469, but viewed from a new angle.

2 Dipping a large sable brush in clear water, the artist takes up a slight amount of color from the pan. Cadmium yellow deep and cadmium red light are used to mass in the figure lightly. The artist is thinking in terms of mass rather than line.

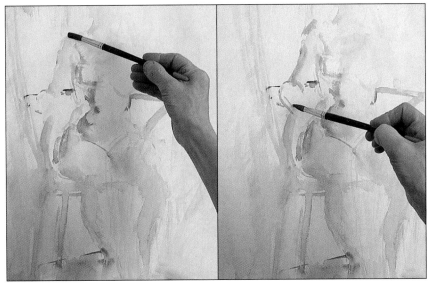

3 He then picks up some cerulean blue and cobalt green light to describe volume and to begin to define the chair. It is important to consider the chair at this stage rather than leaving it as an afterthought, hoping that it will still fit in. The paint is damp and some slight bleeding should be allowed to occur.

4

5

6

4 Keeping the paint wet, some attention is given to the model's immediate surroundings. The artist begins to define the walls and floor using cadmium yellow deep (very dilute) and *stil de grain* (a warm, slightly golden color) for the light areas, cerulean blue, ultramarine, and cobalt green dark for the shadows. He then returns to work on the figure.

5 The form of the figure is further defined using a fairly neutral mixture of cadmium red and cobalt green deep, especially around the legs. A mixture of cadmium yellow and red gives greater strength to the torso.

6 The model's right leg is more clearly defined by a bold stroke of cobalt green dark down the inside of the calf.

7 Taking a finer sable and a mixture of pozzouli earth and ultramarine, the artist uses some linear work to create greater clarity of form, notably under the breasts, around the thighs, and in the area of the head.

8 Using a sable brush, he applies areas of color to the floor and wall at the bottom of the picture and adds warmer tones to the figure's right leg.

10 In order to broaden the form—it is becoming somewhat fiddly—the artist takes a large hog-hair brush and, with plenty of clear water, washes out some of the form in the head and left leg.

9 Using lots of wet paint, the artist applies even more color around the floor and wall areas. He creates further slabs of form in the figure with cadmium red deep, which is cooler than the yellow/orange areas and pushes the form back. He is not afraid of the wet paint, because as long as he does not use too much color he has ample opportunity to build up and alter the form. By now most of the earlier paint layers have dried and something of a glaze technique will operate.

11 Using the hog-hair brush the artist re-establishes some of this form, and redraws into it using a sable brush. He is careful to think in terms of mass first and line second: he finds the form through mass, and linear definition follows. For example, he applies a slab of cold color to the left thigh and then draws into it with a sable brush.

12 Having allowed the paint to dry a little, and consequently to lighten, he begins to define the carpet edge and floor.

13 He introduces some white body (opaque) color in gouache into the wall area, giving a sense of light, and further defines the form of the figure.

14 Finding that some of the color on the figure is now too heavy and is flattening the form, he takes a sponge and pulls some of this wet paint away to increase the sense of light.

CHAPTER SEVENTEEN
Taking it Further

A useful exercise and practice to keep paintings feeling fresh and spontaneous is to work on more than one painting simultaneously. This way we are likely to preserve the freshness of the initial painting that is so often lost when the picture is finished.

Take a piece of board or paper and work on one painting for a few minutes until you feel the freshness going and you are wondering what to do next. At this point begin a second picture. That will go well for a while, and when it begins to go stale look at the first picture and carry on with that and so on, working alternately on each.

WORKING ON MORE THAN ONE IMAGE

These two small watercolors were worked on in this way. They are both
8 x 6 in. (20 x 15 cm) and painted on off-white, acid-free mount board. This is an
excellent surface to work on as it will neither cockle nor chew. The palette is
French ultramarine, viridian green, cadmium lemon, cadmium yellow, cadmium
red, and white (gouache). It is in fact bordering on a gouache technique, as white
is extensively used, giving the paint body. The model is seated on the floor, and
the full figure was done first.

1 The gouache was applied as thinly as
watercolor at first, warm and cold pinks
and yellows being used for the flesh.
Linear work and definition came second,
with the use of a dark gray-violet
(ultramarine, cadmium red, and white)
and gray-green (viridian with a touch of
cadmium red and white). These are
complementary to the yellows and pinks.
Body color is added to the model's right
arm, breasts, and hair.

2 As the painting began to "die," the
second picture was started, giving a
stronger impression of form and the
model's personality. The whole form is
brought forward so that it fills the
picture surface.

ABOVE This series of small watercolor head-and-shoulders studies was conceived in a similar way. They are mounted together, and are examples of the same model painted in different ways, sometimes with a light glaze technique, other times with more wet-into-wet and with body color.

1

2

Although the pose of these two standing figures, painted in oils, is slightly different they were painted *alla prima* in the same evening.

1 The first, with the figure set back a little, is a perfectly acceptable Impressionist study.

2 The second, however, has more verve and movement and feels less fiddly. The bold primary colors around the figure and the green shadow seem more inventive, and there is a good sense of the harshness of the electric light on the upper part of the figure's torso.

MOVING INTO MIXED TECHNIQUES

Watercolor moving into gouache suggests other combinations of water-based techniques. Pure watercolor exploits the white of the paper and sometimes the color of the paper. Essentially it is a transparent medium and it is for these qualities that it is valued. Once "body" color is introduced, gouache techniques, which are more akin to those of oil paint, begin to apply. The paint can be moved around flexibly and free overpainting can occur. Additional techniques are possible with the introduction of other water-based materials.

ABOVE The reclining figure with arm stretched, by the author, was begun In watercolor and gouache. All the main areas of figure and space were washed In with large brushes (in some cases oil-painting brushes). Pastel was worked into this, and fingers and brushes pushed it in to give body to the form. Pastel sticks are held together with water-soluble gum and they can be brushed into the painting with water. In this way large areas can be covered with color. In the final stages of this painting, dry pastel was used to impart a crispness and clarity to the form.

ABOVE The almost Fauvist standing figure by the author employs the same technique. Large areas of simple space were washed in with pastel, water, and gouache. The figure was established with a light, warm yellow wash. Blue, chalky pink, and lemon yellow pastel were worked into this and linear work was done with a dark gray chalk. Heavy drawing was worked in around the head. A final highlight down the leg was made with an eraser, pulling off some of the dense color and revealing the warm ground underneath.

LEFT The nude holding the cat was painted by the author using yellow and pink washes of gouache and pastel. The bed was painted with large brushes. Pastel is "scumbled" over this. Where it becomes too insistent it is washed into the surface and further layers are built up to give a translucent effect.

WORKING FROM DRAWINGS

Working from drawings is a very long-established practice. It helps to train the visual memory and indeed gives direction to the drawings being made. They need precision and eloquence if they are to provide sufficient information for the subsequent painting, The great Post-impressionist painter Bonnard (1867–1947) said he felt weak in front of nature and his practice was to make small drawings from life and re-live the experience in the studio, painting the subject at a later date or time. Sickert's (1860–1942) favored working method was to make small drawings and studies of his subjects. He enlarged these for the finished painting which was executed away from the motif.

SEATED MAN

D A V I D   C A R R

In this sequence the artist used the technique described above. It is important to ask the questions: "Can I paint from this drawing? Does it tell me enough about the subject?" This concentrates the mind and helps you to make clear informative drawings. Painters often make color notes on the actual drawings to aid their memories. The palette for this painting was French ultramarine, viridian green, yellow ocher, raw sienna, cadmium red, alizarin crimson, and titanium white.

1 A careful study was made of the seated figure as well as a small drawing of the head. Quite extensive color notes have to be made on the drawing as the black skin is reflecting both warm and cold light from the interior lighting and daylight.

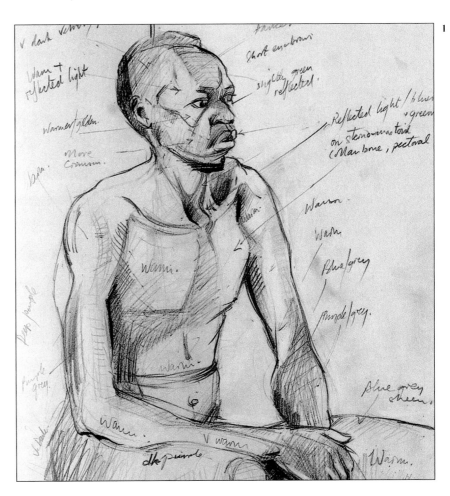

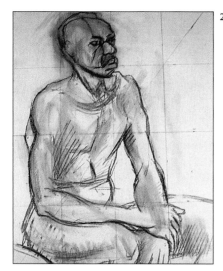

2 Having been as clear as possible about the planes in the figure, as well as the light, the artist squares up the drawing (in this case with a squared-up piece of tracing paper) and transfers it in charcoal to a larger board with the same proportions.

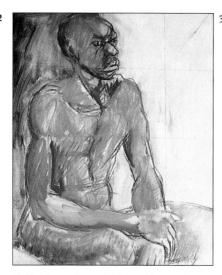

3 The figure is washed in with raw sienna and then a heavier layer of cadmium red and raw sienna. Gray-violet (mixed from alizarin crimson, French ultramarine, and raw sienna) is rubbed in for darker tones.

4 All this is blended together with titanium white, and a little viridian green is introduced into the chest.

5 The artist refers to the color notes on his drawing all the time.

6 Much more work is done around the figure: the artist concentrates on the volume of the head, working wet-into-wet, adjusting and balancing the warm and cold light, and deciding what is reflected light and what is body color. He begins to pull it together with some yellow ocher and a pale green reflection on the chest is established.

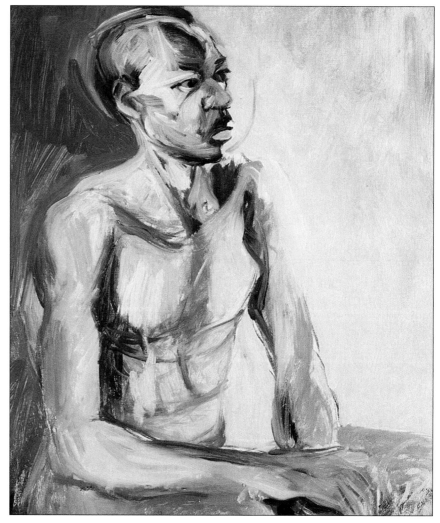

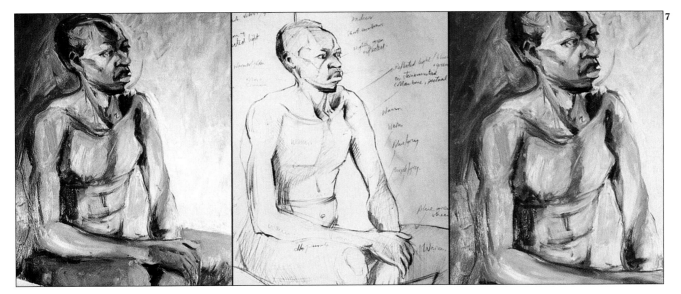

7 By constant reference to the drawing the artit is gradually able to resolve the structure of the head, neck, and shoulders and build up the color in the body.

8 Practice in these techniques can enable you to make finished pictures of subjects where you have only limited time for direct study.

WORKING AT HOME

There is ample opportunity to work from the figure by joining a life-drawing class at a local art school. Tuition, advice, and contact with other painters can be invaluable.

The life room, however, can often seem artificial, although many fine paintings have been produced there. Working at home and in domestic surroundings offers a much more natural setting. The work of Bonnard (1867–1947) and Vuillard (1869–1940) springs to mind, as well as that of Sickert. Hiring a model yourself or asking a friend to pose can often produce more interesting images than art school studies.

ABOVE The reading figure, painted by the author, was sitting naturally at a window. Again there is an economy of means here. This is watercolor with added white body color. Warm orange—cadmium yellow and red —for the main body area was overlaid with thin transparent planes of the same mixture with white added. Touches of viridian in the hair and around the head helped to create a sense of light along with the cool paint on the wall.

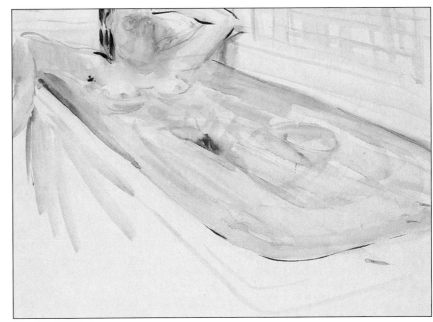

ABOVE The artist, Kay Gallwey, asked her
model to take a bath and produced these
four fresh watercolor images using two
colors in the main, burnt sienna and
French ultramarine, with a little sap green
in the water and burnt umber to
emphasize the drawing.

LOOKING AT OTHER PAINTINGS

The persistence of themes and archetypes, of myths and legends, of the great religious subjects throughout the history of art has already been referred to. The practice of looking at other paintings and copying them is most rewarding. As well as getting to know paintings more thoroughly, you can gain an understanding of underlying compositional devices.

ABOVE The story of Susanna and the Elders has exercised many a painter's imagination. In essence, two lecherous gentlemen proposition Susanna, whom they have been watching bathing for weeks. She refuses their advances and it is ultimately only the wisdom of Daniel that saves her. It is a wonderful opportunity to contrast the naked female form with clothed figures and landscape. In a sense, Manet's *Déjeuner sur l'Herbe* of 1863 exploits the same idea, except that there the naked lady seems happy to enjoy her picnic with the gentlemen in morning dress. This small oil is a copy of one of Rembrandt's versions of the story. One elder is just discernible to the right in the bushes as Susanna clasps her clothes around her in alarm.

ABOVE In this small gouache copy of Rubens's treatment of the subject, the elders are much more forthright as they crowd over the fearful Susanna. As one speaks, the other ominously warns her to be silent.

ABOVE In his painting *Pietà*, Tintoretto (1518–94) places the dead Christ at the foot of the cross in his Mother's lap as the other Mary looks on with arms outstretched. The shaped panel, the semi-circular rhythms of the body, the draperies, the arm and Mary's shoulders echo each other in this closely knit composition. This copy was done in gouache on board.

ABOVE Exploring and copying works has been carried out by all the great masters of the past. Titian's great masterpiece, *The Entombment*, in the Louvre was copied by both Delacroix (1798–1863) and Gericault (1791–1824). The composition harks back even further to a relief carved on the side of an antique sarcophagus. The disciples hold the weight of the dead Christ. The rhythmical curve of their backs and the wonderful echoed movements of the arms make a memorable composition, while the grief-stricken Marys look on. This study was painted with gouache on board.

Painting Flowers

Introduction

Flowers are a symbol of love and life, freshness, and
vigor. To paint them is the ultimate pleasure. Flowers
offer to the painter a subject of the utmost variety in a
form that is part of our everyday life, not only in garden
and countryside, but adapted into designs and
patterns. Ceramics, textiles, and advertising all make
use of this simple image. The flower is a constant and
compelling source of inspiration.

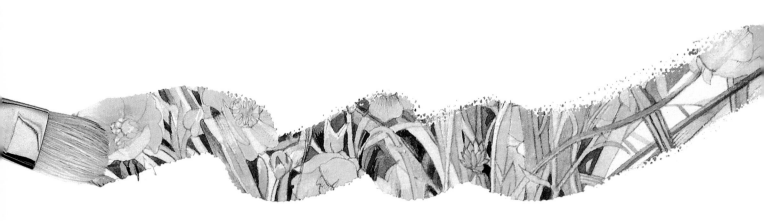

The overwhelming quality of flowers is that they live and breathe. The painter meets them at a particular point in their life cycle and tries to capture that instant. Each describes it in his or her own particular way—a carefully observed study of a single flower in a jam jar can be as potent an image as a swirling explosion of brilliantly colored blooms. Each image is the individual expression of the painter, a response to shape, or color, or mood.

As a subject, flowers have obvious advantages; the range is vast, the cost minimal. Exotic azaleas, once only accessible after months of trekking into the Himalayas, can be bought easily on any high street corner. Landscape and portraiture have their own specific problems, but a flower composition can be instantly set up in the corner of a room with a few roadside flowers, arranged at will and painted at leisure.

There are less obvious benefits—longer contemplation and closer investigation of flowers will uncover shapes and colors and hidden landscapes unimaginable at first glance. Painting flowers is a journey of exploration traveled by some of the greatest painters in history. Close observation reveals the personality of a plant, the gestures it makes and the detail that gives character to the whole. Looking also makes you aware that what you are seeing is not what you think you see, that a leaf presenting itself to you at an acute angle is not the expected oval but a thin triangle, that a white flower against the light becomes in part dark gray.

The principal purpose of this book is to encourage you to develop these skills of observation, to offer basic information on materials and technique, and to show how different artists compose, create, and arrive at a finished painting. The ways of applying paint are limitless. Experimenting with different materials and exploring new methods can trigger fresh ideas and fire the imagination. The ultimate aim is to instill an urge in you to pick up a brush and confidently put into paint an interpretation of the vision that is in us all.

BELOW These beautiful poppies by Rosemary Ieanneret capture fully the delicacy of the petals and stems.

CHAPTER ONE
Flower Painting in History

Flowers have been painted from the earliest times, ever since man first began to represent the forms he observed in nature. Basic shapes of trees and plants were daubed on cave walls in colors made from burnt sticks and colored mud. Images of flowers and plants decorated the tombs of Egyptian Kings and nobles to enhance their life after death. The lotus and papyrus were the source of decorations of all kinds.

Early societies like those of the Minoans, Greeks, and Romans painted flowers as a record of sources of food and medicine, and long periods of social stability enabled botanical art to flourish. Then came the collapse of the Roman Empire and chaos. The thread of botanical knowledge was carried by Arabic scholars who copied and re-copied old manuscripts, and it re-emerged in the monastic world many centuries later. Monks drew inspiration from their gardens to create floral jewels to enrich manuscript borders for the glory of God.

The thirst for knowledge was one of the principal features of the Renaissance. Scientists and artists alike set about investigating the nature of things, and in Leonardo da Vinci the two disciplines were combined. As a scientist Leonardo studied, among other things, phyllotaxy, or the arrangement of leaves on a stem; as an artist and draughtsman he tried to capture in drawing the energy of life force, for he believed that "Nature rather than man had the key to the.Universe." At the same period, Albrecht Dürer in Germany produced watercolor studies that are breathtaking. Most people are familiar with his study of a clod of turf with plantain leaves, sagging dandelion heads, and spiky grasses, This was painted after Dürer had spent a long period of illness indoors—it was perhaps his spontaneous reaction to growing things and to the vigor of life.

In the East, flower painting had been practiced for thousands of years and had developed a different identity—less concerned with botanical exactitude, more with aesthetics, symbolism, and the quality of life. Sweeping brush strokes captured the essence of the living plant. The techniques were part of everyday life; skills with

ABOVE Flowers were used for the border decoration of manuscripts. They were painted in meticulous detail and are somewhat formal In design. Opaque pigments were used, sometimes derived from the flowers themselves. This beautiful border painted around 1500 in watercolor by an unknown Flemish artist is from the Victoria and Albert Museum, London.

RIGHT *The Great Piece of Turf* by Albrecht Dürer was completed in 1502 and hangs In the Albertina, Vienna. The worm's eye view of a clod of meadow turf shows his ability to combine close scientific analysis with a creative and tender response to the wonders of the natural world.

A B O V E *Flowerpiece with Monkey and Parrot* by Jean Baptiste Monnoyer combines a fresh delicacy of touch with rich color and form. The painting Is held in the Alan Jacobs Gallery, London.

B E L O W Flowers were an ideal subject for the Impressionists. Pierre-August Renoir's *La Seffe* was painted around 1900. Renoir was a prolific flower painter and roses were a favorite subject.

brush and ink were acquired at an early age and developed to the point where a whole branch could be described in one elegant, dextrous sweep of the brush.

With the arrival of traders and explorers, East and West met. When examples of this highly developed and radically new style of flower painting arrived in Europe, the impact was enormous. The fluid simplicity of Japanese and Chinese art, and the wealth of detail and pattern developed by Indian and Persian artists was, and continues to be, an inspiration to artisans of all kinds, not least painters.

The same degree of artistic wizardry was achieved in the Netherlands in the 17th century,

though the style and motive could not have been more different. Freed from the constricting Spanish Catholic influence and blessed with enormous economic prosperity, rich merchants demanded showy flowers such as rare tulips rather than the more modest herbs around at the time, tracked them down to the four corners of the globe and encouraged artists painting them to greater and greater heights of artistic dexterity. This was the supreme period of flower painting—art for the appetite.

Botanical art flourished in the centuries that followed. Gardens were created and no expedition traveled without its own artist. The wealth of new plants collected was recorded by some of the finest botanical artists of all time, names like Bauer and Redoute, and engraved and printed images of these newly discovered plants became available to a wider audience. Later, as travel became easier, there were also amateur travelers, wealthy enthusiasts who traveled the world fearlessly and recorded its flora with an enthusiastic wonder.

In the 19th century flower painting developed in new directions. For the French Impressionist painters the natural world was a source of untold riches. Flower studies were part of their investigation of color—paintings of gardens and landscapes were used as a means of expressing their impressions of light. These artists reaped the rewards of great technological progress. Many new colors were developed, the invention of paint tubes meant that artists could paint outside their studios, and the development of the flat brush ferrule enabled paint to be dabbed

A B O V E Odilon Redon's flowers are blossoms of the imagination. In *Portrait of Mademoiselle Wolette Hayman* the profile of a young girl is set against a panoply of brilliant color.

and stroked into animated, expressive textures. The results were revolutionary and the fruits familiar to all—Monet's paintings of his garden and ponds, full of flickering light and huge sweeps of color, Odilon Redon's dream-like flower studies and portraits, and Renoir's soft hazes of massed flowers. Van Gogh painted numerous studies of flowers as explorations of color, including the series of brilliant yellow sunflowers to decorate his house in Arles for Gauguin's visit.

The 19th century was also the age of the great American flower painters, expressing visually the natural wonders of the New World; of the Pre-Raphaelites, seeking, in minute botanical detail, the purity of a lost age of gold; and of the artists who were part of the Arts and Crafts Movement, trying to abstract

the linear vigor of plant growth and adapt it into design. "Art is the flower—life is the green leaf" was a principle followed by artists such as Charles Rennie Mackintosh whose close studies of plant form were adapted into a stylistic code of design and translated into fabrics, furniture, and buildings.

Flowers have been painted for so many purposes and in so many ways; everyone has their own particular favorites—often in the form of dog-eared reproductions religiously treasured. It pays dividends to look afresh at flower paintings we love, or those whose image has stuck in the mind. It is an invaluable exercise to study what makes a painting work for you. Is it the vigorous texture of paint, or colors coming together with an explosive zing, or the way the subject is composed and how and why the eye is led to certain parts? By analyzing what appeals in "past masters," we can more readily negotiate a path to our own artistic expression.

CHAPTER TWO

Materials and Equipment

A successful flower painting depends in part upon
choosing an appropriate medium. Each has its own
distinctive qualities. The delicacy and translucency of
watercolor is well suited to capture the transient character
of flowers and to create a soft haze of color, while the
curious patterns and unpredictable merging of paints give
a feeling of movement and life. Gouache tends to be more
solid, lending itself to pattern and shape. Oil paint is rich
and vibrant—the perfect medium for vigorous brush work,
or flickering dabs of paint. The basic advice is that you
should feel confident and comfortable with the medium
you choose, that you should continue to explore and
build up a knowledge of the materials available.

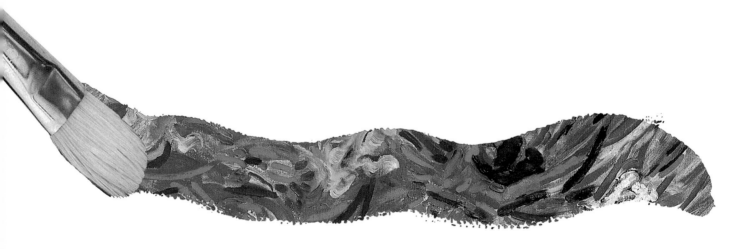

In technical terms, painting is the manipulation of ground pigment in a binding medium, on a receptive surface, by an appropriate tool—a rather clinical description that gives little hint of the vast range of brushes, papers, colors, and other materials developed by artists' manufacturers over the centuries. But a great deal can be accomplished with the minimum of materials, and it is a good idea to start off with a few good quality basic brushes and paints rather than to spend a great deal of money on an extravagant collection you may never use.

USING WATERCOLOR AND GOUACHE
Paints

Most painters remember the excitement of receiving a huge rainbow box of paints and the frustration of desperately rubbing a stubby black brush into a little lozenge of paint and finding that little color appears on the paper. In watercolor, more than any other medium, price reflects quality—quality means glow, transparency and, to a certain extent, permanence.

Watercolor consists of extremely finely ground pigment mixed with a binder. it is the oldest painting medium—originally natural earth, soot, or chalk, bound by gum, starch, or honey. Nowadays it consists of natural or chemical pigment, mixed with gum arabic and a little glycerin as moisturizer. The different characteristics of the pigment add to the excitement—some earth colors granulate, stay on the surface, and separate from

BELOW A selection of watercolor and gouache materials including a box of half pan watercolor paints, some tubes of gouache, a fine sable, and a medium flat brush. Also shown are gum arabic, which can be used to thicken paint and produce a slight sheen, and masking fluid, which will reserve white or pale-colored areas when washes are applied.

others; some chemical colors sink instantly into the paper and make permanent stains. It is only by experimentation that the personalities of individual colors and combinations emerge.

The decision whether to choose semi-moist pans or half pans, tubes, or liquid depends on preference. A box of half pans is easy to carry around and generally has its own mixing area. Tubes are easier for releasing larger amounts of paint for large work and washes. Liquid watercolor or inks have an initial brilliance but also a tendency to fade, though this can be prevented by mixing with Chinese white. In terms of quality, students' colors are fine for sketching but contain lower quality pigment, so artists' colors are a must if funds allow.

Colors from different manufacturers can vary a great deal. Well-established names include Winsor & Newton, Rowney, Schminke, and Grumbacher, and most artists probably use paint from several different manufacturers. It helps to keep a chart pinned to the wall in your working area showing blocks of color of all the paints you have in their dense and dilute forms and labeled with name and manufacturer, grade, and permanence rating. Details of any new paints can be added to this chart.

When you buy paints assess the permanence rating and check the color on the sample sheet, bearing in mind that the name sometimes does not describe the color accurately. Permanence of color is coded by manufacturers, generally with a star rating. Colors marked with few stars are "fugitive," and many of them are in the pink and purple range. Fugitive colors tend to fade when exposed to light.

Gouache paints are the opaque version of watercolors, ground slightly less finely and with the addition of an inert white pigment. Gouache has an innate brilliance which reflects this white pigment rather than depending on the luminosity of white paper as in watercolor, and it tends to rest on the surface of the paper. Its advantages are that it can be used thickly or thinly, it can be worked from dark to light, scraped to create texture or mixed with paste to make an "impasto" surface. A home-made chart of gouache paints is useful because the color changes a great deal when dry.

Watersoluble crayons are another option. it is possible to buy thick or thin crayons; use them as they are or wet the crayonned marks to make watercolor.

LEFT A small box of watercolors, ideal for outdoor work.

Brushes

Watercolor brushes range from inexpensive, synthetic fiber, through middle-range squirrel hair and goat hair wash brushes, to expensive sable, which is, weight for weight, worth more than gold, Pure sable, made from the hairs of a Siberian mink, has a body that holds a good deal of paint and a flexible, springy tip. It is the ideal painting tool, capable both of placing paint in a solid block and trailing to a fine point.

Large mops are good for washes, as are wide flat brushes. Flats and the softer Oriental version, the hake, can be twisted to make interesting leaf shapes, spread for dry brush work, or used on edge for lines and stems, though they tend to produce "corners." The rigger is a useful brush for flower painting. With its long hair it can drop a large amount of paint into a small point, and make long trailing stems and fronds.

Brush sizes range from a very fine 000, consisting of a few hairs, to the large size 12. Flat brushes are sometimes graded by width, for instance $^3/_{16}$ inch or 1 inch.

BRUSH MARKS

E L I S A B E T H   H A R D E N

This sketch of tulips shows how different brushes can be used to make particular marks. It is purely an exercise.

1 The body of the petal is formed with a size 8 sable, laying a flood of color in the bowl and using the point for the fine petal tips.

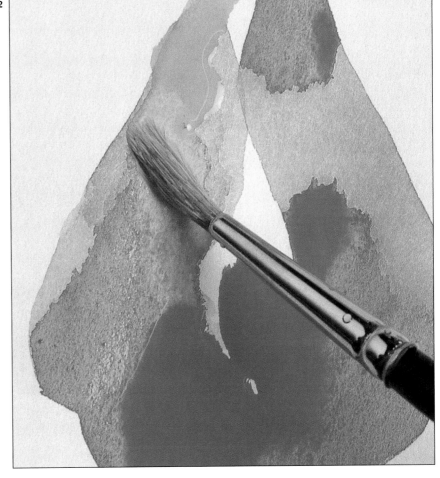

2 A thinner sable, size 4, drops yellow paint into the point of the petal and coaxes it into the drying wash.

3 Flat brushes make fine lines when used along their narrow edge, can be twisted to make very wide marks and then trailed to a point. This is a 1 inch synthetic brush making these marks in one stroke.

4 Other leaves have been formed with the wide brush, sometimes using different colors on each angle of the brush tip.

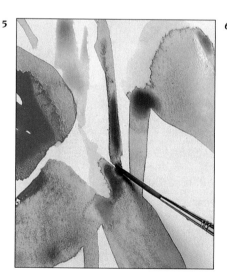

5 A well-loaded rigger brush forms the stems. Riggers hold more paint than the equivalent short-bristled brush and are useful for fine lines and trailing shapes.

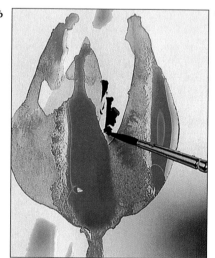

6 For detailed work the delicate point of a fine size 2 sable can accurately pinpoint paint into specific areas.

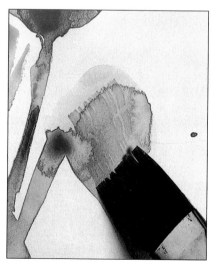

7 Fairly dry paint is stroked onto the leaf with a dryish flat brush.

8 The completed picture—a simple demonstration exercise that succeeds in producing an effective image.

Papers

Papers come in a wide range of quality and price. It is worth investigating the paper trays in a good art store to get an idea of what is available and to ask for advice from staff, who are often artists themselves.

Cartridge paper, a wood-pulp based, strong paper, originally used to hold a small charge of powder for a firearm, is good for sketching and planning, for rough work and for acrylics.

Watercolor paper, made from linen and cotton rag in various proportions, and made with acid-free water for permanence, comes in three categories—Rough, Cold Pressed Paper known as NOT for Not Hot Pressed, and HP for Hot Pressed. Hot pressed is used mainly for line and wash and fine botanical drawings. Its very smooth surface, while ideal for flowing pen lines, is slippery for paint. Cold pressed is the best all-round paper. The texture is smooth enough for detailed work while having enough "bite" to hold large washes, and enough roughness for lively, dry brush strokes. Rough paper can be found with different "tooth" marks, the minute bumps and hollows that bite the paint off the brush. With a dry brush, paint stays on the hills, and with a wet brush it slips into the hollows.

Papers come in different weights and absorbencies. The weight is expressed as pounds per ream (480 sheets) or grams per square meter. Lightweight papers 70–140 lb (150–300 gsm) will need to be stretched, while heavier papers 140–260 lb (300–555 gsm) can be clipped to a board for small work but are better stretched for very large work or heavy washes. Heavyweight papers, up to 300 lb (640 gsm), do not need to be stretched and can cope with plenty of water and vigorous handling.

The absorbency of a paper, dictated by the "size" or sealing agent, can produce interesting effects. On the one extreme, paint sinking and spreading in blotting paper can result in an attractive haziness, and can produce frilled edge lines round pools of paint on semi-absorbent paper. For the beginner a paper with little absorbency is the easiest to work on—paint spreads more fluidly and color can easily be removed from the surface.

A good starter pack would consist of some large cartridge paper, a medium-sized sketch book and a pocket book for ideas, some sheets of 90 lb (190 gsm) cold pressed paper of a quality able to stand up to erasing and heavy washes, and perhaps some tinted paper for gouache.

BELOW Some of the many types of paper available for watercolor. From left to right: Fabriano Artistico Rough, Bockingford Tinted, Arches HP, Saunders Waterford NOT and Bockingford NOT. The brushes surrounding the watercolor mixing palette are, from left to right, Chinese flat brush or hake, size 0 sable, rigger, size 7 sable, Chinese brush, size 16 acrylic brush, and a squirrel hair brush.

STRETCHING PAPER

When you are using watercolor it is important to stretch the paper in preparation for painting.

The sequence of pictures below explains how this should be done.

1 Find the right side of the paper by holding It up to the light—the watermark should read correctly on the right side. Soak it briefly.

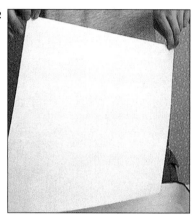

2 Lifting the paper out by one edge, shake it gently to get rid of any excess water.

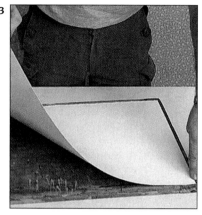

3 Carefully lay the wet paper right side up on the drawing board, making sure that you do not trap any air under the paper and that the paper is completely flat.

4 Cut strips of gummed paper and dampen them with a sponge.

5 Stick all four sides of the paper to the drawing board with the gummed paper. Secure the paper firmly with drawing pins pushed into each corner of the paper, and leave the paper to dry naturally, away from any source of heat.

Other equipment

A good palette for mixing paints is essential and also two flat-bottomed water jars, one for clean water and the other for washing brushes. These should be shallow enough for the brush to go in easily, and made of glass so that you can keep an eye on the state of the water. Other items that are essential are a hairdrier, to speed up drying and push the paint around, and a selection of tools for manipulating the paint—a sponge, toothbrush, twigs, or tissues.

USING ACRYLIC
Paints

Acrylic paint is a supremely adaptable medium, developed early this century by a group of Mexican artists seeking a more versatile, durable, and quick-drying medium for murals, frescoes, and restoration. Ground pigment is dispersed and suspended in acrylic resin, a polymerized resin binder, and can be manipulated thickly like oil or diluted with water or a special medium and used as watercolor. It dries quickly to a waterproof, luminous, matt or gloss finish. The speed of drying is both an advantage and a disadvantage. Layers of paint can be built up quickly, clean, sharp lines made as colors butt each other, and lively textures pulled out of the rapidly drying paint. It is ideal for painting fine details on a dark background, such as cactus spines, or flower stamens. However, the quick-drying paint also means that mistakes can be hard to remedy as it does not allow for paint to be reworked except by overpainting. Most manufacturers make a good range of acrylic paint. Liquitex makes acrylic paint in various forms. Some names of colors are recognizable by names common to oil and watercolor, but extensive research has produced new chemical formulae and new names.

Brushes and supports

Acrylic paints take their toll on brushes. The harsh, stiff paint can wear out the bristles, weaken the ferrule that holds the bristles and transform the brushes into rigid palm trees unless they are instantly washed in warm water. If they are irretrievably rigid, soak overnight in methylated spirits and wash in warm, soapy water. Acrylic is a good medium for old watercolor brushes.

The delight of acrylic paints lies in their versatility. As a support almost anything is suitable—wood, paper, sanded metal, primed walls, canvas; illustration board is excellent. A good range of colors is available in most art stores, and from the wide range of additions on the shelves, an acrylic primer, a medium, and a retarder are essential, plus a good-sized mixing palette. Acrylic paint has a firm texture and needs vigorous mixing to dilute. Speedy cleaning up of everything, not only of brushes, is important- paint on plastic palettes will peel off, but it is a tough medium and sticks limpet-like to anything.

USING OIL

Paints

Oil painting was traditionally the medium for painting flower compositions, and watercolor the preferred medium for botanical studies. The rich colors of Dutch still lifes was achieved by applying layer upon layer of transparent color. Oil paint brings particular qualities to flower painting. It is adaptable and can be moved around the canvas, brushed, scraped, and manipulated with a palette knife to make a textured surface with a rich, lustrous finish.

Oil paints, which come in students' and artists' quality, are made from ground pigment bound with linseed or poppy oil. As with watercolors, a vast number of colors is available, but a selection of basic colors will mix to a very effective range. Most flower and leaf colors can be mixed from the following: titanium white, lemon yellow, cadmium yellow, yellow ocher, cadmium red, cadmium red deep, alizarin crimson, or rose madder, chrome green, viridian, and burnt umber.

Each painter finds his or her own palette pattern and becomes familiar with it, so that a brush can go automatically to a particular color. The pattern often corresponds to the color wheel or, basically, the rainbow and is generally set out with blobs of paint surrounding the central mixing area. It is important to keep this area fairly clear and the paints clean; a rogue streak of red when painting a white petal can be disastrous.

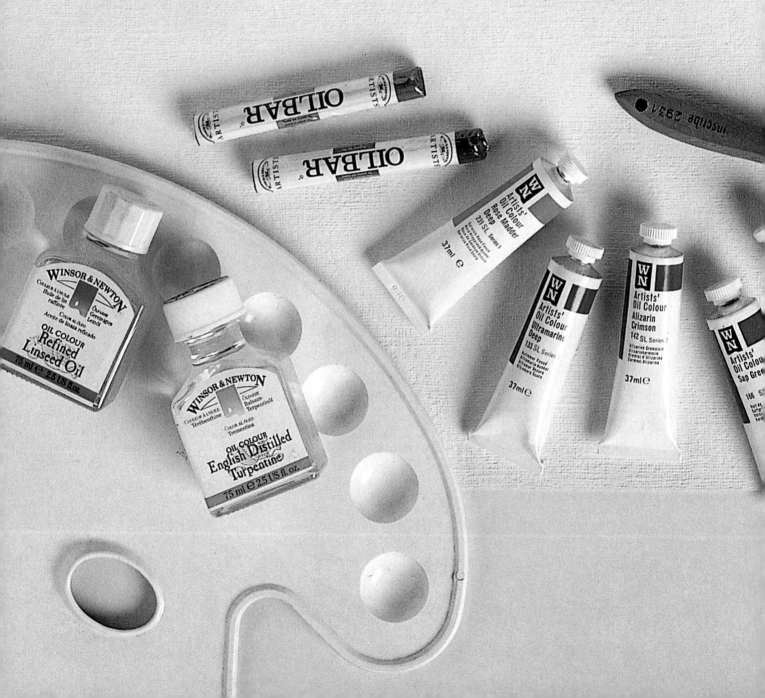

Oil paint is now available in stick form. These bars are easy to use and versatile—try them for laying out a composition, creating texture, or making vigorous drawing strokes in a surface wetted with turpentine.

Oil paints are mixed with a medium, a mixture of distilled turpentine and linseed or poppy oil—1 part oil to 3 parts of turpentine is a good mix but most painters develop their own recipes. This thins the paint to the required consistency, or it can be used straight from the tube.

Brushes

As with paints it is false economy to make do with cheap brushes. Oil painting brushes are generally made from bleached hogs hair, which has split ends to hold the paint, or synthetic fiber. They come in three basic shapes—round, square, and filbert—and a variety of sizes. Sable brushes give a smooth line and are useful for detailed work but are expensive, and soft badger brushes are sometimes used for blending color. Keep turpentine and a rag nearby to keep your brushes clean.

BELOW A selection of oil painting materials. Both acrylic and hog hair brushes are shown in a variety of shapes and sizes. The range, from a size 1 round to a size 8 flat, is versatile enough for most occasions. The fan brush feathers wet paint and blends colors.

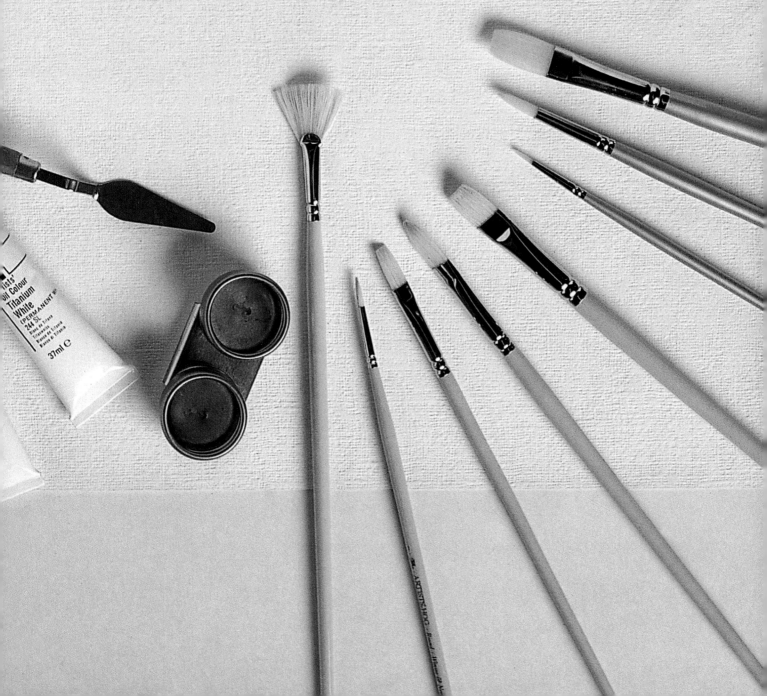

Supports

Wood was one of the earliest painting supports. Wood panels are a luxury item and nowadays wood composition is a satisfactory alternative, with hardboard the best in terms of weight, surface, and cost. The smooth side should be sanded and primed.

Painting on linen dates from Ancient Egyptian times but was widely used in the Renaissance as a lighter support for massive paintings.

Canvas is a wonderful support, providing a subtle "tooth" for paint and a sensitive resistance to the brush, but it is expensive to buy ready-made. A good quality art store will provide you with the canvas and the stretchers, and often the advice on how to make your own. Raw canvas needs to be sealed with glue size and then primed.

A primed ground provides a suitable surface for accepting paint. Ready-made primers do very well; ideally apply two coats, the first white and the second sometimes containing a tint that will show through the paint. An acrylic primer may be used for oil paint, and acrylic paint may be used for quick-drying underpainting.

Other equipment

Palette knives are useful for speedy manipulation of paint, for thick textures or "impasto," or for smoothing large areas. They are also useful for scraping paint off the palette. An easel is the ideal prop for canvas or board.

You will need a palette to work on. Treat new wood palettes with linseed oil. Hardboard ones should be varnished with clear varnish. Many painters now use disposable paper palettes.

OTHER MATERIALS

There are no limits to the materials that can be used to create a painting. Flowers have both a vigorous and a transient quality, and the glow of life. Search around for anything that will express this, notice what methods other painters have employed and try unexpected materials and combinations—colored paper, spray paint, pastels, wax crayons under paint, or metallic paints. The most exciting paintings are often the result of using random materials in a spontaneous way. The outcome may well turn out to be a "happy accident."

THE WORK PLACE

In whatever situation you choose to paint flowers it is important to be comfortable, to have good lighting and to maintain the same situation until the painting is finished. Comfort means space to move about and a drawing board at an angle and height that suits you best, whether it is perched on your knee in a field or on the kitchen table. It also means space nearby for necessary equipment—water, paint, reference sketches—and a source of electricity for a hairdrier and lighting.

Both paper and subject need suitable lighting. A variety of sources—window, overhead lights, or angled lamps will give adaptable variety. Artificial light alters colors considerably, and if you are painting at night, daylight simulation bulbs, which approximate to the blueness of daylight, are available.

If you are painting a group of flowers over a series of sessions, a cool environment will slow down their development. It helps if you can keep the paint area free from random draughts and prowling pets.

CLEANING UP

When painting is finished, brushes and palettes should be cleaned to keep them in good order. Oil palettes need to be covered if they are to be used again, brushes should be wiped on a rag, rinsed in a little turpentine and thoroughly washed under a running tap. The sediment in turpentine can be allowed to settle, the liquid poured into a clean jar for re-use, and the sediment absorbed in paper towels or newspaper.

Brushes used for acrylics dry like leather, so they should be kept wet and cleaned immediately after use. Palettes and board should be speedily washed, or peeled and scraped if dry. The necks of tubes need to be wiped to ensure that they will close tightly.

Watercolor brushes need to be well washed in running water after use, and the bristles gently coaxed to a fine point. Many artists store them upright in a jar, but if you intend keeping them in a roll or container, they should be completely dry. Watercolor paints are expensive and can be reactivated—even by performing a little basic surgery on dried-up tubes. A palette can be selectively cleaned by carefully running water into areas you do not want and skirting round paint that is worth keeping. Plastic wrap will keep the palette damp.

CHAPTER THREE

Basic Techniques

Technique is concerned with the manipulation of
materials. In painterly terms, the description "good
technique" might be applied to a painter who exercises
great skill with a brush and is confident and inventive
in the use of paint. Studying the techniques of the great
masters has always been on the agenda of art students,
and it is interesting to look very closely at paintings you
admire to see what has happened on the surface and
how the artist has achieved a particular effect.

Painting pictures is mostly about ideas, but a knowledge of technique equips you with a visual vocabulary, and a springboard for discovering your own methods of working. Trying some of the different methods of using paint is exciting, and an unexpected result can become the basis of a spontaneous painting.

WATERCOLOR

Additives
Gum arabic added to the water used for mixing paint will give a denser color and a firmer texture. Ox gall (literally the gall of an ox—now happily available in prepared form) reduces surface tension and allows the paint to spread freely.

Back runs
Slightly wetter Paint, worked into a wash before it is dry, will spread into random shapes with hard, serrated edges. It is a distinct characteristic of watercolor. Back runs can also be created and manipulated with a hairdrier by blowing the paint in various directions, and also by tipping the painting board and allowing the paint to flow back over itself. It can be a most useful device in flower painting—blown trickles of paint can create leaves and petals.

ABOVE Back runs created by dropping slightly wetter paint Into a wash and manipulating it by tipping the board or blowing with a hairdrier.

BELOW Paint lightly brushed over paper with a dry brush will produce this lined effect.

Dry brush
A bristly texture or lined effect can be obtained by splaying a fairly dry brush, loading it with a minimum amount of paint, and dragging it over the paper at an upright angle. Experiment on rough paper to gauge the exact degree of dryness, amount of paint, and the type of bristle to use, Stiff, longer hog hair generally works well, as does a flat brush with the bristles spread between finger and thumb, Use this effect sparingly—it is most appropriate for grasses, texture on petals and bark, and sharpening up a landscape foreground.

Hard edges

When a puddle of paint is dropped onto dry paper, the pigment tends to collect toward the edges causing a hard line. The strength of this color can be increased by pushing or blowing the paint into this edge. This hard-edged effect can sometimes be frustrating when unwanted lines of paint appear because the paper has dried too quickly, but it can be remedied by gently nudging the paint lines with a damp brush or sponge. More often, however, it is a wonderful technique, creating natural petal and leaf shapes.

Wash over wash, leaving different areas dry, will create a web of flowing lines, which can be used to suggest shapes and add depth to a painting.

RIGHT Several layers of wash have been applied here, leaving different areas dry in each case, the result being this mesh of flowing lines.

Lifting out

Removing paint to bare the light paper beneath is another possibility. A sponge, crumpled tissue paper or blotting paper, cotton bud, or stiff brushes can be used to lift wet paint from the surface and make a soft-edged shape. Paint can also be lifted out when dry. Water dropped or stroked into strong color pushes edges back and can be mopped out to form paler stems and veins. Obviously a lightweight paper will cope less well with vigorous "lifting out."

LEFT A stiff brush has been used to remove areas of paint, leaving soft edges and paler tones beneath.

Indenting

Drawing firmly with a smooth, blank point into thick paper can create a pattern of marks. Dry brush strokes or powdered paint will rest on the surface, revealing the indented pattern.

LEFT A pattern of marks has been indented in the paper with the side of a key and the surface lightly rubbed with pencil graphite on the finger. Oil pastel or chalk used in the same way could give a similar result.

BELOW Masking fluid has been used to reserve white areas under a wash and, when this has dried, more areas have been masked and further layers of paint applied.

Masking

For some people masking fluid is the greatest innovation, removing the need for careful painting around stamens and tiny florets and adding sparkle to a painting. For others it is an instantly recognizable painting trick and they avoid using it.

It is available as a colorless fluid or with a yellow tint, which is easier to see as the painting builds up, and it is applied by splattering with a toothbrush or painted in with a brush. However, this can be a disaster for bristles unless the brush is thoroughly and instantly washed in warm, soapy water.

When the masking fluid is dry it can be painted over. Paint settling round masked areas tends to create sharp edges, and more paint can be dropped in to heighten the sharpness of contrast. When the painting is finished the masking fluid can be removed easily with a finger or soft eraser.

Scraping and scratching

A scalpel or sharp blade can be used to remove paint or to scrape back to the paper. In watercolor it can be used for adding sparkles, removing mistakes, and creating highlights such as stems or specks of sunlight. Once paper has been scraped it cannot take any more paint.

Gouache, acrylic, and oil can withstand more vigorous treatment and blades or points or sandpaper can alter the surface, remove areas of paint, or even create a base for further layers.

Spattering

Speckles of paint can be sprayed onto a surface by scraping the thumb or knife across the bristles of a paint-loaded toothbrush. Masking will restrict the spattering to particular areas, and by partially damping the paper with a brush or by spraying with water, interesting textures can be created. This is an effective method of painting black poppy dust-speckled petals, and for breaking up flat areas. The Impressionists' technique of making a sparkling surface can be imitated by flicking complementary colors over each other. In acrylic and gouache, the paint's opacity allows pale colors to be speckled over darker ones.

Sponging

Paint can be sponged on or sponged off. Natural sponge produces a less regular effect. Squeezed almost dry, dipped into paint and dabbed lightly onto paper, a sponge will create its own texture. A saturated sponge will spread a wash quickly and smoothly. A dry sponge pressed onto paper will suck in paint, and leave cloud-like blanks. A sponge is an essential tool for softening edges and mopping up over-wetted areas. With skillful manipulation it can be used to pull strong paint from one area into another.

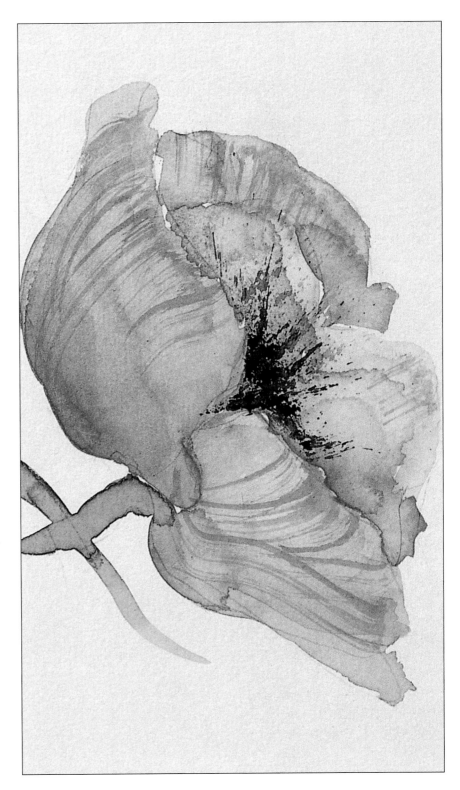

ABOVE Here hard edges have been created round the petals by blowing the paint with a hairdrier against dry areas. The ridges on the petals were made by softly stroking on paint from a dry brush. By masking certain parts, dark paint spattered from a toothbrush has been directed to the center of the flower.

ABOVE A wide, flat brush with different colored paint on each edge of the tip has been articulated to produce these two-color bamboo leaves. On its edge the brush will produce fine lines but when pressed and turned it will splay out into flowing shapes.

Variegated color

Bi-colored shapes can be made by filling the brush with one color, drying the tip, dipping it in a strong concentration of another color, and applying the two colors to the paper simultaneously. A firmer two-color stroke can be made by dipping each corner of the bristles of a flat brush in a different color.

Wash

The wash is the principal technique of watercolor painting, and its luminous character is created by laying thin veils of color on top of each other.

Wet-on-wet

Heavy or stretched paper, dampened but not soaked, is the best surface for the random and unpredictable technique of wet-on-wet. As a liberating exercise it is unsurpassed; as a component of a painting it needs to be controlled. It can establish an atmospheric background or mass of color but requires the sharpening effect of strong brushwork to add form and substance. It is a technique that repays experimentation. The basic wash should be damp but not wet. Paint dropped or painted in will spread. As the paper dries slightly, more paint can be fed in and manipulated into the planned pattern. See the step-by-step sequence on page 548 which demonstrates the technique.

The hazy-edged result is invaluable for backgrounds and for the mass of a multifloral head, later sharpened with detail. For landscapes, gardens and multitudes of flowers, the wet-on-wet technique can describe dense areas of color without diverting the eye from the focus.

Texture and pattern

Texture and pattern can be achieved by many methods. Fabric or crushed foil, pressed into paint and lifted when dry, can form interesting textures. Spread paint on a surface, press paper into it, and then peel it off. Coarse salt sprinkled onto a fairly dense wash will absorb the wet paint and leave a speckled effect. Painting over wax or oil pastels produces interesting results, and stenciling color through open-weave fabric such as net is a speedy method of creating checkered patterning.

GOUACHE

Since gouache is watercolor with added body, most watercolor techniques can be used easily. The thicker consistency of gouache also lends itself to other techniques.

Additives

Gum arabic added to gouache gives it a sheen. Adding paste makes a thick, malleable paint that lends itself to interesting textures.

Gradating tone

Ribbons of color placed close to each other and differing slightly in tone can produce a rippling rhythm.

Washing out

This method of using ink and gouache is an unusual one that lends itself well to floral images. it is best described by demonstration, so look at the following step-by-step sequence on page 520.

RIGHT Fine ribbons of gouache paint, each varying slightly in tone, have been painted next to each other to give a sense of flowing movement to these plant shapes.

LEFT Candle wax rubbed over paper and color painted over will produce interesting effects.

WASHING OUT TECHNIQUE FOR GOUACHE AND PERMANENT INKS

F A I T H   O ' R E I L L Y

This technique exploits the properties of permanent ink and gouache. The black ink intensifies the color, and the final result looks rather like a color lithograph or etching without recourse to expensive equipment.

1 Poinsettias are chosen as the subject for this because of their brilliance of color and distinctive form, and they are set against a dark background. The artist concentrates on a small area of the flowers.

2 Using paper with a rough surface to absorb the color and of sufficient strength to withstand scrubbing under a tap, the artist applies thick gouache using little or no water. The design can be drawn lightly on the paper as here, but pencil marks may show through so it is better to use unaccompanied brush strokes. Experience will give you the confidence to do this.

3 The quality of the paint is important—try to use only artists' quality or poster paint in pots and look for permanence marks. This is because the color will bleach out as the ink washes off. Any areas left without paint will be black in the final image. White gouache can be used in any areas that are to remain white. At this stage greens have been added to the background behind the red flowers.

4 When all the colors have been applied, make sure that all areas you do not want to be black are covered in colored or white gouache.

5 After allowing the paint to dry, preferably overnight, apply black Indian ink over the whole surface—other dark-colored inks can be used as long as they are permanent. The ink is applied quickly using a large brush so that the underlying paint is not disturbed too much.

6 The work is left to dry for half an hour. Then it is gently washed under a tap until the ink begins to lift off. A shower can be used to give more control to the lift-off process. Various results will ensue, and a nailbrush or washing-up pad can be used with a light scrubbing action to make textured marks on the image.

7 The wet paper is then stretched on a flat board, stuck down with gummed paper, and cut off the board when dry.

ACRYLIC

The substance of acrylic is more akin to watercolor and gouache, and many of the techniques already mentioned can be used. By diluting the paint with water or acrylic medium it can be manipulated in similar ways. Acrylic paint dries rapidly to an insoluble film, and this speed of drying is one of its principal assets.

Glazing

Acrylic paint is ideally suited to glazing. Because it dries rapidly, thin washes of color can be laid over each other in rapid succession, producing a subtle translucency. It is particularly effective in the initial stages of a painting, and a combination of glazes and thicker opaque areas will produce a lively surface with depth and body.

Hard edges

Because of its body and speed of drying, acrylic paint makes crisp edges, either butting up against other color, or by using tape or paper mask.. It is ideal for fine lines such as stamens, hairs, feathery leaves, or thin stems.

OIL

Oil paint is a most versatile, easily manipulated and long-lasting medium. There are two basic methods of applying paint.

Alla prima is a simple and direct method of applying paint, in which the work is usually completed in a single session, using the spontaneous application of thick color, generally on a white ground, without later manipulation. This was the technique that was used by the Impressionists, who painted mainly out of doors, often in full sunlight, using pure color on a white ground.

The second method is the "traditional" one—the more carefully conceived method by which layers or strokes of paint are built up slowly, "lean to fat"—starting with very thin layers of paint and gradually applying it more thickly, either adding more oil or using paint straight from the tube.

Oil painting techniques include the following.

ABOVE A palette knife is an effective means of applying paint thickly, speedily and smoothly, and a useful complement to brush painting. Here both methods are combined to create a lively, richly textured, picture by Shirley May.

OPPOSITE This detail of a large composition shows *alla prima* painting—the method beloved of the Impressionists—which Is the spontaneous application of thick color over a white ground without later manipulation. It is a fast, vigorous, and fresh method of working.

Frottage
Non-absorbent paper, either smooth or crumpled, pressed into the surface of the paint will leave a rich, patterned texture.

Glazing
This is the technique used by the Old Masters. Paint with little body color, thinly applied in several layers, builds up a subtle variation of color and a rich sheen. This gives a luminous quality to the surface because light is reflected out of the painting from the opaque pigment below the glaze.

Oil bars
Oil paint is now available as thick or thin sticks. They can be dipped in turpentine and used for drawing, or used in conjunction with conventional paint.

Scumbling
A layer of opaque paint is laid over a layer of dry paint of another color or tone, in such a way that some of the lower layer shows through. The paint can be applied with brush, rag, palette knife, crumpled paper, or any method that ensures that the paint is uneven.

CHAPTER FOUR

Looking at Plant Form

There is a rhythm and pattern in the natural world, and discovering this can make drawing a complicated form surprisingly easy. The study of this pattern and rhythm has occupied many artists, and the adaptation of these elements has formed the basis of innumerable designs. Classical Greek architecture is richly embellished with acanthus leaves; the fan-shaped lotus was both a prolific design source for the Ancient Egyptians and a symbol of eternal life; and the entire Art Nouveau movement—its architecture, painting, furniture, and jewelry—is rooted in the sinuous lines of flower and leaf.

Let us start by analyzing plants with the scrutinizing eye of a botanist. If you look at the way a plant holds itself, the manner in which it stands, climbs or spreads, a personality will be revealed, vigorous and erect, soft and inclining, undulating and invasive. This manner of growth will give you the skeleton. Closer analysis will unravel the structure of the components—the composition of the flower head, the shape and texture of petals, the way the leaves join the stem, the roots and fruits—and the way they all fit together. A picture will emerge from this investigation of a singular identity with pronounced characteristics.

There is another equally important way of looking at plants. It is the exploration of what you actually see before you, the jigsaw of shapes made by plants facing you at odd angles with petals overlapping and leaves and stems twisting, bending, and crossing. You will see colors and patterns made by shadows, and by leaves set against the light. Analyzing the plant in this way will reveal a group of shapes, some of which bear no resemblance to the conventional flower shape you think you know, but which are the reality of what you actually see.

LOOKING AT THE WHOLE PLANT

Life force nudges the plant from the ground and causes it to grow upward, extend into the air, and spread itself to light and sunshine. This channel of energy, the spinal cord of the plant, develops in a manner that suits the plant's particular needs—sometimes vigorously thrusting and spreading, sometimes winding or bending. This continuous line of growth extends right to the flower heads and branches out to the tips of the leaves. The character of the plant lies in this line and to follow it in a logical way helps construct what you are painting. When drawing the plant it also helps to draw from root to tip rather than the other way round.

It is a good exercise to analyze in a few lines the basic skeleton or to see the plant in silhouette. Think of particular gestures—the feathery haze of gypsophila flowers formed by continuous branching and dividing from the main stem, the sentinel stem and bursting blooms of the amaryllis, the fan of an iris rising from a sheaf of sword-like leaves, a cactus flower resting like an unexpected butterfly on a prickly dome. Some plants cling or crawl, and the stem winds at extraordinary angles to reach support. The characters of some plants depend on their mass—a network of grasses, or a clump of rock flowers—and if this is missing when you draw the plants, no amount of meticulous detail will compensate. So it is important to think carefully about this characteristic identity.

BELOW **Many designs have their origin in plant form. The Ancient Greeks used the acanthus as a source of decoration. Carvings like this are found throughout Greek architecture.**

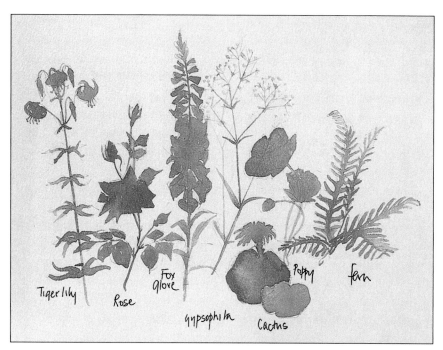

Tiger lily
Rose
Fox glove
gypsophila
Cactus
Poppy
fern

ABOVE The shape and structure of some plants is so distinctive that they are instantly recognizable even without the clues of color and detail. A silhouette highlights the features that give rise to this recognition.

BELOW Behind these silhouettes an intense background throws into relief the three groups of plants by Christine Holmes, emphasizing the tilt of each flower head and the different qualities of the leaves. The papery flower bulb and twine support are as much part of the identity of a potted hyacinth as the blooms themselves.

At various times in the life of plants the growth pattern alters and the structure changes—buds break out, exploratory tendrils lead the plant in a different direction, and flowers erupt into bloom. Later in its life the energy wanes and causes petals to shred at the edges and vivid colors to fade; seed pods appear, and the plant bends, sags, and fragments. These different aspects of the plant's life are just as interesting as the flower in full bloom, and incorporating these in a flower painting will add an extra dimension.

The identity of a plant also lies in its rhythm, the repetition of shape and line. A profusion of tiny daisies has a rhythm in the massed repetition of shape, and the winding stems of some plants, although each has its own distinctive curve, creates a repetitious pattern of movement which is a distinguishing feature.

LILIES, TULIPS AND GRASSES

E L I S A B E T H   H A R D E N

Combining contrasting shapes, color, and textures can make a simple group more interesting. In this watercolor exercise a few flowers, chosen for their differences are combined. The palette on this occasion is Naples yellow, yellow ocher, raw sienna, cadmium yellow, sap green, cadmium orange, cadmium red, Hooker's green, raw umber, and viridian.

1

1 The flowers are arranged to display the different shapes of the plant to best advantage, using the orange flowers as the focus and the darker leaves to give diagonal balance. The lighter and more delicate flowers are arranged to give a freer feel to a fairly conventional composition.

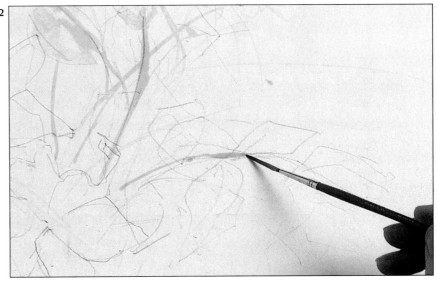

2

2 A rough drawing is made to establish tones and general rhythms in the composition and this is copied lightly to the working surface—in this case stretched, medium-weight watercolor paper with a NOT surface. The main rhythm of the piece is painted in with very dilute green paint. These lines will either stay as stems or parts of stems, or will disappear under darker paint.

3

4

3 The feathery flowers of the cow parsley and flower stamens are blocked out with masking fluid. This allows fast and fluid washes to be used with freedom, and avoids having to paint laboriously around very detailed areas.

4 The shape of the lilies is blocked in with a light cadmium orange wash.

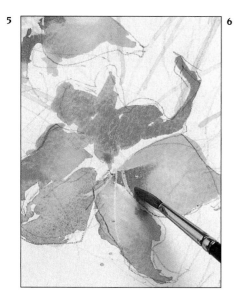

5 A darker cadmium red is dropped into the drying base wash. This building up of color begins to give form to the petals and definition to the masked-out stamens.

6 The group is still a muddle of shapes and lines, so the artist applies a light wash of Naples yellow round the flowers and vase, and drops a darker ocher in as it dries. Now the form of the whole can be seen and the shape built up.

7 Light sap green with a touch of yellow is used for the paler leaves. Much of the work is done with a flat brush, which is twisted and turned to form the strong shapes of the tulip leaves.

9 Taking an overall view it becomes clear that various areas need weight and definition. The vase is given more substance—white patches are left where the light falls and the reflected color of the drapery adds weight to the shadows. The tulips are painted wet-on-wet, adding touches of red where the petal tips emerge from the bud, and emphasizing the line of the stems, which leads the eye to the left of the composition.

8 A darker green is introduced. This throws the red lilies into relief and defines their shape and color. It also adds weight to the lower half of the group.

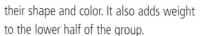

10 The focus of the group is the lilies. A stronger and darker red picks out the areas of more intense color and shadow to build up their shape.

11 The shadow under the vase gives a weight to the whole, and the artist is in a position to make a considered assessment of the composition. The masking fluid is removed and details painted on the cow parsley with a fine rigger brush. The same type of brush adds the thin grasses and pattern on the tulip leaves.

12 The lilies need more color, some indication of the ridges on the petals and a sharp definition of the distinctive stamens.

13 Critical assessment is a valuable learnig process. The rhythm of the piece works well, but possible further improvements would be to give the central area more depth of tone and to anchor the vase of flowers more firmly by increasing the substance and definition of the background.

LOOKING MORE CLOSELY AT PLANTS

It is very easy to look at a plant and see it in terms of flowers and leaves, to draw the most distinct features and then haphazardly join them. The structure of a plant is in some ways like that of the human skeleton, so it makes much more sense to draw the plant's basic skeleton along what might be called its spinal cord, and move outward via the all-important joints and angles toward the flowers and leaves. Head, hands, and fingers move in all manner of ways, but they are dependent upon the extension of the joints—shoulders and hips—and they have little identity when drawn unless this join is convincing. The equivalent of head, hands, and fingers are petals and leaves; the hips and shoulders are the junctions.

Junctions

One of the key areas in a plant is the junction. Branches, flowers, and leaves and stem are joined to each other in distinctive ways, and these junctions hold the key to the structure and posture of the plant.

Sometimes this attachment is simple, leaf stalks springing from a simple bump. Sometimes the junction is a complicated knot of twisting foliage.

Points to notice when constructing junctions are how the collection of leaves and stems fit together, what goes over what, the angle of the join, and whether the leaves or flowers spring from the stem or unwind from a wrapping. All this will alter at various stages in the life cycle. The color at a junction may be different from the rest of the plant, and the texture and width of the stem may vary above and below this point.

BELOW LEFT Cow parsley has the most complex junctions, both ridged and bulbous, and the feathery leaves spring out in all directions. This detail is part of a larger drawing in which the shape of background plants was made by using leaves themselves as a mask for spraying.

BELOW RIGHT This detail is part of a larger composition by Rosemary Jeanneret (see page 553). One of the features of stems is that they are often seen bunched together, crossing and twining, losing their singular identity, but forming a distinctive mesh.

Notice also the junction at the base of the plant, the way the plant grows from the root—as a single column or as a mass of stems—and the way the flower is attached to the stem. Once you are familiar with the junction, the rest will follow easily.

Stems

When looking at the junctions keep an eye open for different types of stem—angular, sinuous, woody—and the marks on them—leaf scars, speckles, peeling tissue, thorns. Look at the texture—fleshy, flaky, hairy, smooth—and the color, which in many cases may be totally different from the leaves and stem. Look also at the way light defines a stem, and how the gradation from pale to dark can emphasize the roundness or squareness of the stem, and how the repetition of dark and light shadows on the curves creates movement as they thicken and taper. The stem is a very useful element in a loose flower painting; color dropped into wet paper, creating hazy shapes can be given a structure by simply painting in a few stems.

Leaves

The basic shape of the leaf may vary enormously. The important point to look for in a leaf is the central spine. The leaf growing along this spine may be a simple oval shape or more complex and divided into fingers. The edges may be smooth or frilly, serrated or prickly; the texture may be hairy or shiny and glossy.

Many leaves are complex, with leaflets placed on either side of a central stem. Look at the way these are arranged, opposite each other or alternating, and the way they join the central stem. Look at the angle at which leaves grow, unwinding from a central stem, like the iris,

ABOVE Using watercolor to investigate a plant takes advantage of the medium's particular behavior. Dark paint leaching into the paler leaves expresses the crispness and rustiness of dying leaves in this study by Jane Dwight better than any amount of labored drawing.

stabbing upward like a sword or inclining with age. Establish the line of growth and the rest will follow.

Leaf veining is often responsible for the pattern on the surface. Even a small area of veining can identify the whole. Notice the texture of the leaf surface and its underside— bristly, waxy, hairy—and the coloring, which may vary in different parts of the leaf. Young leaves are frequently pale; stalks and leaf edges are often a different color. Variety of leaf shape can add pattern to a painting.

BELOW A group of ivy leaves collected to examine the considerable variety of color in one genus of plant. The veins are an important part of the pattern of this plant and help define the line of growth.

Flowers

There are thousands of different categories of flower for the botanist, but the flower painter need only become familiar with several basic shapes. The majority of flowers have regular petals radiating from a center. The petals may be limited to a few, like the magnolia, or there may be many, as in the daisy. Knowing that the plant is composed of, say five petals, makes drawing a great deal easier.

Some radiating plants are more complex and have a mass of tubular florets surrounding a central dome, itself composed of tiny florets. The daisy and the sunflower are examples of this arrangement of petal. The petals of chrysanthemums and roses spiral from a tight center, becoming larger and paler toward the edge. In the sunflower, the central dome has a distinct pattern, a spiral of dark shapes that change radically through the life cycle, ending as a huge cluster of seeds.

Another shape of flower is the bell. Tubular flowers radiate or incline from a central point, or hang at various points down a stem. The foxglove comes into this group of flowers. Look at the way the flower heads are arranged, the way they face and the pattern at their edge. Sometimes they are exotically frilled, sometimes the edge is a different color from the flower itself. Look inside a bell-shaped flower where the patterning is designed to attract insects to the pollen, and you will find dots, speckles, and sometimes intense depths of color.

ABOVE The sunflower is a radiating plant both in name and nature. It is composed of a halo of yellowy florets surrounding a large pad of disk florets which grow in a spiraling manner. The sunflower is particularly interesting at all stages of its life cycle and is one of the most dramatic flowers to paint.

Apparently complex flowers like the orchid and iris also have distinct structures. The pattern of an iris is basically a "Y" with another "Y" crossing it. What looks like a haphazard jumble of different shapes can turn out to have an identifiable pattern.

Patterning itself can be a distinctive feature of a flower. Snake's head fritillaries have a checkerboard on their petals. Some flowers develop patterns to mimic the qualities of insects. Dried seedheads have recognizable patterns, and berries and fruit add spherical shapes to a group.

Skilled manipulation of paint can play a real part in capturing the texture and ephemeral quality of petals. For watercolor painters, water dropped into paint can make frilled petal edges, and enable shading from an intensely colored flower center to its pale tip. Two colors on a brush delineate a multicolored petal in a stroke. Paint on a dry brush can be used to draw thin grasses and the lines and veins on leaves and petals. Dryish oil paint and acrylic brushed lightly over a surface can create ephemeral flakes of petal. Thick impasto paint can mold leaves and petals, buds, and berries. Spatter creates pollen and speckled markings, or a haze of tiny blooms.

HOW THE PLANT PRESENTS ITSELF TO YOU

This close analysis of plants identifies their components and how they are arranged. How flowers present themselves to us and how we see them are two different matters altogether. If we look at the human hand spread flat, the structure is five fingers joined to a palm and so on. But looking at this same hand, say, holding a paint-brush it becomes a different shape completely; no fingers are visible and the silhouette becomes an elliptical rectangle. The same theory applies to flowers.

Flowers can be simplified into basic shapes—circles, stars, or bells. These shapes are dramatically altered by perspective. A circle seen at an angle becomes an ellipse. A group of daisies will contain a variety of forms depending whether the flowers are facing you, some full head and circular, or whether they face upward and appear as an ellipse, presenting larger petals toward you with only the hint of petals on the other side of an oval dome. A flower seen from the back will reveal the joining of the stem and the calyx set against the underside of the petals.

The general inclination of leaves is to face upward toward the source of light. This means we sometimes see them as a thin line, or an undulating thread. A curving leaf will reveal part of the underside is often different in color and texture from the upper surface.

Plants seen against each other create patterns of light and color. To give identity to this jigsaw, find the dominant element and set other things against it. Look at this main element, perhaps a large leaf or flower head. Notice how its shadow falls on the leaves behind, how stems cross in between, and how small patches of light appear in the spaces. Notice how the colors behind may be weaker in tone and intensity.

Observation and an understanding of the make-up of plants should be used as a back-up to the emotional response that must be at the heart of a picture. This knowledge will give a sense of familiarity with the flowers you intend to paint and, thus, a confidence in capturing the particular qualities that inspire you to paint them. Matisse's paintings of dancers, for example, capture the essence of rhythmic movement, but behind this perfect spareness of line and shape lies a vast storehouse of observation, study and knowledge.

LEFT When a round daisy head faces away from you it will appear as a different shape, the circular form altered by perspective to an ellipse. One very helpful technique for drawing flowers is to draw these basic ellipses, in this case the central dome and the shape of the flower surrounding it. The petals will then radiate from one to the other.

A BOWL OF ICELANDIC POPPIES

R O S E M A R Y   J E A N N E R E T

The papery petals and wanton growth of Icelandic poppies have a particular appeal for an artist. They seem to encapsulate the very essence of life and movement, and their texture and subtle coloring reward detailed examination. This group was chosen to illustrate the disposition and character of the plants, and was painted and drawn with watercolor and gouache and watercolor pencils.

1 The poppies are arranged in a glass vase to echo the splay of branching stems, and the arrangement is set against a white background to show off the delicacy of the flowers.

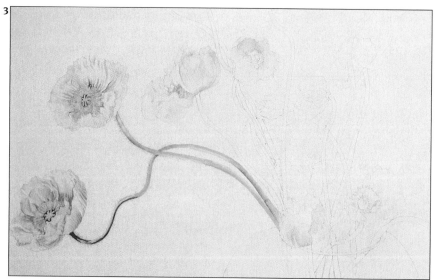

2 A brief sketch is used to plan the general pattern on the paper. The artist then lightly draws the first flower with a fine, hard pencil on Fabriano Artistico paper. Thin washes are painted to build up the delicate tones. While the first flower is drying, the artist starts work on the second flower and, moving from one to the other, builds up with pencil, crayon, and wash. The intense concentration on these two flowers is part of this painter's way of working. She builds up a familiarity with the shape and identity, and finds that this establishes a rhythm for the whole composition and that other flowers will then slot easily into place.

3 The bend of the stems is extraordinary and distinctive. Using thin paint and a medium sable brush she follows their lines back to the vase and then starts to fill in the other plants in relation to these. The whole structure is now sketched in.

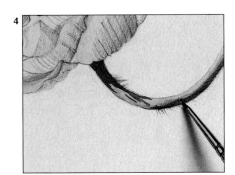

4 Fine brush work and crayoning picks out the shadow and texture of this stem. The work seems painstaking but the artist works with a fluid rhythm and knows exactly what is needed where.

5 Moving backward and forward the flowers are blocked in and built up, the artist paying particular attention to the angle of the head and subtlety of color. Here you can see the fine texture of the petals being put in with a watercolor pencil.

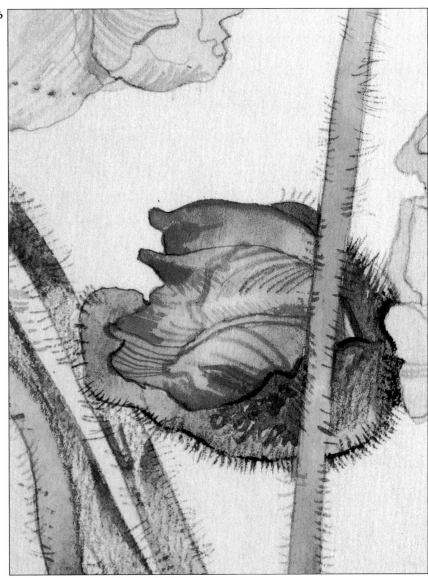

6 Watersoluble crayon is used to draw the shape of this particularly lovely unfolding bud. Water applied to some areas creates controlled areas of intense color.

7 The whole composition depends very much on the careful interlacing of stems. When a group of flowers has been completed the background stems are woven into the overall pattern.

8 A fine brush picks out detail in the center of a flower.

9 Here, the artist is paying particular
attention to the join of stem to flower.

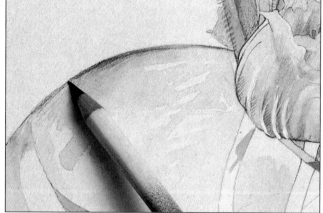

10 The painting of the flowers is
completed, but the vase needs to be
worked on.

11 Painting glass needs intense
concentration. An underlying wash
sketches in the delicate patches of
shadow, and crayoning sharpens the
tone and defines edges.

12 The shape of the stems in the vase echoes the spread above, but reflection and deflection create their own abstract pattern, a mesh of unexpected shapes and colors.

13 The painter takes a careful look at the whole and makes adjustments. Some stems are strengthened, and more intense areas of color built up round the neck of the vase. A web of shadow painted in watercolor echoes the flower shapes and unifies the whole.

CHAPTER FIVE

Sketching and Developing a Sketch

For the flower painter, sketching can serve many purposes. It is essentially a direct rather than contrived response and, as such, has spontaneity, freedom, and vigor in its favor. No preparation is needed, so there is none of the nervous apprehension that sometimes accompanies the first brush stroke of a painting. What happens on the paper matters not one jot and can be developed, discarded or just enjoyed.

SKETCHING AS AN INSTANT RECORD

Sketching can be an immediate recording of a visual image that appeals and is fundamentally a very personal impression. What may appear as a jumble of lines that are unintelligible to others is crystal clear to the artist as the essentials of a plant or the key structure of a group, sufficient to call it to mind at a future date. As well as recording physical images, a sketchbook can be a means of recording aide-memoires and thought processes, which can be explored and developed without their being subjected to the criticism of others.

Ideas are fickle and elusive phenomena. They make unannounced appearances, rarely when faced with a pristine sheet of stretched paper or canvas and a ready brush, but often at particularly inappropriate moments when germs of ideas scudding around in the mind clarify. Having the means of sketching instantly accessible, even

ABOVE This sketch became the basis of a print. Oriental poppies have a wonderful inclination of stem and looseness of flower head, and the two characteristics make a lively combination. The drawing has vigor and excitement, and the artist wove a mesh of flowing lines to find the rhythm of each stem.

BELOW This series of thumbnail sketches by Lynne Moore explores flower composition in terms of brilliant color. She will later use these as a basis for large prints. By working in small scale she can see how the colors and shapes balance each other.

if it is only a scrap of paper and a fiber-tip pen, allows you there and then to lot down the idea or the essentials of a visual image that might otherwise be lost.

The limitation of time can add excitement—a five-minute sketch with a ballpoint pen can have tremendous energy and impact. Sketching will develop as a visual shorthand that is useful when extracting the essentials of an image in the time available, translating the quintessence into swift strokes, outlines, and pattern. There may be an opportunity to fill in the details, either at the time or by returning at a later date, but the main structure and perhaps the color and texture of this image will be on record.

So a sketchbook at the ready can become an essential item and develop into the most precious of possessions. It will be of full of clues that instantly conjure up a scene or moment in time, and these can prove far more potent than a photograph because in sketching

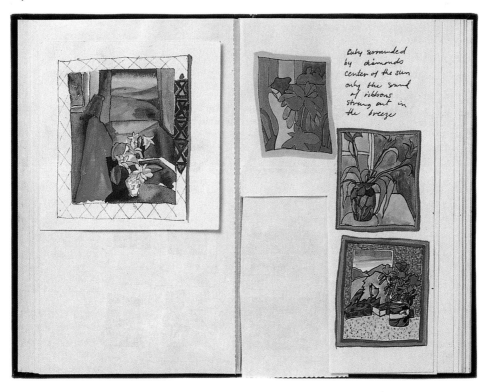

ABOVE This five-minute sketch in pencil and water-soluble crayon tries to catch the thrust and strength of a spray of shaggy chrysanthemums.

the image the eye has traveled over each line and shape and imprinted them on the mind. You may choose to use the sketchbook to build up a storage system of material that might be relevant to a proposed painting—references such as cuttings from catalogs, detailed sketches, notes of colors, pressed flowers or leaves, rapid scribbles of an interesting leaf pattern, or distinctive markings, and names of flowers. All this will be on hand as a source of stimulus and a visual banking system that will pay high dividends.

SKETCHING FOR FAMILIARITY

Sketching can be used to get to know a subject, to build up a familiarity prior to painting and to see it in new ways. Try thinking laterally and approaching the subject from a distance and close up, as if with a wide angle or a zoom lens. Are you are looking for a broad view and a general impression or for details? It will affect the way you look. Think of the image in terms of shape and color and tone, the gradation from dark to light.

Detailed sketching is an exploration that offers the thrill of meeting something new and of not knowing what you are going to find. Starting to investigate the flower

head of a geranium, for example, the eye might become attracted to the knotted joints, or a pair of overlapping leaves farther down the stem whose shape is exciting. Sketching allows you to move where you will and brings a confident familiarity. Looking carefully at the geranium and allowing the eye to travel will ensure that you are well acquainted with the flower and are familiar with its five-petalled bursts of florets and its scalloped leaves. When you set about painting it, the brush will flow more freely.

BELOW After making a fairly detailed study of this geranium, the artist decided to paint it in color to pick up the touches of red throughout.

SKETCHING TO DEVELOP TECHNICAL DEXTERITY

Drawing and painting can often be hampered by the necessity of producing finished work, paintings that will work well, accurately recording a new image, and perhaps producing something that will stand up to the comments of others. All these requirements place inhibitions upon the artist and stifle and tighten freedom of expression.

Sketching is free of these constraints, and offers a chance to be loose and unrestrained, to explore at will and to exercise the hand and eye, thus developing technical dexterity.

Draw freely, regardless of the result. Try making fast impressions of a flower group in different media knowing that you will discard them —you can always change your mind if something remarkable emerges. Tape a stick of charcoal to the end of a long stick and sketch on the floor or on an easel, smudge the result into a tonal study, strengthening the dark areas and rubbing out the light.

ABOVE This sketch in ink and wash tries to capture the rhythm of a mass of bluebells. The artist plced the container to the side of the composition to emphasize the flow of the stems.

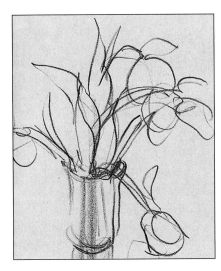

Try also drawing in charcoal or crayon without letting your hand leave the paper, and without taking your eye off the subject, not even for a fractional glance. This serves to concentrate the entire attention upon the subject, following the contours and angles without breaking the attention to look at what is happening on the page. The results may surprise you, the maze of lines will reveal unexpected shapes of great vigor. Assess what is there and see if you can develop it.

Be messy with paint—spread it freely with your fingers or rags; squirt it straight from the tube and mix it around with water or sticks; drop color onto wet paper or onto a glass surface, and take a print by pressing a sheet of paper onto this paint. The possibilities are endless and will help to overcome the terror of the blank page and fear of failure. Vary the size, texture, and color of paper or painting surface. One antidote to staleness is to paint the same subject in different media.

DEVELOPING FLUIDITY OF LINE

Freedom of expression will add to the vitality you capture from the plant. In most plant forms there is a definitive flow in the shape of leaves and petals and the curve of stems. The curve in particular can be notoriously difficult to draw, yet this is a very important element in flower painting and is also seen in the ellipses of flowers and the rounded lips of containers. Stems are perhaps the most tricky of all, however. Some have pronounced bends, others gentle curves. Some are perfectly straight for the most part, then erupt into a shape. The direction of growth is often quite different from the way your arm naturally moves, and the effect of light means that they are dark and thick in some parts and light in others. Swing your arm like a windmill and let the curves flow.

There is an inclination to make branches join at exactly the same angle, to paint leaves all the same size. There is enormous variation even among the leaves from a single plant. Mix up some color and paint different sized leaves splaying at different angles, varying the color and strength. Do not be afraid of the paper. If your sketch does not work, try again.

BELOW Janet White has employed two techniques here to create a mesh of bamboo foliage. The basic image Is drawn lightly and the leaf shapes left by painting a blue background around them, making a negative space. A twig dipped in household bleach adds a further web of lines, which leach the color and form finer details.

SKETCHING AS A LEARNING PROCESS

One tried and tested method of learning and developing skills is to study the work of other artists whose works you admire. Copying allows you to register a painting in your mind, to analyze the rhythm and pattern of the whole and perhaps to discover an underlying pattern, unseen at first glance. It enables you to see how the painter has handled color and overcome problems that are inherent in any subject.

Sketching at an exhibition or gallery can be a permanent record of particular favorites; copying from reproductions is an adequate second best, allowing you more time and a greater selection of materials. Copying a reproduction and then searching out the original can be an enlightening and invigorating experience.

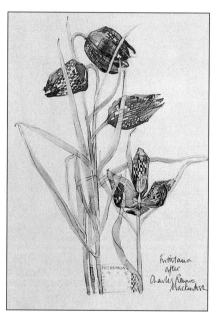

ABOVE The artist was so inspired by an exhibition of the work of Charles Rennie Mackintosh that she copied a plate in the catalog. What had particularly appealed was the strong sense of pattern both in the flower heads and in the arrangement of the whole group. Mackintosh used plant forms as a basis for his remarkably individual style of architectural decoration.

ABOVE Emil Nolde made gardens wherever he settled. His paintings combine the love of flowers with the energy and brilliancy of the German Impressionists. The artist made this copy from a small reproduction of Nolde's to imprint a favorite image in her mind.

LEFT Preliminary sketches help to assess whether a composition will work. The compositional lines formed by the dresser would normally pull the eye out of the picture, but the dark shades and tonal contrast of the flower group hold the attention.

MATERIALS FOR SKETCHING

Arm yourself with a variety of materials, and enough paper to allow for plenty of discarding and big enough to work large. For sketching outdoors equip yourself with a drawing surface small enough to fit in a pocket or bag and sturdy enough to withstand water and time—a well-bound sketchbook will keep your collected jottings together for years whatever media you use.

ABOVE, LEFT, AND OPPOSITE
A florist's shop can be the most magical source of stimulation to the flower painter, the whole atmosphere an overwhelming assemblage of perfume and color. This series of sketches was made prior to a composition, to collect images and ideas and perhaps make a rough layout for a painting. The artist supplements these with photographs and details of flowers from catalogs and tries the ideas in many forms to create a firm structure in the mass of color and texture.

WET-ON-WET PAINTING—CARNATIONS

ELISABETH HARDEN

Wet-on-wet painting can be a most exhilarating exercise. Color added to damp wash has a mind of its own, and the painter has only limited control. This unpredictability is part of the charm, but persistence is needed to work through and discard several failures while waiting for the moments of magic to appear. The palette used for this sketch is rose doré, vermilion, alizarin carmine, permanent rose, oxide of chromium, sap green, and cobalt green.

1 Carnations and gypsophila are arranged in a simple group, crowding the flower heads together to give an intensity of color.

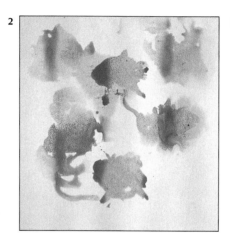

2 Stretched watercolor paper, 140 lb (300 gsm) with a NOT surface, is dampened with a sponge. Even the sturdiest of papers will buckle after a while. Blobs of paint have been dropped onto the paper and the buckles have caused them to pool. The artist will try and utilize this variation in color for the tones of the flowers.

3 A softish green, oxide of chromium, is painted between the flowers. The paper is starting to dry at this point so the paint can be manipulated with a flat-headed brush into shapes of leaves and butted up against the flowers to give definition to the edges.

4 Flower shapes are made by removing paint from the semi-dry surface with crumpled tissue. This forms the basic outline of some flowers. At the same time the paints are mixing and merging together to create areas of soft color.

5 The artist paints strong areas of alizarin carmine. Where the paper is dry it will make a crisp edge, forming the petal edges of the pale carnation. On damp patches it will merge to give a soft effect.

6 The spiky nature of the carnations is beginning to emerge. Redamping, painting in, and removing paint with tissue builds up a loose definition of the plant. Some patches will work better than others, and by concentrating on these, the "happy accidents" can be exploited.

7 A pale yellowy green is washed in and pushed with both brush and hairdrier into sharp edges which form the outline of the palest flowers. This is a way of using "negative space" to form the body of the flower. The predominant color in the two pale carnations in the foreground is a pink frill that forms the edges of the petals. Threads of paints are applied with a fine brush.

8 A third shade of green, cobalt green, forms the stems, flower calyxes, and establishes the rudiments of a jug. A light spatter of white paint gives an indication of the gypsophila. Reassessing the exercise, the artist feels that texture rather than composition has been the more successful outcome. At a second attempt she would avoid the row of three flowers in the foreground, give the jug more substance and spatter a stronger sparkle of white gypsophila with acrylic paint. But, after all, trial and error is part of the painting and sketching process.

CHAPTER SIX

Basic Composition

The urge to paint flowers can be triggered off by almost anything. Perhaps it is a glimpse of a stunning combination of colors that cries out to be painted or a group of flowers whose shape is particularly appealing. Perhaps you just need to paint. Whatever the reason for creating a picture, it will be both easier to paint and visually more successful if the composition is carefully considered. Composition is the arrangement of visual information in a manner that pleases the eye. It is the arrangement of the subject and the space around the subject within defined boundaries—the edge of paper, board, or canvas.

Composing is sometimes just a starting point and things happen along the road that alter the original concept—a mass of color that becomes too overwhelming as the painting progresses, an object that does not seem to fit in, perhaps a flower head altering dramatically by opening up or inclining with age. Accepting that changes might happen adds an excitement to the project. Being prepared to alter the plan as the painting progresses is likely to produce a more satisfactory and fresher painting in the end.

CHOOSING AND ARRANGING THE SUBJECT

For the flower painter choosing a subject is easy. But pause a little before making a decision. There is a temptation to set about painting a complicated arrangement of a large variety of flowers in the assumption that such mass of color and shape is essential for a complete picture. Very often, too large a group can result in overkill; too many shapes and colors bombard the eye and leave it bemused. A few flowers in a simple vase can have great impact, allowing the plant to display itself fully—the inclination of its stem, the shape and texture of leaves, and the subtler aspects of its personality.

Flower painting need not be limited to blooms. Grasses, seed pods, twigs, and dead heads have distinct shapes that make a pattern in themselves. Alongside his exuberant fresh sunflowers Van Gogh drew a series of gnarled dead flower heads, which make an even more potent image than the brilliant yellow blooms.

As an alternative to fresh flowers, dried flowers can capture to some extent the character of their living equivalent. The desiccated quality adds a particular dimension to a painting, even though the living flow of life is missing. The colors of dried flowers are interesting, too, and this type of painting utilizes the subtle earth colors in the palette that are infrequently used.

Flower painting need not be

ABOVE The flowers occupy a central position in this painting by Elisabeth Harden, but by cropping the jug the artist draws the eye into the group, and by the elliptical arrangement of the daisies among the cornflowers strikes an asymmetrical balance. Subtle touches of color enliven the whole—the yellow center of the flowers is echoed in the soft ocher background. There Is considerable variation in the strength of color used for the cornflowers. Basically the same ultramarine blue is used, but in its intense form for the closer flower heads and very dilute in the background. The same color mixed with indigo is used for the decoration on the jug.

limited to a conventional arrangement. We find them in many situations and painting a plant as found sometimes makes a more unusual composition. A bunch still in wrapping paper spread across a page could combine the fluidity of flowers and the geometric shapes of creased paper. Painting flowers outside can sometimes make the most of their amazing quality of popping up in the most unexpected places, tucked into a pavement crack, or stoutly defying the elements on a precarious cliffside, although painting in such situations is not without its hazards.

One last point to bear in mind when choosing a subject is to assess the amount of time you have. Do not attempt to paint a whole bouquet in a two-hour slot. If you cannot complete it all at one sitting recognize that flowers are living things, that they grow, expand, and wither, and will inevitably have done quite a lot of this if a long period of time elapses between painting sessions. Cézanne took so long over his paintings, sometimes many weeks, that he often resorted to using silk flowers and wax fruit as his dummy subjects.

LEFT This group of bluebells by Elisabeth Harden was painted initially outdoors where a vast carpet of flowers made a compelling subject. Wildflowers are generally best painted as a mass and their delicacy described by a few crisp details in a body of tone.

HOW TO ARRANGE THE FLOWERS

Every flower has a personality of its own. Part of this identity is related to the way it grows naturally. It helps to echo this in arranging a composition, letting the flowers flow as they do in nature. Consider the drooping habit of some plants like tulips, the erect nature of lilies and irises, the blowsy, tumbling quality of roses, or the shaggy legginess of chrysanthemums. Wild flowers work best as a haphazard mass, jam-packed into a simple jug or basket, while orchids need singling out to exhibit their extraordinary exoticism. So the arrangement of the flowers is vital in showing them to best advantage.

The choice of container for flowers depends very much on personal taste, and often the painter has accumulated a collection to suit many purposes. The size, shape, and color of the container must complement the flowers, neither overwhelming them by its bulk nor dominating them by its color. If the lines of the flowers and the flow of stems are echoed in the container it will add a unity to the whole.

Different containers have particular qualities that can enhance a composition. Ceramic will absorb color and show shadows; curved metal will reflect light and distort shapes. Glass containers can become a painting subject in their own right, with reflections, distortion, and transparency. A plant in a flowerpot has a different identity—the thrust and flow from its roots embodies the essence of the living plant.

ABOVE This bowl of cyclamen, painted by Sue Merrikin, captures the vigor of the growing plant—the thrust of the stems and the inclination of the flowers.

LEFT Rosemary Jeanneret painted this remarkable study of buttercups. The group loses nothing of its freshness by being described in such detail. The delicacy of the tiny flowers and their particular manner of straggling, haphazard growth is accentuated by their mass. There are definite lines of composition; the wilting grass leaves on the right lead the eye down to shadows and through these into the bulk of the flowers.

COMPOSING THE GROUP

When you have decided what you wish to paint, think about the balance of the group and the arrangement of color. If there are only a few flowers, or if particular flowers become the center of attention of the group, then choosing an odd number rather than an even one tends to make for better balance. Try using more than one container in the composition or adding objects that enhance by their shape or color—perhaps some fruit or vegetables. Another option is to see how the group looks when you lay some of the flowers beside the container.

Generally, painters set their arrangement on a table below eye level. This allows the curve of the container to give the composition a more three-dimensional appearance. It also allows the surface on which the group is standing to be used in the composition, utilizing the texture of the surface or the patterning or folds of a cloth.

There are certainly no hard and fast rules about composition, so move things around until the arrangement pleases you. Setting up should never be hurried—it is yet another aspect of the pleasures of painting flowers.

A B O V E Jeni Sharpstone's oil painting of daffodils contrasts the delicacy and haphazard petal growth against the dark, formal patterning of an Oriental carpet.

L E F T Foxgloves and roses combine to make a riot of soft color in this glorious composition by Sue Wales. Cropping the top of the group makes it more intimate, and allows the eye to focus on the darker depths rather than follow a divertingly busy contour. Placing some of the flowers beside the vase gives the group a feeling of richness and plenty. She has orchestrated the colors in a masterly way and unified the composition by repeating the soft pink throughout.

HOW TO LIGHT THE SUBJECT

For a simple group side lighting, perhaps from a window, will give sufficient variations of tone and will establish shadows that give a composition weight. Take these cast shadows into consideration because they can become an important part of the pattern. You can of course experiment with other types of lighting and this is dealt with in detail in Chapter 8.

BACKGROUNDS AND SETTINGS

A question that is often asked is "What shall I put as background?" In complicated compositions the shapes and colors in the background form an integral part of the pattern as a whole. This will be considered on page 597.

For a simple composition the background is secondary to the main group and its sole purpose is to enhance color and shape and to set the composition in space. Looking at the work of other painters with a particular eye to background will show the means they have chosen and how it has worked. The sumptuous flower groups painted by Dutch Old Masters tended to have dark, plain backgrounds to show off the intricacy and brilliance of the flowers. The flower studies of the Impressionists were generally very simply composed, backed by soft colors, and with perhaps a few lines of a table described to set the composition in space.

BELOW In a simple group the background often takes a secondary role. This case is different. Sue Pendered has created as a foil to this group, *Hydrangeas and Amonite*, a background of subtle complexity. She uses various materials, pressing them into drying paint and experimenting and reworking until the desired effect is achieved.

A GROUP OF ANEMONES PAINTED IN OIL

FAITH O'REILLY

Oil paint is an excellent medium for capturing the brilliant colors of anemones, and the ragged nature of their growth. There is no definitive palette of colors for painting flowers, and for the pinky/purple shades of this group Faith O'Reilly chooses a specific palette of titanium white, chrome lemon, Naples yellow, aureolin yellow, cobalt blue, sap green, oxide of chromium green, Mars violet, cobalt violet, alizarin crimson, scarlet lake, Italian pink, and rose madder. This gives a good range of pinks and reds to create the different tones of the flowers. The paints are mixed with distilled turpentine or used straight from the tube.

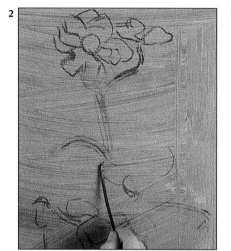

1 The anemones are arranged in a white jar to relieve the heaviness of a dark-tone surface, and set against a yellow background to complement the predominantly purple coloring of the flowers. Sometimes it helps to do a quick watercolor sketch at this stage, to help establish the range of colors needed for the desired effect.

2 The stretched canvas is prepared with an undercoat suitable for oil or acrylic, and on top of this is painted a thin layer of alizarin crimson and ultramarine to create a tonal background for the group. The composition is sketched with charcoal, starting with the basic structural lines.

3 The advantage of using a mid-toned background is that the artist is working "up" to the lights and "down" to the darks. This both saves time and adds a particular richness or complexion to the finished work. Here, the lightest tones are painted in.

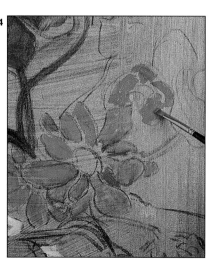

4 The basic colors of the anemones are painted to establish the color balance of the group, and to create areas of tone. The purple flowers are fairly dominant in tone, but the effect is balanced by the strong area of red and pink, which will jump forward toward the eye.

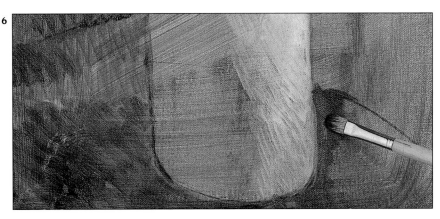

5 The principal colors of the group have been painted in and the main color balance established.

6 Here, a dark underpainting of the surface has been worked using vigorous "scumbling" brush strokes. This lively application of paint will give texture and variety of tone to the otherwise plain area of color.

7 The artist paints a thin layer of Naples yellow over the background. Having established the whole color balance she paints in the smaller flowers and a green-tinted reflection of the tablecloth on the side of the white pot.

8 By painting the purple and red flowers on the left of the group, the artist has created a color balance in the whole with a trio of darker colored flowers setting off the brilliance of the reds and purples. Oxide of chromium green is painted around the base of the pot, and its form is modeled by dragging the paint lightly from one side to the other with a soft brush, allowing the underpainting to show through.

9 Detail is added with a fine brush, to delineate the flicker of light on stems and the feathery leaves round the flower heads. Modeling the flower heads with darker tones and picking out the flower centers gives them dimension, sets each one against each other and indicates the way they are facing.

10 The palette knife gives a particular texture to oil painting, allowing smooth areas of paint to be applied quickly and creating a rich background for the flowers. This builds up a thin ripple of paint around each flower and smooth patches in the background. Here a brighter yellow is being added to the background.

11 At this stage the painter assesses the work. All the components are in place, and it is time to stand back and decide what needs to be changed and where most detail is required.

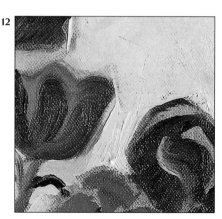

12 More color is added to the background and flecks stroked onto flowers to denote petals catching the light.

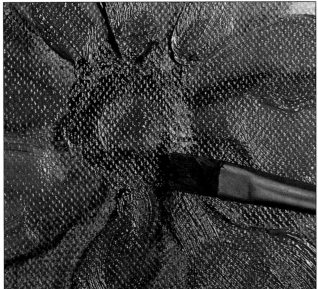

13 A thin brush is used to add detail to the centers of the flowers.

14 Again the palette knife is used to apply large areas of paint with vigorous speed, allowing the underlying color to shine through. The final green of the cloth gives a lighter note to the base of the composition, but the color of the two underlying layers adds grain and density to the flat area of color.

15 The finished painting has an energy that captures the vitality of the flowers. The apparent simplicity of the setting is given depth and dimension by the layers of color, with underlying tone appearing throughout the work to give harmony to the whole.

TRANSLATING THE COMPOSITION TO PAPER OR CANVAS

Once you have chosen the subject, and combined it in a way that pleases, with lighting that defines and gives weight, look carefully at it as a potential picture. In transposing a three-dimensional group onto a two-dimensional surface, some basic rules of composition can be used to simplify the process.

Use the arrangement of objects to control the way the eye looks at the picture. Lines of movement can be created that will lead the eye to the point of focus. These lines of movement can be made by the inclination of stems, the shape of a shadow of the fold in a cloth or by anything that gives the feeling of line. Look for the lines in a group and observe where they lead. A line through the center of a group, dividing the group horizontally, vertically or diagonally, will direct the eye out of the picture and create equal divisions that will confuse the eye.

If the dominant object is placed right in the center, the eye can become confused by the equal space all around. So, in principle, an unequal balance makes a group more interesting.

Avoid also straight lines that lead the eye out of the picture; a curved or broken line leads the eye in. The eye should be enticed in by interesting pointers to the heart of the painting.

There are also unseen lines of structure and rhythm. Placing emphasis on particular lines of construction will serve to underline other qualities. Accentuating the vertical will give a feeling of strength; paying particular attention to the horizontal, spreading quality will emphasize solidity; diagonal lines stress movement, and cross-hatching or intertwining creates the illusion of density. Utilize these lines as well as the directional lines of composition. One way of composing is to use a viewfinder. Cut a rectangle in a piece of stout card and use it as photographers do to isolate particular areas.

RIGHT An unequal balance in a composition will make a subject more interesting. Rosemary Jeanneret has set the jug of mistletoe at the bottom of her paper and uses the space above to give a feeling of airiness and light.

ABOVE The lines in this composition are very strong. They radiate in from three directions to the oval shape made by the plate and through the color to the bunch of shaggy nasturtiums that form the theme of this painting by Elisabeth Harden. A harmony Is made by the use of complementary colors. Orange and blue are the dominant combination, and a soft green offsets the sparks of dark red. Pale yellow in the surrounding area is balanced by a gentle touch of violet at the top of the brushes and a darker mauve in the shadows.

THUMBNAIL SKETCHES IN LINE AND TONE

Using the specific passages of the subject you are seeing through the viewfinder, make thumbnail sketches. Look at the subject from a distance, with the whole group included, and see what is happening. Position the focus of attention off-center, or in one corner so the composition is asymmetrical. Pick up on lines that draw the eye in and curves that

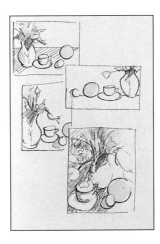

swing into the composition. Look at the patterns shadows make, and experiment.

LEFT AND BELOW These thumbnail sketches (left) show various groupings. From the top downward, the flrst separates the objects, the second places them in a line, and the third cuts the objects too dramatically. The chosen grouping (bottom) links each object and uses a high viewpoint to emphasize the roundness. This works well, as can be seen in the finished painting (below).

WHAT SIZE, WHAT MEDIUM

The decision to use a particular painting medium may well have been decided by your preferred technique or the materials available, but size is a consideration at this point. This will partly be guided by the subject—a busy subject painted too small will lose impact, though a single flower painted much larger than life can take on a new dimension—and partly by personal preference and the amount of time you have.

LEFT This small study of weigela measures only 5 x 5 in. but the painted image appears large because it completely fills the space.

TRANSFERRING THE IMAGE TO THE PAINTING SURFACE

Some artists can paint straight from a thumbnail sketch, but it is often useful to sketch the composition in roughly. Heavy pencil drawings will leave marks on the paper and pencil lines will show through pale colors, so for a subtle watercolor structural lines in a pale color which blends with the general scheme are best. Charcoal can be used to sketch in the structure of an oil or acrylic.

Begin by positioning the main focus of attention with reference to the sketch—the biggest flower or area of most activity—and fit in everything else around. Work on a larger surface than you think you need. This eliminates the danger of going off the paper or board and allows for altering the composition if the extremities prove interesting.

RIGHT Shirley May began this piece as a composition of flower heads using a horizontal or landscape format. During the course of painting she decided to extend the group, so added paper and completed this lively and expressive work as a vertical or portrait shape.

STARTING TO PAINT—WHAT TO LOOK FOR IN A COMPOSITION

Now that you have a group of flowers positioned in a setting, shut your eyes, then open them and look at your arrangement in a completely different way. Study it with the seeing side of the brain—the side that sees the pattern rather than the objects. Leaves and flowers will relate to each other, overlap and cast shadows. There will be a shape all round the arrangement, sometimes creating curious harsh edges, sometimes merging into a soft haze. There will be indefinable angled shapes in the group, perhaps pale spaces between the petals and leaves and dark spaces between stems, or vice versa. These strange shapes are vital to the composition. They form the negative shape around the positive. Try putting out of your mind completely the idea that before you is a shaggy yellow sunflower. What you are seeing is a complicated arrangement of shapes, locking into each other like a puzzle. What is not there sets off what is there.

SKETCHES AS SOURCES

Sketches are often the bedrock of composition, though perhaps less so in the case of flower subjects, when secondhand information may lose vitality. However, by using sketches as a basic structure, moving the shapes around, experimenting with color, and supplementing them with visual information, what emerges may be a pleasing reconstruction of a fleeting vision.

SETTING UP THE WORKING ENVIRONMENT

Painting is in some ways like cooking. The important ingredients should be close at hand because searching for some essential in the midst of a complicated procedure or when the current of creation is in full flow, is frustrating and disturbing. Assessment is an important part of the painting process. If you do not know which direction to take, leave the work for a short period of time and this will allow you to review it with new eyes. Stopping work can be very difficult; there is an inclination to worry a painting, to fill in the whole surface, to add too much detail. If you find you are doing this without achieving anything then stop—the painting may be complete.

ABOVE In this sketch the background behind the image has been colored to form a series of interesting shapes, using the line around the picture as part of these forms. The unity of positive and negative shapes as patterns in their own right will help you compose a picture.

ABOVE The components of a composition are the positive shapes, the objects, set against "negative space," the empty area. The concept of negative space utilizes this space as a positive, solid entity. This sunflower, which fills the picture area, is set against a white background.

ANEMONES IN WATERCOLOR

E L I S A B E T H   H A R D E N

This is a watercolor study of the same group of anemones as in the preceding step-by-step on page 556. The artist's concern is to capture the shaggy quality of the plants and their haphazard manner of growth. The colors are permanent magenta, violet alizarin, rose madder, cobalt blue, ultramarine blue, alizarin carmine, alizarin crimson, Naples yellow, raw sienna, raw umber, and Hooker's Green.

1 The composition of the group differs slightly from the previous one in a number of ways; the dark cloth has been removed from the table because it was felt to have too strong a tone for the composition, and the flowers have been repositioned so that the flow of the stems is more exaggerated.

2 Purples and pinks are notoriously difficult in watercolor, so a number of different shades in these tones were mixed to see if they approximated to the color balance of the whole.

3 A thumbnail sketch of the whole, to establish basic balance and tone is transferred lightly to the painting surface—stretched Saunders NOT watercolor paper—and the stem structure sketched in with watery green paint. A pale wash lays in the basic shape of the purple anemones, forming a negative shape around a space for the brilliant pink flower. The wash is very pale at this stage, and sharper edges are formed by dropping water into the painted shapes. If too many hard edges result they can be softened with a sponge as the painting progresses.

4 More concentrated color is dropped into the drying paint, tipping the board and using a hairdrier to control the position of the color. The behavior of paint depends very much on the dampness of the paper and only experience will ensure confident control.

5 Basic stems and blooms are in place. At this stage it helps to stand back and see where the next shape is needed to give balance to the piece. The flowers seem to float in space so they need to be anchored into a structure.

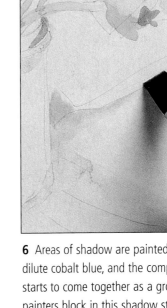

6 Areas of shadow are painted with dilute cobalt blue, and the composition starts to come together as a group. Some painters block in this shadow structure at the beginning of the work and it acts as a scaffolding, holding the different components together.

7 A wash of Naples yellow is painted round the whole. This complementary tone to the predominating purple defines the white vase and adds a warmth to the whole. At various points during the drying more color is flooded in so that the soft background is a haze of shades and shapes.

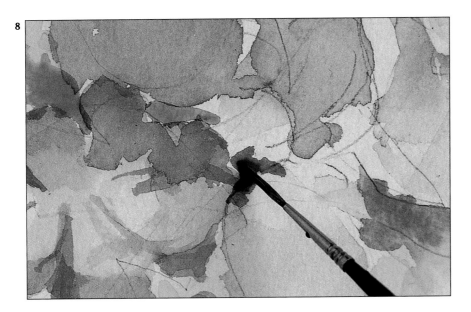

8 The whole group is pale and needs definition. Hooker's green is painted around and between the flowers, giving a sharpness to their outline, and throwing them forward in space.

9 Watercolor painting is very much a process of building up layers of color and modifying tones in relation to each other. More concentrated color is painted into the flowers and the stems, and the dark interior of the vase is given more definition and weight.

10 Here, the artist concentrates on the heart of the flowers. Often this stage will unexpectedly bring life to the whole painting. A fine rigger brush paints in the dark centers and stamens. It helps to look very closely at the centers, often the petals are a lighter color than the surround, and the stamens grow in a distinctive way that identifies a particular flower.

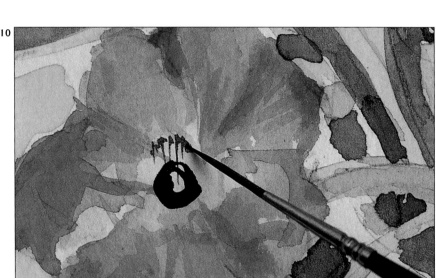

11 The flowers have an identity now and the positioning of the dark centers establishes which way each flower is facing.

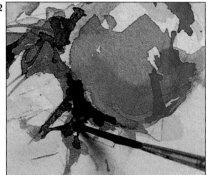

12 A thicker rigger brush, chosen for its dragging qualities, is used to drop in and pull darker paint into the shaggy shapes surrounding the flowers. The darker green is made by mixing Hooker's green with a touch of alizarin crimson. The flower has been painted very loosely, and the artist feels that this ruff of dark leaves is sufficient to establish its identity.

13 The composition still seems to float, so a diagonal of raw umber wash is swept across the composition. Very often, leaving the painting for a period of time will enable you to look with objective eyes and pinpoint the areas that need defining or strengthening.

14 The completed painting, which succeeds well in conveying the way in which these flowers seem to reach out from the vase, their stems twisting and bending.

CHAPTER SEVEN

Color and How We See It

Flowers and color are inextricably linked. It is no coincidence that many colors are described by flower names—rose pink, periwinkle and cornflower blue, violet, buttercup yellow, lily white. These names evoke an emotional response and a vivid mental image of specific color.

The palette of nature can be brilliant and bold, with kaleidoscopic masses jostling for attention, or infinitely gentle, with soft, muted shades that merge imperceptibly. There is color where you would least imagine; the petals of a seemingly white flower can yield variety of shade and tone.

In nature vibrant colors in proximity do not clash and a superabundance of flowers is thrilling rather than visually excessive. In paint brilliant colors can overwhelm each other and a huge mass of flowers can lose identity and structure. In other words, the perfection of flowers in nature becomes, in effect, one of the principal problems for the flower painter; to adapt this apparent flawlessness into a painting needs careful composition and an appreciation of the power and possibilities of color. It is impossible to reproduce the brilliant effect of light with pigment. We must rely on the effects of colors against each other—the interaction of color—and on the use of tone. Much of the work of the Impressionists, the Post-Impressionists and the Fauve movement was to this express purpose—creating with color the brilliance of light itself.

COLOR IN SCIENTIFIC TERMS

In scientific terms color is the breakup of light into the visible spectrum. A beam of white light passed through a glass prism separates into the bands of color familiar to us as the rainbow, and described by Sir Isaac Newton in the 17th century as violet, indigo, blue, green, yellow, orange, and red. Since that time many light-wave frequencies outside that rainbow spectrum have been investigated, notably infrared at the yellow end of the range and ultraviolet at the other. Ultraviolet is the light that enables insects to home in on plants but is impossible for humans to see.

An object has no color until it is illuminated by light. White light comprises all colors. Most materials and substances consist of pigment that will absorb certain ranges of the light spectrum and reflect others. For example, a yellow sunflower is yellow because it contains pigment that will reflect yellow light wavelengths and absorb all others. An extremely dark flower contains very little reflective pigment so most of the light rays are absorbed. Black objects—in flowers perhaps the patterning or the stamens—absorb all light.

Blue and orange

Red and green

Purple and yellow

THE COLOR WHEEL

The spectrum of color is often arranged as a color wheel. This is a device created by color theorists to explain color behavior. The three primary colors—red, blue, and yellow—are placed as segments of a wheel so that each primary faces a mixture of the other two primaries, a secondary color. Opposing colors on the wheel are said to be complementary to each other. Red has green as its complementary; yellow has violet; and orange has blue. Complementary colors, as the term suggests, enhance and intensify each other.

This color pattern can be extended farther. Where primaries and secondaries merge into each other they create more subtle hues, and can be placed to great effect against the blend at the opposite side of the wheel, a yellowy green complements a pinky red.

Considering this in relation to flower painting, and in very general terms, orange flowers are enhanced by blue flowers or blue-toned foliage, for example, and red or pinks and green are mutually enhancing. The least effective of the

LEFT These Illustrations show each of the three primary colors with their complementary. Various subtleties of each color have their balance in the equivalent complementary colors.

THE COLOR WHEEL

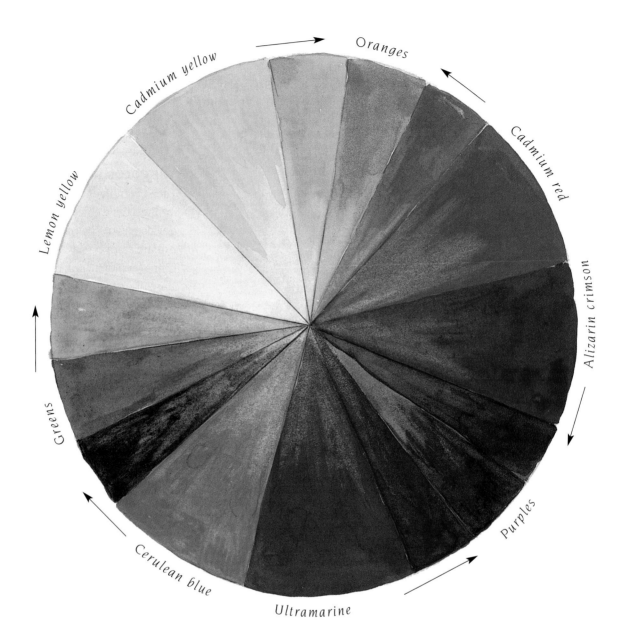

Oranges

Cadmium yellow

Cadmium red

Lemon yellow

Alizarin crimson

Greens

Purples

Cerulean blue

Ultramarine

complementary combination is violet and yellow; since one is pale and the other relatively dark, the two colors are a strong tonal contrast and this can undermine the complementary effect.

Another use of the theory of complementary colors is to employ it in a softened or muted form to make the main color more intense. Mixing a tiny touch of orange with its complementary blue will push it toward a gray, and when this is used as a soft background it will create a subtle harmony while adding brilliance to the main color, orange, which is pushed forward in the composition.

ABOVE The color wheel Is a device created by color theorists to explain color behavior. The three primary colors are placed as spokes of a wheel, each primary being opposite the color mixed from the other two primaries—a secondary color. Further subtleties are created as further mixes are made. For Instance an orangey red is the complement of a greenish blue and serves to enhance and heighten its effect.

ABOVE Two colors leap out of this composition *Blue Teapot* by Sue Wales—the brilliant blue of the teapot and the luminous patches of orange. On closer examination the painting reveals a complicated web of color worked round the subtle nuances of these colors. The eye is drawn to areas of pattern and texture and finds echoes of the complementaries in the flowers, curtain fabric, and tablecloth, and even the plate of cookies. A sharp green flickers in the shadows and draws the eye to the bowl of red and green tomatoes. Color and line combine to make a fascinating and vibrant painting.

LEFT This sketch shows the effect of using a muted version of the complementary color as a background. The soft lilac intensifies the luminosity of the yellow flower.

HUE AND TONE

Color is also defined in terms of saturation, hue, and tone. Saturation means using color at full strength to obtain maximum intensity; desaturation means diluting the color and reducing the intensity. Flower painters in the East used to paint with saturated colors to show shadow rather than adding darker pigments.

The term hue indicates the tint or shade of color and its variations, how much white or black the color contains. The top illustration on this page shows a study in gouache using only hues of cadmium yellow.

Tone is the quality of light and dark. When a colored picture is reduced to shades of gray on a photocopier we can see the tonal values clearly. As we have said, yellow tends to be light in tone and violet dark, but other colors on the color wheel that lie between them—orange, red, green, and blue in its lighter hue—are fairly similar in tone. Assessing tone is one way of obtaining a balance in a picture.

Balance can also be achieved with color by utilizing the affinity of two related colors, say red and orange, and balancing them with a complementary color, like blue, which is darker in tone and is the complementary of orange.

ABOVE Gouache colors can be mixed with white and black to make a whole range of hues. Here cadmium yellow has been used in its pure form and mixed in various proportions with black and white to make this wide variety of colors, from pale primrose to dark olive.

RIGHT This tonal painting of nettles uses only the shades from black to white to capture the slightly menacing and ominous quality of a dense clump of nettles. Brilliant white catches the rather cruel, jagged-edged leaves and the luminosity of a glowering sky beyond. Various shades of gray and black and textures of paint and ink explore the intricacies of the dense undergrowth.

CHRISTMAS ROSES—A STUDY WITH A LIMITED PALETTE

ELISABETH HARDEN

The purpose of this exercise was threefold: to explore the subtleties of white flowers; to paint using only a limited color range; and to compose the group so that its arrangement within boundaries made a pattern in itself. Christmas roses are flowers of great delicacy of shape and subtlety of color, ranging from intense plummy purple to the almost white. There is always a green tinge to their complexion. Stretched Saunders NOT 140 lb (300 gsm) paper is the painting surface and the palette is cadmium yellow, May green, Hooker's green, cobalt green, and olive green.

1 The flowers are arranged on a white surface. They languish out of water so the painting needs to be completed quickly.

2 A viewfinder is a useful aid. A rectangular shape approximating to the proportions of the composition is used to help fit the image into the space. Masking tape is stuck gently round the edge of the composition to create a border and this enables the paint to be freely washed against the edge.

3 Delicately colored flowers painted in watercolor depend very much on the subtle application of thin layers of paint. Building up these layers gradually reveals the roundness of the form and here this process is shown at an early stage. Masking fluid has been used to reserve white details.

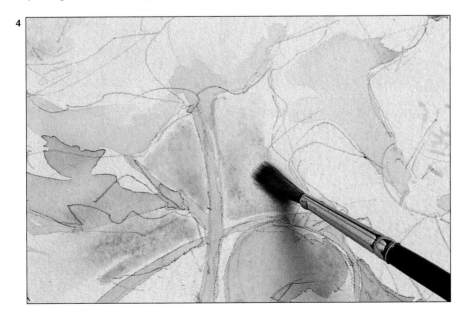

4 Cobalt green is a curiously oily color, but it has a wonderful fresh tone and precipitates into the hollows of textured paper in an intriguing way. Here it is painted loosely with a medium sable brush to define the petals of the flowers and add a contrasting background.

5 Cobalt green has also been lightly brushed over petals to give them some shadow. The main shape of the composition is becoming clearer, but it seems pallid overall and the tonal values need adjustment.

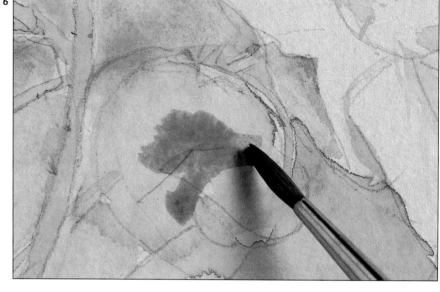

6 A denser green is painted and dropped in, emphasizing the areas of shadow and giving the whole painting more substance.

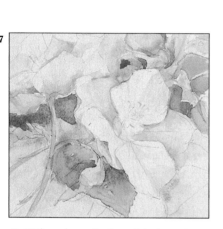

7 With each application of darker paint the artist needs to look at the whole pattern and adjust accordingly. Here you can see how the form is emerging.

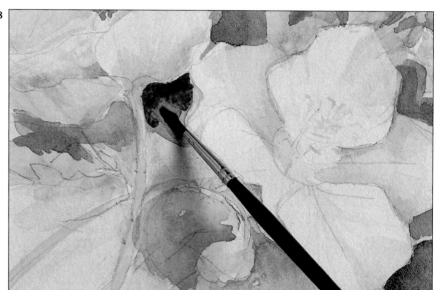

8 The artist looks at the subject carefully and tries to discover the areas of darkest tone. These will both throw the pale flowers into relief and create depth. It is interesting to see that in this case the area with the most paint recedes and the part with no paint jumps forward.

9 Soft washes of color are built up, and stronger paint introduced into the center of the flower.

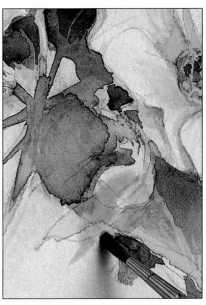

10 A very fine brush is used to pick out the dark parts of each flower center, the masking fluid is rubbed off and the details are readjusted. The flower centers are now the point of focus for the whole painting.

11 The whole image seems intensely green, so a few touches of a warm toning color are added.

12 The masking tape is removed when the painting is complete. The resulting white surround tends to concentrate the eye more closely on the subject, and makes interesting shapes round the edge.

Having described color as light reflected or absorbed by pigments, it is interesting to consider briefly these pigments themselves and how they have evolved by trial, error, invention, and development into the wonderful range available nowadays.

Earliest paints came from the earth itself, ochers and siennas, and pulverized minerals. Later the Ancient Egyptians tried baking these minerals and found that other colors resulted. Medieval monks sometimes used the plants themselves—the best gold for use on manuscripts was made of celandine petals and mercury (fine, as long as they did not lick their brushes). Pigments came from the most extraordinary sources: Indian yellow arrived in Europe in stinking lumps from the markets of Bengal, the dried urine of cows fed on mango leaves; painters in the 16th and 17th centuries were known to use a brown called "Mummy brown," which was made from powdered Egyptian mummies. Plants yielded all manner of coloring; madders, indigo, gamboge, and sap green. Animal sources were the whelk, which produced the Tyrian purple beloved of Roman emperors; carmine came from the cochineal beetle. Painters must have worked under extremely difficult conditions, coping with the fugitive nature of the colors, the toxicity of some pigments and the cost of others.

Now all has changed. Sophisticated chemistry has produced a kaleidoscopic range of colors that are easily available, varied and, for the most part, colorfast.

The basic range for a painter consists of a warm and cool version of the three primaries. Cadmium red and alizarin crimson in the reds; French ultramarine and cerulean blue in the blues; and cadmium and lemon for the yellows. These mix to an adequate variety of shades. By adding some earth colors such as yellow ocher or raw sienna, the more

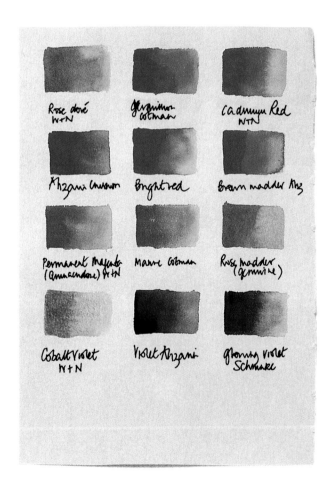

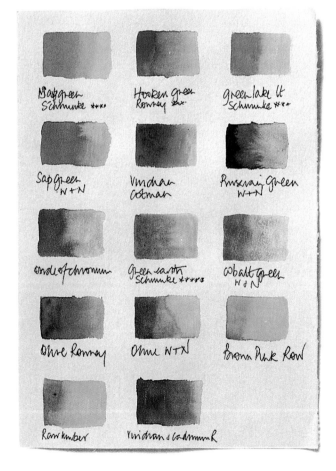

translucent burnt sienna, raw and burnt umber, and a dark gray-blue such as Payne's Gray, a huge range of colors is available. Oil, gouache, and acrylic require a good quality white, usually titanium white.

The flower painter has specific requirements, and needs to be able to mix a wide range of greens, and obtain very particular colors in the red/pink areas, where mixing colors tends to dull their brilliance. Mauves and violets can also be difficult, and often the identity of a plant is linked to a very specific color. Happily, most manufacturers offer an extensive range of colors.

Useful additions to the basic range might include rose doré, a warm pink; carmine, a rich dark red, permanent rose, a blue-based brilliant pink, and brown madder. In the purple and violet range you could add permanent magenta and cobalt violet, alizarin violet, and glowing violet. These colors are varied, brilliant and generally colorfast.

A good range of greens can be mixed from the basic palette, using the combination of the warm and cool primaries. However interesting additions extend the range: viridian, which used alone is very strong and staining, but mixes well and can be toned down with its complementary red to a dense black-green; terre verte; cobalt green, a thick turquoise green; olive green; Hooker's green; and brown pink, which is a yellowy olive color.

With some experience and experimentation each artist will arrive at an appropriate palette. It is interesting to take note of what each painter in the step-by-step demonstrations has used. Their palettes will include particular favorites that are used much more than others and which contribute to that unquantifiable quality— individual style.

OPPOSITE AND BELOW A color chart is an Immensely useful and speedy reference. Painters often build up a collection of paints—even though they will generally use only a limited number—and record the details of each color, in its saturated and dilute form, with the maker's name and permanence rating. Flower painting sometimes requires specific colors In the pink/red and green ranges, which are difficult to achieve by mixing.

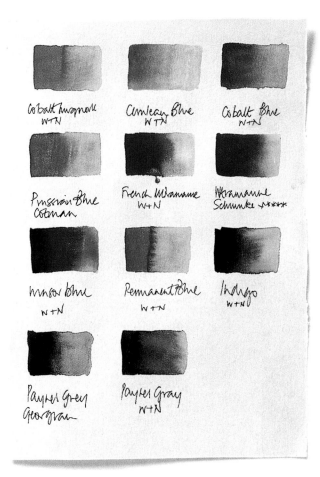

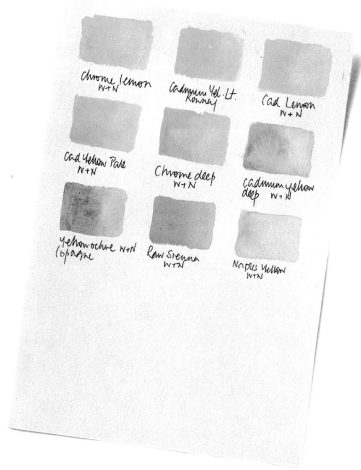

SUBJECTIVE COLOR—WHAT IT MEANS TO DIFFERENT PEOPLE

Scientific analysis of color is interesting, and theories can solve certain problems, but color also has an emotional, spiritual, and social dimension in life and art.

Color means different things to different people. The Ancient Greeks identified it with universal harmony, and associated various gods with particular colors. Tibetans link color to geographical direction.

Australian aborigines respond to only a few colors, principally the earth and sky colors that surround them. Eskimos, perceiving their world against an overwhelmingly white background, are able to differentiate between a great number of shades of white.

Color has long been used for healing, with specific hues affecting different areas of the body and mind—pink for instance is said to produce beneficial effects on the eyes.

Goethe called the hues from red to green the "plus" side, and the hues from green to violet the "minus" side, suggesting that one is associated with a mood of zest and liveliness, and the other with more subdued and contemplative feelings.

B E L O W This group is composed in colors from within a limited range. Soft and bright shades of blue, highlighted with white, are set In a warm surround of ochers and yellows.

USING COLOR FOR PARTICULAR EFFECT

Color can be used to manipulate the eye, to lead it round a painting. Dramatic combinations of brilliant colors are exciting. Faced with two bright colors of similar tone, the eye cannot decide where to rest and flickers between the two.

Bright color can pull the eye to a certain area, and this can sometimes be an effective extension of the composition of a painting. The basic structure of lines and tone will direct the eye to a certain point or points, but it can then be manipulated to another area by the insistent pull of a patch of brilliant color.

A painting using colors from a very limited area of the spectrum, and using a great variety of subtle tones, will create an atmosphere of harmony. Subtle combinations of tone allow the eye to rest and to be led into an area, to explore the deeper tone. This gives the surface of the picture a three-dimensional appearance. Sometimes the addition of a spot of bright color catches the eye and brings this area to the forefront.

ABOVE The excitement of this composition *Red, Red Amaryllis* by Shirley Trevena, lies partly in its abstract nature—a loose indication of what it portrays, inviting the viewer to explore and imagine. The stimulation of two bright colors of equal tone causes the eye to flicker between the two, unable to decide where to rest.

LEFT The accepted rules of composition are often defied in a spectacular way. At first glance the three regular pots seem to be the subject of this composition of *Anemones on Shelf* by Rosemary Jeanneret. The eye is then led round the burst of flowing blue anemones and suddenly discovers a pinpoint of red and pink at the farthest extremity. Another look at the picture reveals echoes of this brilliant alizarin crimson throughout the composition, in shadows, stems and petal tips.

COLOR IN WHITE

Painting white flowers in some media is easy and effective, particularly when they are set against a dark background. On a darker tone, tiny sprays of flowers can be flicked with white paint, or a fragile petal stroked onto the canvas as a broken brush stroke, the starkness of contrast giving sparkle to the group. But this effect is only as you see it at the time: in reality, white is rarely white.

Look very closely at a white flower in various lights. Place it on a sheet of white paper and you will see the infinite subtleties. There will be different shades within each petal, perhaps a greener tone in the center and a brownish tinge toward the tip. If there is light above, the petals underneath will have a shadow and this shadow will be made up of different colors. Colors nearby reflect onto the white.

Hold the flower against a window and look at the tones; the outside petals will appear pale and fragile, but where they cross one another the tone will be darker, and in the center the color will be anything but white, perhaps a bluey gray. Painting white flowers against light requires a firm hold on the mind to paint what you see rather than what you think is there.

Creating the form of white flowers can sometimes be difficult, especially in watercolor. Negative painting is a useful technique to use. Another device is painting a darker color round the whole or part of a flower, which will reveal the silhouette, then adding a flower center and perhaps a touch of shadow which will create an apparently solid form in a white space. Masking fluid can be used to great effect.

ABOVE *White Tulips,* by Shirley Trevena shows how leaving blank white paper in a painting can make a very solid form, and that only a hint of shadow and detail is needed to reveal the dimension of these shapes. Their purity of shape and color stands out against an infinitely subtle background, where flickers of white and pale pattern lend a unity to the whole.

ABOVE *White Daisies* by Sue Wales shows to great effect how a white form is seen in different situations. The daisies set against dark tones are bright and stark, their petals shown in great definition; in the shadows the form Is less distinct and certain parts of the flower take on various degrees of blue shadowing. In deeper shadow the flowers are very indistinct and their identity merges totally with the atmosphere of melting shadow.

CHAPTER EIGHT

Light

Without light there is no color. It is light that creates color, models form and establishes mood. An understanding of the effects of light, and a knowledge of how to use it can create magic out of the mundane.

Light failing on a surface is in part absorbed and in part reflected by pigments within. Each pigment reflects back particular light rays, and this is known to us as the color. When less light falls on a surface the color is fainter and less true. A shadow is created when light is blocked from a surface. In this way light creates a variety of colors from differently pigmented objects and, by the arrangement of these objects in relation to the light source, makes a variety of tones and patterns.

The interplay between light and shade gives a painting its life, a pattern to its surface and a weight and dimension to the subject. It is a means of expressing a three-dimensional subject within the two-dimensional limits of a painting. Light can add excitement —a sparkle of light as it catches a petal edge, or shines through leaves— and, by contrast, give dark passages a rich density and an air of mystery.

Consider the effect of a different light direction on a simple group. A bunch of flowers, placed in a jug on a flat surface with a facing light, say a window, will look bright and clear but flat. The whole group will be uniformly lit and there will be a lack of dimension.

The same subject obliquely side-lit will look totally different, This is the traditional method of lighting a group, used by painters for centuries, either from a window, or by candlelight, and is the most effective way of establishing form and bulk. Parts facing the light source will be pale with white highlights, merging round the form to very dark areas where the subject receives no light. Shadows are cast, adding weight to the composition, and the pattern they make is often as exciting as the original subject.

Lit from the back the subject becomes even more dramatic. Deep colors and tones, barely indicative of their normal color, will contrast strongly with a surrounding aura of light and a pale hazy background. The mood is theatrical and the effect dramatic. Inky shadows are cast in the foreground, leading the eye into the intensity of the picture. Color and tone change in an unexpected way when seen against the light.

Hold a light-colored flower

LEFT These sketches of a hydrangea head show the effect of light striking it from different directions. At the top right front light picks out each flower but tends to make the whole look rather flat and uniform. At the top left light coming from high on the right bleaches color from the facing florets and throws the underside of the flower head into deep shadow. At the bottom back light dissolves the form of surrounding petals and gives a density of tone to areas away from the light source.

ABOVE Sunshine pouring through a large window gives an atmosphere of light and warmth to this piece. The artist, Elisabeth Harden, painted it over a period of three days, returning at the same time each day to catch the particular effects of bleaching brightness in certain areas and the patterns of cool, deep color in the shadows. The flowers were painted freely using a Chinese brush, and a flat brush to create stripes and streaks and wedges, blending the whole with soft washes. Shadows were built up using alizarin crimson with a touch of ultramarine.

ABOVE Shirley Ttevena's *Iris and Sewing Box* captures the brilliance and intensity of a back-lit scene. The outer petals of the flowers are hazy and indistinct, soft forms in subtle colors that contrast with the stark shapes of the unlit flowers. Light catches various surfaces throughout the composition and creates luminous areas of shape and pattern. The color scheme adds to the drama, a surround of subtle purple and brown linked by a gentle patterning of red to the concentration of color in the center. Yellow detail enhances the brilliance of the lilacs and purples.

against a bright window. Some petals will be sufficiently transparent to allow the light to pass through them; in some parts the light will create a halo that merges with the form. Where the subject is denser, the petals thicker or overlapping, the pale color disappears and becomes a succession of deeper and deeper tones, giving dark shadow with unexpected blues and grays.

Light is one of the elements over which an artist can have a great deal of control in the creation of a picture, with the power to direct and readjust the source of light until exactly the right effect is achieved. By utilizing an interesting source of light, the pattern made by light and dark can become a principal feature of the painting, bathing an area in lamplight while pushing the background into murky shadow, or using a chink of light to create a brilliant spot of color, or stripes of brightness that ripple over the form, giving it a different identity.

Assess what sources of light you have at your disposal; window, top light, or spots. An angled lamp is perhaps the most useful. Direct the light source either singly or perhaps in combination to give the group softness, drama, highlighting, patterned shadows— whatever will suit your ideas.

If a painting is going to take some time it is preferable to paint in constant light conditions, but a flower painter hoping to finish painting a group in the same light the following day may occasionally find only a bunch of sagging dead heads and a pile of petals. A reasonably good approximation of daylight can be achieved by using daylight simulation bulbs.

ABOVE This sketch by Jane Dwight shows a group of fruit and flowers on a sunlit windowsill. The artist was Intrigued by the warm yellow light flooding the fruit with brilliance and touching the petals of the flowers.

ABOVE Candlelight can be an interesting source of light. It has a warm, yellowish glow, illuminating only a small intimate area and creating dense inky shadows. The light flickers and gives the feeling of catching the scene for a very limited time. This sketch by Jane Dwight contrasts the halo of gold round the light source with the dense cool purple of the shadows. Threads of gold illuminate the light-facing edges.

EXTERIOR LIGHT

Painting outside can be a different matter altogether. The weather rather than the artist is in charge of the light source, and patterns of light and shade will change all the time.

The light at different times of day has a dramatic effect. Morning light is tinted with the blue tones left from the cooler atmosphere of night. Bleaching midday sunlight from above, which bleeds out color and leaves intense shadows, can in an instant give way to broken light or the uniform flatness caused by cloud.

At the end of the day pinks and golds of sunset and the dust in the air leave a glowing haze. Photographers tend to do much of their outdoor work in the morning and evening because of the softer, more forgiving light.

BELOW Elisabeth Harden started to paint this composition, *Lobelia and Geranium*, as a view down a garden, but became increasingly attracted by the patterns and colors created by the brilliant overhead sunlight. It became necessary to paint the lobelia as an overall mass and then to pick out details, otherwise the plant would have become bitty and fussy. The areas of pattern on the pot are echoed in the patches of shadow and light on the table and the patterning on the fabric. Subtle reflections of color are echoed round the composition.

LIGHT AND ATMOSPHERE

In the 17th and 18th centuries, Claude Lorraine in France and Turner in England started to paint atmosphere in terms of light. Turner's canvases—flecks and swirls of color creating a haze round an indistinct form—are a powerful evocation of atmosphere. It was not until the time of the Impressionists in the late 19th century, and later, that the nature of light itself was investigated. Painters such as Monet, Renoir, and Manet created luminous, glowing paintings of flowers and gardens using many flickering colors as a means of expressing the atmosphere of light.

Light is linked very closely with atmosphere. Atmosphere is a rather unquantifiable quality. It describes different weather conditions, times of day, seasons, amount of dust or water vapor in the air, and temperature, all of which can vary the appearance of a subject. The resulting light conditions in turn affect the mood of a piece. Atmosphere is also linked with the way you feel about a subject, scene, or situation.

Compare the mood of a composition of pastel-colored flowers, illuminated with a soft diffused light, and a group lit with stark light from a specific source. The first has a mood of calm and tranquillity and subtle nuances of color flicker in a misty glow. The other is sharp and brilliant; flowers stand out starkly against shadows.

BELOW This composition tries to capture the speckled effect of brilliant sunlight on blossom. The Impressionists often painted with dots of color, using them to describe the flickering light round a form rather than the object itself.

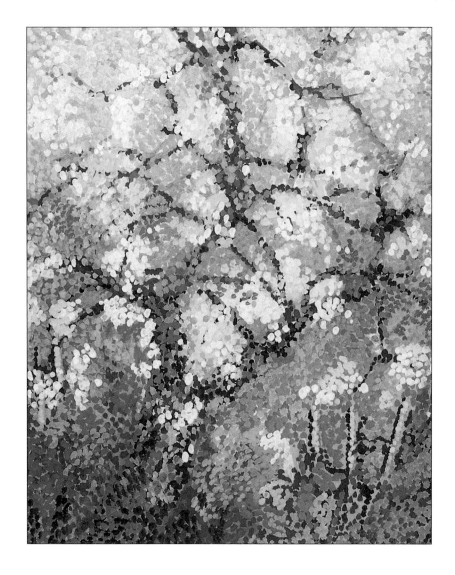

ABOVE The atmosphere of *Last Summer Posy*, a gouache by Sue Wales, is gentle and contemplative. The artist has avoided any dramatic source of light and created infinite subtleties of shade within the group. The haze of cool light emphasizes the luminous colors of the flowers, and leaves some forms as indefinable shadows. The background Is a subtle mix of deeper color, giving a loose form to some objects and an overall air of mystery.

LEFT Here the artist has chosen to Illuminate the composition with a brilliant front light. *Night Flowers* by Shirley May uses the intensity of night to throw up the silhouettes of the shaggy chrysanthemum, but has employed subtlety of shade and vibrant flecks of color to enliven what could be a flat background.

SHADOWS

For each source of light there is an appropriate shadow and each shadow has an identity of its own. Shadow is not, as might appear at first glance, a uniform dark area on the opposite side of light. It is made up of umbra (total shadow) and penumbra (partial shadow), and in each part there can be great variety of tone and color, contrary to the frequently held assumption that shadow is made up of tones in the gray/black range. Look at the shadow to find where the darkest part is and see how it is colored, look at the subtleties and pattern in the palest part, and see how the whole merges with the light, sometimes creating a stark line, sometimes a gentle fusion. Take particular note of shadows in flowers and the particular colors you find there. Painting grays and blacks can often deaden the life in a flower. Shadow is, in principle, a more neutral tone, which throws the bright part into relief. Using a deeper tone of a color, for instance alizarin crimson to make shadows in brighter red, and adding touches of blue, or perhaps the complementary green, will emphasize the brilliance of the brighter parts, and throw the subject into relief without dulling and deadening the appearance.

As mentioned previously, observing how other painters have coped with problems is often revealing. Botanical painters in the past used color in its saturated form to create shadows areas. Other painters, such as Toulouse Lautrec, used brilliant, cool colors like turquoise and purple to make the darker areas recede. Shadows

help establish the spatial location of an image, and in doing so can help fill dead areas like that at the base of a vase of flowers. They can also be an interesting part of the pattern in their own right, and the effects of light passing through different shapes can be used as an important patterning device. Light through lace curtains creates freckles of darkness on a surface, and using the patterns of light and shadow created by reflection in glass, mirrors, and shiny surfaces, can be fascinating and complex. Light is one of the key components in a composition; experiment with using it in different ways and enjoy the result.

ABOVE A jug of daffodils waiting on a kitchen surface inspired this study of reflection by Elisabeth Harden. The various layers of shadow and reflection that make up the abstract pattern of shape give only a hint of the identity of the flowers above, but this is part of the attraction of the whole. Ambiguity in a painting Is intriguing; not knowing exactly what a subject is takes a composition out of the area of reality and into the realms of the imagination.

LEFT Rosemary Jeanneret has used shades of lilac and blue to create the subtle pattern and varied layers of these shadows. This is a detail of *Buttercups*, and shows the meticulous care with which the artist has observed the nuances of pattern created by light. Shadows vary enormously in their intensity depending on a number of factors —brightness of light, distance from the surface, and how the object faces the light. Notice also the patterns of light and shadow on the glass jug and the colors the artist has used to portray it.

BELOW Light can create exciting shadow patterns that can become an integral part of a composition. Christine Holmes' work depends very much on flat pattern, and she articulates the surface of her paintings into a fascinating jigsaw of shape and color. In this composition her use of dark gray shadows has an enlivening rather than a deadening quality, adding dimension to the shapes, echoing their form and anchoring the varied objects into a whole. If you tried to consider this composition without the shadow it would be confusing to the eye.

CHAPTER NINE

Composing Pictures in a Setting

Once you feel confident painting a simple group it is interesting to move on to something more elaborate—to paint flowers in a setting tht forms an integral part of the composition, or to group the flowers with other objects whose shape, color, or particular significance enhances the pattern and mood of the whole. The same planning decisions must be made as with a simple composition in terms of balance, color, and tone, but the boundaries are wider, and other criteria are involved such as distance, perspective, and the relevance of the flowers when they may not be the main focus of attention but an important part of a wider scheme, an interior, landscape or even a portrait.

THE LANDSCAPE OF THE INTERIOR

Consider what you want from the group; what you want the painting to say. Are you inspired by an atmosphere of hazy color in soft light, stark contrasts of brilliance in a garden border, or the excitement of interesting juxtapositions? Perhaps you just happen upon a scene that begs to be painted, a pail of flowers in a kitchen sink waiting to be arranged. Keep the "why" of wanting to paint it at the forefront of your mind because it is the emotional surge that will give vigor to the painting.

Sometimes you can paint there and then; more often the components need to be arranged, and the best viewpoint chosen. Setting the composition is the most important and often the most time-consuming operation. By using a viewfinder to look at the composition from all angles you will see that shadows, unrelated shapes and parts of other objects can be used to make up a pattern within the confines of the frame. Choose objects that complement the group, scour around for interesting things that relate either in shape or color, or will add

RIGHT *Wallflowers and Oriental Carpets* is part of a series of paintings In which the jeweled colors of wallflowers are set against the more subtle and somber patterning of Eastern textiles. One type of wallflower is actually named Persian Carpet, and seeing this on a seed packet may have triggered the initial Idea. Gouache has been used because of Its smooth, matt quality, and the whole composition has been abstracted into a series of flat areas of pattern, highlighting features such as the radiator for its corrugated shape rather than its rather mundane identity.

ABOVE A *Bunch of Tulips* by Rosemary Jeanneret Is more a composition of geometric shapes than a portrait of flowers. It Is the subtle juxtaposition of these shapes and colors that gives the painting its vigor—the slightly off-center metal jug with its delicate reflections, the diagonal thrust of the bunch of tulips in its harlequin wrapping and the flowing stripes of the cloth echoing this diagonal. Each color reappears In the regular patterning of the Oriental carpet chosen as a background.

ABOVE A large arrangement of flowers in
the foreground is used here as a device to
lead the viewer into the heart of the group.
The blue-striped canvas serves the same
purpose. The artist painted this sketch
from a video of a friend's wedding and,
using flower catalogs as a reference for the
flower group, developed the idea into the
basis of a lithograph.

pattern and texture. Fabric and
folds can make interesting areas of
tone, and newspapers and the
printed word make interesting
patterns. Add objects that might
seem unrelated but will add a
frisson to the composition and a
new dimension of meaning.

If you use a viewfinder to look at
the composition from all angles you
will see that shadows, unrelated
shapes, and parts of other objects
can be used to make up a pattern
within the set confines.

The next decision must be to
make a calm appraisal of the
subject matter before deciding what
will be the point of focus. This need
not necessarily be in the
foreground; indeed, leading the eye
all round a painting en route to the
point of focus in the distance is a
method employed by many painters
and can make the composition
much more interesting.

Use blank space and solid blocks
of color as elements in the jigsaw,
and make use of the contrast of
areas of great activity where there
are lots of busy shapes or
complicated patterning against the
calm areas of single or no color.
Move the viewfinder up and down
and from side to side to place the
point of focus at the top or side of
the frame, letting the large space
left become a structural element in
the jigsaw.

LILIES, ANEMONES, AND GLASSCLOTH

S H I R L E Y   T R E V E N A

In this composition Shirley Trevena has arranged a few flowers and household objects in such a way that their pattern and disposition become the most important elements in the composition and the simple objects themselves take on a new meaning. She finds a visual excitement in seeing certain colors together and exploring the spatial relationship between objects and spaces. The large areas of white paper in this composition are a significant feature of the whole. Her palette is cadmium yellow, sap green, olive green, Winsor green, permanent rose, indigo, purple madder alizarin, sepia, raw sienna, and black.

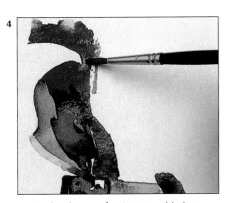

1 Setting up the group can take a considerable amount of time. Each part is carefully placed so that color, shape, ellipse, line, and pattern relate in the jigsaw of composition.

2 The artist uses a combination of watercolor and gouache. Here, strong green paint is dragged into the lines of the leaf with a twig.

3 Cadmium yellow paint is fed into the wet green paint.

4 Further layers of paint are added to create more leaves and the stark outline of the lily petal. A strong purple defines more of this petal and is encouraged to melt into the drying green paint below.

5 The same purple paint is led into the shape of the flower, allowed to merge in some parts and in others used sharply to define the form. At the same time, the flower center is painted and the petals scraped to create a radiating pattern.

6

6 The form of the group as a whole now begins to appear.

7 Yellow paint is concentrated in the flower center and allowed to spread into a few of the petals.

8 As the form is built up, more leaves are added. A squirrel brush is used to soften shapes, remove paint, and blend color.

9

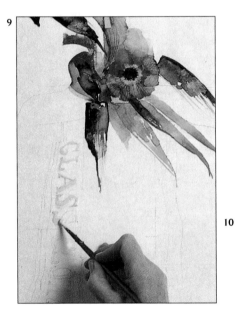

9 The lower parts of the painting are now lightly sketched in. The letters on the glasscloth are carefully drawn, and the parts intended to remain white are painted with masking fluid.

10 While the masking fluid is drying, stamens are drawn in the heart of the lily. In some cases the intense color of the anthers is allowed to flow into the softer green stamens. A pale gray wash adds shadow to the underside of the flower.

7

8

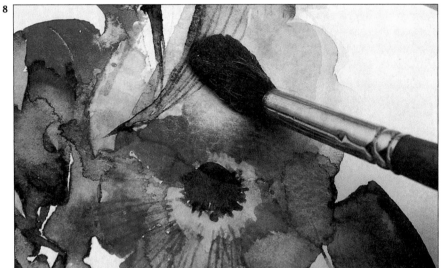

10

11 An important part of the whole composition is the strong horizontal. A dark sepia wash across the composition throws into relief the oblique thrust of leaves and stems. More leaves are added to emphasize this diagonal.

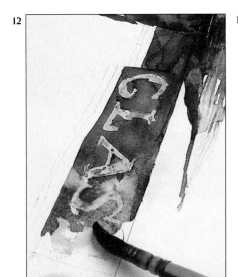

12 An indigo wash is painted over the masked letters to form the stripes of the glasscloth and differing values of tone are used to bring out the ripples and folds of the cloth.

13 The masking fluid is removed by gently rubbing with the finger.

14 Dark paint flicked with a brush adds sharpness to the center of this anemone.

15 Moving from the dense area of activity at the top of the picture, the artist uses indigo paint to shape the cup and saucer, defining only the part of its form and using the lines on the glasscloth to tie it into the whole structure.

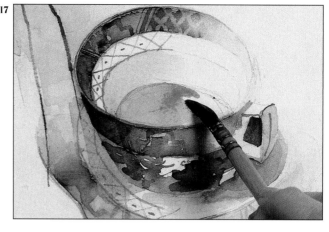

16 Detailed painting with stronger paints adds pattern and definition to the cup.

17 When the blue paint is completely dry, a thin sable brush is used to draw the fine decoration, and a thicker squirrel brush floods a wash of raw sienna paint into the cup, carefully manipulating it and adding more color as necessary.

18 The finished painting is a wonderful mix of rich color and shapes of white. The artist has deliberately left the flower containeras a blank rectangle, forcing the eye to flicker between the intensely colored area at the top of the composition and the cup and saucer, and their echoes of color.

PAINTING A LARGER LANDSCAPE

Painting flowers in an interior or as a group with other objects, the painter is for the most part in control of the arrangement and can shift and add as he or she pleases. If you choose to paint a wider landscape, and this may be a flower store or market garden, or a meadow, the components are already there, perhaps in abundance. The most important task is selection, and the principal aim must be to achieve a harmonious balance between foreground and background. Thus the composition becomes an intriguing combination of flower study and landscape.

One of the great pitfalls when faced with, say, a flower-filled garden border or an orchard of blossom, is to try and paint it all. But in reality, the eye does not see it all at once. It will rest on a particular area, home in on a few blossoms, and the mind will be aware of a haze of color and light, or perhaps a dense, receding undergrowth. Just as when walking through a landscape the eye registers certain objects at first and then is led along paths of discovery and starts to notice other things, a landscape painting needs a pattern that will lead the eye "in and round and through."

RIGHT A field of oil seed rape is the subject of this painting by Mary Faux Jackson. The overwhelming brilliance of a vast expanse of the acid-colored flowers was the inspiration. The artist has overcome the problem of giving depth to this expanse of yellow by softening the color toward the distance and clarifying a few of the foreground flowers with patterns of dark greenery. The line of the edge of the field and the distant building anchors the composition in space.

ABOVE This sketch was a quick response to a mass of daffodils and narcissi grown in an orchard. A few details identify close, individual flower heads, but the overall impression is of an abundant sweep of massed spring growth.

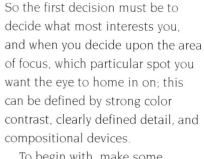

ABOVE This painting by Christine Holmes, *Lilies on a Pond*, is typical of the artist's meticulous method of working. The particular characteristic of each plant is carefully observed and expressed in a subtle variation of color. This order gives the eye a clear route round a busy composition, focusing on the wide-open lilies in the foreground and the black depths of water between them, and then leading it further back in the picture to the two pink flowers, which stand as stark silhouettes in the dense shadows.

ABOVE The scene is a view into a backyard, where the features of an urban landscape are enlivened by a pot of brilliant orange flowers. The color of this tiny feature draws the eye, and it is emphasized by the delicate mix of blues and green surrounding it.

So the first decision must be to decide what most interests you, and when you decide upon the area of focus, which particular spot you want the eye to home in on; this can be defined by strong color contrast, clearly defined detail, and compositional devices.

To begin with, make some preliminary drawings. These will clarify in your mind how you want to control the structure of the composition. It will help you to pinpoint areas that need to be highlighted and also the areas where soft tone and lack of detail will take them out of the area of concentration.

When you start painting, fill in areas of color broadly, perhaps working wet-on-wet, until the basic shape appears, then home in on key areas with stronger colors and crisper shapes. Use the receding quality of blue tones to pull areas into the distance, and the brightness of reds and oranges to make features spring forward out of the composition toward the eye.

ABOVE Francesca Lucar-Clark uses watercolor in a very free and fluid manner to describe the effects of light in the landscape. Very few of the flowers in this painting are represented in any detail, but their identity is clear from the shape of a clump, the line of a stem and the odd hint of recognizable features.

ABOVE The painting and the one opposite, top left, have plants and water as their theme. Both are painted in gouache, but the style and use of paint could not be more different. This luminous painting, *Irises by a Pond*, by Shirley Trevana, combines criss-crossing leaves and stems and bursting flowers, sharpening the image with jutting sheaths of bud and disks of reflection on the water beyond. Water is very much a part of the texture of the painting—floods of loose color give a watery feel, and the soft, spattered paint has the appearance of drops of rain on a window.

PAINTING IN THE LANDSCAPE

Painting on location involves other considerations. Having all the essentials with you is a priority, and keeping a list and a bag of basic materials saves time. There is a great deal of equipment on sale for outside work, but traveling light is much easier. Basic paints, in an easily transportable form, and with sufficient space for mixing are essential; a container for water or medium, and ideally a source of the former at hand are needed. Brushes need their bristles protected, and polythene bags act as a good cover for both oil and watercolor. Oil board itself acts as support, and watercolor blocks or paper pinned to a board give something to lean on.

The principal requirement, though, is somewhere comfortable to sit; a small folding stool will increasingly reveal its value as the painting session proceeds, and reduce the effects of damp and cramp. A hat helps, and insect repellant is sometimes surprisingly useful, though the suffering endured by the botanical painter Sydney Parkinson in the 19th century is now unlikely. When sitting on a beach in Tahiti he was overwhelmed by a cloud of flies which not only obscured his view, but consumed the pigment of his painting.

THE LANDSCAPE OF FLOWERS

The American painter Georgia O'Keeffe created wonderful images of the heart of a flower—close-up views expanded to such dimensions that they had the effect of making the viewer lose sight of the details of structure and concentrate on the essence or soul. She painted a series of paintings of "Jack in the pulpit." Each successive image in the series draws closer and closer to the heart of the flower, recognizable features disappear and the heart becomes a surreal and magic landscape.

Treating the interior of a flower head as a landscape in itself can be fascinating and revealing. A basic flower head is instantly recognizable. We think we are looking closely when we get very near the flower, but how often do we look right inside and imagine that thumbnail interior as a large landscape in its own right?

RIGHT The artist uses subtle gradations of tone in gouache paint to explore the folds and rhythm of a cluster of apple blossom. The exercise was not principally intended as a description of the features of the plant, but rather as an exploration of the flow and movement of petal growth.

ABOVE Jane Dwight captures in this
watercolor the soft, luminous tones and
shades in the heart of a rose. Clarity of
color and sharp areas of dark paint
describe the form with vibrancy and
freshness. This watercolor is large, and its
size gives this close-up great impact.

RIGHT This painting is very large and is
based on an enlarged photocopy of part
of a painting of poppies by the artist.
Expanding the flower to fill the whole
range of peripheral vision brings us right
into the heart of the flower and excludes
the distinguishing characteristics of
external structure, which iIdentify it
conventionally in our minds.

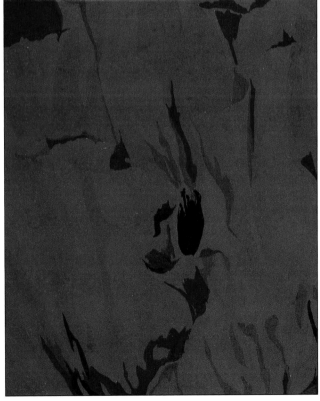

CHAPTER TEN

Finding Your Own Vision

A final chapter in this section of the book is in principle a round-up of the ideas explored. It is easy and satisfying to assume that, having investigated these ideas, built up an experience of materials and techniques, developed a basic confidence in the use of paints, and a knowledge of the subject, that would be the end of the story. But it is only the beginning. Looking back over the previous chapters will confirm that the ways in which flowers can be painted are as varied as the flowers themselves. Painters have explored the fundamentals involved in creating a painting and developed these ingredients into a very personal means of expression.

Experience of materials and techniques allows choice. It enables a painter to choose the medium that suits the purpose and the colors that particularly appeal, to develop a personal palette, and to manipulate those colors into a harmonious and satisfying fusion. Taking steps forward and extending choice is not necessarily expanding the range of flowers painted, but perhaps confining and limiting, using shapes and forms with which we have built up a confident acquaintance, liberating us from a hesitant encounter with something new.

Many artists return again and again to a particular theme, using the same favorite objects, colors, and shapes. Familiarity enables them to push the idea to the limits and to discover new means of artistic expression. The painter Jennifer Bartlett has expanded and evolved a single subject, a garden in the South of France, into a colossal series of works, expressing in a variety of media her direct response to this setting under varying conditions, from different points of view, and developing the theme in concept and scale into more varied media still—woodcut, silkscreen, and metal.

Consider works already completed and experiment in varying the interpretation. Many artists find that reworking an image in another medium is a good means of dismissing the staleness of familiarity. Trying a new medium will force you to explore and concentrate on different elements, and can be liberating and thought provoking.

Watercolor depends upon the luminosity of white paper shining through thin veils of paint, upon the often haphazard pattern made

ABOVE The patterning and colors of this group of primulas touched a chord in the artist's mind and linked them with particular images and objects. A much-loved wooden elephant makes an appearance in the composition, and the image of an Indian figure from a postcard is repeated in triplicate. One of the artist's favorite subjects is the medieval angel seen at the back of the group. Christine Holmes has used flat patterning in the manner of Oriental manuscripts to create a rich and evocative image.

ABOVE *Irises, Fish, and Lemons* by Christine Holmes started life as an exercise to try to make a composition from three objects whose identities and form were very varied. She has painted several versions of this interesting mix, combining the three into a recurring pattern, intertwining the characteristics of each imto an abstract jigsaw, but retaining patches of their particular identity.

ABOVE Shirley Trevena abstracts the visual essence of a few flowers and fills this composition with their brilliant colors. The title of the work is *Blue Glass Jug of Flowers*, but the exciting element is the abstract disposition of all the pieces. We are not sure which flowers are in the jug and which are outside, but it does not matter; the feeling of the whole is of the exuberant vibrancy of flower form.

by water and paint and upon a certain amount of considered planning. Try the same subject in gouache on toned paper, using the denser paint to build up dabs and dots of broken color and allowing the tone of the paper to show through. Gouache allows great subtlety of pastel shades, and the chance to travel up and down the tonal scale, and also a greater intensity of color than watercolor. Oil paint and acrylic will each add another dimension to the same subject, brilliance of color, and the rhythm of textured brush strokes.

With acrylics whole areas can be altered at a stroke and random splashes of color and brilliant highlights added at will.

However, the choice of a particular medium does not mean that you have to stick rigorously to it. Combining different materials can produce interesting and exciting results that emerge through the trial and error of experimentation, though some media combine much more happily than others.

Soft pastel used over watercolor can add vigor of line and surface

texture, though it should be used with a light touch.

ABOVE Shirley May's painting of *Freesias* combines watercolor, gouache, and pastel, using the matt, chalky quality of the pastel to add streaks of broken color, and the sparkle of varied texture to the surface of the painting. The artist works very fast, often making numerous images of the same subject, and builds up her composition by responding instinctively to the flowers with a variety of materials rather than trying to capture an accurate, definitive record of her subject.

Crayon and watercolor used in combination delineate form and can give a more controllable subtlety of color. Water-soluble crayons can be wetted to make fluid paint or used in a linear manner. A good example of this successful combination can be seen in the step-by-step demonstration on page 536.

Acrylic and watercolor used together can exploit the qualities of each, merging the stronger, denser tone of the water-diluted acrylic into the watercolor, and using its clarity of line and strength of color to pick out sharp detail. Combining patches of rich, matt color with soft fluidity can be very effective.

Other combinations work well. Often the need to use different media will arise in the course of a painting, and you should never hesitate from adding as seems fit. Mixed media can combine the most unexpected of bedfellows and the spontaneity of creation can inspire you to utilize and incorporate the most mundane of materials.

Trying different media and combining materials does not necessarily mean the purchase of a new set of equipment. Some of the best and most exciting materials may be close at hand. Twigs can be used to pull paint in different directions, to print lines or to manipulate oil paint. An image drawn in candle wax or oil pastel will show through thin water-based paint. Paint sprayed over leaves will leave a silhouette on the paper.

ADDING MATERIALS TO THE SURFACE

Collage can be used to extend the third dimension that comes from thick impasto paint and the build-up of texture. Utilize rough edges of torn paper for petals, add patches of tissue and watch how they crumple and leach their color when water is applied. Oil paint is a good medium for supporting materials like dried leaves or for imprinting textures. The moving force should be innovation and experimentation. Some ideas will be disastrous; others will work well.

ABOVE Collage is used for this picture of tangled growth, *Old Man's Beard*, by Elisabeth Harden. The artist has used cut paper, ink, paint, tissue paper, and chalk to generate this maze of ancient stems, and built up the collage by cutting up drawings, intertwining the pieces, and working on the resulting image with whatever materials seemed appropriate.

ABOVE The artist wanted to recreate the atmosphere of a confetti of blossom dispersing in the wind, and used cut, tinted paper to create this illusion.

DESTROYING THE IMAGE

As well as adding to an image by building up the surface, a painting can progress through destruction of the image. If, after due consideration, you feel unhappy with a gouache or watercolor, think about washing it out. Radical measures such as this require a firm heart and a strong paper—anything insubstantial might dissolve into pulp—but the result may hearten you. Stretch the washed paper on a board, or leave it to dry as it is, and work into the resulting soft color.

Acrylics and oil paint can always be painted over, but distressing the surface by scratching or sand-papering will create textures as a base for further work, or reveal patches of tone below. One of the exhausting elements of creating a picture is that the artist is directly responsible for the way work progresses. Introducing the chance element can be stimulating and unexpected. Perhaps a painting torn up and discarded can be reassembled. Blowing up a painting on a photocopier will give the subject a totally new character. Concentrate on a particular area of the photocopied image and see what emerges. Patterns will appear and small areas of shadow take on a large tonal identity, faint lines and details become the essential elements of structure. It is interesting to subject creative work to this mechanical process of alteration and then to return to creativity to develop the result.

What has perhaps also emerged is that this expression is not an imitation of nature but a personal interpretation—nature's impression upon the artist. Because the reality of nature is constantly changing, moving, and growing, this should

BELOW A discarded painting, torn up and relegated to the rubbish bin, has been resurrected and reconstructed. The artist, Shirley May, felt that fragmenting the image had given it a new life.

be the essence that we must chase. Unlike the study of buildings and, to some extent, landscape, whose reality is relatively constant, over-concentrating on the structure of the plant and trying to portray it with devout accuracy, often excludes the more important elements of spontaneity, vigor, and movement.

What pleases us in the natural world is that impressions are like perfumes—fleeting and immediately evocative—like capturing a butterfly in the hands for an instant, looking and then letting it fly away. As Matisse said, "The painter must feel that he is copying nature and even when he consciously departs from nature that is only the better to interpret her."

ABOVE This image has been painted on silk by Francesca Lucas-Clarke, using a resist medium to separate the different areas of color. This pale outlining of form has given the catkins, flower heads, and rose hips a clarity that ties their varied forms into a pleasing arrangement of color and shape.

TULIPS—MIXED MEDIA

ALISON MILNER GULLAND

Alison Milner Gulland works very freely, drawing an image out of an apparently haphazard mêlée of painted textures and working into this image to reveal energetic and lively plant forms. She uses a combination of printing inks, acrylic paint, acrylic medium, and watercolor.

1 Brilliant red and yellow tulips are used as a basis for the composition but mainly as a source of reference rather than as a specific subject.

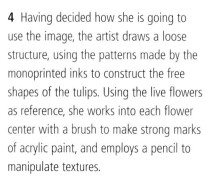

2 An acetate sheet is placed on top of white paper and used as a non-absorbent working surface on which to manipulate the colors. The artist uses printing inks, choosing whatever is appropriate from a wide collection, and manipulates them on the acetate. Diluting the ink with turpentine creates paler pools. Acrylic paint could be manipulated with water in the same way, and glass or formica would serve as a surface. A strong, smooth watercolor or printing paper is placed over the pattern of paint, pressed into the surface to move and spread the paint and then gently peeled off.

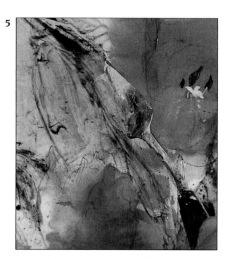

3 This monoprinting technique can be unpredictable, and success depends on experience. The resulting image is left to dry and then considered carefully to discover the flowers within.

4 Having decided how she is going to use the image, the artist draws a loose structure, using the patterns made by the monoprinted inks to construct the free shapes of the tulips. Using the live flowers as reference, she works into each flower center with a brush to make strong marks of acrylic paint, and employs a pencil to manipulate textures.

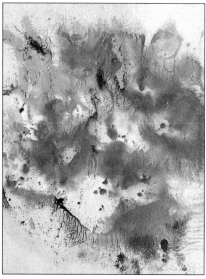

5 Dark leaf shapes are clarified and created with loose brush work. These are given texture and dimension by manipulating thick opaque paint with a palette knife.

6 The yellow background is extended and the shape of the leves and the detailed flower centers give a sharpness to the composition.

7 Two shades of blue paint are spattered onto the paper with a toothbrush and larger drops are flicked on from a brush.

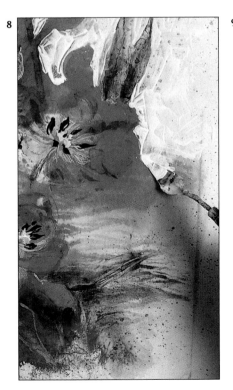

8 The artist decides at this stage to use a coat of acrylic medium to silhouette some petals and give form to the flowers in the background.

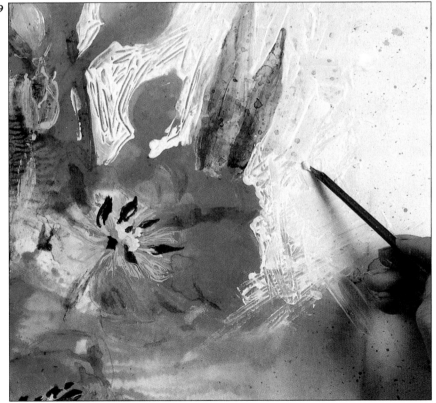

9 The artist then scrapes into the medium to give rhythm to the surface and leave a vigorous basis for further paint.

10 The blocking in of certain areas has changed the whole appearance of the composition, defining the fluid shapes of the flowers in the foreground and revealing a silhouette of shapes behind.

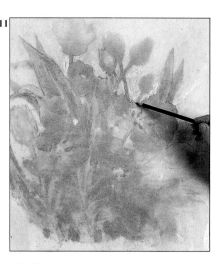

11 The painter decides to cool down certain parts. She traces the outline of the areas she wishes to remain as they are and cuts a stencil.

12 This stencil is taped in position and watercolor paint is sprayed in gentle bursts over the top half of the image with a paint diffuser.

13 The final painting is a wonderful explosion of color. The stenciling has produced areas of cool tone, and formed a background of shaded flower forms and interesting pale silhouettes.

Painting
Landscapes

Introduction

Light, ever changing, is the key to all landscape painting. Objects that make up the natural world are constantly altering their appearance as the light changes. The seasons, too, can bring dramatic differences to a familiar scene, as autumn tints disappear beneath a blanket of snow or driving rain reduces a spectacular view to a few indistinct shapes. The color of light on objects modifies their intrinsic color. Everyone is familiar with the way light affects the appearance of a mountain range, for instance, at different times of day and in varying weather conditions.

ABOVE *Hunters in the Snow* is one of the *Months* series painted by Pieter Bruegel the Elder in 1566. The icy weather can almost be felt in the dull color of the sky.

Rapidly changing light caused by unstable weather conditions gives rise to irritation and frustration in painters anxious to "get it down before the light changes." Light can also elicit an emotional response. A bright sunny day with clear blue skies induces a sense of joy, happiness, and peace, whereas a dark, overcast, cold day usually suggests menace, despair and a sense of isolation.

Artists can evoke these sensations through the use of colour that corresponds to light. We can only see the colours in nature through the effects of light—they are inseparable companions.

In this book I will concentrate mainly on the modern conception of landscape in art. Landscape in medieval Europe was largely a vehicle for a narrative representing biblical or mythological scenes rather than a representational end in itself. There are similarities here with modern painting, where landscape is used to convey a psychological or painterly response to nature.

The first representational landscapes were painted in the 15th century during the Italian Renaissance. Until then landscape outside the city walls was generally seen as a hostile environment from which man needed protection. Cultivated walled gardens were used as a kind of theatrical backdrop to figure paintings.

TOPOGRAPHY

As towns and cities grew and the wild forests were tamed and cut down, so the interest in the wider environment grew. It is obvious from paintings done in the Middle Ages, that location studies involving intense observation were being made. Dürer (1471-1528) and Altdorfer (c 1485-1538) were two German artists who produced drawings and paintings where figures were reduced to a minor role in a highly detailed study of nature. Dürer himself is credited with painting the first townscape. In Italy the two Renaissance artists Giovanni Bellini (c 1430-1516) and Piero della Francesca (c 1410-1492) also sought to elevate the importance of landscape to the level of figure painting.

PAINTING LANDSCAPES

NATURALISM

Dutch 17th~century painting was the first European movement to establish the art of landscape in its own right. Dramatic chiaroscuro effects of light and dark were combined with the depiction of commonplace domestic scenes as Dutch society celebrated the rise of bourgeois living.

Landscape became an accepted subject to paint. The architectural arrangement of shapes in space, the balance of horizontal against vertical and the overall stillness of paintings by Poussin (1593-1665) embody the principles of the classical tradition in landscape. This line proceeds down through Cézanne and into the abstractionists of the mid-20th century, such as Mondrian.

During the 19th century the Romantic movement developed. The Romantic artists were concerned with mood, emotion, movement, and effect rather than the purely formal aspects of balance and symmetry in landscape. Nevertheless, the best paintings usually contained elements of all these qualities.

OPPOSITE ABOVE Jacob van Ruisdael showed how to color the northern landscape and the northern sky, with Claudean poetic resonance.

OPPOSITE LEFT *Orpheus and Eurydice* (1650) by Nicholas Poussin uses a landscape formula of dark idealized landscape receding in parallel planes which structure the depth of the painting, while clear vertical and horizontal accents give increased stability to the work. This underlying geometry gives the scene its elegant serenity.

TURNER AND CONSTABLE

These two very different painters continued the naturalistic tradition albeit in their own individual ways. Turner (1775-1851) produced grandiose subjects like *The Fighting Temeraire*, while Constable (1776-1837) painted pastoral, almost parochial subjects such as *The Haywain*.

Turner saw the elements of landscape as a unified whole, suffused with an overwhelming light, which merged sky, water, and land as one luminous, swirling form. Constable, infatuated with

ABOVE *Great Falls of Reichenbach* by Joseph Mallord William Turner. This magnificent view of Alpine scenery painted for exhibition in 1804 reveals Turner's use of watercolor for the expression of a vast and solemn romantic theme. The strong tonal contrasts and swirling forms enhance the sense of natural drama.

ABOVE In works like *The Haywain* (1821), Constable struggled against the academic tradition with its Italianate landscapes. He worked extensively directly from nature, before the subject, painting rapidly, with separate strokes, and blobs of paint.

the countryside around Dedham Vale in Suffolk realized the importance of the sky in his work. His use of spectacular tonal contrast, combined with superb brush work, integrating the sky and land, finally overcame the landscape artists' traditional problem of the "two halves." He loved all the detail of landscape, proclaiming that he had "never seen an ugly thing in his life." The work of Constable and Turner had a profound influence in France, particularly on Gustave Courbet (1819-77), a realist, who painted nature directly as he saw it.

IMPRESSIONISM

Courbet's example led directly to Impressionism. The approach of these artists was not only realistic; their concern was to capture the effect experienced on first seeing a view—in its totality and without undue attention to detail. It was the first movement to be expressly concerned with light. The principal artists were Monet, Renoir, Pissarro, Sisley, Seurat, and Morisot. These painters worked largely out of doors and on location. To seize the precise effects of light and atmosphere on color meant spending long hours enduring the elements. They had to be hardy individuals!

Apart from working directly from the environment, their principal revolutionary development was in the use of color, which they used more purely and brightly than their predecessors. For example, they saw that the shadows in nature are not simply the neutrals, black, or gray, but blue, violet, and dark green.

Seeurat introduced a system known as Pointillism. He called it "ma méthode." Instead of mixing his tones on the palette he mixed them optically on the canvas. This he did by placing small brush strokes of pure color alongside one another to produce planes of brilliant, vibrating colour, when viewed at a distance. For example, he placed dots of primary red alongside pure blue, which then merge in the spectator's eye, to appear as violet.

LEFT *Autumn at Argenteuil* (1873) by Claude Monet. This Impressionist painting superbly captures the effect of the sun, low in the sky, on the gold coloured tree foliage at the left of the picture.

BELOW There is a charm and warmth in *Apple Picking* (1888) by Camille Pissarro, which may have been an attempt by him to make his work more popularly acceptable. At the same time, the painting reflects the trend in the 1880s toward the depiction of more solid and larger figures which dominate the scene, and the deployment of more "scientific" theories of color, derived from the example of Seurat.

POST-IMPRESSIONISM

Cézanne (1839-1906) was dissatisfied with the lack of formal considerations in the work of his Impressionist contemporaries. Cézanne's theory that all forms in nature are based on the cone, the sphere, and the cylinder gained him the reputation of being "the father of modern painting". He saw and interpreted the scene in front of him in these terms. He worked on location in the hills around Aix~en~Provence in southern France, using Impressionist color, but he was also influenced by Poussin and the classical tradition in art.

Van Gogh (1853-90) is credited as being the precursor of the entire Expressionist tradition in modern art. To him the subject was a starting point for his personal response through color to that subject. He has been quoted as saying that he was more concerned with the colors on his palette than those in front of him. Gauguin (1848-93), who started as an impressionist, developed the principles of symbolism. His color and shapes were simplified to produce a more "primitive" effect. He constructed his paintings largely in the studio. Both artists drew their inspiration directly from nature and human experience, rather than from the preconceptions about art held by petit~bourgeois society.

Along with many other artists in the latter part of the 19th century, Van Gogh and Gauguin were influenced by Japanese prints. Flatter, purer color enclosed by a black outline was the manifestation of this influence in European art.

The research into the nature of color by the French scientist Chevreul was to have a major impact on European art. The principle of simultaneous contrast caused artists to substitute the colors they saw before them for colous which make harmonious contrasts. This led directly to the brilliant primary colours used by the Fauvists.

BELOW The Provençal landscape provided the subject matter for hundreds of Cézanne's paintings and Mountains in Provence (c 1885) is a perfect summary of the preoccupations and achievements of Cézanne at the beginning of his maturity. Cézanne's concern to give expression to the qualities of the landscape was always balanced by an equal concern for the language of painting. All the features in this composition have a clearly defined role and create an overall harmony in such a way that the removal of any element would destroy the equilibrium.

ABOVE Van Gogh has used long
expressive brush strokes in *Road with
Cypress and Star* (1890), transforming the
surface of this work—as can be seen in
his paintings during his stay in the
assylum at St Rémy—in a way that has
been attributed to the series of
breakdowns he had suffered.

MODERNISM

From the end of the 19th century, attitudes to landscape painting diverged into a variety of different styles and concepts. Representation for its own sake had been thoroughly explored to the point where sheer observation of nature was no longer sufficient. The invention of photography was another major factor in the movement away from Naturalism. The photograph was seen as both a threat and a blessing to painters. On the one hand it provided a quick, accurate record of nature and events; on the other it liberated artists from the burden of pure representation. From this point painting was never to be the same again.

CUBISM

Braque (1882-1963) and Picasso (1881-1973) took Cézanne's formula of the sphere, cone, and cylinder as a starting point. They, as it were, dissected nature and recomposed it as a series of interlocking planes, the object being to include more than one aspect or angle of a subject in a single picture. The rectangular picture plane was divided into flattish smaller planes involving the elimination of spatial depth.

The Expressionist wing of modernism emerged in France, led by Matisse (1869-1954), and in Germany with Kandinsky (1866-1944) and Franz Marc (1880-1916) as its leaders. Both the French Fauvists and the German Blue

Riders saw nature in terms of pure color. Their painting was characterized by expressive brush work and violent tonal contrasts. Unlike the Cubists, who never entirely forsook representation, the Germans moved toward abstraction, particularly Kandinsky, who is credited with painting the first entirely abstract picture in 1913. From this point on, new directions for landscape painting began to proliferate. Paul Klee (1879-1940) reduced it to a

BELOW *Smoke Drift* by Timothy Easton. This oil painting beautifully evokes the effects of sunset in autumn. The scene is essentially back lit putting the objects into silhouette against a bright sky. The leaves on the spruce trees are scumbled with touches of rich color over the background.

series of textural diagrams. Futurism and Surrealism arrived and treated landscape as a symbol for psychological expression. Concepts about the content from within replaced the observable world without. The introduction and juxtaposition of incongruous images within landscape created a shock reaction with the public. The appearance of the Surrealist movement in Europe was a major force throughout the 1920s and 30s, involving a large number of artists: Breton (1896-1966) and followers in France, Magritte (1898-1967) in Belgium and the flamboyant Spaniard Dali (1904-89) just about everywhere. André Breton is credited as being the founder of the Surrealist movement. Paradoxically he was a poet, not a painter!

The new industrial power becoming visible in the environment inspired Marinetti (1876-1944) and the Futurists in Italy to produce images of dynamism.

The migration of the Surrealists to the USA at the outbreak of World War II caused a revolution in American art, culminating in the appearance of Abstract Expressionism. Landscape was used as a vehicle to express notions about color and brush work, harking back in some cases to its use in medieval Europe.

The fascination with the constantly changing visible world has maintained its hold on painters everywhere, although the discoveries of the last hundred

ABOVE Hazel Soan's watercolour *Kudo at Goas* creates the arid effects of a watering hole in the African bush. The wet-in-wet technique used for the sky and background contrasts with the dry brushed trees and animals.

years have influenced style and approach. Photography, originally seen as the usurper of representational art, is now widely used as a valuable means of obtaining source material for painters. The Photo~realists actually copy photographs at very large size in minute detail. The photograph is now almost as indispensable to the travelling artist as the traditional sketchbook. Finally, Leonardo da Vinci said that "drawing is the root of all science". It is also the prerequisite of all good painting, so do lots of it!

Materials and Equipment

The range of materials and equipment available to the artist is vast, and here I will concentrate only on the essential items that will enable you to attempt similar landscape projects to those demonstrated later. I am also concerned that artists should not be overwhelmed by the sheer variety and complexity of all the possible technical aids to painting.

Technical virtuosity is not an end in itself. The most successful paintings have been made with limited materials and equipment—five colors, three or four brushes, a simple piece of board or paper—and plenty of inspiration.

Expense is another good reason for restricting the range you start out with. Art materials are not cheap. Care and proper use of materials and equipment are very important. If they are looked after they will go further and last longer.

SKETCHBOOKS

An essential item of equipment for any painter is the sketchbook. It should be like a good companion—always there when needed, providing a reservoir of information and ideas. The type I prefer is spiral bound and contains sheets of 70 1b (150 gsm) cartridge paper (acid-free) for quick sketches, size 5¾ X 8¼ in. (A5). This can be carried with you and used for getting down details, notes on color, and ideas for future paintings. There is also a large range of watercolor sketchbooks;

these are ideal for working on location or in the studio and are available in a variety of sizes from 5¾ X 8¼ in. (A5) to 23¼ X 16⅜ in. (A2). A good quality watercolor book containing sheets of 140 1b (30Ogsm) acid-free paper can be used for the final paintings.

ABOVE *Allotments* by Mike Bernard. This pencil drawing demonstrates the range of tone and texture that can be achieved solely with the use of a 3b pencil.

BELOW *Reservoir in the Wye Valley*. Watercolour by the author. Done on location, this sketchbook study utilises both the wet-in-wet and wet-in-dry techniques to create the effects of light.

OILS

Paints

I suggest a range of colors that will serve you for a variety of subjects in different light and weather conditions: Permanent Violet, Alizarin Crimson, Cadmium Red Light, Cadmium Yellow Medium, Naples Yellow, Burnt Sienna, Permanent Green, Chrome Oxide Green, Cerulean Blue, Ultramarine Blue, Cobalt Blue, Yellow Ocher, Burnt Umber, Sap Green, Cadmium Orange, Payne's Gray, Lamp Black, Titanium White.

Palettes

As well as wood, there are also plastic (plexi~glass) palettes, masonite board coated with acrylic primer, and tear-off paper palettes. These are useful for location work. I use a large wooden palette for studio work and a lightweight masonite board when working outside.

Brushes

Brushes are all based on three shapes: round, flat, and filbert, with a special fan shape for texturing and blending tones. They are all produced in hog's hair bristle, sable, or synthetic bristle. The best quality are hog's hair and sable, but the synthetics have improved in quality over recent years and they are quite satisfactory. The price is usually a good indicator of quality and durability. Most brush ranges are made in both "long hair" and "short hair" versions. Long-hair hog bristles are the best for applying large areas of color and for accentuated brush marks. Use the sables for smoother effects and putting in fine detail.

ABOVE Glazes of color are the basis of this picture, *The Church at Wareham*, by the author.

ABOVE *Distant Bonfire in the Iris Field*. Oil by Timothy Easton.

Palette knives

Palette knives are made in a variety of shapes and sizes. They serve two main purposes: mixing the paint on the palette and applying paint to the canvas. The broad or flat design is for mixing and the pointed, angled type is for knife painting. A useful item for your studio is a mahlstick. This is a length of wood dowel with a soft pad at one end. Its function is as a hand rest when painting straight lines or fine details.

Solvents and Binders

The most commonly used and readily obtainable solvents and binders for oil painting are linseed oil, poppy oil, and refined spirit of turpentine. They can be used separately or mixed together for thinning paint. Mixing pure linseed oil with your paints produces a glossy, lustrous effect, but it is slow drying. Turpentine on its own leaves the painting matt and flat in appearance, although it will dry faster. The "household" type of untreated turpentine or white spirit is not suitable for paint mixing and should be used only for cleaning brushes.

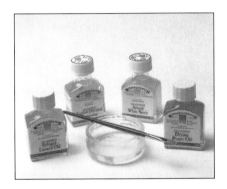

ABOVE Solvents for oils: refined linseed oil, distilled turpentine, white spirit and poppy oil.

Supports

Any material that can be primed and prepared may be used for oil painting: fabric, wood, cardboard, masonite, or paper. The primer commonly used is white acrylic. There are a variety of ready-made supports available, including stretched canvas, canvas boards, and canvas paper. Canvas boards and canvas pads are handy for location work where portability is important. The traditional oil-painting support is primed cotton canvas stretched over a wood frame.

Easels

An easel is essential for any painter working directly from observation. Having the support vertical enables the artist to make instant comparisons with the subject and the painted image. There are a number of different types and sizes of easels. Small portable metal easels are lightweight, but tend to be unstable in windy conditions. Wooden fold-up easels with telescopic legs are ideal for location work. The ultimate for portability is probably the combination sketch-box easel. When unfolded and set up, this device comprises a paint-box with drawer and a small vertical easel with adjustable legs. For studio work involving larger paintings, there are the radial easel and the studio easel. For those who prefer sitting down, an artist's donkey is useful.

ABOVE *The Park in Autumn.* Oil by the auther. An example of the alla prima technique.

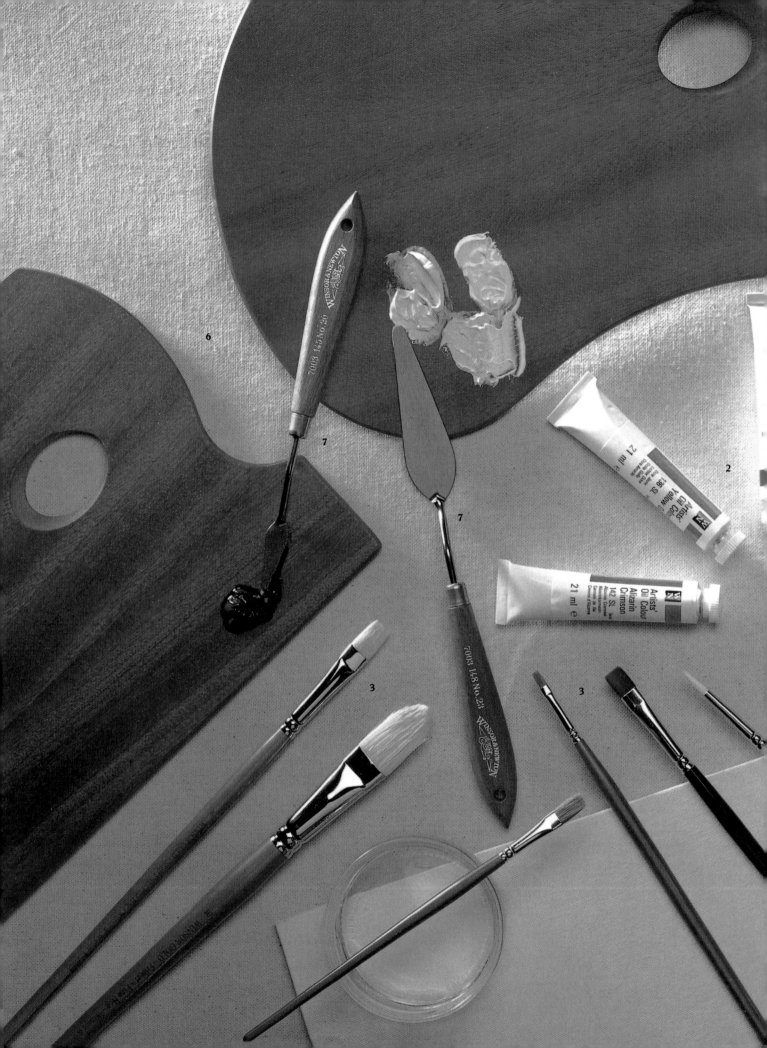

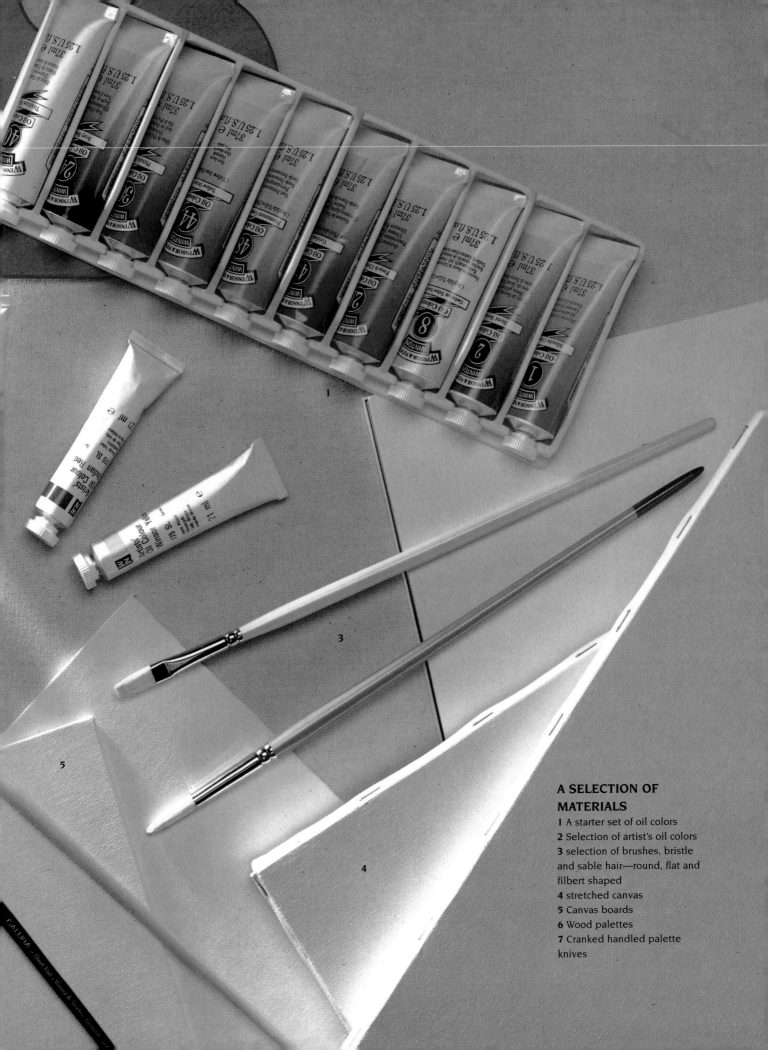

A SELECTION OF MATERIALS

1 A starter set of oil colors
2 Selection of artist's oil colors
3 selection of brushes, bristle and sable hair—round, flat and filbert shaped
4 stretched canvas
5 Canvas boards
6 Wood palettes
7 Cranked handled palette knives

ACRYLICS

Acrylic paints were first developed by Mexican mural painters in the 1930s. These artists were seeking a durable paint that would withstand harsh weather conditions. Acrylics consist of pigment bound in a synthetic resin. They are quick drying and when dry they are light-fast and produce a hard matt surface. In warm temperatures an acrylic painting will dry within minutes, so that it can be taken off the easel and packed away in the time it takes to wash the brushes. This fast-drying characteristic makes acrylics a good choice for location work. There is a retarder available to slow down drying, which is essential if you wish to blend colors on the canvas. Acrylics have most of the characteristics of oil paint. Their quality is comparable and they offer a similar range of colors. Acrylics may be used for underpainting, impasto, and palette-knife work. However, due to the drying speed, you have to work quickly, because you cannot easily scrape the paint off and start again, Used straight from the tube acrylics behave in a similar way to thick gouache paints. Heavily diluted with water they can be brushed on in broad washes achieving virtually the same effect as with watercolor. Generally acrylics are cheaper than oil, making them attractive to students and those on a limited budget.

Paint

It is advisable for all painters to use a consistent range of colors in all media; therefore, I would suggest the same selection as listed in the oil section on page 628.

ABOVE *The Garden in Spring.* Acrylic by the author. Planes of color overlaid with sparks of brilliant color create the seasonal feel.

Palettes

There are two kinds of palettes suitable for acrylics: plastic and the "wet" palette. Wood is not recommended, because it is more difficult to clean when the paint has dried. The "wet" palette is an ingenious device designed to keep the paint workable for longer periods. It is basically a plastic box with a layer of blotting paper placed on the inside. This is then soaked with water and a second sheet is placed on top, so retaining a damp surface on which to lay out the colors. If the lid is replaced when finishing for the day the colors can remain workable until the following morning.

Mediums

Various mediums are available for acrylics. They are: gloss, matt,

ABOVE Gerry Baptist's contrasting, brilliant primary colors give a luminosity and overall glow to this acrylic painting *Provençal Landscape*. The use of diagonals and triangular shapes in the buildings produces a dynamic composition.

retarder, and gel. They are mixed in specified proportions with the paint according to your preference.

Supports

As with oil, almost any surface can be used for acrylic painting: canvas, wood, metal, masonite, cardboard, and paper. It is not essential that a primer is used, except on porous surfaces such as canvas and cardboard. The universal primer is acrylic primer.

Brushes

The same range of brushes may be used for acrylics as for oil painting. Keep your brushes in a jar of water while working and wash them out thoroughly afterward. Paint-hardened brushes can be softened by soaking in methylated spirits for about 12 hours.

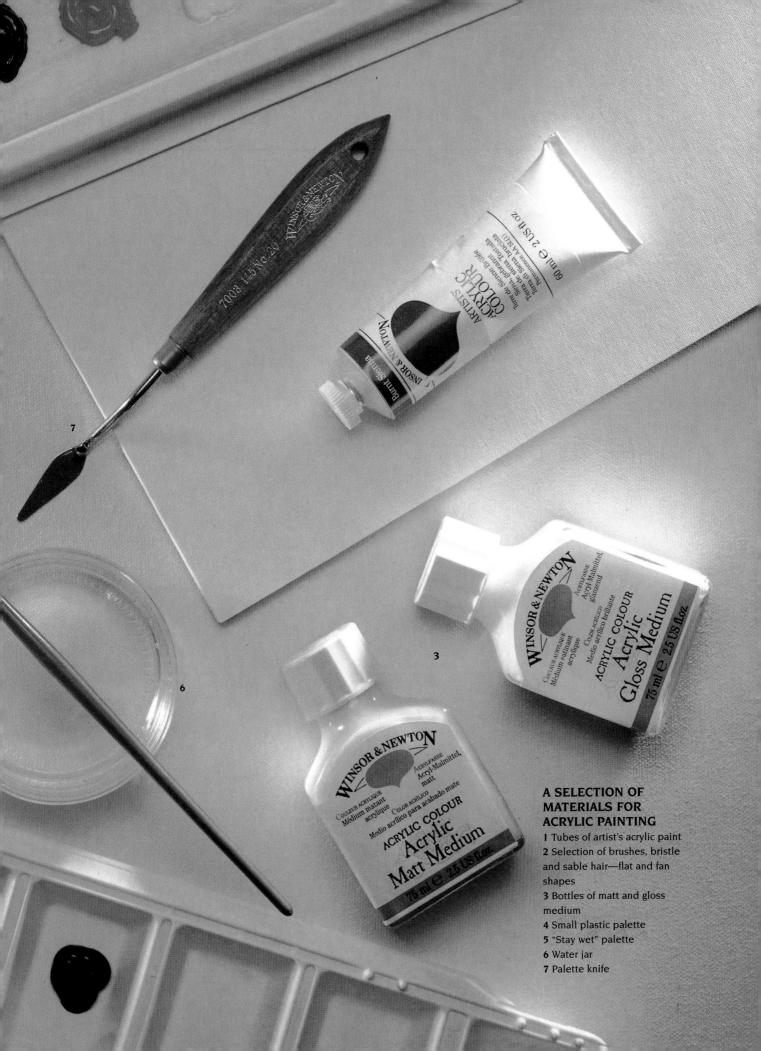

7

3

6

A SELECTION OF MATERIALS FOR ACRYLIC PAINTING

1 Tubes of artist's acrylic paint
2 Selection of brushes, bristle and sable hair—flat and fan shapes
3 Bottles of matt and gloss medium
4 Small plastic palette
5 "Stay wet" palette
6 Water jar
7 Palette knife

WATERCOLOUR AND GOUACHE

Paints

The quality of watercolors varies considerably and so it is advisable to buy from reputable manufacturers. Check that the term "Artists'" appears somewhere on the label, then you can be assured of good quality. Watercolor is pigment, finely ground, and suspended in water with gum arabic as the binder. As a general rule it is not necessary to have as many colors on the palette as with oils or acrylics, because of the "wash" characteristic of watercolors. Working wet-in-wet produces tints and shades by the very nature of the medium. Some distinguished watercolorists of the past have not used more than six or seven colors. Again, select your colors from those that you use for other painting media or from the list for oils on page 628.

Watercolors are available in small cakes (called half pans), tubes, and bottles. Both tubes and half pans can be bought separately or in tin boxes, which also serve as palettes. They are all fast drying and do not change their color value when dry. Gouache paint can be described as opaque watercolor. It has this opacity through the addition of an inert white pigment, which gives it a handling quality similar to matt acrylics. As with acrylics, it is fast drying, but unlike acrylics it can be soaked off for changes or corrections. Watercolor obtains its pure brilliance through transparency, whereas with gouache the flat, bright color is reflected back from the surface of the paint itself. Both watercolor and gouache are suitable for making quick, on-the-spot studies. Watercolor is preferable when the object is to capture the transient qualities of light and mood.

I prefer gouache for small-scale color compositions that are to be scaled-up later into larger paintings in oil or acrylics. Water-soluble crayons are also a useful medium for quick studies. They produce an effect similar to watercolor, but involve less equipment. All you need is a small container for water and a brush to move the color around after you have made a sketch.

Palettes

Most watercolorists carry with them a box, which also functions as a palette when opened out. These are available in various sizes, some large enough to contain one or two brushes. For studio use larger ceramic or plastic palettes are also available, but a large dinner plate is as good as anything.

ABOVE *Fish River Canyon.* Hazel Soan's watercolor combines sensitive drawing with delicate color washes.

Brushes

Brushes are made in a variety of types from broad flat squirrel, and goat hair to very fine pointed sable brushes. The type of brush you use will directly influence your style and the final effects obtained. The finest quality brushes are the sables. These are made from mink fur and are expensive, but they are the most durable and long lasting. A good, fine-pointed sable brush is ideal for washes and fine detail. Flat, chisel-shaped sables are also produced specially for paintings requiring large areas of wash color. Because of the adaptability of the pointed sable, it is not generally necessary to buy very small sizes; sizes 2 to 12 will do most tasks. If funds are low, you can try out some of the synthetic brushes, but beware that you do not end up with the poorest quality, because they will not be capable of achieving the subtle effects you may want.

Water

For the perfectionist, distilled water is safer than tap water. Tap water can be too hard or too soft and it can affect the paper and paints. Always have at least two containers: one for mixing paint, the other for cleaning your brushes.

Papers and boards

A lot of work can be done directly in watercolor sketchbooks—especially when working on location. These are available in a variety of papers, as described on page 627. The range of both papers and papers mounted to board is extensive. They are obtainable under the following headings referring to their manufacturing technique: Hot Pressed, Cold

ABOVE *Mist in the Mountains*. Watercolour by Kenneth Swain.

Pressed, or NOT and Rough. Hot pressed has a smooth surface and is suitable for line and wash paintings, but the absence of grain makes it less attractive to watercolor painters, who prefer the "tooth" of the other two. Hand-made papers are expensive, but they are of high quality. They are normally made of pure linen rag. There are also a number of more "exotic" papers found in specialist stores. Among them is Japanese rice paper, which is absorbent and has to be handled delicately.

The weight and thickness of watercolor paper is an important consideration. Paper weights for watercolor range from 90 1b (190 gsm) to 300 1b (640 gsm). The heavier weights 150 1b (325gsm and above) may be worked on directly, but the lighter or thinner papers must be stretched to avoid buckling when washes are applied to the surface. The best weight and surface for general use would be a 1001b (20Ogsm) cold-pressed surface cartridge paper. To avoid the need for stretching some papers are produced in board form. The paper is mounted to a cardboard support, which guarantees that the surface will remain flat from the start to the finish of a painting.

A SELECTION OF WATERCOLOR AND GOUACHE MATERIALS

1 Tubes of artists' watercolor paint

2 A boxed set of watercolor tubes

3 Tubes of designers' gouache color

4 A watercolor box (containing half-pans, palette, water bottle, a brush, and a sponge)

5 A selection of sable brushes

6 One wash brush

7 A ceramic palette

8 A ring-bound watercolor sketchbook

9 a sheet of watercolor board

10 A piece of wax

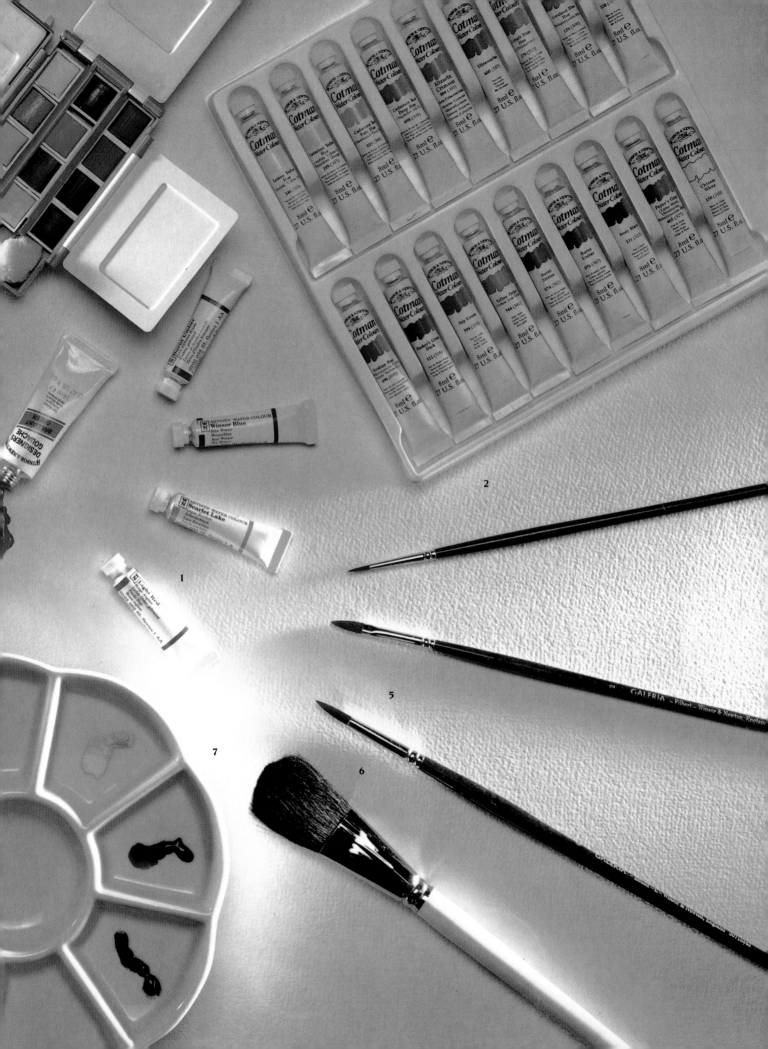

2

1

5

7

6

PASTELS

Colors

A very wide range of colors, numbering hundreds, are manufactured as pastels. They are produced as square or round sticks of pigment, and as pencils. A large number of colors are made because pastels cannot be mixed on a palette. Thus the artist needs a wider range of tints than is the case with watercolor or oils.

Pastels can be purchased either singly, or boxed in sets. A reasonable range for those just starting to use pastels would be a boxed set of 48 tints. Pastels are manufactured in three grades: soft, medium, and hard. The soft grade, as its name suggests, is best suited for laying large areas of color and overlaying, while the hard versions are intended for linear drawing. Oil pastels are an alternative to the traditional type. They are growing in popularity because they are stronger and less likely to break when in use. The oil pastel produces an effect akin to oil painting, which makes it ideal for preliminary sketches on location.

Sketching with pastels

Pastels are lightweight and easily portable. They are fast to work with and, of course, there is no drying time involved. These qualities make them an ideal medium for color sketching without the paraphernalia of oil or watercolor painting.

Supports

Watercolor paper or rough cartridge paper, Ingres paper, and various cover papers are used as a support for pastels. in fact, any paper or board that has a textured, fibrous surface that will accept the pastel grains can be used. Papers tinted with a neutral color are also popular with pastel artists, who often prefer to work on a base color rather than pure white.

Equipment

A drawing board or an easel may be used. It is advisable not to work flat, as the pastel dust tends to accumulate and obscure the picture as it progresses. When using a drawing board, set it at an angle, so that the dust will fall downward, away from the picture. Other items you may need when working are: a tightly rolled piece of paper to use as a pastel spreader, a soft duster, a kneaded putty rubber, a sharp knife, and a fixative spray.

ABOVE *Pastel* by Nancy Green. This picture demonstrates the richness and subtlety of pastel skilfully used.

RIGHT Painting outdoors can be one of the delights of landscape painting, but do plan ahead to make sure you have everything you need.

CHAPTER TWO
Basic Techniques

Technique is not a thing which can be taught—it has to be discovered. Every artist has to find the method of painting a picture which suits them best. This takes time and willingness to experiment with and understand the medium that is being used.

Your technique becomes your style and your personal style is the quality that distinguishes your own work from that of others. Study the technique of good artists and note the methods they use to obtain their effects. There are a wealth of explanatory art books and magazines which can serve as a guide to this.

The ability to develop a repertoire of techniques is essential as an aid to expression in the creative process. It is important also to gain a knowledge of the possibilities as well as the limitations inherent in the different media. When all these factors are understood, the artist can then be fully in control of the means of expression, rather than being controlled by them!

What follows is a description of the basic techniques, which are, as it were, the classic methods that have evolved throughout the long history of painting. The demonstrations later on in this section illustrate a number of other techniques which have been adopted by contemporary artists working in the various media.

USING OILS AND ACRYLICS

There are two basic methods of painting a picture in oils or acrylics: alla prima and glazing.

Alla prima

This is the most direct method. The painting is usually completed from start to finish in one session. It is particularly widely used for landscape, where working on location under changing light and weather conditions is always a hazard. The exact method adopted by different artists varies a little, but I will explain the generally accepted procedure.

No preliminary studies are done other than a lightly sketched drawing in charcoal or thinned paint applied directly to the painting support. The support is

usually white with no base color. The paint is applied right across the picture, either in small brush strokes or in broad areas of colors, followed by blending and joining tones, with a few touches to finish the work. As the painter is working quickly with this method the viscosity (liquidness) of the paint is important. It has to be rather like double cream—supple, yet at its full brilliance. To achieve this the paint should be diluted with a little oil and turpentine on the palette before starting the painting. This technique was the one favored by the *en plein air* Impressionists.

BELOW *Picnic in the Park* by the author. Painted in oil alla prima, the band of shadow under the trees, broken with dappled light, contrasts with the sunlit background.

Glazing

Glazing involves working with successive transparent layers of diluted paint, so that each layer allows the color beneath to remain visible. For those who prefer to build up their picture by stages, glazing is the classic method. With a few exceptions, all painters since Van Gogh have worked in this way. As this technique takes longer to execute it is normally used for painting in the studio.

It may involve scaling up a sketch or study for transfer to the full-size painting support. The drawing is then made using charcoal or diluted paint. This is followed by a thinned layer of paint indicating areas of light and dark. When this is dry the entire painting is covered by successive layers of paint, except for the very lightest areas. It is important to allow each layer to dry sufficiently before adding the next; this prevents the underpainting from being disturbed and "muddied." Finally, highlights and definition lines are applied using thicker, impasto paint. Usually white is absent from the glazes to retain their transparency.

Glazing is suitable for oil, acrylic and watercolour painting.

BELOW *Girl by the Edge of a Wood*. The author used successive glazes of thinned oil color to achieve richness and tonal depth. Finally, bright patches of thick color create the effect of dappled light.

Impasto

Impasto is normally the final stage in a painting. Paint is mixed thickly, sometimes straight from the tube. This technique is frequently used as an overpainting to enrich the color and give texture to a picture produced by glazing. It is suitable for oil and acrylic painting.

RIGHT A vigorous impasto painting by the author. *Summer Garden* began with a base drawing in thin color onto which thicker paint was applied. The layers were gradually built up before employing the palette knife for the final touches.

BELOW *Autumn in Hadley* is another impasto oil by the author. This time the method first used was alla prima, beginning with all the violet and blue areas behind the foliage. A variety of browns and yellows were mixed in thicker paint for the foreground foliage.

Palette knife

A version of impasto painting, but applied with a knife, this technique is generally used as an overpainting to increase surface texture. Large amounts of paint are first mixed on the palette, then applied to the support using an angled, pointed palette knife. Sand or sawdust is sometimes mixed into the paint to increase its bulk and texture. The result usually has the appearance of a spontaneous, expressionistic style. Suitable for oil and acrylic.

RIGHT *St. Paul's from Ludgate Hill.* Oil by Kenneth Swain. This splendid picture has been produced almost exclusively with the palette knife. The red London buses serve both as a focal point and a lead-in to the dome of St. Paul's in the background.

RIGHT *Chania Harbour* by the author seemed to demand the use of the palette knife to achieve the scintillating reflections of brightly lit buildings seen in the water of this Cretan port.

Scumbling

Frequently used by the Impressionists, scumbling is the best method for putting the finishing touches to a painting. It is suitable for subjects requiring bright highlights to appear on water. The method is to drag, or roll, a brush heavily loaded with dryish paint across the required parts of the picture leaving the underpainting visible. Suitable for oil and acrylic.

ABOVE *The Poplars, the Four Trees* (1891) by Claude Monet. Monet built up his painting in layers, usually allowing parts of the previous layer to show through by separating his brush strokes. The final layer utilizes thick, purer color flicked and dragged onto the surface.

RIGHT *Autumn Trees* by the author. The nature of this subject is ideal for the scumbling technique. The tree trunk and the tree shape were first drawn in thinned oil color and when dry, thick paint was dragged or dabbed across the foliage to produce the pure autumn tints.

Scratching

This is simply scraping off paint to reveal the underpainting and leave a textured effect. The point of a palette knife or the tip of a brush handle was frequently used by the Cubists to draw into wet paint. This is difficult with acrylics where drying time is so short. Most suitable for oil.

RIGHT This detail of *Autumn at Argenteuil* by Claude Monet shows his use of scratching at the completion of the painting. The paint layers have been scored back to the canvas surface, probably because he felt that the tones were too dense and he wanted to stress the effect of movement and reflected light.

BELOW Extensive use of scratching with the tip of a palette knife is evident in Kenneth Swain's dramatic oil *Welsh Chapel*. The technique has been used to stress the shape of the angular forms and to create texture.

USING WATERCOLORS

Watercolor is probably the oldest painting medium in the history of art. It dates back over thousands of years to the ancient Egyptian civilization. If you are prepared to persevere with the technique and the handling of the material watercolor can also be one of the most satisfying. The pigment is finely ground and suspended in a binder of gum arabic. It is transparent, contains no white and, in the hands of a skilled artist, can produce the most subtle and delightful effects. This very transparency, however, means that every mark will show through successive washes of paint—a characteristic that led a painting teacher of mine to remark that "when you put down a line, you're stuck with it."

There are several other forms of water-based media including distemper, fresco, and gouache.

The two principal techniques involved are wet-in-wet and glazing.

Wet-in-wet

Paint is applied in diluted washes to damp or dry paper. Additional washes of varying color are then worked into the first wash before it is dry. The extremely fluid nature of this method makes it difficult to predict exactly the outcome, but it can result in a "happy accident."

ABOVE *The Fisherman* by Kenneth Swain. Watercolor washes of delicate color have been applied to a dampened surface. The figure and its reflection were put in when the background was dry.

BELOW The paper was first dampened in this garden study by the author. Washes of color were dropped onto the surface before applying stronger tints for the blossoms and foliage.

Glazing

This is the classic watercolor technique, that is more precise than "wet-in-wet." A light sketch drawing is made onto white paper. Successive washes are applied, starting with the palest overall color, leaving the bright highlights white. The washes progressively darken and enrich the surface until the final wash is applied only on the areas of deep shadow.

RIGHT This example of glazing with watercolor by the author demonstrates the richness of color and depth of tone that can be achieved. The study also includes some wet-in-wet technique in the foreground. Some initial planning is necessary when using the glazing technique.

Line and wash

This is a good technique for sketching on location, because you can make a study quickly. Only a minimum of color is needed, with line added to define forms.

There are two methods of approach:
1 Make a preliminary line drawing on the support, then apply washes of color up to the boundary lines, still retaining the line beneath.
2 Apply color washes first, then when dry draw the lines on top to accentuate the forms and indicate shadow areas. Pencil, ink, conté or charcoal may be applied for the line work.

RIGHT A camping holiday provided the opportunity for the author to produce a quick line and wash sketch. In this study pale washes were first applied to a damp ground and, when dry, the line was added to define the forms and strengthen tone.

Blotting and sponging

Sponges are indispensable for most watercolor techniques, to remove excess paint and lighten tones (natural sponges are preferable). Dipped in paint they can be used to add color to washes and create textures. Blotting paper will soak off washes almost down to the surface.

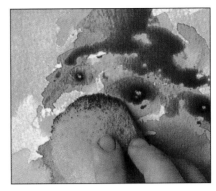

1 The soft, irregular texture of a sponge makes it a highly versatile tool particularly suited to rendering the texture of tree foliage. In this first stage of the painting the artist begins by loosely washing in the shapes of the trees with pale tones of sap green.

2 The artist mixes up a more intense wash of sap green and Payne's gray for the mid-tones of the foliage. A rounded sponge is dipped in clear water, squeezed out until it is just damp, and pressed into the pool of color on the palette and then used to deposit a mottled pattern of dark tones over the dried underlayer.

3 The painting is allowed to dry, after which slightly darker tones of Payne's gray and sap greens are sponged onto the tree shapes and a few slender branches indicated with a rigger brush.

Masking fluid

Masking fluid is employed extensively by some artists. Its purpose is to mask out those areas that are to remain white, or to retain the purity of an underlying color wash. Masking fluid can be painted on, stippled with a toothbrush, or splattered. It dries quickly and can then be painted over. When the painting is dry it can be easily removed by gently rubbing with the finger.

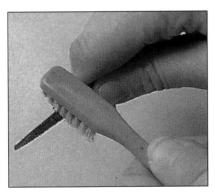

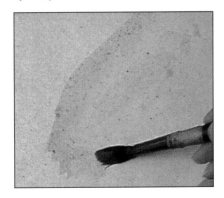

1 A small quantity of masking fluid is lifted from the tinting saucer with an old toothbrush. The loaded brush is dragged against the edge of a palette knife so that flecks of masking fluid are spattered onto the surface of the paper and allowed to dry before overpainting.

2 After dampening the paper, the artist mixes a wash of raw and burnt sienna and uses a broad brush to create an irregular shape on the paper.

3 The paint is broken by the now dry droplets of masking fluid.

STRETCHING PAPER

Light- or medium-weight papers tend to buckle when wet paint is applied, but they won't do this if they are stretched. Stretching paper may seem a chore, but there are two excellent reasons for doing it. One is that you can save a good deal of money, because light papers are considerably less expensive than heavy ones, and the other is that stretched paper is more pleasant to work on—it is frustrating to paint over ridges caused by buckling. Stretching isn't difficult, but you need to do it well in advance of painting. The paper has to be soaked and will take at least two hours to dry thoroughly.

1 Rule light pencil lines about half an inch from the edges of the paper to help you put the tape on straight.

2 Immerse the paper briefly in water, turning it over once to make sure both sides are evenly wetted. You can do this in a bathtub, basin, or plastic tray.

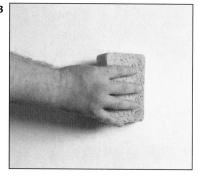

3 Place the paper on the board and smooth it with a damp sponge to remove any creases or air bubbles.

4 Cut four pieces of gummed tape roughly to length and dampen each one just before use by running it over the sponge. Don't make it too wet or it may stretch and tear.

5 Place the strip around all four edges, smoothing it with your hand as you go. Trim the corners with the scissors or a sharp knife, and stand the board upright until the paper is completely dry.

USING GOUACHE

Gouache could be described as the commercial artist's watercolor. It is an extremely flexible medium, which may be used in heavily diluted form like watercolor, or as opaque body color resembling acrylic, or matt oil painting. Thus, all the techniques previously described for watercolor can also be used for gouache painting.

Dry brush

An old brush with splayed bristles, or a fan shaped brush may be used for this technique. Normally the brush is first dabbed on a piece of cloth after dipping it in the paint to prevent overloading and losing the required effect. Dry brush is particularly good for adding textures to grasses, winter trees, etc.

Flat colour

Because of its opacity gouache is ideal for laying flat areas of color. The brush should be well loaded with paint with about the viscosity of single cream. The color is then laid down in horizontal strokes, keeping the edge wet to receive the next stroke. If the edge dries before this the result will be "streaky." However, with gouache it is possible to soak off mistakes and overpaint again.

Gouache lift

This technique produces an effect akin to a lino or wood cut. The principle is based on an underpainting of thick gouache (water based) and a complete overpainting of Indian ink (insoluble). Line and wash board is the best surface to work on. When complete, and absolutely dry, the painting is placed under a running tap and gently "washed off." The gouache dissolves and "lifts" the

ABOVE Two gouache studies by the author show the use of flat color broken with some finer lines to create texture. The red painted gate acts as a focal point.

ink from the surface—except in those areas not first painted with gouache. A black negative effect is left on the board.

ABOVE *Trees* by the author demonstrates extensive use of dry-brushed color. Thick dryish gouache color has been dabbed onto pale background tints creating a sense of transparency.

USING PASTELS

It is important to remember that pastels, unlike oil or watercolor, cannot be mixed on the palette. Different tints of color can only be obtained by using another pastel or, to a limited degree, smudging or blending on the support.

Because pastels cannot be mixed before using, it is essential before starting to select all the colors you will need to complete a painting. They should be laid out according to color and tone. A piece of corrugated cardboard is ideal for this purpose.

The strokes made by a pastel vary enormously depending on the angle at which they are held and the manner in which they are used. Held lengthways and flat to the support, they produce a wide band of color. Held upright, they can be used for medium-width strokes of color and for "Stubbing in" more brilliant dots of color. If broken in half, very fine lines can be drawn with the edge onto the support. Pressing down on the pastel will result in larger amounts of color filling the paper grain and giving a more "solid" look to the mark. Conversely, light pressure results in a smaller deposit of pastel, with more texture and background showing through.

Pieces of pastel can be ground down to make a powder. This can be done with a piece of wood or a metal spoon and then applied to the support with a soft tissue or brush; the technique is useful for obtaining background tints.

Most artists adopt either of two methods of painting:

1 Layering. Broad strokes of pastel are laid one over the other, building up to a rich, dense finish. It is usually necessary to fix each layer before the next is applied, although this can be avoided with soft pastels.

2 Linear. Strokes of pastel are placed all round the picture with little or no attempt to blend. Additional strokes are then applied using different colors until the entire picture is densely covered with long and short strokes. This method is usually adopted for work on a tinted background support, where the intention is to retain the neutral color in the final painting.

Protecting a pastel painting

Pastel is the most vulnerable of the painting media. A picture is easily spoilt if the surface is accidentally touched or if it is placed uncovered in a portfolio. Spray lightly with a fast-drying fixative, before covering the work with a sheet of tissue paper.

The paper should be fixed to the support, or wrapped round it to prevent rubbing during transportation.

Note Be sparing with the fixative, because too much can cause some colors to darken and some, notably white, may disappear altogether.

BELOW Nancy Green's delightful pastel painting is reminiscent of Monet with tints of pink and blue in the background contrasting with green and yellow in the foreground.

CHAPTER THREE
Sketching

Sketches are the principal reference source for the landscape painter. The sketchbook is the artist's personal visual dictionary containing everything that might be used in later works, from thumbnail studies of leaves and grasses to compositional drawings in preparation for large-scale paintings.

Sketching is also a pleasure in itself. Every painter has experience the urge to make a quick visual statement, when suddenly confronted by a superb view or an intriguing object, a scene that demands to be drawn on the spot and with whatever materials are to hand.

Quite apart from compiling your own visual handbook, sketching is vital to the artist's personal creative development. It is like a private sanctuary where experiments can be made and ideas explored, free from public scrutiny. The dedicated artist always carries a sketchbook or a notebook with him wherever he goes. A small A5 ringbound sketchbook is ideal for the purpose as it slips easily into a coat pocket or a small bag.

A phenomenon associated with sketching is that the sketch often appears to be more natural and satisfying than the finished painting made from it. This is because we are stimulated by the first sight of the scene and make the drawing without preconception. We are also in an unconcerned, relaxed state of mind, enabling us to work quickly, without self-conscious thought about quality or "getting it right."

Of course, you can work in any medium to produce a sketch. The quick drawing that we have been discussing is probably best done with a pencil or pen, but color can be used as well. When I decide to make a day of it, I take a small box of watercolors or some water- soluble pencils, even on occasion oils or acrylics and a portable easel. The difference between setting up to do a full-scale painting and a sketch is

that I will move my position several times during the day. That is why I need the most portable of equipment. Many "plein air" artists, including some of the impressionists, have the practice of sketching in the whole picture loosely in thinned color. They finish the painting with thicker, more brilliant color in their studio with the support of sketches and studies.

ABOVE *Trees and a stretch of water on the Stour* (1836-7) by John Constable. Here we can see the influence Constable's treatment of light had on the French painters.

Water-soluble pencils and felt-tip pens are very handy tools for doing quick color and tonal sketches. You need a small screw-top water container and a brush to dissolve the color and spread the tone.

ABOVE Another quick pen sketch by the author sitting on the quayside. A fountain pen was used for the line drawing and then the ink was smeared and spread with a piece of damp cloth to create tone and to soften the line.

ABOVE *Houses by a Canal* by the author. This study is another example of the line and wash technique. The line drawing was made first using a 2b pencil. Only the basic shapes of the houses and canal bank were indicated lightly. Watercolor was then washed in over the line.

LEFT Fishing boats beached at Hastings, England, were the inspiration for this rapid pen sketch.

LEFT Having an idea for a painting, the author made a preliminary sketch in pastel of the view through the window. The pale blue sky is echoed in the stronger blue of the right hand door. By contrast, the warm, pale tints on the lefthand door reflect the sunlight.

PENCIL SKETCHING

Graphite pencils are available in a wide range from very hard to very soft. The soft range 2B to 6B is suitable for sketching. The softer the lead, the broader the mark you can make. It is best to keep your pencils sharpened roughly to a point so that it is possible to vary the line from thin to thick by changing the angle at which you hold the pencil. The technique generally used is cross-hatching.

RIGHT This charcoal sketch was executed by the author in under 10 minutes. He then had to flee the driving wind and rain!

ABOVE Planes of light and dark tone in the hillside houses were the inspiration for this study. The author used a 3b pencil.

ABOVE The spherical shape of these trees make a suitable subject for pencil cross hatching.

ABOVE The author used a soft pencil for this drawing.

HATCHING

The drawing is made by a build-up of short lines placed at a regular angle across the paper. The angle of the pencil is then changed and the lines crossed again. This process continues until the drawing is "complete." Alternatively, the initial sketch can be made with a very soft pencil, after which the lines are "smudged" with the finger to move the tone around and create areas of light and dark.

The same technique may be used with charcoal. Again, this medium is produced in hard and soft form, both as a pencil and in sticks. Charcoal is ideal for "smudging," where large areas of tone can be created very quickly.

HARVEST, NEAR DATCHWORTH, HERTFORDSHIRE, ENGLAND

ENID FAIRHEAD

Enid Fairhead is from the tradition of *en plein* air painters. She searches for her motifs and when she has found inspiration works directly on the spot and without preliminary studies or drawings. She writes, "I am fortunate to live in Hertfordshire in England in the midst of lovely countryside—the source of my inspiration as a landscape painter. Visually, one of the most exciting times for me is the harvest—seas of vibrant tawny golds, bleached grasses and bright greens giving way to blue purple and bronzed greens."

Author's Notes

What fascinates this artist about this view is the way the lines of corn and stubble converge at the large trees in the middle distance. This makes for a natural focal point, which she is careful to place slightly off center. She is intimately concerned with light and its effects on color, which changes according to the time of day. "It is always better to paint landscape up to mid-morning and from mid-afternoon, when the shadows are angled, accentuating form. This can disappear in the flattening noon light".

Enid normally prefers to work on a colored ground, because this provides a key for color and tonal unity at the start. She uses well-diluted paint to apply glazes across the picture, gradually using her paint more thickly with each glaze. She never completely covers the preceding layer, but allows tints of translucent color beneath to remain and contribute to the overall subtlety.

1 A quick charcoal sketch of the scene.

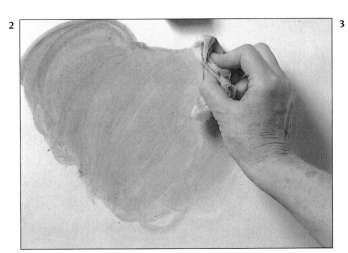

2 The ground is prepared with a wash of light red diluted with turpentine.

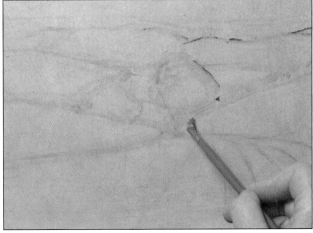

3 Drawing the main lines of the composition with thinned raw sienna. A No. 4 filbert bristle brush is used for this.

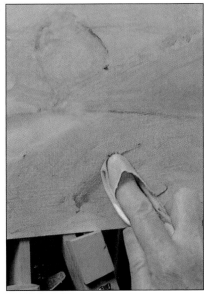

4 Patches of color, ultramarine mixed with white and a little crimson are worked into the sky with a No. 6 flat bristle brush.

Yellow ocher, cadmium orange, raw sienna and light red are brushed into the cornfields, using turpentine only.

5 The artist occasionally rubs in colour with a rag to spread the tones more quickly.

6 The first glaze of warm tints is complete.

7 Ultramarine and raw sienna are mixed to make a cool green to mark the trees. The horizon line is indicated with a mix of ultramarine and lemon yellow, then rubbed down with a cloth.

8 Thicker glazes are now being used, following the "fat over lean" principle. Furrow lines are drawn into the mid-distance field with a pointed sable brush dipped in turpentine.

9 A No. 4 bristle brush is well loaded to paint a mix of thick yellow ocher and white for the bright corn tops.

10 The corn stubble lines are drawn in using the edge of a flat bristle brush.

11 A No. 2 pointed bristle brush is employed to touch in the tractor with a mixture of cadmium orange and light red.

12 A mix of thick pale yellow is applied to the tops of the corn increasing contrast and introducing more texture.

13 The painting is almost finished and the artist decides that some final touches of blue and pink are needed in the sky.

14 More touches of violet and blue are scumbled in the distant horizon to add more atmospheric perspective.

15 The finished painting.

PEN SKETCHING

Any type of pen (and there are many) can be used for sketching. Keep a felt tip or ballpoint pen handy for making quick notes. Ink cartridge sketching pens are a good investment, because you do not have to carry bottles of ink around with you. They can produce a variable thickness of line similar to the dip pen. Using water-soluble ink enables you to produce tone as well as line, simply by moistening parts of the drawing and then spreading the ink with your finger. Many artists still prefer the dip pen, because of its quality of line and the fact that tonal areas and texture can be created by dipping tissue paper or a sponge into the bottle.

All the sketches on this spread were done by the author. The pens used are different in each case. They were selected to suit the subject and the type of study being attempted.

OPPOSITE TOP A fairly quick cross-hatched study of a copse of trees focuses on structure, form and tone. A felt-tip pen was used.

OPPOSITE BELOW Here, interest lies In the relationship between the geometric shapes of the buildings set against the textural masses of the trees. Line combined with hatched fountain pen was the method used.

ABOVE Cyprus trees set against the spherical shaped tree in the center provide the visual interest in this dip-pen sketch.

LEFT This ball-point pen sketch of a stream running through woodland is the first study for a future painting.

BRUSH DRAWING

Sketching with a brush dipped in paint or ink can produce delightful effects. Rembrandt and Constable were masters in its use, when they wanted to catch the effects of large, contrasting areas of light and dark. If you are prepared to carry the necessary equipment—brushes, a palette, some paint, and cloths—it is possible to produce dramatic tonal drawings quite quickly.

RIGHT *Fishing boats in Hastings*, by the author. A rapid sketch in acrylic color on prepared paper.

BELOW The author made this watercolor study overlooking an inlet on the Cornish coast. Both wet-in-wet and wet-on-dry techniques were used.

ABOVE The center of interest for the author in this scene is the surf breaking on the rocks. Watercolor heightened with white gouache (for the surf) has been used.

ABOVE Both these brush and ink sketches by the author are of the same scene. They are the first studies for a painting. The sketch at the left zooms in closer to the couple on the bench so that less background is included than the sketch on the right.

ABBEY VIEW

TED GOULD

This mural is now installed in the foyer of a development in Watford, Hertfordshire, England. It was produced in the studio and is the culmination of severalstudies done on location during Fall.

Author's Notes

The title *Abbey View* is also the name of the high-rise flats where the mural now hangs and it is the *raison d'être* of the picture. From the top of the flats it is just possible to see the tower of St Albans Abbey projecting above a line of trees, about 8 miles (12km) distant. It was obviously not feasible to work so far away from the subject, so I made a trip to St Albans to seek out a much closer position. I discovered that the view across the lake in front of the abbey is quite delightful and offered all the elements for color and composition that I could desire. I immediately sat down to make a watercolor study and also take some photographs. The next task was to return to my studio and collect everything that would be necessary for at least two days' painting out of doors.

When working far from my means of transport I find that a shopping trolley suits my needs perfectly. All the materials are contained either inside the bag, or strapped to the outside and the whole ensemble fits easily into the car boot and the trolley wheels are robust enough to cope with fairly rough terrain.

The kit I take for an oil-painting expedition includes: a portable easel; a paintbox with compartments for brushes, palette and solvents; a collapsible chair; a sun umbrella; a viewfinder; sketchbooks; and some rags for brush and palette cleaning. I also pack a guy rope with a couple of tent pegs to hold the easel down in windy conditions. A flask of hot coffee is a must!

An important consideration is clothing. Even when the weather looks fine it can change. It may feel warm when walking, but having to keep still for a couple of hours can

1

2

1 Photograph of St Albans Abbey seen across the lake.

make you more susceptible to the slightest breeze. So I normally take a hat, warm jacket and sweater, thick socks and strong shoes—even, on occasion, gloves!

2 Watercolor study done on the spot.

3 Traveling to the painting location with my "kit".

4 Before unpacking and setting up the easel etc. I use the viewfinder to survey the scene and find the best position.

5 Set up and making a start. The picture is drawn with charcoal and the viewfinder is used to find the positions and directions of the main composition lines.

6 I continue to draw. The sun umbrella is now up, giving shade to the white support from strong sunlight.

7 The palette and the detachable palette rest. The solvent containers are also detachable from the palette, but I like to keep them close to the color. One contains pure turpentine, the other a linseed oil and turpentine mix.

8 The first washes of color being applied: cerulean blue with a little white for the sky, cadmium yellow and violet for the screen of autumn trees. A No. 7 filbert bristle brush is used.

9 The completed painting. Separate studies were made of the swans, which were added later in the studio. The painting has been done in exactly the same proportion as the intended mural—that is, it is exactly the same shape, but much smaller.

The next stage is to "scale up" the painting to the same size as the larger mural. The support for the mural is cotton canvas, stretched over a wood frame and primed with acrylic white. The size of the mural is 6 x 7 ft. (1.8 X 2.1 m).

Scaling-up was achieved by drawing a grid of squares onto tracing paper and laying this over the painting. Exactly the same number of squares was drawn onto the mural support using charcoal. It was then possible to draw the basic composition onto the mural support, using the squares overlaying the painting as reference points.

10 The finished mural painting.

11 Detail of the mural.

The use of the camera as an aid to painting is still the subject of debate. Many artists feel that photography is a different medium altogether and its use by painters leads directly to mere copying and the loss of drawing skills. However, the photograph has been used by artists for almost a hundred years now. Any medium that a painter uses or borrows from has its own intrinsic qualities, which can change the character of the work. Degas, the Impressionist painter, made extensive use of the photograph, which opened up new possibilities in composition for him.

One advantage of the modern camera loaded with high-speed film is that it is now possible to record forms in motion: the running figure, a racehorse, etc. For the landscape artist skilful use of

the camera can provide a very useful reference source of complex details that would take hours to draw.

ABOVE AND BELOW The author discovered this scene while looking for subjects to paint. Two overlapping photographs were taken to act as reference for the oil painting below.

GARDEN LANDSCAPE

KAY GALLWEY

Kay Gallwey does not use the traditional pastel painter's method of "layering." That is to say that she does not "blockin" areas of color and then work over and into them. She prefers bold strokes of color, using the thin edge of the pastel. For her it is essential to stay in touch with the ground, never entirely covering it.

Author's Notes

This picture, vibrant with color and movement, was not done on location, but was produced from a magazine cut-out that took the artist's eye. No preliminary studies were made—the painting is entirely spontaneous and executed on the spot. The artist works fast, continually standing well back from the painting, so that she can assess the progress of the whole. Long strokes of color appear right across the picture to start with. She does not "dally" in any particular area, and when changing to another color, continues to use it, finding the right places for it all over the picture.

The work progresses by adding more lines, occasionally smudging an area to prevent it becoming dominant, introducing a pink here to add richness and a more neutral violet there to unify areas of color. Finally, Kay puts in some touches of fluorescent pastel, to give the painting its ultimate brilliance.

1 A spread from a garden magazine was the inspiration for the painting.

2 The artist does not start with a neutral base drawing. She launches straight into the picture, placing patches and flicks of color right across the surface.

3 Broad strokes of yellow with the pastel held lengthways indicate the field and sunlit foliage.

4 Light green is applied in rapid strokes around the painting, changing to a complementary pink and light blue.

5 Touches of white are added to keep the color key light.

6 Strokes of dark green are added to some areas in shadow, gradually increasing the contrast with the light pinks and blues of the flowers.

7 Black is employed here to provide a link between the surrounding contrasting tones.

8 More pink is applied to the flowers progressively, making the picture more dense and saturated with color. Note that the artist never completely covers the background paper with solid color.

9 Dark blue is added to the green of the foliage to increase contrast with the yellow bushes in front.

10

10 Gently rubbing the pastel in the background bushes softens the forms and increases the sense of atmospheric perspective.

11 To increase the contrast between foreground and background, dark violet is applied between the bright tones. This also has the effect of creating more spatial depth to the picture surface.

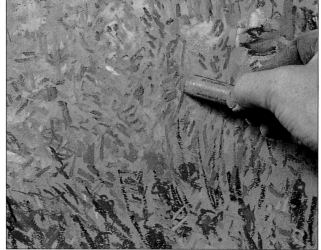

12 Touches of fluorescent pastel have been placed in the flowers and foreground foliage. This gives the picture a little more "sparkle." The painting is nearly complete and the artist considers the finishing touches.

13 A few more strokes of blue to the central part of the painting and some touches of violet create more spatial depth.

14 The finished painting.

CHAPTER FOUR
Color and Light

Color and light are inseperable elements in all painting. We cannot see color without light and the color of light itself affects all the local colors in our field of vision.

A peculiarity of landscape painting, and an essential consideration for the artist, is the effect on color caused by atmosphere. This is negligible when painting portraits or a still life but, where distance is involved, the atmosphere will make a radical difference to the color and tone of an object. For example, a house near the horizon will appear light and grayish, almost disappearing on a misty day, by comparison with a similar building in the foreground.

COLOR THEORY

There are only three basic colors red, blue, and yellow. From these three primary colors all the other colors are mixed. This sometimes comes as an astonishing fact to those just starting out as painters.

Secondary colors are obtained by mixing the primaries in equal quantities.

Tertiary colors are obtained by mixing different quantities of the primaries together:

| 2 parts yellow with 1 part red = yellow/orange |
| 2 parts red with 1 part yellow = red/orange |
| 2 parts blue with 1 part yellow = blue/green |
| 1 part yellow with 2 parts blue = green/blue |

Of course, the theory is based on the colors that are produced by light. In painting we use colors that are found in the earth or are manufactured in a chemical laboratory.

ABOVE Painting color triangles like this one is a good way of learning the different mixtures that can be obtained from the three primary colors, red, blue, and yellow. These, which cannot be mixed from any other colors, are placed one at each corner. The first inner triangle shows the secondary colors, mixed from any pair of primaries, while within this are the tertiaries, the neutral colors mixed from the secondaries. This triangle shows cobalt blue, cadmium yellow, and alizarin crimson, but you can vary the primary hues, which will give a different set of mixtures.

VISCOSITY

The degree to which paint is diluted is important for different working situations and the various stages of a painting. Like the Impressionists, most location painters use heavily diluted paint to assist them to work quickly. The "fat over lean" principle (thicker paint applied over thinner) means that less diluent is used the further a painting progresses, until areas of impasto (straight from the tube) are used in the final stages.

A graphic demonstration of the use of primary colour is in front of you as you read this book. All the color illustrations have been printed using only the three printing primaries—magenta, cyan blue, and yellow—plus black for definition. The mass of different tones are achieved by printing tiny dots of pure color alongside each other.

DIRECTION OF LIGHT

Apart from the color of light, the other important factor in landscape painting is the direction of light. There are four directions from which light can illuminate a scene: front, side, back, and top. On cloudy, overcast days the direction is usually from above. The tops of objects are the lightest, casting a pool of soft shadow beneath. The absence of sunlight reduces contrast both in color and tone, producing a generally muted effect.

TOP LEFT Back lighting occurs at the extreme ends of the day, at dawn and at sundown. In this case the light is coming directly toward the painter from low in the sky. The sky itself is the brightest area in the scene, reducing all the objects between the sky and the artist to silhouettes, with long vertical shadows In front. In this study the girl carrying the basket has fine highlights on her head, the side of her basket and the edge of her blouse.

LEFT Side lighting. This study assumes that the light is coming from the left and fairly low down. The sun is bright in a cloudless sky, causing the trees, figure and building to be seen three-dimensionally and in sharp relief. Shadows are cast diagonally from the right side of the objects. Strong side lighting illustrates Cézanne's thesis that all nature is based on the sphere, cone and cylinder.

BELOW LEFT Front lighting. The position of the sun is directly behind the artist in this study. The effect is to increase the color temperature to its warmest and flatten the shapes of everything. The angle of the light source is high, so that the shadows are underneath the forms.

Using the landscape study described in these exercises, do three studies of your own in acrylic or oil demonstrating the points made in the text.

Color temperature

We tend to think of color as either warm or cool, with reds and yellows at the warm end of the spectrum, blues and violets at the cool end. colors themselves can be made warmer or cooler in mixing. For example: red mixed with very little blue becomes cool red; green mixed with more yellow becomes warm green.

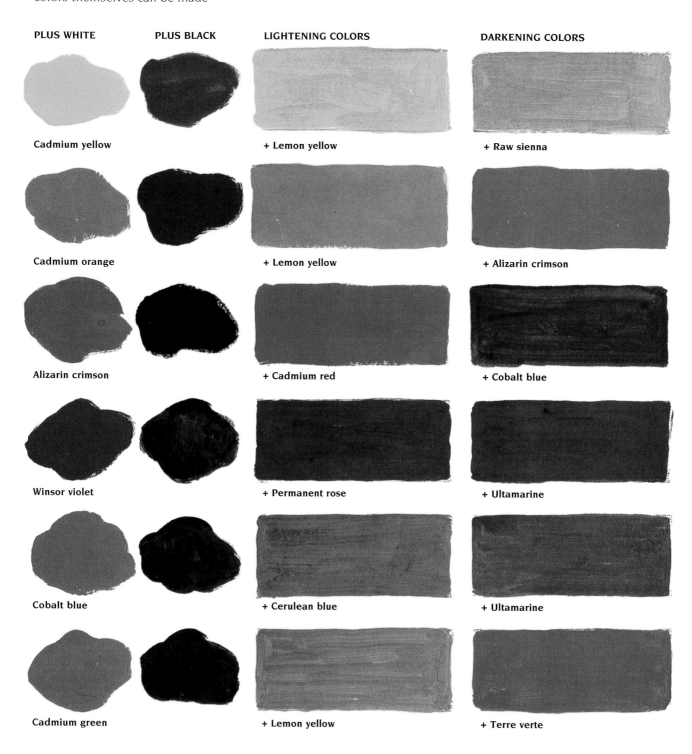

PLUS WHITE	PLUS BLACK	LIGHTENING COLORS	DARKENING COLORS
Cadmium yellow		+ Lemon yellow	+ Raw sienna
Cadmium orange		+ Lemon yellow	+ Alizarin crimson
Alizarin crimson		+ Cadmium red	+ Cobalt blue
Winsor violet		+ Permanent rose	+ Ultamarine
Cobalt blue		+ Cerulean blue	+ Ultamarine
Cadmium green		+ Lemon yellow	+ Terre verte

Neutral tones

These can be described as warm, or cool grays. In painting, neutrals can be mixed from the primary and secondary colors laid out on your palette; for instance, orange mixed with blue and broken with a little white, will produce a mid-gray. Payne's Gray can be described as a mid-gray that can be made warmer or cooler by the addition of Red or Blue.

Neutral tones are very important as a link or a division between pure, brilliant colors, particularly in landscape painting. They also have the effect of unifying the whole composition.

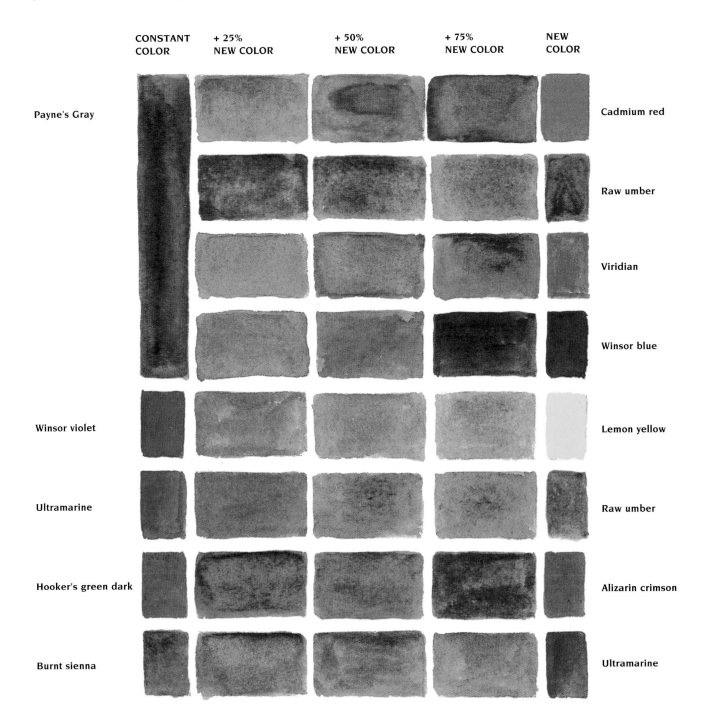

	CONSTANT COLOR	+ 25% NEW COLOR	+ 50% NEW COLOR	+ 75% NEW COLOR	NEW COLOR	
Payne's Gray						Cadmium red
						Raw umber
						Viridian
						Winsor blue
Winsor violet						Lemon yellow
Ultramarine						Raw umber
Hooker's green dark						Alizarin crimson
Burnt sienna						Ultramarine

BOY MEETS OCEAN

KENNETH SWAIN

The boy is the artist's son Jonathan. This oil painting is not the result of hours spent on location working in front of the subject. Although it is hard to believe that a picture so full of light, color, and atmosphere, was not painted on the spot, it was actually done from start to finish in the studio.

Author's Notes

The idea for the painting came several weeks after the event when Ken saw a photograph taken while he was introducing his son to the water. This gray, monochrome image was enough to activate the color sensations that had been stored in his mind through acute observation.

There are no preliminary studies or drawings made. The artist has launched directly into the full-size painting, making a simple charcoal sketch first and then applying patches of dry color into the sky and water. The color areas are rubbed down, repainted, and generally modified until they approximate to the image in his mind. In fact, there are only two main stages to this work. The first, as described above, continues using dryish color, until all the forms are balanced against each other across the entire painting. The second stage is impasto. The artist employs a palette knife, a smallish bristle brush to apply modeling and texture to the underpainting.

1 This monochrome photograph served as the only reference for this picture.

2 The artist begins with a light charcoal drawing outlining the main color and tonal areas. A touch of diluted flesh color is used to position the figure. No base color has been applied, because the intention is to use high-key, pure color throughout this painting.

3 The color of the sky will set the key for the entire picture. Washes of Prussian blue broken with a little white and black are brushed in, using a No. 10 flat bristle brush.

4 Pinkish tints are added near the horizon line. The Prussian blue is used in the sea, reflecting the color of the sky and then broken with lemon yellow to produce a translucent green. The color is used thin and "rubbed" into the white canvas.

5 Patches of diluted color are now placed all around the painting following the principle that a picture should look somewhat finished at every stage. Yellow ocher, crimson, cadmium red, and burnt umber are added to the palette. They are mixed and still used thinly to establish the waves and rock shapes. Bristle brushes sizes 4 and 10 are used. The artist uses a cloth to rub down certain areas.

5

6

7

7 Mixing darker tones of Prussian blue and burnt umber. The rock forms are stressed and divided into sharper planes of color.

8

8 The sky area has been modulated with thicker paint using tones of pink, blue, and yellow. The child's torso is more finely washed with warm tints of orange.

6 From now on the palette knife is brought into use to apply thick color, which is then "scratched and scraped" back with the tip of a penknife. The child's figure represents the focal point of the painting, so the artist builds up the color here first. Similar warm tints of yellow ocher and red are then "found" in the rocks, reflections in the water and the sky.

9

9 White is worked into the sea forms and to the surf, to soften and "feather" the color. A No. 4 round bristle brush is used with the palette knife to create texture.

10 The penknife is again being employed to scratch through the impasto and expose the colors beneath.

11 Adding more tones of pure color. Chrome orange is used here with the palette knife to create the skin tones reflected in the water. Burnt umber is worked into the child's figure and the rocks to stress form. Colors are now used straight from the tube without first being mixed or diluted.

12 The picture is nearly finished and it is time to take stock and decide where the final touches and alterations should be made.

13 A little more impasto white occasionally broken with tints of blue, green, and pink is applied to increase the sense of atmosphere and light.

14 The finished painting.

USING COLOR

Painters always strive to reproduce the effects of light on color in landscape. Only an approximation can be achieved with paint, which, after all is simply a pigment suspended in a binder. The colors in a scene on a wintry, misty day will generally be at the cool end of the spectrum. On a clear, sunny day the same scene will be dominated by colors toward the warm end.

RIGHT AND BELOW Two oil studies employing cool and warm palettes:
RIGHT Prussian blue, violet, burnt umber and yellow ocher.
BELOW Venetian red, orange, cadmium yellow and chrome green.

OLIVE TREES WITH DONKEY

T E D   G O U L D

The idea for this oil painting came as the result of a short trip to Crete
during early summer. As usual I had a small sketchbook with some tubes of
gouache and my camera. We came across an area of the island that was
given over to cornfields and olive trees, interspersed with the occasional
melon grove. Here and there I could see a donkey sheltering from the midday
sun. The scene was made even more attractive by a range of mountains
running behind the fields and parallel to the horizon. I sat down right away
to make a quick study and to take some photographs.

Author's Notes

There are two dominant color
complementaries running
throughout this landscape: yellow
and blue/green, which create
something of a counterchange
pattern. The whole is held together
by the bright cerulean blue of the sky
and the blue/violet of the mountains.

After the underpainting is
complete areas of thicker more
textural paint are applied using a
knife. The term palette knife properly
applies to those with long handles
used for mixing paint on the palette.
Painting knives have short broad
blades with "cranked" handles to
keep the hand out of the wet paint.
They feel flexible and springy and
produce a variety of effects, always
wonderfully spontaneous and bold.
There is almost a sense of modeling
the paint onto the canvas. Light is
reflected off the strokes and
textures, keeping the surface lively.

Dragging the knife at an angle
with firm pressure spreads the paint
in a transparent layer with thick
"edges," rather in the manner of
spreading soft butter on bread.
Using the point with short, sharp
patting movements produces a
raised texture of points. Fine lines
can be drawn while simultaneously
turning the knife to score through
the surface layers in a sgraffito effect.

1 A photograph of the area.

2 A base drawing in charcoal and yellow ocher diluted with turpentine is the first stage. This places the shapes in space and indicates the main composition lines.

3 Beginning the underpainting. The intention is to paint the entire picture with thinly diluted paint first, then when dry, to work over the top using palette knives. Starting at the top with cerulean blue, mauve, and chrome green, the sky, mountains, and foreground tree are brushed in lightly. A No. 5 filbert bristle brush is used.

4 The figure and donkey are brushed in using a mix of mauve and yellow. Parts of the drawing are lost during this process and then restored by drawing back with ultramarine and mauve.

5 Yellow ocher and Indian yellow are mixed for the cornfields, which are painted as a flat wash. A No. 5 filbert bristle brush is used.

6 The underpainting is complete. A soft cloth has been used to rub down wet areas and spread the color. The painting is left to dry for a few hours.

7 The palette knife painting is begun by mixing cerulean blue with a little white and a touch of linseed oil, working broadly across the sky using a large pointed knife.

8

8 The mountains are indicated with mauve and ultramarine added to the cerulean. This is broken with white and a touch of yellow ocher toward the base, which creates a heat-haze effect.

9

9 Tree foliage is painted with a mix of chrome green and ultramarine, keeping the knife well loaded with color and changing the angle continually to create texture.

10

10 The tip and edge of the knife are employed to put in the cypress trees in the background.

11

11 A good thick mix of yellow ocher, Indian red, and a touch of mauve is applied to the cornfields. The knife is turned regularly and used to scratch and scrape back to reveal the underpainting.

12 Modulating the colors in the middle ground.

13 A small pointed palette knife is used to model the foreground tree foliage and to create texture.

14 Black is added to the deep shadow areas such as tree branches. Final touches of Indian red and mauve are mixed to add texture to the grasses and shadow areas under the trees.

15 The finished picture.

FISHING BOATS

T E D   G O U L D

This study of fishing boats in a Portuguese harbor is the result of a brief visit to a little harbor in the Algarve region. The fishermen were repairing their nets in preparation for the next day and they were all busy in their brightly colored boats.

Author's Notes

Standing on the quayside I took some photographs before moving on to the next stop on the journey. When I saw the prints later I was reminded of the vibrating image of reflected light and decided to make a bleach drawing to attempt to recreate the sensation.

1 The photograph that provided the reference for the drawing.

2 Watercolor board is covered with a good wash of ink using a flat sable brush. When this has dried thoroughly, the composition is sketched in with conté pencil.

3 Starting with a cotton swab dipped in bleach the light areas are etched back. Only a little bleach is used at first, because if the swab is too heavily loaded it will clean the ink off right down to the board's surface.

4 The swab is used all over the light areas, gradually applying more bleach to increase the contrast between light and dark.

5 Finally a pen dipped in bleach is employed to draw in the details and highlights.

Color used to unify a painting

As already stated, neutral colors have the effect of creating unity. Adopting a limited palette of colors close together on the spectrum is an aid to achieving a unity of the whole picture. It is also advisable for those just starting to paint.

R I G H T Smooth washes of color in this seascape by Robert Tilling give an impression of great space and depth. A limited palette of three or four colors has been used with strong tonal contrasts providing the visual interest.

Using a bright complementary as a focal point

Bring out a point of particular interest in a picture by using a complementary color in contrast to the general color scheme.

R I G H T A rapid oil study by the author done while on holiday in Dorset. The inspiration for the picture was the backdrop of the dark, ominous sky set against the warm sandstone church tower. The red boat anchored in front of the church provides a strong focal point.

Contrasting high-key color

Complementary colors can be used alongside each other when outlined, or separated by a neutral. Such color was the basis of the Fauvist movement and, of course, Van Gogh's work.

LEFT *Poplars*. This acrylic by Gerry Baptist brilliantly exploits the complementaries, pink, blue, and yellow, to produce a vibrant painting full of light. The neutral black is cleverly used as a unifying factor. The composition counterpoints the verticals in the trees with the horizontal fields.

BELOW *West Herts College*. A gouache by the author which makes use of the primary colors blended together in washes of diluted color. A neutral gray with black lines encloses the central forms to make something of a frame for the composition.

OASIS IN TUNISIA

TED GOULD

A simple postcard which dropped through my letterbox one morning is the basis for this picture. The distinctive shapes of the palm trees standing vertically on the rippled sand dunes make them a "natural" for the gouache lift technique

Author's Notes

I decided to use colored gouache to evoke the atmosphere of the desert. Three colors are used: cerulean blue, yellow ocher, and violet. The support is NOT surface watercolor board. Do not use a smooth surface paper or board because you will find that the textures are disappointing and the ink may lift off as well.

As can be seen, the gouache lift technique produces a similar effect to that achieved by a lino or wood cut. However, it is much quicker to do than either of those two methods, but, of course, you end up with just one original, whereas with lino or wood you can make dozens of prints.

1 The postcard that inspired the picture.

2 A light pencil drawing is made onto the board. This defines the areas of light and dark and indicates the areas for painting in the gouache. Do not draw the lines too heavily, otherwise they may be visible in the finished painting.

3 Full-strength color has been applied straight from the tube. Note that these colors will be lighter in tone when "washed off." Those areas where no ink is to penetrate have been painted thickly. The edges and some other parts have been dry brushed for texture. Remember that those parts left white will be black in the final picture. The paint should be left to dry completely. A No. 4 pointed sable brush was used.

4 The entire painting is now covered with an even layer of waterproof black ink, using a No. 8 pointed sable. The brush is well loaded with ink, which is applied as quickly as possible to avoid disturbing the gouache beneath. The ink layer must be left to dry completely before "washing off."

5 The final "washing off" stage is best done under a slow-running cold tap. The gouache slowly dissolves and lifts the ink off the painted areas. This process is assisted by gently rubbing with a large sable brush until all the surface gouache has been removed.

6 The finished picture.

TREES AT STE. FOY (BORDEAUX REGION)

G E R R Y   B A P T I S T

Gerry Baptist likes to travel, particularly in the warm Mediterranean climate
—not for him the cool greens and dark grays of the English landscape.
He acknowledges the influence of the Fauves on his color, but the
expressive power of this acrylic painting contains echoes of the German
"Blaue Reiter" group.

Author's Notes

A quick comparison of the painting with its reference demonstrates the fact that the photograph has been used as little more than a starting point for the picture. The scene was originally glimpsed from a car window as the artist was traveling through the area, resulting in the photograph on page 700.

Before starting the final painting various studies are made exploring different color schemes. These are important in the process of translating the greens and grays in the photograph to the bright sensuous colors used in the picture.

The artist likes to establish bright, contrasting base colors for his pictures. They function as the color key for the entire work. In this painting there are three complementary base colors. He then draws the main forms and lines of the composition and expands the shapes with thicker paint. Further planes of color are applied, usually complementaries of the one beneath. More glazes are overlaid as the picture grows and changes, often leaving some of the underlying colors "exposed." As well as glazing, he "feathers" some of the layers one into the other to create gently receding or advancing planes. The picture is "finished" when he feels that he cannot add anything more and the work appears to have its own independent existence.

1 The reference photograph which provides the starting point for the painting.

2 A preliminary study for the picture.

3 A base painting is prepared indicating broad horizontal areas of color, which the artist will continually modify throughout the painting. Emerald green, chrome orange, acra red, magenta, chrome green yellow, pthalo blue, and cerulean blue are mixed and applied with a size No. 14 bristle brush.

4 The base painting is complete and left to dry.

5

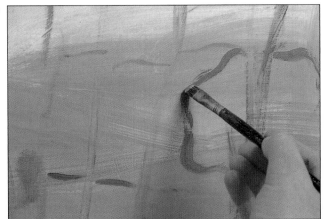

6

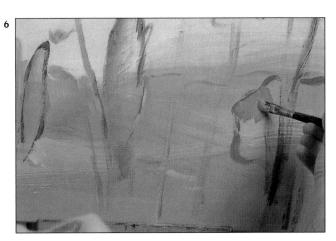

5 and **6** The foreground trees are brushed in with green, changing to violet mixed with white and red for the righthand tree in the middle distance.

7 More dryish color has been brushed into the sky background and trees, which are worked alternately. Yellow, white, and cerulean blue are the principal colors used for this.

7

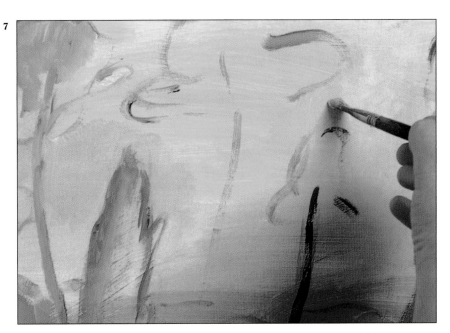

8

8 Detail Green tones are added to the foliage, contrasting with the violet in the trees behind.

9

10

9 More green is brushed into the foreground against the complementary pink. The whole picture is assessed by the artist at this stage.

10 Thicker pink is dry brushed onto blue, producing a violet fringe to the form. Matt gel medium is added to the colors at this stage to thicken them.

11

12

11 Some yellow is dry brushed and then feathered over the pink form. The artist moves from one area to another applying complementaries over previous colors.

12 This picture shows how the painting has changed by continually working different colors over the top of previous glazes. The paint is thick but dry, so that it can be scumbled onto the surface and feathered.

13 Forms in the foreground tree are built up with blue and blue green mix to pull them into the foreground. A No. 8 bristle brush is still being used.

14 The picture is nearly finished. More pale yellow has been brushed into the sky and the tree foliage has been modulated with a little more pink and yellow.

15 The finished painting.

CHAPTER FIVE
Composition

Painting is largely about the organization of shapes, colors, and lines in a satisfactory and pleasing manner. Composition is the difference between making a sketch and creating a picture, bringing order to apparent chaos. Some artists reconstruct from studies of the subject until they feel that all the elements of the picture are in harmony. Others, working on location, take time and great care to choose a view which fulfills all their needs for composition. In this the viewfinder is invaluable. Make one for yourself using mount board, black one side. You should make sure that the window is exactly the same proportion as the painting support being used.

When choosing a subject, and probably after a good deal of searching around, you sometimes find that the resulting painting is a disappointment. This is not simply that you cannot get down what you see, or that you have made the wrong color choice. It is because the subject itself, although attractive, is not suitable for painting as it stands. When painting any aspect of nature the artist is actually translating a three—dimensional subject into two dimensions. Translation means interpretation and this is precisely where composition studies are so important, because you are translating objects in space into lines, shapes and colors on a flat rectangular plane.

PLANNING A PAINTING

When planning a painting it is advisable to work to a small scale. The sketchbook is useful for this. Do several studies for each subject—monochrome studies to work out the tonal contrasts and color studies to decide on your final palette. When working out your studies, consider the points listed below.

ABOVE AND RIGHT This photograph of the river at Salisbury was taken with the aim of making an oil painting of the scene. The pencil study, by the author, made from the photograph compresses the image into a more compact, vertical composition. It also functions as a tonal analysis of the subject.

ABOVE AND RIGHT Both photograph and gouache sketch of olive trees were done on the spot by the author. The subject contains contrasts between the blue/green of the tree foliage and the yellow/brown of the fields. The photograph provides more details than can be achieved in a quick study.

Subject

For your first landscape choose a view that is interesting without being too complex, one that contains both verticals (trees, buildings) and horizontals (fields, pathways etc.).

RIGHT *Winfrith Newburgh*, oil by the author. This is an example of a classically based composition. The trees set in the foreground represent verticals which form a contrast with the horizontal cottages behind. The green foliage of the trees also contrasts with the pinks and browns of the buildings.

Contrast of scale

A contrast of scale adds impact and visual interest. You could place a large tree or rock in the foreground, a row of cottages in the middle distance all against a backdrop of hills or mountains in the background.

BELOW The large tree in the foreground of this gouache study, by the author, cuts both top and bottom edges of the picture plane, increasing the sense of space and depth to the house in the middle distance.

Diagonals

Angled shapes or lines add a
sense of movement to a picture.
They also function as a visual link
between one part of a painting and
another.

RIGHT The figures in this gouache study
by the author, make a triangle with the
apex at the top of the picture plane. They
rest on a diamond shaped cloth near an
angled tree trunk. In fact, all the forms in
this composition are placed at an angle to
the edges of the picture, nothing is simply
horizontal or vertical.

BELOW Several strong diagonals running
parallel to each other emphasize the
slope of the hillside on which this gouache
study was made. The counterchange
between light and dark areas creates a
pattern which is bisected by the curving
tree trunks going off the top of the picture
plane.

ROCKS ON THE ATLANTIC COAST

HAZEL SOAN

The artist discovered this beautiful stretch of coastline during one of her
visits to South Africa. At the time she was not primarily concerned with a
painting location, but with finding a suitable bathing spot for herself and her
family. However, when she happened upon this series of inlets on the Cape
Peninsula she was inspired by what she saw—setting off immediately to
explore the whole area for the most interesting views.

Author's Notes

The Cape Peninsular is on the
Atlantic seaboard. It consists of a
series of inlets interspersed with
boulders and rocky outcrops,
incised by coves of almost pure
white sand. Much of this coastline
is backed by high cliffs and a ridge
of mountains in the background. A
strong contrast is made between
the rocks, piled up in many strange
configurations and the smooth
planes of sand cutting between
them. This is the visual inspiration
for the picture.

Hazel Soan uses a variety of
watercolor techniques in this
painting; wet-in-wet, wet-on-dry,
glazing, masking, sponging, and
waxing. She works intuitively,
preferring to keep all her options
open as the work progresses. As
can be seen from this
demonstration, she starts simply
and broadly. A few light pencil
marks are made to indicate key
points in the composition and
then light washes of color are
added to establish the tonal areas.
These are then textured, and
further washes are laid in a
progressive build-up to the finale.

1 The main composition lines have been sketched in lightly with an HB pencil. Masking fluid is applied to the sketch to preserve the highlight areas all round the picture. A No. 3 pointed sable brush is used.

2 Candle wax is gently rubbed onto selected areas—particularly the rocks, to produce texture as the color washes are applied.

3 A broad wash of diluted yellow ocher covers most of the paper, apart from the sky. This provides a warm key to the picture. A No. 14 pointed sable is used for this.

4 The sky area has been damped with clean water and diluted Prussian blue has been "touched in" to blend with the still wet yellow ocher.

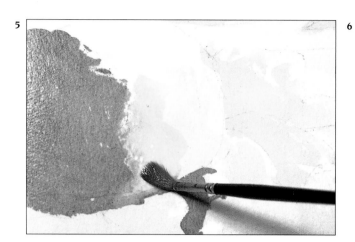

5 The blue has been brought down into the foreground rocks. Wax has been applied to the edge of the rock and yellow ocher is being washed over. The effect is to give a rough edge to the changing planes of color.

6 A little alizarin crimson has been added to the Prussian blue to create warmer cast shadows in the rocks.

7 The blue and violet areas are completed by "soaking off" some color toward the base of the mountains, thereby creating a misty effect.

8 Laying a glaze of slightly thicker yellow ocher over the rocks, making them warmer and defining their shape. "Spots" of alizarin crimson are dropped into the wet paint.

9 Deeper color is "dropped" into wet areas producing a "little explosion" effect. Wax is drawn into the rocks to protect previous washes and increase the textured effect. Alizarin crimson, yellow ocher, and Prussian blue are used.

9

10

10 A variety of techniques are now employed in painting the rocks—wet-inwet, wet-on-dry, and wax. Darker tones of scarlet and blue are added to stress shape and color.

11

11 The broad washes are now completed and the masking fluid is being removed with a putty rubber.

12 The complete picture so far.

13 Yellow ocher and Prussian blue are mixed to apply small wet-on-dry washes to the mountains and the rocks in the middle distance.

14 The artist has decided to modify a portion of the picture by taking out one of the rocks. Using a sable brush and clean water, she soaks off the color until it is almost obliterated and then retouches the area to leave it like the rest of the beach.

15 Pale Prussian blue is mixed to add ripples to the water and shadows around the mid-ground rock. A No. 7 pointed sable brush is used for this.

16 A natural sponge dipped in a mixture of Prussian blue and alizarin crimson is dabbed onto the foreground rocks to add surface texture.

17 The completed picture.

Light and dark

The balance of light and dark is a very important consideration. The dark or shadow areas of a picture set off the light, brightly colored areas. The one emphasizes the other and creates a sense of depth and contrast.

TOP and MIDDLE The trees in both these pastel sketches had deposited half their leaves on the ground. The visual sensation thus created was one of light yellow/brown contrasted with green/black.

BELOW Before starting a full-size painting I frequently produce a tonal study of the subject analyzing it in terms of light and dark. The importance of this is to establish a satisfactory composition for a fairly complex subject.

Focal points

Some painters find it essential to create a clear focal point, or center of interest, others prefer to see their work as an overall pattern of shapes and colors, sometimes called architectural composition.

Two artists who saw composition as being of prime importance were Poussin and Cézanne. Both were acutely aware of the rectangular support in front of them and sought always to create a perfect balance within it—in the abstract sense. Let us aim for the same!

ABOVE A trawler sheltering in a bay off the Cornish coast prompted the author to attempt this watercolor study. The boat occupies a central position in the picture, leading the eye directly to it and creating a natural focal point. The distant hills behind provide a tonal link with the trawler.

WHERE THE WATERS CROSS

TIMOTHY EASTON

This oil painting is of a view across a pond attached to a moat surrounding a country farmhouse. There are two islands to the left and right, and the sun rises on the left of the composition, creating some interesting shadows and highlights that help give distance across the water.

Author's Notes

During the warmer months of the year there is usually a degree of certainty that successive days will be available when a painting can progress outside. The artist finds that he can work on a number of canvases during a day so the first session will start at 6.00 a.m, progress to 10.00 a.m., and the next will begin at 10.15 a.m. going on to the lunchbreak. This pattern can continue until 10.00 p.m. The paintings will be returned to for as many days as are required to complete each one. The canvas used here is double primed on linen, which is washed over with a mid-tone wash of color.

MATERIALS USED

BRUSHES: Hog hair sizes 1–5.
Preferably filberts. Sable brushes
finest quality No.7 (Winsor & Newton)
short-handled.
COLORS: Titanium white, cadmium
yellow, yellow ocher, Indian yellow,
burnt sienna, burnt umber, cadmium
red, permanent magenta, permanent
sap green, olive green, cobalt blue,
cerulean blue, and French ultramarine.
OTHER EQUIPMENT: Palette knife for
pre-mixing only.

1 The initial view.

2 In the nuttery on the left-hand island is a flowering cherry tree, and it was anticipated that the picture would incorporate this, as well as the blossom that would come out a week later when the cherry blossom was over.

3 The canvas is covered with a base color of thinned olive green paint that allows both light and dark tones and color to register against a mid-tone color. This base color must be totally dry before work begins. The composition is then drawn in with a sable brush using thinned olive green paint.

4 Some broader areas of color are blocked in using a No. 3 hog's hair brush to give some idea of the balance of light and dark areas. No medium is used on the house and sky areas, but the color used on the water areas has been thinned out with turpentine.

5 The garden gateway is drawn in using a fine No. 2 sable brush and a mahistick to steady the hand.

6 The sky and water areas are further established to give an overall impression of the light and dark masses. The sky is dry-brushed with some additional olive green lines to suggest the form of the main tree branches.

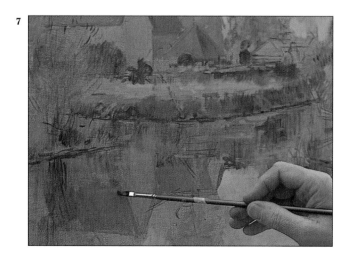

7 The mid-tone of the house roof reflected in the water is established using a No. 3 filbert hog's hair brush.

8 The colors along the top edge of the palette. Start with the light colors on the left: Yellows through to ochers then to the reds: *mid-way* next to cadmium red are the complementary colors of sap and olive green, continuing on to blues. The colors below these are initially premixed using a palette knife. These two rows take up half the palette, leaving the other part free to be used for additional mixing as work progresses.

9 After one and a half hour's work, with the early morning sun creating strong contrasts in light and shade, the light areas are heightened to contrast with those in shadow.

10 The sky is further reworked using dry color, and into this the blossom of the flowering cherry tree is worked up using small dry dabs over the mid-tone areas of paint below. This detail shows the suggestion of the branches and leaves of the middle tree in the composition.

11 Adjustments are made to the color and proportions of the house, and the windows are added. There is a further reworking of the roof and blossom.

12

13

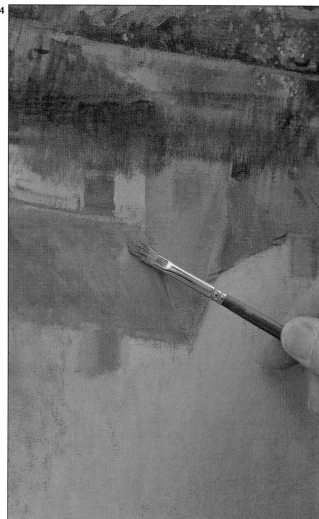

14

15

12 The light across the lawn showing between the gaps in the hedge is further heightened and the water is also reworked, for greater contrast.

13 Having broadly established the tone, color and contrast required, some smaller details are painted in using fine sable brushes.

14 Hog's hair brushes are used to define the water reflections.

15 A wind was driving the petals across the pond. The water is disturbed and the arching of the may petals helps to lead the eye across the pond from the bottom left-hand corner toward the bend in the moat.

16 More raking light is introduced into the part of the moat coming from the left, behind the nut trees and cherry.

17 The cherry blossom has now gone but the may tree has fully flowered on the right side. The may blossom is added between young trees on the small island to the left of the picture. The chance arrival of the white duck offers a small detail in the foreground. Working on a picture over several days, with changing moods in the weather, means there are always incidents the artist can take advantage of. These "happenings" add interest to the composition. A painting done from a photograph captures only one moment in time, whereas a painting completed outdoors evolves over some time.

18 The finished picture. The top of the sky has been strengthened once more with a darker blue and some clouds introduced to reflect something of the light wind movement expressed in the arching petals on the surface of the pond.

MT. ASPIRING

MARK TOPHAM

Mark Topham has chosen one of the classic landscape scenes for this gouache demonstration. Mountains framed by trees with a broad river meandering between verdant hills make for a challenging subject. The snow-capped mountains and sandbanks contrast sharply with the dark green water.

Author's Notes

The artist has a precise approach to his work. He takes time, before starting to do a visual analysis of the subject. He makes mental notes of the light and dark areas and the warm and cool colors he will need. He then indicates these areas on the support using a soft pencil. Choosing from a large range of colors he assembles those he will need. Mark prefers to work with a greater number of pure colors, rather than mixing from a limited range. His experience has given him the ability to wprk with and control more colors than would be recommended for a beginner.

The painting proceeds initially with diluted washes, leaving the very lightest areas white, until he has completed a delicate underpainting of the whole picture. He uses fairly small brush strokes, varying the tints as he goes. The process is then one of a gradual build-up of thicker paint, culminating in touches of white for highlights. The artist uses both the wet-in-wet and dry brush techniques, with some stipple and blotting for texture.

1

2

3

1 The painting is an interpretation of this photograph, which is the sole reference.

2 A base drawing of the main forms in this composition has been made using a 6B pencil. The sky is being washed in with a diluted mix of cerulean blue, ultramarine blue, and monastial blue. The paper has been slightly dampened and the artist is pulling the wash down with a squirrel hair brush.

4

3 *Detail* Changing to a No. 7 synthetic sable brush, patches of color have been placed in the mountains using diluted pale violet. Green mixed with yellow ocher is being brushed into the mid-ground hills down to the shore line with the squirrel brush.

4 Thinned washes of blue with a little green are mixed for the water tones. Violet is added for the shadow areas. The artist has returned to the mountains, working with orange, white, burnt umber, and violet. The hills are lightened with white to create aerial perspective. This is done with a No. 7 pointed sable brush.

5

6

5 The first glazes are finished. Thicker paint will now be used mixed with some acrylizing medium to give body to the color.

6 The sky has been re-worked with blue and white to define the clouds. Darker tones of viridian green and raw sienna are mixed to paint the tree in shadow. More tones of dark green, blue, and raw sienna are used to finish the tree.

7

8

7 The picture looks one-sided at the moment—darker tones must be carried over to the mid-ground hill on the right.

8 Texture in the right-hand hill is being applied with a No. 7 pointed sable brush. This is "feathered off" toward the horizon.

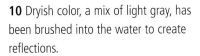

9 Still using the No. 7 sable brush, with a mix of green, blue, and raw sienna, the shadows and ripples are painted on the river.

10 Dryish color, a mix of light gray, has been brushed into the water to create reflections.

11 Now some light gray is dragged across the snow and rocks with the finger.

12 White with a little pink, used thickly, is applied to the banks and to suggest snow floating in the water. Some white is scumbled onto the foreground to indicate ripples.

13 Final touches for highlights are added to the tree and the painting is finished.

14

14 The picture represents a beautiful study of the cool atmospheric effects of this region.

PERSPECTIVE

Perspective is the means by which an artist can create the illusion of depth in a painting. It is an important aid to the landscape painter, although it should not be allowed to displace the principles of good composition. There has been an awareness of these principles since the time of Ancient Egypt. These were not fully developed until the Italian Renaissance, when Paolo Uccello and Leonardo da Vinci became interested in the theory of and made extensive use of perspective.

ABOVE A splendid example of singlepoint perspective Is provided by Paolo Ucello's *The Rout of San Romano* (1397-1475). The direction of the fallen lances indicates a fairly high eye level, with the vanishing point near the center.

BELOW This drawing by Leonardo da Vinci shows the grid system he developed on which to construct his perspectives.

Main principles

If you stand looking out through an upstairs window, the point directly in line with your vision is the eye level. The window frame in front of you is your canvas or picture plane. In single-point perspective the point on the eye level, straight ahead, is the vanishing point (see fig. 1), where all lines parallel to your line of vision will converge. This is known as linear perspective.

Aerial perspective concerns color and tone and is governed by the effects of light and atmosphere. We realize that hills and trees in the far distance are indistinct and light in tone, whereas a tree that is close up in the foreground is sharply focused with rich, contrasting color.

I have illustrated here the four main situations in which the painter will need to have a knowledge of perspective. They are: one-point, (high and low eye levels), two-point and three-point perspective. Note what a radical difference the position of the eye level makes to the same scene.

ABOVE Single-point, low eye level.

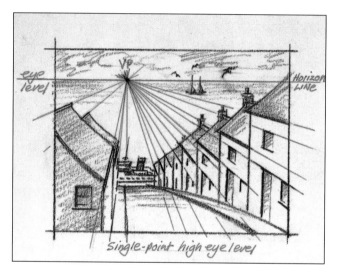

ABOVE Single-point, high eye level.

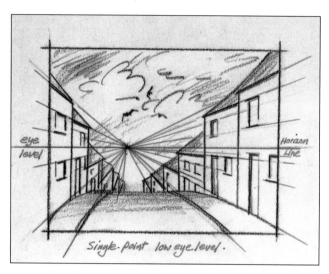

ABOVE Two-point, low eye level.

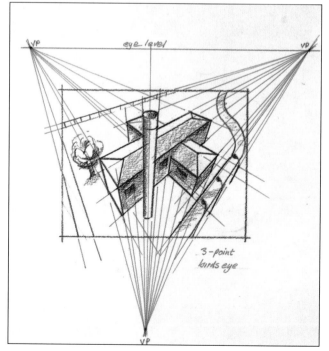

ABOVE Three-point, birds eye view.

ABOVE *Cornfields and Roses*. This oil by Timothy Easton is a *tour de force* of landscape painting. His delicate, sure brushwork combines with an unerring sense of tone and color which results in an immensely accomplished picture.

GLOSSARY

Abstract painting Relying on color, pattern, and form rather than the realistic or naturalistic portrayal of subject matter.

Abstraction The creation of an abstract image by the simplification of natural appearances.

Action painting Splashing and dribbling paint on canvas. The technique is supposed to be derived from Leonardo's suggestion of using stains on walls as a starting point for a design.

Advancing colors Colors which appear to be near the viewer. Warm, strong colors seem to advance whereas cool colors recede.

Aerial perspective The use of color and tone to indicate space and recession. Warm colors, clearly defined forms, and sharp contrasts of tone tend to advance toward the picture plane whereas cool colors, less clearly defined forms, and tonal contrasts appear farther away.

Alla prima Completing the painting in one session with neither underdrawing nor underpainting.

Aqueous A term which refers to a pigment or medium soluble, or capable of being suspended, in water.

Binder The fixative with which powdered color is mixed.

Blending Merging adjacent color areas so that the transition between the colors is imperceptible.

Blocking in The technique of roughly laying out the forms and overall composition of a painting or drawing in terms of mass and tone or color.

Body color Pigments such as gouache that have been rendered opaque by the addition of a white substance like chalk.

Broken color This is an effect achieved by using colors in a pure state, without blending or mixing them, and dragging paint of a stiff quality across the support so that previous layers can be seen through the new application.

Bottega The workshop or studio of an artist, specifically where the pupils and assistants worked on commissioned production, from and usually signed by the master.

Brush work The personal handwriting of a painter. May be thick or thin, gentle or vigorous depending on the form of expression of the artist. It may be aesthetically pleasing in itself.

Calligraphic A term referring to a linear style of painting or drawing characterized by flowing, rhythmic marks.

Charcoal A drawing material made by reducing wood, through burning, to charred, black sticks. All charcoal tends to powder but sticks are available in different thicknesses so the qualities in a charcoal drawing can be varied.

Chiaroscuro This term literally means "light-dark" and originally was used in reference to oil paintings with dramatic tonal contrasts. It is now more generally applied to work in which there is a skillfully managed interplay of highlight and shadow.

Collage A work put together from assembled fragments.

Contre-jour Painting against the light.

Complementary colors Colors that lie opposite each other on the color wheel and have the effect of enhancing their opposite.

Composition The organization of color and form within a picture area.

Covering power This term refers to the opacity or transparency of a paint. Some paints are transparent and are therefore more suitable for glazing whereas opaque paints are used for areas of dense color or where it is important to obliterate underlying color.

Cross hatching A technique of laying an area of tone by building up a mass of criss-cross strokes rather than with a method of solid shading.

Design Roughly has the same meaning as composition, but applies also to artefacts and decorative objects, and functional equipment. Also has the same meaning as the Italian word *disegno* to mean drawing.

Diluent A liquid such as turpentine which is used to dilute paint. It evaporates completely and has no binding effect on the pigment.

Drawing The simplest way to plot out an image; to organize shapes and tones preparatory to painting or designing. To put down what is seen in an ordered way so that it is immediately understood. The way artists and designers think about their work. The artists' way of making notes and observations for future reference.

Distemper Powdered color mixed with glue size. Because of its relative simplicity and cheapness was often used as a household paint for decoration, but since superseded by acrylic paints. Not to be confused with tempera.

Dry brush In this technique dry paint is dragged across the surface of a painting, so that it adheres to the raised areas, creating broken areas of color.

Fat Possessing a high proportion of oil to pigment.

Ferrule The metal section of a paintbrush which holds the hairs.

Figurative This term is used in referring to paintings and drawings in which there is a representational approach to a particular subject; as distinct from abstract art.

Fugitive Applied to dyes and paints which are short lived in intensity, especially in sunlight.

Foreshortening The effect of perspective in a single object or figure, in which a form appears considerably altered from its normal proportions as it recedes from the artist's viewpoint.

Fresco Wall painting with a medium like watercolor (but without any binder) painted on to wet plaster which when dry acts as the binder by "locking-in" the paint. Absolutely permanent when favored by a dry and warm climate.

Gesso Name of the ground used for tempera painting, and sometimes oil. Not recommended for acrylic.

Glaze Transparent film of pigment over a lighter surface or over another.

Glazing The application of a transparent film of color over a lighter, opaque color. It is sometimes used to modify darker colors.

Gouache Opaque watercolor known variously as poster or designer's color. Often used as a substitute for oil paint, but lacks the sparkle of acrylic to do it well.

Graffito Lines produced by scratching the pigmented surface to reveal another.

Grain The texture of a support for painting or drawing. Paper may have a fine or coarse grain depending upon the methods used in its manufacture. Some heavy watercolor papers have a pronounced grain which can be exploited to achieve effects of highlights and broken color in painting.

Graphite A form of carbon which is compressed with fine clay to form the substance commonly known as "lead" in pencils. The proportion of clay and graphite in the mixture determine the quality of the pencil, whether it is hard or soft and the density of line produced. Thick sticks of graphite are available without a wooden pencil casing.

Ground The surface preparation of a support on which a painting or drawing is executed. A tinted ground may be laid on white paper to tone down its brilliance.

Gum arabic Hardened sap of acacia trees, used as a binder and to thicken paint and add gloss.

Half tones A range of tones or colors which an artist can identify between extremes of light and dark.

Handling The name given to the most personal part of the work—the actual execution.

Hatching A technique of creating areas of tone with fine, parallel strokes following one direction.

Hot color Color which tends to be reddish in hue.

Hot pressed paper Paper is produced by the "hot pressed" method.

Hue This term indicates the type of color in terms of its blueness, redness, or yellowness. About 150 different hues can be recognized.

Impasto Paint applied thickly, so that brush and palette knife marks are evident.

Key Color is said to be high or low in key according to whether nearest to white (high key) or black (low key).

Lean Paint containing little oil in proportion.

Linear perspective A method of creating an illusion of depth and three dimensions on a flat surface through the use of converging lines and vanishing points.

Local color The inherent color hue of an object.

Luminosity The effect of light appearing to come from a surface.

Mahl stick A cane used for steadying the painting arm when putting in fine detail. One end is covered with a soft pad to prevent the point from damaging the support.

Marouflage Process of affixing canvas to a wall by means of cement. Can also mean gluing canvas to a support.

Masking The technique of covering areas of the support (with either masking fluid or tape) in order to create a hard edge to the area being painted. The artist is free to use loose brush strokes, while at the same time protecting the covered area.

Medium Substance mixed with pigment to make paint, and with acrylic and oil to ease manipulation.

Modeling The three-dimensionality of objects in painting or drawings, suggested by various methods including the variation of tones.

Mixed method Originally oil glazes over a tempera under-painting, but can also mean mixing compatible mediums like collage and paint; painting over drawing with inks,

acrylic, and vice versa; adding three dimensional objects to a flat surface etc.

Monochrome A painting executed in black and white, or black, white, and one other color.

Mural or wall painting is a term to describe any kind of wall decoration. Not interchangeable with fresco.

Negative space The space round an object, which can be used as an entity in composition.

NOT Paper with a slightly textured surface, meaning "not" hot pressed.

Ochres Earth colors derived from oxide of iron in a range from yellow to orange-red.

Opacity The quality of paint which covers or obscures a support or previous layers of applied color.

Optical color mixing Creating new colors by mixing pigments optically on the canvas rather than on the palette. The Pointillists placed small dots of unmixed color on the canvas so that viewed from a distance the dots are no longer visible and, for example, dabs of yellow and red would combine in the eye of the viewer to create orange.

Paint quality One of the desirable visual attributes of a finished painting. The term does not refer to good or bad ingredients.

Paint quality is intrinsic for material beauty or skillful handling, but often helped by the paint concerned—like acrylic, which has a sympathetic paint quality.

Palette The implement on which a painter mixes his colors, but can also refer to a selective assortment or group of colors, chosen for use in painting technique.

Pastel A drawing medium made by binding powder pigments with a little gum and rolling the mixture into stick form.

Picking-up What happens when a color is laid over another incorrectly, so that the two colors combine and become muddy.

Picture plane The defined surface area being painted.

Pigment Coloring matter, the basis of paints, from natural or synthetic substances.

Plein air A French term meaning "open air" used to describe pictures painted out of doors.

Precipitation The grainy effect produced when pigment separates from the medium.

Primary colors The colors red, yellow, and blue, which combine to form the complementary colors.

Priming Also known as ground, this is the layer or layers of materials applied to a support to make it less absorbent or more

pleasant to paint on. A suitable priming for canvas could consist of a layer of size, followed by an oil ground.

Renaissance The cultural revival of classic ideals which took place in Europe from the fourteenth to the sixteenth centuries.

Resist Using materials which protect a surface from the action of paint; paper, masking tape, and masking fluid all fulfill this purpose.

Saturation The strongest possible concentration of pigment.

Scumbling To drag or dab thick paint onto the support.

Size Used as both a noun and a verb. Size is the solution that is used to coat a support in order to render it less absorbent. To size is to carry out this process.

Spatial depth This is created by changing the tones of color on receding planes.

Sponging The application of paint with a natural sponge to produce a textured surface.

Stipple The use of dots in painting, drawing, or engraving, instead of line or flat color.

Support A surface for painting or drawing, which could be canvas, board, or paper.

Tempera Any kind of binder that will serve to temper powdered pigment and make it workable.

Tint A color either diluted or mixed with white.

Tone The degree of lightness or darkness. The tone of a color is assessed independently of its hue.

Tooth Texture or roughness of paper or canvas, allowing paint to grip the surface.

Underdrawing The preliminary drawing for a painting, often done in pencil, charcoal, or paint.

Underpainting The preliminary blocking-in of the main forms, colors, and tonal areas.

Unified colors Colors close together in the spectrum.

Value The character of a color as assessed on a tonal scale from dark to light.

Wash An application of thinly diluted paint.

Watercolor Paint consisting of pigment bound in gum arabic, requiring only water as a medium.

Watermark The symbol or name of the manufacturer incorporated in sheets of high quality watercolor paper.

Wet in wet The application of wet paint to an already wet surface.

Whiting-out or repriming is the process of covering a painting or part of a painting that has "gone wrong" with a semi-transparent layer of white or tinted paint.

INDEX